Ready®
Common Core

8 **Reading**
INSTRUCTION
Teacher Resource Book

Advisors

Crystal Bailey, Math Impact Teacher, Eastern Guilford Middle School, Guilford County Schools, Gibsonville, NC

Leslie Blauman, Classroom Teacher, Cherry Hills Village Elementary, Cherry Creek School District, Cherry Hills Village, CO

Max Brand, Reading Specialist, Indian Run Elementary, Dublin City School District, Dublin, OH

Kathy Briguet, Retired Curriculum Coordinator for K-12 Literacy, Forest Lake Area Schools, Forest Lake, MN; Adjunct Instructor, Reading Instruction in the Elementary Grades, University of Minnesota, Minneapolis, MN

Helen Comba, Supervisor of Basic Skills & Language Arts, School District of the Chathams, Chatham, NJ

Cindy Dean, Classroom Teacher, Mt. Diablo Unified School District, Concord, CA

Randall E. Groth, Ph.D., Associate Professor of Mathematics Education, Salisbury University, Salisbury, MD

Jennifer Geaber, Kingston Hill Academy Charter School, South Kingstown, RI

Bill Laraway, Classroom Teacher, Silver Oak Elementary, Evergreen School District, San Jose, CA

Susie Legg, Elementary Curriculum Coordinator, Kansas City Public Schools, Kansas City, KS

Sarah Levine, Classroom Teacher, Springhurst Elementary School, Dobbs Ferry School District, Dobbs Ferry, NY

Nicole Peirce, Classroom Teacher, Eleanor Roosevelt Elementary, Pennsbury School District, Morrisville, PA

Donna Phillips, Classroom Teacher, Farmington R-7 School District, Farmington, MO

Kari Ross, Reading Specialist, MN

Sunita Sangari, Math Coach, PS/MS 29, New York City Public Schools, New York, NY

Shannon Tsuruda, Classroom Teacher, Mt. Diablo Unified School District, Concord, CA

Mark Hoover Thames, Research Scientist, University of Michigan, Ann Arbor, MI

Acknowledgments

Project Manager: Claudia Herman
Revising Editor: Rob Hill
Cover Designer and Illustrator: Julia Bourque
Book Designer: Mark Nodland

Managing Editor: Nicole VanderLinden
Director–Product Development: Daniel J. Smith
Vice President–Product Development: Adam Berkin

Table of Contents

Unit 4: Craft and Structure in Literature

Unit 5: Integration of Knowledge and Ideas in Informational Text

Unit 6: Integration of Knowledge and Ideas in Literature

Language Handbook

Conventions of Standard English

Knowledge of Language

Vocabulary Acquisition and Use

Ready® Common Core Program Overview

Ready® **Common Core** is an integrated program of assessment and data-driven instruction designed to teach your classroom the Common Core State Standards (CCSS) for English Language Arts. The program teaches and assesses all the tested CCSS in the Reading and Language strands. You can use the program in a supplemental way to address specific standards where your students need instruction and practice, or in a more comprehensive way to engage students in all the CCSS.

Built for the Common Core. Not just aligned.

Differentiated Instruction and Assessments

Ready Common Core Instruction—provides differentiated instruction and independent practice of key concepts and skills that builds student confidence. Interim reading assessments give frequent opportunities to monitor progress. A Language Handbook gives instruction and practice on the Common Core Language standards.

Ready Common Core Assessments provides extensive practice on the high-rigor items required by the Common Core, giving you a measure of student growth. The three full-length assessments will strengthen students' skills, build their confidence, and ensure that they are ready to show their mastery of the Common Core.

Teacher Resource Book and Teacher Toolbox

Ready Common Core Teacher Resource Books support teachers with strong professional development, step-by-step lesson plans, and best practices for implementing the CCSS.

Ready Common Core Teacher Toolbox (Teacher Toolbox sold separately) provides online lessons, prerequisite lessons from previous grades, and targeted best-practice teaching strategies.

i-Ready® Diagnostic

Built on the Common Core and integrated with the **Ready** program, **i-Ready Diagnostic** helps teachers track student growth, pointing teachers toward the correct **Ready** lessons to use for remediation. See page A22 for details. (**i-Ready** sold separately.)

Features

 Built with brand-new content

 Uses a research-based gradual-release instructional model

 Employs higher-rigor test questions, requiring students to cite text-based evidence to support answers

 Includes complex, authentic texts from a wide range of genres

 Embeds thoughtful professional development

 Integrates teaching of language arts standards at point of use

 Engages students with high-interest themes for passages, drawing in commonly studied science and social studies topics

NEW 2014 Edition

- More high-rigor test items reflecting latest guidance from Smarter Balanced and PARCC
- New Language Handbook covering the CCSS Language strand
- Updated item Depth of Knowledge (DOK) levels based on latest guidance

The Common Core State Standards (CCSS) were developed to make sure that by the time students graduate from high school, they are college- and career-ready. Therefore, the creators of the standards started with the expectations they had for students at the end of 12th grade and worked down to kindergarten. As a result of this backward design approach, the CCSS are more rigorous than most current standards. The creators of the standards want students at every grade to be creative and critical readers and writers. At the end of each grade, students are expected to independently read and comprehend increasingly complex text. Not only are most current textbooks lacking alignment to the CCSS, they also lack the levels of complex text identified in the CCSS. ***Ready® Common Core*** is here to help.

Because every Common Core reading standard has been addressed with a clear, thoughtful pedagogy, you can use the ***Ready*** program as the main structure of a year-long program. Any other materials aligned to the CCSS can be easily woven into the curriculum.

Each ***Ready*** lesson covers the entirety of a particular skill, so classrooms can work through any lesson independently from the rest of the book. This gives teachers in states transitioning to the CCSS enormous flexibility, knowing that ***Ready*** lessons can be pulled out and applied to any implementation plan.

Keep Up to Date with *Ready®* Teacher Toolbox

The online ***Ready*** Teacher Toolbox gives you access to a host of multilevel resources, such as instructional support, online lessons, and lessons for prerequisite skills. (See pages A20 and A21 for more.) You can access the latest version of ***Ready Assessments*** there, as well.

Smarter Balanced Assessment Consortium (SBAC) and the Partnership for Assessment of Readiness for College and Career (PARCC) are state-led consortia developing assessments aligned to the Common Core. They are creating higher-rigor, innovative item types and assessments that can measure a student's mastery of the Common Core. (See page A14 to see the higher-level DOK items in ***Ready***, matching the consortia approach.) To match the differing approaches of the two consortia, we have created custom versions of ***Ready Assessments***, one for PARCC and one for SBAC.

The situation will be changing rapidly as the consortia complete their work. We will make sure that ***Ready Assessments*** addresses the most recent information released by the consortia. You can ensure you have access to the latest updates by visiting the ***Ready*** Teacher Toolbox (*www.teacher-toolbox.com*).

Helpful Resources for the Transition to the Common Core

http://www.corestandards.org/
The main website for the Common Core. Here you'll find the full text of the standards, plus frequently asked questions and resources.

http://www.smarterbalanced.org/ and ***http://www.parcconline.org***
The testing consortium creating Common Core assessments for future implementation.

http://www.ascd.org/common-core-state-standards/common-core.aspx
A helpful list of all of ASCD's resources on the Common Core, as well as link to ASCD's free EduCore digital tool, which was funded by a grant from the Bill & Melinda Gates Foundation. A repository of evidence-based strategies, videos, and supporting documents that help educators transition to the Common Core.

http://www.reading.org/resources/ResourcesByTopic/CommonCore-resourcetype/CommonCore-rt-resources.aspx
Links to helpful articles about the Common Core from *Reading Today Online*.

THE DEMANDS OF THE COMMON CORE	HOW *READY*® DELIVERS
Text Complexity: Students must engage with texts of sufficient complexity to prepare them for college and career.	All texts in **Ready** have been carefully leveled to meet Common Core requirements for complexity. See more on page A11.
Intentional, Close Reading: Careful, close readings of complex texts teach students how to gather evidence and build knowledge.	All **Ready** lessons contain activities requiring close reading, re-reading, and frequent interactions with text. On-page guidance models the good habits that successful readers employ. See more on page A12.
Text-based Evidence: Students' interpretations and comprehension of the text must be supported by the words in the text.	All the questions and activities in **Ready** lessons require students to cite evidence directly from the text. Instruction and hints throughout the lesson reinforce the importance of quoting from the text to substantiate interpretations.
Wide Range of Genres, Emphasis on Nonfiction: Students must read a true balance of authentic literary and informational texts. Success in college and the real world requires that students master the skills needed to read a wide range of genres.	**Ready** passages encompass the range of genres and text types cited in the Common Core, including articles, poems, historical text, technical text, scientific text, and dramas. 50% of **Ready** lessons focus on informational texts. See more on page A13.
Building Content Knowledge: Students should view reading as an opportunity to learn new information. As much as possible, therefore, have students read text on related topics that allow them to deepen their understanding.	All passages in a **Ready** lesson are thematically linked. Many of the themes relate to grade-appropriate science and social studies content, others to high-interest, appealing topics. Theme activities provide opportunities for students to see relationships between topics and deepen their content knowledge.
High-Quality Texts: It's important that students are exposed to well-crafted texts that are worth reading closely and exhibit exceptional craft and thought or provide useful information.	**Ready** lessons include authentic texts that students will see in the real world, including text and images from websites, and newspaper and magazine articles from such publications as *The New York Times*, *National Geographic*, and *Highlights*.
Integrated ELA Instruction: Use the texts as a source of rich language arts instruction, as opposed to isolated skill instruction.	**Ready** integrates Speaking & Listening, Writing, and Language activities with every Reading lesson.
Use of Technology and Digital Media: Students learn to use technology thoughtfully and efficiently to enhance their reading.	Specific **Ready** Media Features and lessons allow students to integrate audio and visual media into their reading experience. They learn to evaluate the pros and cons of various media and to employ the best medium to achieve a particular purpose.

The Importance of Text Complexity

Research has shown that the complexity levels of the texts in current classrooms are far below what is required for college- and career-readiness. A major emphasis of the Common Core State Standards is for students to encounter appropriately complex texts at each grade level in order to develop the mature language skills and conceptual knowledge they need for success in school and life. Instructional materials should meet this challenge with texts of appropriate complexity at each grade level.

A Three-Part Model for Measuring Text Complexity

No single formula can provide an accurate measure of text complexity. For that reason, the CCSS has developed a balanced three-part model that takes into account the following three ways of assessing text complexity:

Qualitative Measures:
The purpose of the text, the structure and clarity of the language, and background knowledge demands

Quantitative Measures:
Standard readability formulas, such as Lexile and Flesch-Kincaid

Reader–Task Consideration:
Including the reader's motivation and experience, as well as the complexity of the task assigned and questions posed

Text Complexity in *Ready®*

All passages in **Ready** conform to the leveling criteria outlined by the CCSS. We used quantitative formulas to place texts within the grade-level bands recommended by the Standards, which are more rigorous than those of the past. We also had an experienced team of teachers and literacy specialists apply the qualitative and reader–task measures described above. Through the scaffolded instruction in **Ready**, students develop the strategies they will need to comprehend this challenging text.

Academic Vocabulary

The CCSS categorize types of vocabulary in a three-tier model similar to the one developed by Beck, McKeown, & Kucan in *Bringing Words to Life*. (Beck, McKeown, & Kucan, 2002) Tier One Vocabulary are the words of everyday speech. Tier Two (which CCSS calls "general academic vocabulary") are the words a reader encounters in rich, complex texts of all types. Tier Three (which CCSS calls "domain specific") are the words particular to a field of study, such as science or history. While Tier Three words are often explicitly defined in a subject-area text, this is not the case with Tier Two words. Their meanings are often subtle, yet they are the most important words for students to learn, since they are generalizable, or applicable to a wide variety of texts.

Unlike reading programs of the past, in which difficult vocabulary was "pretaught" before reading, CCSS emphasizes the use of text-based strategies, such as context and word structure, to determine word meaning. **Ready** provides this type of instruction in the Teacher Resource Book lessons by identifying challenging Tier Two words in a passage and giving the teacher explicit text-based strategies to support students in unlocking their meanings.

A11

What Is Close Reading?

The purpose of a close reading is to unlock the meanings of a text and to probe an author's motivations for writing it. To achieve these goals, readers must

- reread the text (in whole or in part),
- write down questions and observations relevant to the text's meaning and purpose, and
- mark up the text to identify details that help answer those questions and develop those observations.

Internalizing and mastering such close-reading strategies prepares students for college and careers, which is a key goal of the Common Core: "[Research] links the close reading of complex text—whether the student is a struggling reader or advanced—to significant gains in reading proficiency." (PARCC, 2011)

How Do We Apply Close Reading Instruction in *Ready® Common Core*?

Short, rich, complex text: Readers use close-reading strategies with challenging text that are hard to fully comprehend on a first reading. It's this type of complex text you'll find in **Ready**. **Ready** uses short text because we agree with reading experts that "When students are introduced to a . . . strategy through close reading, it's wise to use a short piece of text. Constraining the amount of text under investigation helps students see how to apply that . . . strategy and limits the amount of time required to teach [it]." (Fisher, Frey, & Lapp, 2012)

Multiple readings: In Guided Practice, we explicitly emphasize multiple readings (see page A28). For the first reading, students focus on literal comprehension. In the second reading, students apply close-reading strategies to unlock meaning and practice the lesson's featured standard. Fisher, Frey, & Lapp describe the value of multiple readings: "Sophisticated readers understand that the nature of some text requires that they be read more than once. . . . First and foremost, close reading requires a willingness to return to the text to read part or even all of it more than once." (Fisher, Frey, & Lapp, 2012)

Marking up the text: Our Close Reading activities guide students to mark up the text, helping them remember and make sense of what they read. We prompt students to mark specific evidence in the text that provide answers to the text-dependent questions they will need to answer. As Fisher, Frey, & Lapp describe it, "[b]y annotating texts . . . students learn to slow down their reading to mine the depths of the concepts, arguments, and metaphors used by the writer." (Fisher, Frey, & Lapp, 2012)

Teaching for transfer: Students must take what they learn from the study of one text and apply it to the next. To encourage this transfer, we remove the scaffolds in our Common Core Practice section. See page A30 for a tip activating these metacognitive strategies.

Monitoring Student Progress in *Ready® Instruction*

These ongoing assessment features in the **Ready** program keep you informed about student progress:

Student Lesson

- **Common Core Practice:** Each lesson ends with Common Core Practice. Use these results to identify how well students mastered the specific standard. If students scored poorly, review the lesson and use reteaching support in the Teacher Resource Book.
- **Interim Assessment:** Use the Interim Assessments and Performance Tasks at the end of each unit to see how well students can integrate the skills and strategies covered in that unit.

Full-Length Assessments

- **Ready Assessments:** Three full-length assessments allow you to benchmark student progress on each CCSS throughout the year.

Teacher Resource Book

- **Error Alerts:** This easy-to-use feature allows you to quickly identify and address common misconceptions students experience when applying the targeted standard.

Genres and Themes in *Ready*®

To succeed in college and the world outside the classroom, students must master reading a wide range of genres. *Ready*® ensures students read rich texts linked in meaningful ways by including a variety of genres and by organizing each lesson under a theme. The following chart shows the themes and genres for grade 8 lessons.

Lesson	Theme	Genres
1: Analyzing the Development of a Central Idea	American Cities	History
2: Summarizing Informational Texts	Our Living Language	Essay, Report, Social Studies
3: Citing Evidence to Make Inferences	Light Phenomena	Newspaper Article, Science
4: Analyzing Comparisons and Analogies	Worldwide Food	Economics, History, Social Studies
5: Analyzing Categories	High-Tech Solutions	History, Science, Technical
6: Citing Evidence to Support Inferences	Home and Family	Lyric Poem, Realistic Fiction
7: Analyzing Dialogue and Incidents in Stories and Drama	Doers and Dreamers	Drama, Realistic Fiction, Science Fiction
8: Determining Theme	Teamwork	Legend, Realistic Fiction
9: Summarizing Literary Texts	Views of Other Worlds	Science Fiction
10: Analyzing Word Meanings	Animal Survival	Science
11: Analyzing Word Choice	Challenging Journeys	Biography, History
12: Analyzing the Structure of Paragraphs	The Civil Rights Movement	History, Public Document
13: Determining Point of View	Great Deeds and Minds	Editorial, Essay, Speech
14: Analyzing How Authors Respond	Environmental Review	Editorial, Opinion Piece, Persuasive Essay
15: Determining Word Meanings	The Language of Poets	Free Verse, Lyric Poem, Sonnet
16: Analyzing Analogies and Allusions	Arts Alive	Free Verse, Realistic Fiction
17: Comparing and Contrasting Structure	The Many Forms of Poetry	Elegy, Free Verse, Lyric Poem, Sonnet
18: Analyzing Point of View	Unexpected Moments	Realistic Fiction
19: Evaluating an Argument	Innovation and the Future	Editorial, Essay, Persuasive Essay
20: Analyzing Conflicting Information	Innovations: Benefits and Consequences	Science, Technical Account
21: Analyzing Elements of Modern Fiction	From Myth to Modern Fiction	Fantasy, Legend, Myth, Realistic Fiction

Depth of Knowledge Levels in *Ready*®

The following table shows the **Ready**® lessons and sections with higher-complexity items, as measured by Webb's Depth of Knowledge index.

Lesson	Section	Item	DOK	Lesson	Section	Item	DOK
1	Guided Practice	3	3	15	Common Core Practice	1	3
1	Common Core Practice	4	3	15	Common Core Practice	2	3
3	Guided Instruction	—	3	15	Common Core Practice	3	3
3	Guided Practice	3	3	16	Guided Instruction	—	3
3	Common Core Practice	4	3	16	Guided Practice	1	3
4	Guided Practice	3	3	16	Guided Practice	2	3
4	Common Core Practice	4	3	16	Guided Practice	3	3
5	Guided Practice	3	3	16	Common Core Practice	1	3
5	Common Core Practice	2	3	16	Common Core Practice	2	3
5	Common Core Practice	4	3	16	Common Core Practice	3	3
Unit 1	Interim Assessment	1A	3	16	Common Core Practice	4	3
Unit 1	Interim Assessment	1B	3	17	Guided Instruction	—	3
Unit 1	Interim Assessment	2	3	17	Guided Practice	2	3
Unit 1	Interim Assessment	6	3	17	Guided Practice	3	4
Unit 1	Interim Assessment	7	3	17	Common Core Practice	1	3
Unit 1	Interim Assessment	8	3	17	Common Core Practice	2	3
Unit 1	Interim Assessment	9	3	17	Common Core Practice	3	3
6	Guided Instruction	—	3	17	Common Core Practice	4	3
6	Guided Practice	1	3	17	Common Core Practice	5	4
6	Guided Practice	2	3	18	Guided Instruction	—	3
6	Guided Practice	3	3	18	Guided Practice	3	3
6	Common Core Practice	2	3	18	Common Core Practice	1	3
6	Common Core Practice	3	3	18	Common Core Practice	4	3
6	Common Core Practice	4	3	Unit 4	Interim Assessment	2	3
7	Guided Practice	3	3	Unit 4	Interim Assessment	4	3
7	Common Core Practice	4	4	Unit 4	Interim Assessment	6	3
8	Guided Practice	3	3	Unit 4	Interim Assessment	7	3
8	Common Core Practice	4	3	Unit 4	Interim Assessment	8	3
Unit 2	Interim Assessment	5A	3	Unit 4	Interim Assessment	9	3
Unit 2	Interim Assessment	5B	3	Unit 4	Interim Assessment	10	4
Unit 2	Interim Assessment	6	3	19	Guided Instruction	—	3
Unit 2	Interim Assessment	8	3	19	Guided Practice	2	3
Unit 2	Interim Assessment	9	3	19	Guided Practice	3	3
10	Guided Instruction	—	3	19	Common Core Practice	2	3
10	Guided Practice	3	3	19	Common Core Practice	3	3
11	Guided Instruction	—	3	19	Common Core Practice	4	3
11	Guided Practice	1	3	20	Guided Instruction	—	3
11	Guided Practice	2	3	20	Guided Practice	1	3
11	Guided Practice	3	3	20	Guided Practice	2	3
11	Common Core Practice	1	3	20	Guided Practice	3	3
11	Common Core Practice	3	3	20	Common Core Practice	2	3
11	Common Core Practice	4	3	20	Common Core Practice	3	3
11	Common Core Practice	5	3	20	Common Core Practice	4	4
12	Guided Practice	3	3	Unit 5	Interim Assessment	4	3
12	Common Core Practice	4	3	Unit 5	Interim Assessment	5	3
13	Guided Instruction	—	3	Unit 5	Interim Assessment	6A	3
13	Guided Practice	1	3	Unit 5	Interim Assessment	6B	3
13	Guided Practice	3	3	Unit 5	Interim Assessment	7	3
13	Common Core Practice	2	3	Unit 5	Interim Assessment	8	4
13	Common Core Practice	3	3	Unit 5	Interim Assessment	9	4
13	Common Core Practice	5	3	21	Guided Instruction	—	3
14	Guided Instruction	—	3	21	Guided Practice	1	3
14	Guided Practice	1	3	21	Guided Practice	2	3
14	Guided Practice	2	3	21	Guided Practice	3	4
14	Guided Practice	3	3	21	Common Core Practice	1	3
14	Common Core Practice	1	3	21	Common Core Practice	2	3
14	Common Core Practice	2	3	21	Common Core Practice	3	3
14	Common Core Practice	3	3	21	Common Core Practice	4	4
14	Common Core Practice	4	3	Unit 6	Interim Assessment	1	3
Unit 3	Interim Assessment	1A	3	Unit 6	Interim Assessment	2	3
Unit 3	Interim Assessment	1B	3	Unit 6	Interim Assessment	3	3
Unit 3	Interim Assessment	4	3	Unit 6	Interim Assessment	4	3
Unit 3	Interim Assessment	6	3	Unit 6	Interim Assessment	5A	3
Unit 3	Interim Assessment	7	3	Unit 6	Interim Assessment	5B	3
Unit 3	Interim Assessment	8	3	Unit 6	Interim Assessment	5C	3
Unit 3	Interim Assessment	9	3	Unit 6	Interim Assessment	6	4
15	Guided Instruction	—	3	Unit 6	Interim Assessment	7	4
15	Guided Practice	1	3	Unit 6	Interim Assessment	8	4
15	Guided Practice	2	3	Unit 6	Interim Assessment	9	4
15	Guided Practice	3	3				

Cognitive Rigor Matrix

The following table combines the hierarchies of learning from both Webb and Bloom. For each level of hierarchy, descriptions of student behaviors that would fulfill expectations at each of the four DOK levels are given. For example, students can show how they evaluate by citing evidence or checking multiple sources, but there isn't a lower-rigor (DOK 1 or 2) way of truly assessing this skill.

Depth of Thinking (Webb) + Type of Thinking (Revised Bloom)	DOK Level 1 Recall & Reproduction	DOK Level 2 Basic Skills & Concepts	DOK Level 3 Strategic Thinking & Reasoning	DOK Level 4 Extended Thinking
Remember	• Recall, locate basic facts, definitions, details, events			
Understand	• Select appropriate words for use when intended meaning is clearly evident	• Specify, explain relationships • Summarize • Identify central ideas	• Explain, generalize, or connect ideas using supporting evidence (quote, text evidence, example . . .)	• Explain how concepts or ideas specifically relate to other content domains or concepts
Apply	• Use language structure (pre/suffix) or word relationships (synonym/antonym) to determine meaning	• Use content to identify word meanings • Obtain and interpret information using text features	• Use concepts to solve non-routine problems	• Devise an approach among many alternatives to research a novel problem
Analyze	• Identify the kind of information contained in a graphic, table, visual, etc.	• Compare literary elements, facts, terms, events • Analyze format, organization, & text structures	• Analyze or interpret author's craft (e.g., literary devices, viewpoint, or potential bias) to critique a text	• Analyze multiple sources or texts • Analyze complex/abstract themes
Evaluate			• Cite evidence and develop a logical argument for conjectures based on one text or problem	• Evaluate relevancy, accuracy, & completeness of information across texts/sources
Create	• Brainstorm ideas, concepts, problems, or perspectives related to a topic or concept	• Generate conjectures or hypotheses based on observations or prior knowledge and experience	• Develop a complex model for a given situation • Develop an alternative solution	• Synthesize information across multiple sources or texts • Articulate a new voice, alternate theme, new knowledge or perspective

SBAC, 2012; adapted from Hess et al., 2009

Using *Ready®* Common Core

The **Ready®** program provides rigorous instruction on the Common Core State Standards using a proven-effective gradual-release approach that builds student confidence. It also prepares students for more complex assessment items with full-length assessments and interim assessments. With the Teacher Resource Book, you get strong support, step-by-step lesson plans, and best-practice tips to learn new approaches to teaching the Common Core. The Teacher Toolbox gives you access to invaluable, easy-to-use resources to differentiate instruction with a host of online materials, all in one place.

Using as a Supplement to a Textbook

The textbook you use in your classroom may not have been developed for the Common Core. It may not have all the resources you'll need to meet these challenging standards. In addition, the passages in textbooks don't reflect the levels of text complexity required by the Common Core, and the activities and questions don't reflect their rigor. By supplementing with **Ready**, you'll be able to address all of these gaps and deficiencies.

Using with a Balanced Literacy/Reading Workshop Curriculum

Because every standard in **Ready Common Core** has been addressed with a clear, thoughtful pedagogy, you can use the **Ready** program as the main structure of a year-long English language arts program. Any other materials aligned to the Common Core can be woven into the curriculum, using the four easy steps on this page as your map.

Using with *i-Ready®* Diagnostic

If you are an **i-Ready** subscriber, you can administer the **i-Ready Diagnostic** as a cross-grade-level assessment to pinpoint instructional needs and address them with **Ready Common Core Instruction**. For more on this, see page A22.

1 Measure Growth

- Use Assessment 1 from **Ready Assessments** to establish a baseline for measurement and to focus instructional plans. Use Assessments 2 and 3 to measure growth as students work through the program. These tests give students practice with more complex items that match the rigor of the Common Core.

2 Instruct

- Administer each **Ready Common Core Instruction** lesson, using the Pacing Guide on page A17 as a guide. Language Handbook lessons are also listed to show how the Reading and Language lessons can be used together.

- At any time during the instructional program, refer to the Teacher Toolbox to review prerequisite skills and access lessons from previous grades for remediation.

3 Monitor Progress

- Use the Interim Assessments at the end of each **Ready Instruction** unit to pinpoint student progress on the standards they have most recently learned and diagnose problem areas.

4 Differentiate Instruction

Provide differentiated instruction for your students using the rich and varied resources in the Teacher Toolbox. Here you'll find links to prerequisite skills from earlier grades of **Ready**, as well as links to highly interactive animated modules that will deepen students' understanding of skills and strategies. See page A20 for more on using the Teacher Toolbox.

Year-Long Pacing Guide for Grade 8

Week	*Ready® Common Core Instruction* Lesson	Days	Minutes per Day	Language Handbook Lesson(s) (allow 20 minutes per lesson)
1	Assessment 1	3	60	
2	Lesson 1: Analyzing the Development of a Central Idea	5	30–45	13
3	Lesson 2: Summarizing Informational Texts	5	30–45	14
4	Lesson 3: Citing Evidence to Make Inferences	5	30–45	15
5	Lesson 4: Analyzing Comparisons and Analogies	5	30–45	16
6	Lesson 5: Analyzing Categories	5	30–45	–
	Unit 1 Interim Assessment	1	30–45	
7	Lesson 6: Citing Evidence to Support Inferences	5	30–45	1
8	Lesson 7: Analyzing Dialogue and Incidents in Stories and Drama	5	30–45	2
9	Lesson 8: Determining Theme	5	30–45	3
10	Lesson 9: Summarizing Literary Texts	5	30–45	4
	Unit 2 Interim Assessment	1	30–45	
11	Lesson 10: Analyzing Word Meanings	5	30–45	5
12	Lesson 11: Analyzing Word Choice	5	30–45	6
13	Lesson 12: Analyzing the Structure of Paragraphs	5	30–45	7
14	Lesson 13: Determining Point of View	5	30–45	8
15	Lesson 14: Analyzing How Authors Respond	5	30–45	9
	Unit 3 Interim Assessment	1	30–45	
16	Assessment 2	3	60	
17	Lesson 15: Determining Word Meanings	5	30–45	17
18	Lesson 16: Analyzing Analogies and Allusions	5	30–45	18
19	Lesson 17: Comparing and Contrasting Structure	5	30–45	19
20	Lesson 18: Analyzing Point of View	5	30–45	–
	Unit 4 Interim Assessment	1	**30–45**	
21	Lesson 19: Evaluating an Argument	5	30–45	10
22	Lesson 20: Analyzing Conflicting Information	5	30–45	11
	Unit 5 Interim Assessment	1	30–45	
	Media Feature 1: Evaluating Presentation Mediums	5	30–45	–
23	Lesson 21: Analyzing Elements of Modern Fiction	5	30–45	12
	Unit 6 Interim Assessment	1	30–45	
	Media Feature 2: Comparing Media: Evaluating Artistic Choices	5	30–45	–
24	Assessment 3	3	60	

Ready® Common Core Instruction was created to help students develop proficiency with the Common Core State Standards (CCSS). Each lesson uses scaffolded instruction, beginning with modeled and guided instruction, and then gradually releasing the student into fully independent practice of the skills and strategies behind the Common Core. Use in conjunction with the Teacher Toolbox, which allows you to access additional resources—see page A20 for more information.

Weekly Pacing

Year-Long Program: Use *Ready Common Core Instruction* as the foundation of a year-long English language arts program or a year-long supplement to your basal program. The Year-Long Sample Week (below) shows a model schedule for teaching one Reading lesson per week. The Year-Long Sample Week, *Ready Common Core* Language Handbook table on page A19 shows a model schedule for teaching five Language lessons per week. Use the Year-Long Pacing Guide on page A17 for a specific week-to-week schedule integrating Reading and Language instruction.

Intensive Test Preparation: Target *Ready Common Core Instruction* lessons based on *Ready Common Core Assessments* results to focus learning during test-preparation. The Intensive Test Preparation chart on page A19 models teaching two Reading lessons (lessons A and B here) per week.

Year-Long Sample Week, *Ready Common Core Instruction*

	Day 1	Day 2	Day 3	Day 4	Day 5
Core	Part 1: Introduction (20 minutes, includes Tap Students' Prior Knowledge from TRB)	Part 2: Modeled Instruction (25 minutes)	Part 3: Guided Instruction (45 minutes, includes Answer Analysis discussion from TRB)	Part 4: Guided Practice (45 minutes, includes Answer Analysis discussion and Integrating Standards activities from TRB)	Part 5: Common Core Practice (45 minutes)	Part 5: Common Core Practice Answer Analysis: discussion of test results (20 minutes, from TRB) Integrating Standards activities (25 minutes, from TRB)
Optional		Genre Focus (TRB)	Tier Two Vocabulary (TRB)	ELL Support (TRB)	Theme Connection (TRB)	Additional Activities (TRB)

Key:

Whole Class/Small Group

Individual

Lessons Built for the Common Core

Each grade level in **Ready® Common Core English Language Arts Instruction** provides targeted instruction on the Common Core State Standards for ELA.

Ready Instruction, covers the following strands:

- Reading Standards for Literature: Key Ideas and Details, Craft and Structure, Integration of Knowledge and Ideas
- Reading Standards for Informational Text: Key Ideas and Details, Craft and Structure, Integration of Knowledge and Ideas

The Ready Language Handbook covers the following strands within the CCSS Language Standards:

- Conventions of Standard English
- Knowledge of Language
- Vocabulary Acquisition and Use

The correlations chart beginning on page A39 provides an in-depth look at how **Ready Common Core Instruction** correlates to the CCSS. The passages and questions in **Ready Instruction** reflect the rigor and complexity required by the Common Core.

Intensive Test Preparation, *Ready Common Core Instruction*

	Day 1	Day 2	Day 3	Day 4	Day 5
In Class	*Lesson A* Introduction (15 minutes) Modeled Instruction (30 minutes)	*Lesson A* Guided Instruction (15 minutes) Guided Practice (30 minutes)	*Lesson B* Introduction (15 minutes) Modeled Instruction (30 minutes)	*Lesson B* Guided Instruction (15 minutes) Guided Practice (30 minutes)	*Lesson A* Review concepts and skills (20 minutes) *Lesson B* Review concepts and skills (20 minutes)
Homework (optional)		*Lesson A* Common Core Practice		*Lesson B* Common Core Practice	

Year-Long Sample Week, *Ready Common Core* Language Handbook

Day 1	Day 2	Day 3	Day 4	Day 5
Introduction (10–15 minutes)	**Introduction** (10–15 minutes)	**Introduction** (10–15 minutes)	**Introduction** (10–15 minutes)	**Introduction** (10–15 minutes)
Guided Practice (10–15 minutes)	**Guided Practice** (10–15 minutes)	**Guided Practice** (10–15 minutes)	**Guided Practice** (10–15 minutes)	**Guided Practice** (10–15 minutes)
Common Core Practice (10–15 minutes)	**Common Core Practice** (10–15 minutes)	**Common Core Practice** (10–15 minutes)	**Common Core Practice** (10–15 minutes)	**Common Core Practice** (10–15 minutes)

Connecting with the *Ready*® Teacher Toolbox

Designed for use with the ***Ready*® *Common Core Instruction***, the Teacher Toolbox provides a host of multilevel resources teachers can use to differentiate instruction. If you purchased the Teacher Toolbox, you should have received an insert with access codes and information. Please contact Customer Service at (800)-225-0248 if you need this information. Visit *www.teacher-toolbox.com* to get started.

The Common Core builds on skills covered in the previous year's standards. Of course, many students will not have mastered those standards, and most students could use a review. ***Ready Common Core*** allows you to access lessons from previous ***Ready*** grades through the Teacher Toolbox.

How Do I Use the Teacher Toolbox?

Lessons are conveniently organized to match your print materials, making it easy to find additional resources for teaching the skills and standards associated with each lesson. All of these resources are perfect for use with any interactive whiteboard or other computer projection screen.

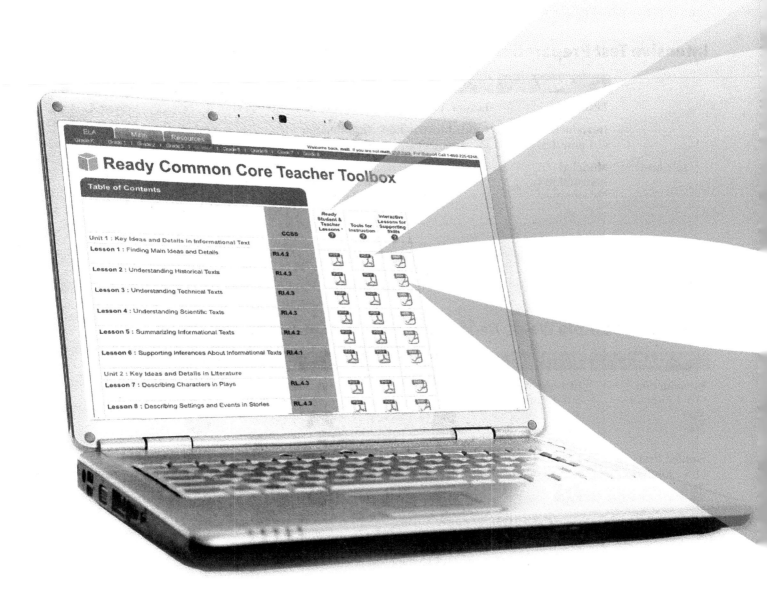

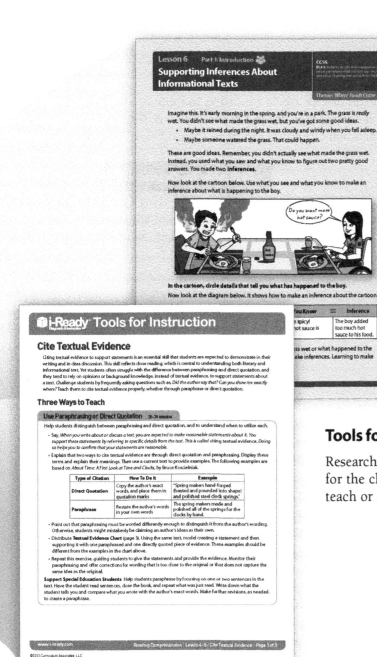

Ready® Lessons

Ready® lessons make it easy for teachers to focus on particular skills, or even reteach skills that students may not have mastered at earlier grade levels. What you get:

- Every lesson in this book is available as an individual PDF file, which you can project for whole-class and small-group use.

- Prerequisite student lesson PDFs—and the accompanying Teacher Resource Book lesson—from prior grades are available to administer as remediation.

- All three full-length **Ready Assessments** are available for easy measurement of student growth.

Tools for Instruction

Research-based, best-practice routines and activities for the classroom and small groups provide ways to teach or review standards and prerequisite skills.

Guided Interactive Tutorials

Guided interactive tutorials give teachers another engaging way to provide whole-class or small-group instruction. Lessons follow a consistent structure of explicit instruction and guided practice. Immediate corrective feedback continuously supports students.

Using *i-Ready® Diagnostic* with *Ready® Common Core*

If you have already purchased *i-Ready® Diagnostic*, you can use its robust reporting to monitor students' overall and domain-specific reading proficiency as they move through *Ready® Common Core Instruction*. Specifically, use the Student Profile report and the Instructional Grouping report to identify Next Step skills for student instruction.

Student Profile Report

Available for Grades K–8

The **Student Profile** report shows teachers students' performance levels for each strand and why they are struggling. Plus, it provides detailed recommendations and resources to support teacher-led instruction.

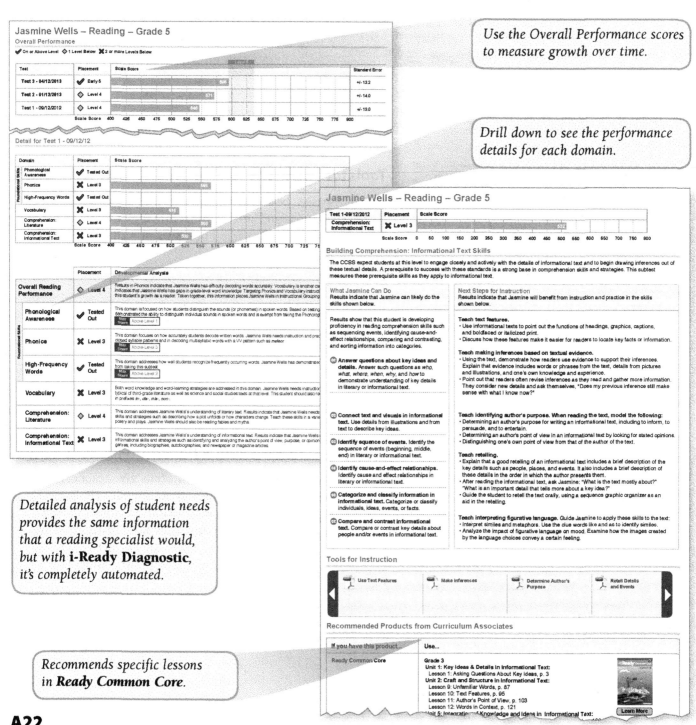

Use the Overall Performance scores to measure growth over time.

Drill down to see the performance details for each domain.

*Detailed analysis of student needs provides the same information that a reading specialist would, but with **i-Ready Diagnostic**, it's completely automated.*

*Recommends specific lessons in **Ready Common Core**.*

Instructional Grouping Profile

The **Instructional Grouping Profile** report shows teachers exactly how to group students so that students who are struggling with the same skills get the most out of small-group instruction. The report also gives effective instructional recommendations and resources for each group profile.

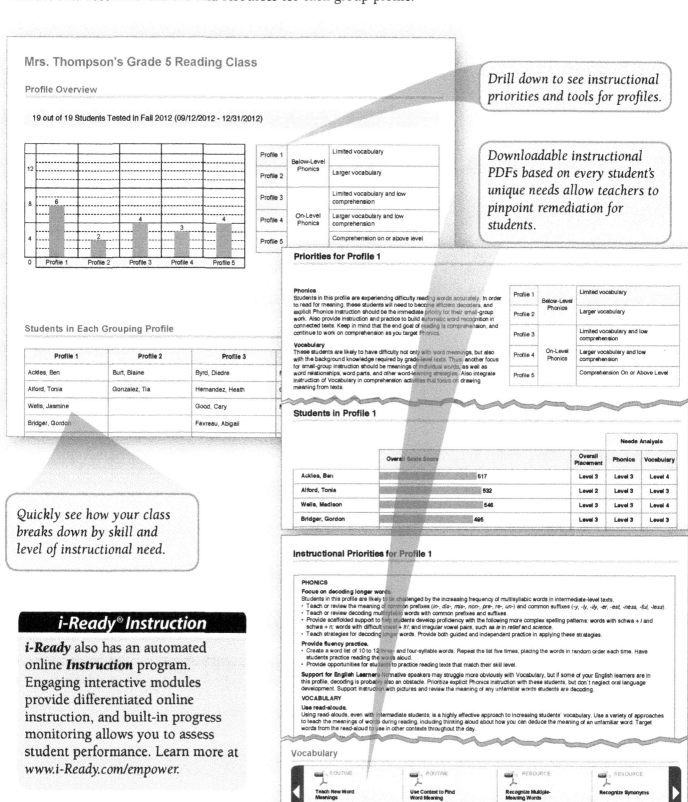

Drill down to see instructional priorities and tools for profiles.

Downloadable instructional PDFs based on every student's unique needs allow teachers to pinpoint remediation for students.

Quickly see how your class breaks down by skill and level of instructional need.

i-Ready® Instruction

i-Ready also has an automated online **Instruction** program. Engaging interactive modules provide differentiated online instruction, and built-in progress monitoring allows you to assess student performance. Learn more at www.i-Ready.com/empower.

A23

Features of *Ready® Common Core Instruction*

This section guides teachers to the key features of the Student Book and Teacher Resource Book. Numbered boxes call out and describe the key features. Use this section to familiarize yourself with the overall structure of a **Ready® Common Core ELA Instruction** lesson.

Each unit in the Student Book opens with an engaging text and visual to introduce the main focus of the unit. A Self-Check allows students to check their knowledge of each standard before the unit and again after each lesson.

Teacher Resource Book

Each lesson begins with a full page of orientation on the standards covered in that lesson.

1 Lesson Objectives identifies specific skills goals for students.

2 The Learning Progression helps teachers see the standard in context, how it builds on the previous grade, and how it leads to the next year's expectations.

3 Prerequisite Skills lists critical concepts and skills required for success with a given lesson.

4 Tapping Students' Prior Knowledge provides quick warm-ups and discussion activities to activate students' prior knowledge of prerequisite and related skills, laying the foundation for the featured standard.

5 The **Ready** Toolbox chart provides an overview of related resources available online in the *Ready* Teacher Toolbox.

6 CCSS Focus identifies the Common Core State Standard featured in the lesson, as well as Additional Standards covered in activities in the Teacher Resource Book.

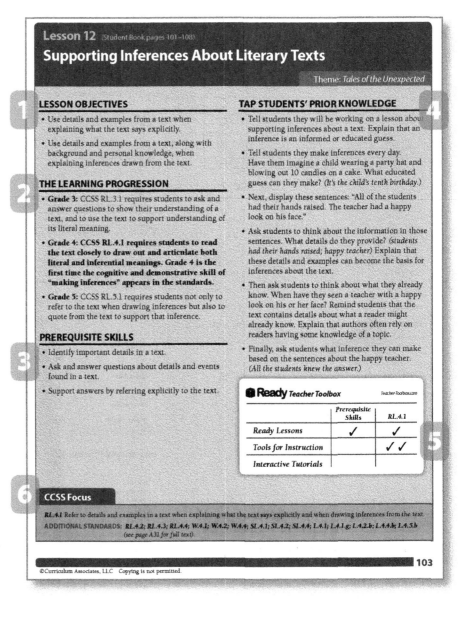

Lesson 12 (Student Book pages 101–108)

Supporting Inferences About Literary Texts

Theme: *Tales of the Unexpected*

1 LESSON OBJECTIVES

- Use details and examples from a text when explaining what the text says explicitly.
- Use details and examples from a text, along with background and personal knowledge, when explaining inferences drawn from the text.

2 THE LEARNING PROGRESSION

- **Grade 3:** CCSS RL.3.1 requires students to ask and answer questions to show their understanding of a text, and to use the text to support understanding of its literal meaning.
- **Grade 4: CCSS RL.4.1 requires students to read the text closely to draw out and articulate both literal and inferential meanings. Grade 4 is the first time the cognitive and demonstrative skill of "making inferences" appears in the standards.**
- **Grade 5:** CCSS RL.5.1 requires students not only to refer to the text when drawing inferences but also to quote from the text to support that inference.

3 PREREQUISITE SKILLS

- Identify important details in a text.
- Ask and answer questions about details and events found in a text.
- Support answers by referring explicitly to the text.

4 TAP STUDENTS' PRIOR KNOWLEDGE

- Tell students they will be working on a lesson about supporting inferences about a text. Explain that an inference is an informed or educated guess.
- Tell students they make inferences every day. Have them imagine a child wearing a party hat and blowing out 10 candles on a cake. What educated guess can they make? (*It's the child's tenth birthday.*)
- Next, display these sentences: "All of the students had their hands raised. The teacher had a happy look on his face."
- Ask students to think about the information in those sentences. What details do they provide? (*students had their hands raised; happy teacher*) Explain that these details and examples can become the basis for inferences about the text.
- Then ask students to think about what they already know. When have they seen a teacher with a happy look on his or her face? Remind students that the text contains details about what a reader might already know. Explain that authors often rely on readers having some knowledge of a topic.
- Finally, ask students what inference they can make based on the sentences about the happy teacher. (*All the students knew the answer.*)

5 **Ready** *Teacher Toolbox* — *Teacher-Toolbox.com*

	Prerequisite Skills	RL.4.1
Ready Lessons	✓	✓
Tools for Instruction		✓✓
Interactive Tutorials		

6 CCSS Focus

RL.4.1 Refer to details and examples in a text when explaining what the text says explicitly and when drawing inferences from the text.

ADDITIONAL STANDARDS: **RL.4.2; RL.4.3; RL.4.4; W.4.1; W.4.2; W.4.4; SL.4.1; SL.4.2; SL.4.4; L.4.1; L.4.1.g; L.4.2.b; L.4.4.b; L.4.5.b** *(see page A31 for full text).*

©Curriculum Associates, LLC Copying is not permitted. **103**

Introduction

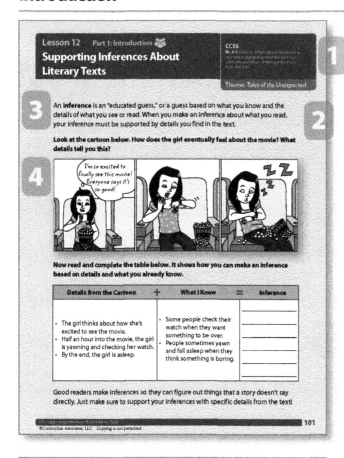

The Introduction builds student confidence and motivation by gradually introducing students to the lesson standard. Most pages begin by having students explore how they apply the strategy in non-text based ways. This page is meant to be teacher directed.

Student Book

The CCSS covered in the lesson are given, and the theme for the lesson is identified.

This page gives a student-friendly overview of the skills, concepts, strategies, and vocabulary of the covered standard(s).

Key vocabulary appears in boldface.

Visual aids—such as cartoons, tables, charts, and graphic organizers—engage struggling readers and visual learners.

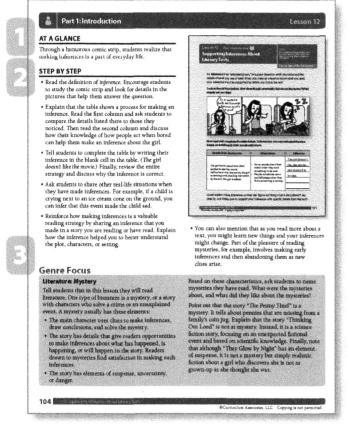

Teacher Resource Book

At a Glance provides a brief overview of what students do in each lesson part.

Step by Step provides an explicit walk-through of the steps for guiding students through each lesson part.

Genre Focus provides a student-friendly introduction to one of the genres featured in the lesson.

Modeled Instruction

The teacher models how a good reader goes about the process of answering a question. The teacher begins by reading the passage aloud, and then, using the think-aloud support in the Teacher Resource Book, guides students through answering the question. Depending on the support your students need, you may choose to do this page together with the class or first have students independently complete the activity, and then review it together.

Student Book

1 The genre for each passage is identified by the Genre tab.

2 Students begin by applying the strategy to a short piece of text.

3 Clearly stated steps walk students through the thought process for responding to the question.

Teacher Resource Book

1 A detailed Think Aloud models the thought process for answering the question.

2 The ELL Support feature targets language concepts that students who are learning English may need reinforcement on, including compound words, prefixes, suffixes, contractions, homophones, multiple-meaning words, and regular and irregular verbs.

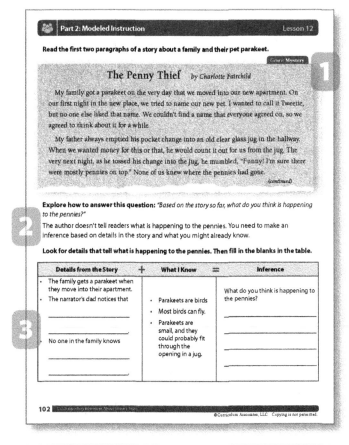

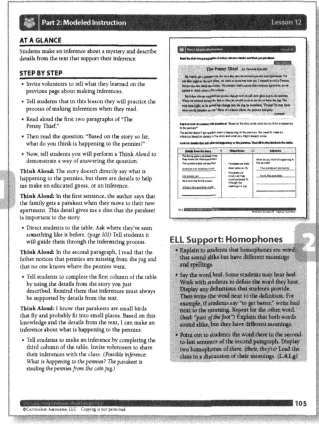

Guided Instruction

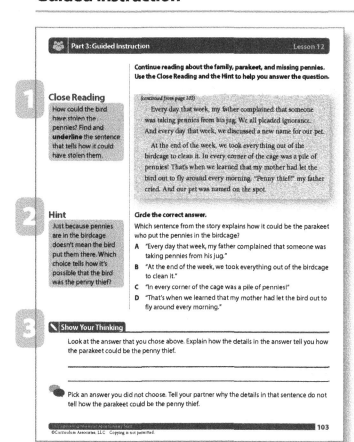

Students work through a sample question. The Close Reading and Hint provide strong guidance. After students respond to the question independently and respond to the Show Your Thinking prompt, partners discuss the reasons for their answers. Finally, the teacher discusses the steps leading to the correct answer, and discusses why the other choices are not correct.

Student Book

1 Close Reading encourages students to interact with the text, often directing them to mark up the text by underlining, circling, or note-taking.

2 The Hint provides clues to help students respond to a specific question.

3 Show Your Thinking challenges students to explain why the answer they chose is correct. A thoughtful open-ended question is posed for discussion.

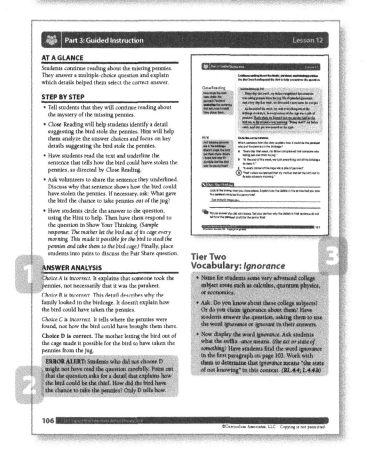

Teacher Resource Book

1 Answer Analysis explains why an answer is correct and identifies the types of errors students commonly make in choosing incorrect answer choices.

2 Error Alert addresses common errors or misconceptions that lead students to an incorrect answer.

3 Tier Two Vocabulary gives guidance on helping students use text-based strategies to understand a given word. Tier Two (or general academic) words are more common in complex texts than in speech. Since they occur in many types of reading, a knowledge of Tier Two words is a powerful aid to comprehension.

x

Guided Practice

The Study Buddy, Close Reading, and Hints provide guidance as students read a longer passage and answer several questions. After an initial reading with students, the teacher checks literal comprehension by asking the questions in the Teacher Resource Book. After the second reading, students and teacher discuss the Study Buddy and Close Reading activities, then students use the Hints to answer the questions.

Student Book

1 Students apply the targeted reading strategy to a longer piece of text.

2 The Study Buddy is the student's reading coach, modeling strategies proficient readers use to access text.

3 Close Reading activities continue to guide students.

Teacher Resource Book

1 Written by experienced teachers, Tips provide thoughtful and practical suggestions on how to deepen students' understanding and appreciation of the target strategy.

2 ELL Support continues to appear at point of use.

3 Multi-paragraph, full-page passages are read and then reread, enforcing the good habits of close reading.

Teaching Tip: Read the Study Buddy prompt together with students and discuss how it relates to the text.

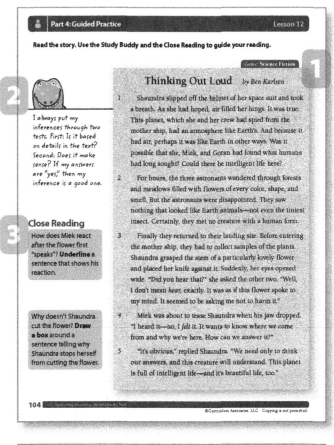

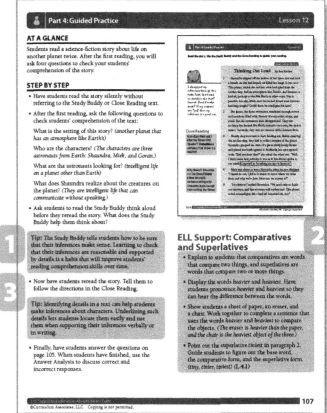

Guided Practice

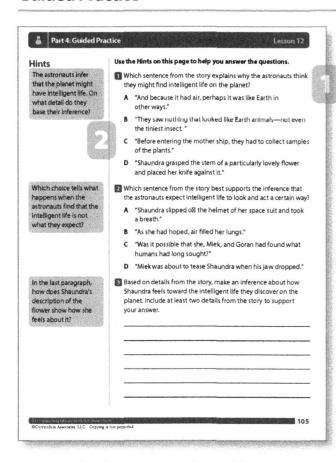

Student Book

1 Students answer a series of multiple-choice and/or short-response questions on the targeted skill.

2 Clues in the Hints draw students back to the text to find text-based evidence.

Teaching Tip: As you review the answers to each question in the Guided Practice, ask students how the Close Reading activity helps them answer the question. Probe how and why the parts of the text they marked up are evidence that they can cite in their answer.

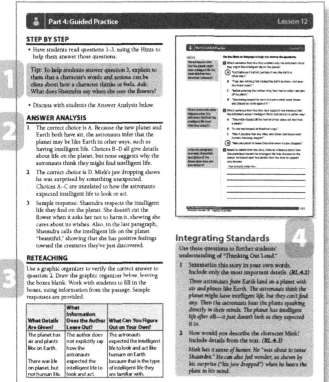

Teacher Resource Book

1 The Tip helps teachers extend one or more of the Hints.

2 Answer Analysis provides detailed discussion of why each answer choice is correct or incorrect, as well as a sample answer for the open-ended questions.

3 Reteaching reinforces and deepens students' learning by using a graphic organizer to visually depict and verify the correct answer to one of the questions.

4 Integrating Standards helps teachers integrate standard instruction by providing specific questions and short activities that apply standards in addition to the targeted one. Standard codes are provided at point of use.

Common Core Practice

Scaffolding is removed. Students work independently to read a longer passage and answer a series of multiple-choice and short-response questions. Students mark their answers directly in the Student Book by filling in bubbles in an Answer Form. After students have completed the questions, they record the number of questions they answered correctly in the scoring box on the right side of the Answer Form. The teacher can use the Answer Analysis to review correct and incorrect answers, encouraging students to discuss the thought process they used in their responses.

Student Book

 Students apply the targeted strategy to a longer and more difficult text.

Teaching Tip: To encourage students to transfer the skills they've learned, have students ask themselves the following four questions, formulated by reading expert Nancy Boyles, as they reflect on the Common Core Practice passage. (Boyles, 2012/13)

- What is the author telling me here?
- Are there any hard or important words?
- What does the author want me to understand?
- How does the author play with language to add to meaning?

Teacher Resource Book

1 The Answer Form on the facsimile of the Student Book pages has the bubbles filled in for easy scoring.

2 Theme Connection provides short questions and activities that help students make connections among the lesson passages and build content knowledge about the lesson theme.

3 Answer Analysis provides detailed discussion of why each answer choice is correct or incorrect, as well as a sample answer for the open-ended questions.

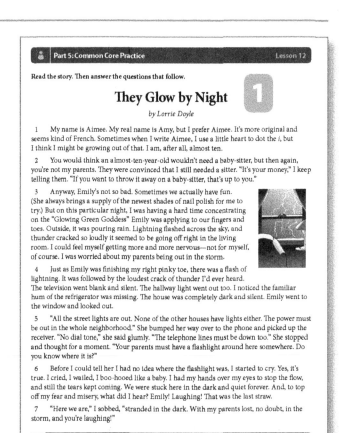

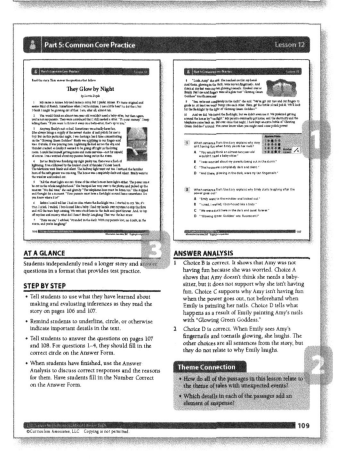

Common Core Practice

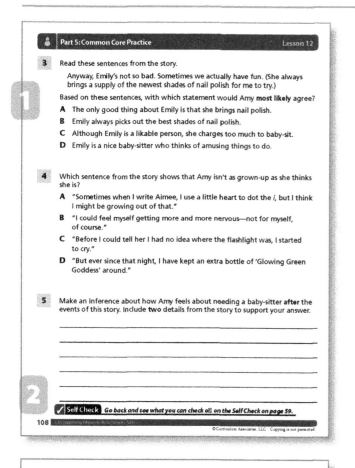

Student Book

1 Students answer multiple-choice and open-ended questions on the Common Core Practice passage.

2 Students are reminded to update their Self Check, located at the beginning of every unit, to reflect the learning accomplished in the lesson.

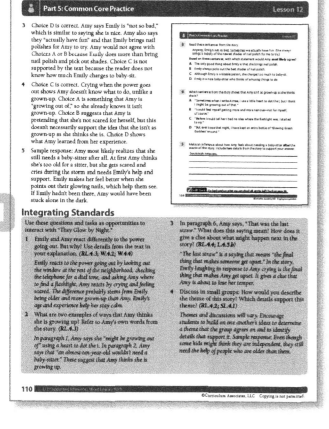

Teacher Resource Book

1 Integrating Standards helps teachers integrate all ELA standards instruction, including appropriate Language, Speaking & Listening, and Writing standards by providing specific questions and short activities that apply to the Common Core Practice passage. Standard codes are provided at point of use.

Additional Activities

Additional Activities provides short activities that allow you to expand on the passages in the lesson with meaningful standards-based Writing, Language, and Speaking & Listening activities. Standards codes are identified at point of use next to each activity, allowing you to easily integrate standards instruction.

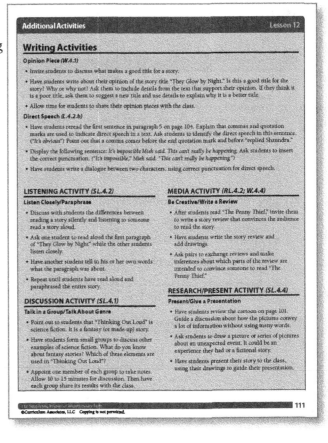

Interim Assessments

Interim Assessments are given at the end of each unit to assess students' understanding of the unit standards and to measure progress.

- Questions include both multiple-choice and short-response items that assess all of the unit's standards.

- A Performance Task—Extended Response asks students to write a longer essay about some aspect of the passage, citing evidence from the text to support their response. This item reflects how the testing consortia apply extended-response essays as a part of their performance-based events.

- In the Teacher Resource Book, correct answers are indicated on the Answer Form. Correct and incorrect answers are fully explained in Answer Analysis.

- Rubrics for the short-response items and Performance Task guide teachers in assigning a score to these items. Sample Responses provide examples of what a top-scoring response should include.

Features of the *Ready® Common Core* Language Handbook

The ***Ready Common Core* Language Handbook** was created to help students develop proficiency with the Common Core State Standards for Language. Each lesson uses scaffolded instruction, beginning with an introduction and guided practice and then moving students into fully independent practice of the skills and strategies behind the Common Core. This section shows the key features of the Student Book and Teacher Guide.

Student Book

Introduction

The Introduction builds student confidence and motivation by introducing students to the lesson standard. This part of the lesson is meant to be teacher directed.

1 The CCSS covered in the lesson are given.

2 This section gives a student-friendly overview of the skills, concepts, strategies, and vocabulary of the covered standard(s).

3 Key vocabulary appears in boldface.

4 Visual aids, such as tables and charts, engage struggling readers and visual learners.

Guided Practice

The Guided Practice activity allows students to apply what they have learned in the Introduction. Students may work with partners in this part of the lesson.

5 The direction lines clearly identify how to complete the activity.

6 The Hint provides guidance to help students complete the activity.

7 Students apply the targeted language concept as they respond to a variety of activities, such as fill in the blanks, circling, and sentence completion.

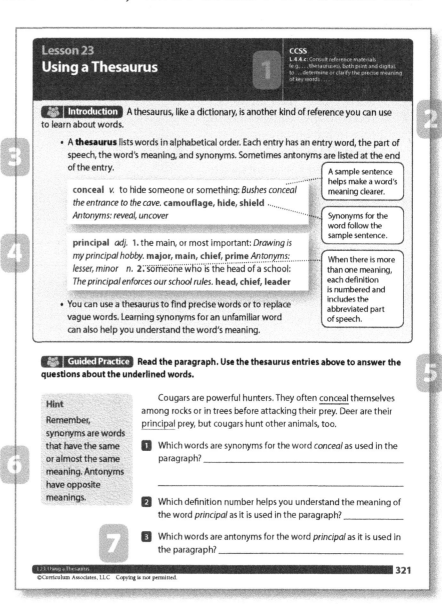

Common Core Practice

In the Common Core Practice section the scaffolding is removed. Students work independently.

8 Students answer multiple-choice questions related to the targeted standard. One lesson has short-response items.

9 Students mark their answers directly in the Student Book by filling in bubbles in an Answer Form. For short-response items, students write on writing lines.

10 Students record the number of questions they answered correctly in the scoring box. The lesson with short-response items has no scoring box.

Student Book

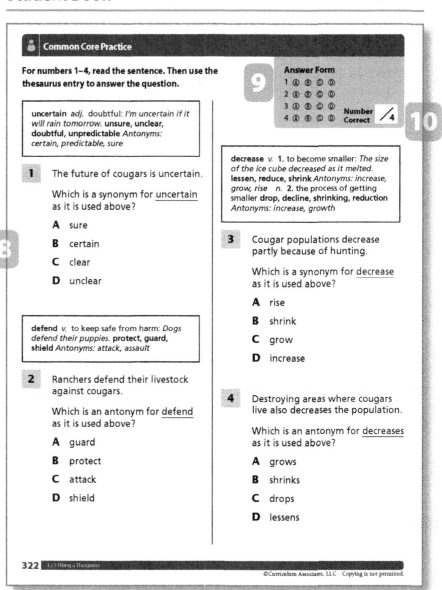

Common Core Practice

For numbers 1–4, read the sentence. Then use the thesaurus entry to answer the question.

uncertain *adj.* doubtful: *I'm uncertain if it will rain tomorrow.* **unsure, unclear, doubtful, unpredictable** *Antonyms: certain, predictable, sure*

1 The future of cougars is uncertain.

Which is a synonym for <u>uncertain</u> as it is used above?

A sure

B certain

C clear

D unclear

defend *v.* to keep safe from harm: *Dogs defend their puppies.* **protect, guard, shield** *Antonyms: attack, assault*

2 Ranchers defend their livestock against cougars.

Which is an antonym for <u>defend</u> as it is used above?

A guard

B protect

C attack

D shield

Answer Form
1 Ⓐ Ⓑ Ⓒ Ⓓ
2 Ⓐ Ⓑ Ⓒ Ⓓ
3 Ⓐ Ⓑ Ⓒ Ⓓ
4 Ⓐ Ⓑ Ⓒ Ⓓ Number Correct ⁄4

decrease *v.* **1.** to become smaller: *The size of the ice cube decreased as it melted.* **lessen, reduce, shrink** *Antonyms: increase, grow, rise* *n.* **2.** the process of getting smaller **drop, decline, shrinking, reduction** *Antonyms: increase, growth*

3 Cougar populations decrease partly because of hunting.

Which is a synonym for <u>decrease</u> as it is used above?

A rise

B shrink

C grow

D increase

4 Destroying areas where cougars live also decreases the population.

Which is an antonym for <u>decreases</u> as it is used above?

A grows

B shrinks

C drops

D lessens

322 L23 Using a Thesaurus

©Curriculum Associates, LLC   Copying is not permitted.

A34

Overview

Ready® Common Core Instruction is founded on research from a variety of federal initiatives, national literacy organizations, and literacy experts. As a result, this program may be used in support of several instructional models.

Ready® Uses . . .	Examples	Research Says . . .
Instructional Strategies		
Close Reading Close reading refers to the slow, deliberate reading of short pieces of text, focusing solely on the text itself, to achieve a deep understanding.	**SB:** Study Buddy and Close Reading features help students focus on the most important elements of the text.	"The Common Core State Standards place a high priority on the close, sustained reading of complex text. . . . Such reading focuses on what lies within the four corners of the text." (Coleman & Pimentel, Revised Publishers' Criteria, 2012, p. 4)
Multiple Readings Through reading a text more than once, students are able to access different levels of its meaning.	**TRB:** In Guided Practice, students read the text first, with follow-up discussion to confirm literal understanding before delving into more complex questions.	"[Close reading] often requires compact, short, self-contained texts that students can read and re-read deliberately and slowly to probe and ponder the meanings of individual words, the order in which sentences unfold, and the development of ideas over the course of the text." (Coleman & Pimentel, Revised Publishers' Criteria, 2012, p. 4)
Text-Dependent Questions Questions that are text-dependent can be answered only by information contained in the text itself, not personal opinion or background knowledge.	**SB:** Questions in each section of the *Ready* lesson are text-dependent. Students are required to support answers with evidence from the text.	"When examining a complex text in depth, tasks should require careful scrutiny of the text and specific references to evidence from the text itself to support responses." (Coleman & Pimentel, Revised Publishers' Criteria, 2012, p. 6)
Citing Textual Evidence The Common Core State Standards require students to provide evidence directly from the text to support their inferences about a text.	**SB:** Questions in the *Ready* lessons and Interim Assessments specifically require students to cite evidence from the text to support their answers.	"Students cite specific evidence when offering an oral or written interpretation of a text. They use relevant evidence when supporting their own points in writing and speaking…" (Common Core State Standards, 2010, p. 7)
Building Content Knowledge Reading multiple texts on a single topic builds knowledge and an increasingly deeper understanding of the topic.	**SB:** Passages in each lesson focus on a single topic or theme. Informational topics align with grade-level science and social studies curricula as well as high-interest grade level topics. **TRB:** The Theme Connection feature helps students make connections among lesson passages. Additional Activities allow students to expand their understanding of the lesson topic.	"Students establish a base of knowledge across a wide range of subject matter by engaging with works of quality and substance." (Common Core State Standards, 2012, p. 7)

Ready® Uses . . .	Examples	Research Says . . .
Instructional Strategies (continued)		
Direct Instruction Scripted lesson plans include explicit step-by-step instruction of reading and learning strategies and lesson objectives.	**SB:** The Introduction gives an overview of the lesson content. Step-by-step directions for answering questions are provided in Modeled Instruction. **TRB:** In the Step-by-Step section, explicit instructions are provided for the teacher.	"The research demonstrates that the types of questions, the detailed step-by-step breakdowns, and the extensive practice with a range of examples . . . will significantly benefit students' comprehension." (Gersten & Carnine, 1986, p. 72)
Scaffolded Instruction Scaffolded instruction is the gradual withdrawal of support through modeled, guided, and independent instruction.	**SB:** Graphic organizers, Study Buddy, and Close Reading provide support in earlier parts of the lesson, allowing students to achieve independence by the Common Core Practice section. **TRB:** The gradual-release model of Modeled/Guided Instruction and Guided Practice provides appropriate support that is gradually withdrawn as students gain mastery of the standard.	"Scaffolded instruction optimizes student learning by providing a supportive environment while facilitating student independence." (Larkin, 2002)
Prior Knowledge Prior knowledge activities activate knowledge from previous experiences.	**TRB:** Tap Prior Knowledge at the beginning of each lesson engages students in a discussion to connect the new skill to what they already know.	"Research clearly emphasizes that for learning to occur, new information must be integrated with what the learner already knows." (Rumelhart, 1980)
An Integrated Model of Literacy The processes of communication (reading, writing, listening, and speaking) are closely connected, a fact which should be reflected in literacy instruction.	**TRB:** Integrating Standards provides opportunities to apply Common Core State Standards beyond the target one. Additional Activities expand the lesson to include activities in the areas of Writing, Language, Listening & Speaking, Research, and Media.	"While the Standards delineate specific expectations in reading, writing, speaking, listening, and language, each standard need not be a separate focus for instruction. Often, several standards can be addressed by a single, rich task." (Common Core State Standards, 2010, p. 5)
Instructional Features		
Complex Text A major emphasis of the Common Core State Standards is for students to encounter appropriately complex texts at each grade level in order to develop the skills and conceptual knowledge they need for success in school and life.	**SB:** All passages in **Ready** conform to the leveling criteria outlined by the CCSS. (See page A11 of this document for more information on these criteria.)	"To grow, our students must read lots, and more specifically, they must read lots of 'complex' texts—texts that offer them new language, new knowledge, and new modes of thought." (Adams, 2009, p. 182)

Ready® Uses . . .	Examples	Research Says . . .
Instructional Features (continued)		
Balance of Informational and Literary Text; Emphasis on Literary Nonfiction at Grades 6–8 The Common Core State Standards align with the requirements of the National Assessment of Educational Progress (NAEP) in calling for a greater emphasis on informational text.	**SB:** Six units in each grade alternate Literary and Informational text. Nonfiction units at grades 6–8 include essays, speeches, opinion pieces, biographies, journalism, and other examples of literary nonfiction. **TRB:** The Genre Focus feature introduces the characteristics of each genre.	"Most of the required reading in college and workforce training programs is informational in structure and challenging in content . . . . the Standards follow NAEP's lead in balancing the reading of literature with the reading of informational texts. . . ." (Common Core State Standards, 2010, pp. 4–5. See also National Assessment Governing Board, 2008)
Answer Explanations for Students As a part of scaffolded instruction, students receive immediate feedback on their answer choices and the reasoning behind correct and incorrect answers.	**TRB:** In the Guided Instruction, Guided Practice, and Common Core Practice sections of each lesson, as well as in the Interim Assessments, answer explanations are given for each question.	Research (Pashler et al. 2007) has shown that when students receive direct instruction about the reasons why an answer choice is correct or incorrect, they demonstrate long-term retention and understanding of newly learned content.
ELL Support Some teaching strategies that have been proven to be effective for English learners include scaffolded instruction, use of graphic organizers, and modeling of language by teachers and peers.	**SB:** Features such as graphic organizers, Close Reading, Study Buddy, Hints, and Pair/Share partner discussions support English learners throughout the lesson. **TRB:** ELL Support boxes provide linguistic instruction at appropriate points.	"Graphic organizers facilitate ELLs' comprehension through visual illustrations of key terms, vocabulary, ideas, and the relationship among them." (Sigueza, 2005) Researchers state that one of the best practices for teaching ELL students is to model standard pronunciation and grammar. (Mohr & Mohr, 2007)
General Academic Vocabulary (Tier Two) General academic, or Tier Two, words are words a reader encounters in rich, complex texts of all types.	**TRB:** Tier Two Vocabulary boxes at point of use support the teacher in helping students use text-based strategies to figure out the meanings of challenging words.	"Tier Two words are frequently encountered in complex written texts and are particularly powerful because of their wide applicability to many sorts of reading. Teachers thus need to be alert to the presence of Tier Two words and determine which ones need careful attention." (Common Core State Standards, Appendix A, 2010, p. 33. The three-tier model of vocabulary is based on the work of Beck, McKeown, & Kucan, 2002, 2008)
Graphic Organizers Graphic organizers are visual representations of a text's organization of ideas and concepts.	**SB:** In the introduction, a graphic organizer is presented to represent the concepts and ideas of the lesson.	"Graphic organizers can provide students with tools they can use to examine and show relationships in a text." (Adler, 2004)

A37

References

Adams, M. J. (2009). The challenge of advanced texts: The interdependence of reading and learning. In Hiebert, E. H. (ed.), *Reading more, reading better: Are American students reading enough of the right stuff?* (pp. 183–189). New York, NY: Guilford.

Adler, C. R. (2004). Seven strategies to teach students text comprehension. Accessed at: *http://www.readingrockets. org/article/3479.*

Beck, I. L., McKeown, M. G., & Kucan, L. (2002). *Bringing words to life: Robust vocabulary instruction.* New York, NY: Guilford.

Beck, I. L., McKeown, M. G., & Kucan, L. (2008). *Creating robust vocabulary: Frequently asked questions and extended examples.* New York, NY: Guilford.

Boyles, N. (2012/2013). Closing in on close reading. *Educational Leadership,* 70(4), 36–41.

Coleman, D., & Pimentel, S. (2012). *Revised Publishers' Criteria for the Common Core State Standards in English Language Arts and Literacy, Grades 3–12.* Accessed at: *http://www.corestandards.org/resources.*

Fisher, D., Frey, N., & Lapp, D. (2012). *Text complexity: Raising rigor in reading.* Washington, DC: International Reading Association.

Gersten, R., & Carnine, D. (1986). Direct instruction in reading comprehension. *Educational Leadership,* 43(7), 70–79.

Hess, K. K., Carlock, D., Jones, B., & Walkup, J. R. (2009). *What exactly do "fewer, clearer, and higher standards" really look like in the classroom? Using a cognitive rigor matrix to analyze curriculum, plan lessons, and implement assessments.* Accessed at: *http://www.nciea.org/cgi-bin/pubspage.cgi?sortby=pub_date.*

Larkin, M. (2002). *Using scaffolded instruction to optimize learning.* ERIC Digest ED474301 2002-12-00. Retrieved from *www.eric.ed.gov.*

Mohr, K., & Mohr, E. (2007). *Extending English language learners' classroom interactions using the response protocol.* Accessed at: *http://www.readingrockets.org/article/26871.*

National Assessment Governing Board. (2008). *Reading framework for the 2009 National Assessment of Educational Progress.* Washington, D.C.: U.S. Government Printing Office.

National Governors Association Center for Best Practices and Council of Chief State School Officers. (2010). *Common Core State Standards for English Language Arts and Literacy in History/Social Studies, Science, and Technical Subjects.* Accessed at: *http://www.corestandards.org/the-standards.*

———. *English Language Arts Appendix A.* Accessed at: *http://www.corestandards.org/the-standards.*

Partnership for Assessment of Readiness for College and Careers. (2011). *PARCC model content frameworks: English language arts/literacy grades 3–11.* Accessed at: *http://www.parcconline.org/parcc-model-content-frameworks.*

Pashler, H., Bain, P., Bottge, B., Graesser, A., Koedinger, K., McDaniel, M., & Metcalfe, J. (2007). *Organizing instruction and study to improve student learning* (NCER 2007-2004). Washington, D.C.: National Center for Education Research, Institute of Education Sciences, U.S. Department of Education. Retrieved from *http://ncer.ed.gov.*

Rumelhart, D. E. (1980). Schemata: the building blocks of cognition. In Spiro, R. J., Bruce, B. C., & Brewer Erlbaum, W. F. (eds.), *Theoretical issues in reading comprehension* (pp. 33–58).

Sigueza, T. (2005). Graphic organizers. *Colorín Colorado!* Accessed at: *http://www.colorincolorado.org/article/13354.*

Smarter Balanced Assessment Consortium. (2012). *General Item Specifications.* Accessed at: *http://www. smarterbalanced.org/wordpress/wp-content/uploads/2012/05/TaskItemSpecifications/ItemSpecifications/ GeneralItemSpecifications.pdf.*

Correlation Charts

Common Core State Standards Coverage by *Ready® Instruction*

The chart below correlates each Common Core State Standard to each *Ready® Common Core Instruction* lesson that offers comprehensive instruction on that standard. Use this chart to determine which lessons your students should complete based on their mastery of each standard.

Common Core State Standards for Grade 8—Reading Standards		*Ready* Common Core Student Lesson(s)	Additional Coverage in Teacher Resource Book Lesson(s)
Reading Standards for Literature			
Key Ideas and Details			
RL.8.1	Cite the textual evidence that most strongly supports an analysis of what the text says explicitly as well as inferences drawn from the text.	6	7–9, 15–18, 21
RL.8.2	Determine a theme or central idea of a text and analyze its development over the course of the text, including its relationship to the characters, setting, and plot; provide an objective summary of the text.	8, 9	6, 7, 15–18, 21
RL.8.3	Analyze how particular lines of dialogue or incidents in a story or drama propel the action, reveal aspects of a character, or provoke a decision.	7	6, 8, 9, 16, 18, 21
Craft and Structure			
RL.8.4	Determine the meaning of words and phrases as they are used in a text, including figurative and connotative meanings; analyze the impact of specific word choices on meaning and tone, including analogies or allusions to other texts.	15, 16	6–9, 17, 18, 21
RL.8.5	Compare and contrast the structure of two or more texts and analyze how the differing structure of each text contributes to its meaning and style.	17	9, 21
RL.8.6	Analyze how differences in the points of view of the characters and the audience or reader (e.g., created through the use of dramatic irony) create such effects as suspense or humor.	18	9
Integration of Knowledge and Ideas			
RL.8.7	Analyze the extent to which a filmed or live production of a story or drama stays faithful to or departs from the text or script, evaluating the choices made by the director or actors.	Media Feature 2	6–8, 18, 21
RL.8.8	(Not applicable to literature)	N/A	N/A
RL.8.9	Analyze how a modern work of fiction draws on themes, patterns of events, or character types from myths, traditional stories, or religious works such as the Bible, including describing how the material is rendered new.	21	—
Range of Reading and Level of Text Complexity			
RL.8.10	By the end of the year, read and comprehend literature, including stories, dramas, and poems, at the high end of grades 6–8 text complexity band independently and proficiently.	All Lessons	

Common Core State Standards for Grade 8—Reading Standards	Ready Common Core Student Lesson(s)	Additional Coverage in Teacher Resource Book Lesson(s)
Reading Standards for Informational Text		
Key Ideas and Details		
RI.8.1 Cite the textual evidence that most strongly supports an analysis of what the text says explicitly as well as inferences drawn from the text.	3	1, 2, 4, 5, 10–13, 19, 20
RI.8.2 Determine a central idea of a text and analyze its development over the course of the text, including its relationship to supporting ideas; provide an objective summary of the text.	1, 2	3–5, 10, 12–14, 19, 20
RI.8.3 Analyze how a text makes connections among and distinctions between individuals, ideas, or events (e.g., through comparisons, analogies, or categories).	4, 5	1–3, 10–12, 14, 19
Craft and Structure		
RI.8.4 Determine the meaning of words and phrases as they are used in a text, including figurative, connotative, and technical meanings; analyze the impact of specific word choices on meaning and tone, including analogies or allusions to other texts.	10, 11	1–5, 12–14, 19, 20
RI.8.5 Analyze in detail the structure of a specific paragraph in a text, including the role of particular sentences in developing and refining a key concept.	12	3, 10, 13, 14, 19
RI.8.6 Determine an author's point of view or purpose in a text and analyze how the author acknowledges and responds to conflicting evidence or viewpoints.	13, 14	10, 11, 19, 20
Integration of Knowledge and Ideas		
RI.8.7 Evaluate the advantages and disadvantages of using different mediums (e.g., print or digital text, video, multimedia) to present a particular topic or idea.	Media Feature 1	1–5, 10–14, 19, 20
RI.8.8 Delineate and evaluate the argument and specific claims in a text, assessing whether the reasoning is sound and the evidence is relevant and sufficient; recognize when irrelevant evidence is introduced.	19	10
RI.8.9 Analyze a case in which two or more texts provide conflicting information on the same topic and identify where the texts disagree on matters of fact or interpretation.	20	3
Range of Reading and Level of Text Complexity		
RI.8.10 By the end of the year, read and comprehend literary nonfiction at the high end of the grades 6–8 text complexity band independently and proficiently.	All Lessons	
Language Standards		
Conventions of Standard English		
L.8.1 Demonstrate command of the conventions of standard English grammar and usage when writing or speaking.	—	2–4, 6, 8, 9, 15, 21
L.8.1a Explain the function of verbals (gerunds, participles, infinitives) in general and their function in particular sentences.	L1–L6	1, 2, 7
L.8.1b Form and use verbs in the active and passive voice.	L7	11
L.8.1c Form and use verbs in the indicative, imperative, interrogative, conditional, and subjunctive mood.	L8	4, 20
L.8.1d Recognize and correct inappropriate shifts in verb voice and mood.	L9	14
L.8.2a Use punctuation (comma, ellipsis, dash) to indicate a pause or break.	L10	15, 16, 18, 21
L.8.2b Use an ellipsis to indicate an omission.	L11	3, 12, 20

*Lesson numbers such as L12 refer to the Language Handbook.

Common Core State Standards for Grade 8—Reading Standards	Ready Common Core Student Lesson(s)	Additional Coverage in Teacher Resource Book Lesson(s)
Language Standards (continued)		
Knowledge of Language		
L.8.3 Use knowledge of language and its conventions when writing, speaking, reading, or listening.	—	6
L.8.3a Use verbs in the active and passive voice and in the conditional and subjunctive mood to achieve particular effects (e.g., emphasizing the actor or the action; expressing uncertainty or describing a state contrary to fact).	L12	—
Vocabulary Acquisition and Use		
L.8.4 Determine or clarify the meaning of unknown and multiple-meaning words or phrases based on *grade 8 reading and content*, choosing flexibly from a range of strategies.	—	14, 16, 17
L.8.4a Use context (e.g., the overall meaning of a sentence or paragraph; a word's position or function in a sentence) as a clue to the meaning of a word or phrase.	L13	1–3, 4–16, 18–21
L.8.4b Use common, grade-appropriate Greek or Latin affixes and roots as clues to the meaning of a word (e.g., *precede, recede, secede*).	L14	1, 2, 5–7, 11–14, 16, 19, 20
L.8.4c Consult general and specialized reference materials (e.g., dictionaries, glossaries, thesauruses), both print and digital, to find the pronunciation of a word or determine or clarify its precise meaning or its part of speech.	L15, L16	5, 7, 9, 13, 17, 20
L.8.4d Verify the preliminary determination of the meaning of a word or phrase (e.g., by checking the inferred meaning in context or in a dictionary).	—	4, 6, 8–11, 14, 16, 18, 19
L.8.5 Demonstrate understanding of figurative language, word relationships, and nuances in word meanings.	—	2
L.8.5a Interpret figures of speech (e.g. verbal irony, puns) in context.	L17	8–10, 17, 18, 20
L.8.5b Use the relationship between particular words to better understand each of the words.	L18	8, 21
L.8.5c Distinguish among the connotations (associations) of words with similar denotations (definitions) (e.g., *bullheaded, willful, firm, persistent, resolute*).	L19	15, 18, 21

Additional Coverage of Common Core ELA Standards, Grade 8	Ready Common Core Teacher Resource Book Lesson(s)

Writing Standards

Text Types and Purposes

W.8.1	Write arguments to support claims with clear reasons and relevant evidence.	3, 5, 7, 10, 11, 14, 19, 20
W.8.2	Write informative/explanatory texts to examine a topic and convey ideas, concepts, and information through the selection, organization, and analysis of relevant content.	2–5, 12–15, 18
W.8.3	Write narratives to develop real or imagined experiences or events using effective technique, relevant descriptive details, and well-structured event sequences.	1, 8, 9, 16, 21

Production and Distribution of Writing

W.8.4	Produce clear and coherent writing in which the development, organization, and style are appropriate to task, purpose, and audience.	1, 2, 5, 6, 8, 9, 11, 12, 15, 17–19, 21
W.8.5	With some guidance and support from peers and adults, develop and strengthen writing as needed by planning, revising, editing, rewriting, or trying a new approach, focusing on how well purpose and audience have been addressed.	13
W.8.6	Use technology, including the Internet, to produce and publish writing and present the relationships between information and ideas efficiently as well as to interact and collaborate with others.	4, 10, 11, 14

Research to Build and Present Knowledge

W.8.7	Conduct short research projects to answer a question (including a self-generated question), drawing on several sources and generating additional related, focused questions that allow for multiple avenues of exploration.	1, 4–7, 9, 10, 11, 13, 15–19, 21
W.8.8	Gather relevant information from multiple print and digital sources, using search terms effectively; assess the credibility and accuracy of each source; and quote or paraphrase the data and conclusions of others while avoiding plagiarism and following a standard format for citation.	2, 3, 5, 8, 9, 12, 13, 15, 16, 20

Speaking and Listening Standards

Comprehension and Collaboration

SL.8.1	Engage effectively in a range of collaborative discussions (one-on-one, in groups, and teacher-led) with diverse partners on *grade 8 topics, texts, and issues*, building on others' ideas and expressing their own clearly.	1–21
SL.8.2	Analyze the purpose of information presented in diverse media and formats (e.g., visually, quantitatively, orally) and evaluate the motives (e.g., social, commercial, political) behind its presentation.	3, 13
SL.8.3	Delineate a speaker's argument and specific claims, evaluating the soundness of the reasoning and relevance and sufficiency of the evidence and identifying when irrelevant evidence is introduced.	19

Presentation of Knowledge and Ideas

SL.8.4	Present claims and findings, emphasizing salient points in a focused, coherent manner with relevant evidence, sound valid reasoning, and well-chosen details; use appropriate eye contact, adequate volume, and clear pronunciation.	1–9, 11–21
SL.8.5	Integrate multimedia and visual displays into presentations to clarify information, strengthen claims and evidence, and add interest.	1, 6, 10, 12, 15, 16, 21
SL.8.6	Adapt speech to a variety of contexts and tasks, demonstrating command of formal English when indicated or appropriate.	1, 2, 4, 5, 11–13, 17

Additional Coverage of Reading Standards for Literacy in History/Social Studies and Science and Technical Subjects, Grade 8	Ready Common Core Student Book Lesson(s)

Reading Standards for Literacy in History/Social Studies

Key Ideas and Details

RH.6-8.1	Cite specific textual evidence to support analysis of primary and secondary sources.	5
RH.6-8.2	Determine the central ideas or information of a primary or secondary source; provide an accurate summary of the source distinct from prior knowledge or opinions.	1, 2

Craft and Structure

RH.6-8.4	Determine the meaning of words and phrases as they are used in a text, including vocabulary specific to domains related to history/social studies.	11
RH.6-8.5	Describe how a text presents information (e.g., sequentially, comparatively, causally).	12
RH.6-8.6	Identify aspects of a text that reveal an author's point of view or purpose (e.g., loaded language, inclusion or avoidance of particular facts).	13, 14

Integration of Knowledge and Ideas

RH.6-8.8	Distinguish among fact, opinion, and reasoned judgment in a text.	19

Reading Standards for Literacy in Science and Technical Subjects

Key Ideas and Details

RST.6-8.1	Cite specific textual evidence to support analysis of science and technical texts.	3

Craft and Structure

RST.6-8.4	Determine the meaning of symbols, key terms, and other domain-specific words and phrases as they are used in a specific scientific or technical context relevant to grades 6–8 texts and topics.	10

Interim Assessment Answer Keys and Correlations

The charts below show the answers to multiple-choice items in each unit's Interim Assessment along with the page numbers for sample responses to constructed-response items. The charts also display the depth-of-knowledge (DOK) index, standard(s) addressed, and corresponding *Ready® Common Core Instruction* lesson(s) for every item. Use this information to adjust lesson plans and focus remediation.

Ready Common Core Interim Assessment Answer Keys and Correlations

Unit 1: Key Ideas and Details in Informational Text

Question	Key	DOK[1]	Standard(s)	Ready Common Core Student Lesson(s)
1A	A	3	RI.8.1	3
1B	D	3	RI.8.1	3
2	C	3	RI.8.1	3
3	B	2	RI.8.2	1
4	D	2	RI.8.3	4
5	See page 47.	2	RI.8.2	2
6	See page 47.	3	RI.8.2	1
7	See page 47.	3	RI.8.3	4
8	See page 47.	3	RI.8.3	4
9	See page 47.	3	RI.8.3	5

Unit 2: Key Ideas and Details in Literature

Question	Key	DOK	Standard(s)	Ready Common Core Student Lesson(s)
1	A	2	RL.8.1	6
2	A	2	RL.8.3	7
3	B	2	RL.8.1	6
4	D	2	RL.8.3	7
5A	B	3	RL.8.2	8
5B	See page 85.	3	RL.8.2	8
6	See page 86.	3	RL.8.1	6
7	See page 86.	2	RL.8.2	9
8	See page 86.	3	RL.8.1, RL.8.3	6, 7
9	See page 86.	3	RL.8.3	7

Unit 3: Craft and Structure in Informational Text

Question	Key	DOK	Standard(s)	Ready Common Core Student Lesson(s)
1A	D	3	RI.8.6	13
1B	B	3	RI.8.6	13
2	A	2	RI.8.5	12
3	D	2	RI.8.6	14
4	A	3	RI.8.4	11
5	D	2	RI.8.5	12
6	See page 134.	3	RI.8.4	10
7	See page 134.	3	RI.8.4	10
8	See page 134.	3	RI.8.6	13
9	See page 134.	3	RI.8.5, RI.8.6	12, 14

[1]Depth of Knowledge measures:
1. The item requires superficial knowledge of the standard.
2. The item requires processing beyond recall and observation.
3. The item requires explanation, generalization, and connection to other ideas.
4. The item requires analysis, synthesis, or evaluation of multiple sources or texts.

Unit 4: Craft and Structure in Literature

Question	Key	DOK	Standard(s)	*Ready Common Core* Student Lesson(s)
1	D	2	RL.8.4	15
2	D	3	RL.8.4	16
3A	A	2	RL.8.4	15
3B	A	2	RL.8.4	15
4	A	3	RL.8.6	18
5	B	2	RL.8.4	15
6	See page 175.	3	RL.8.6	18
7	B	3	RL.8.4	15
8	See page 175.	3	RL.8.4	15
9	See page 175.	3	RL.8.6	18
10	See page 175.	4	RL.8.5	17

Unit 5: Integration of Knowledge and Ideas in Informational Text

Question	Key	DOK	Standard(s)	*Ready Common Core* Student Lesson(s)
1	A	2	RI.8.8	19
2	A	2	RI.8.8	19
3	D	2	RI.8.8	19
4	C	3	RI.8.9	20
5	D	3	RI.8.9	20
6A	See page 198.	3	RI.8.8	19
6B	See page 198.	3	RI.8.8	19
7	See page 198.	3	RI.8.8	19
8	See page 198.	4	RI.8.9	20
9	See page 198.	4	RI.8.8, RI.8.9	19, 20

Unit 6: Integration of Knowledge and Ideas in Literature

Question	Key	DOK	Standard(s)	*Ready Common Core* Student Lesson(s)
1	A	3	RL.8.9	21
2	B	3	RL.8.9	21
3	B	3	RL.8.9	21
4	C	3	RL.8.9	21
5A	A	3	RL.8.9	21
5B	See page 215.	3	RL.8.9	21
5C	See page 215.	3	RL.8.9	21
6	See page 216.	4	RL.8.9	21
7	See page 216.	4	RL.8.9	21
8	See page 216.	4	RL.8.9	21
9	See page 216.	4	RL.8.9	21

Analyzing the Development of a Central Idea

LESSON OBJECTIVES

- Determine the central idea of an informational text.
- Analyze how facts, details, and other evidence develop a central idea.
- Analyze the relationship between a central idea and supporting details.

THE LEARNING PROGRESSION

- **Grade 7:** CCSS RI.7.2 requires students to determine and analyze the development of two or more central ideas over the course of a text.
- **Grade 8: CCSS RI.8.2 builds on the Grade 7 standard by emphasizing how authors develop ideas through the use of supporting details.**
- **Grade 9:** CCSS RI.9.2 has students analyze the development of a central idea, including how it emerges and is shaped and refined by specific details.

PREREQUISITE SKILLS

- Identify central ideas.
- Recognize how ideas develop over the course of a text.
- Understand how details support central ideas.

TAP STUDENTS' PRIOR KNOWLEDGE

- Tell students they will be working on a lesson about how authors develop a central idea in a text. Ask students what a central idea is. (*what an entire text is mostly about*) Tell students they will learn how authors relate facts and information in the text, or the supporting details, to the central idea.
- Display this text for students: *American cities have many unique landmarks. In St. Louis, Missouri, visitors will see the huge Gateway Arch. Tourists can experience the well-known Golden Gate Bridge in San Francisco, California, and the Statue of Liberty, which looks unlike any other landmark in the world, can be viewed in New York Harbor.*
- First, ask students to identify the central idea. (*American cities have many unique landmarks.*) Then ask them to list the supporting details. (*huge Gateway Arch; well-known Golden Gate Bridge; Statue of Liberty, which looks unlike any other landmark*) Discuss how each example develops the central idea.
- Explain that when students are reading an informational text, understanding how all the details connect to the central idea of the text will help them to remember and understand what they read.

▉ **Ready** *Teacher Toolbox*		*teacher-toolbox.com*
	Prerequisite Skills	*RI.8.2*
Ready Lessons	✓	✓
Tools for Instruction		✓
Interactive Tutorials		✓

CCSS Focus

RI.8.2 Determine a central idea of a text and analyze its development over the course of the text, including its relationship to supporting ideas....

ADDITIONAL STANDARDS: **RI.8.1, RI.8.3, RI.8.4, RI.8.7; L.8.1a, L.8.4a, L.8.4b; W.8.3, W.8.4, W.8.7; SL.8.1, SL.8.4, SL.8.5, SL.8.6**
(*See page A39 for full text.*)

AT A GLANCE

By studying an illustration of a scene at a city park, students are introduced to the idea that supporting details relate to a central idea.

STEP BY STEP

- Read aloud the first paragraph, which introduces students to the concept of the central idea.

- Ask volunteers to distinguish in their own words between a topic and a central idea about a topic.

- Encourage students to examine the picture closely and read the caption. Tell them to circle picture details that relate to the central idea expressed in the caption.

- Explain that the chart shows a way of understanding the relationship between the supporting details and the central idea.

- Read aloud the central idea and the two supporting details. Discuss how the supporting details are specific examples of how parks are great places for relaxation and fun. Then have students add another supporting detail from the illustration to the chart. (*Sample response: Young people are playing soccer.*)

- Ask students to share other examples the artist could have included in the picture that would have served as supporting details for the central idea.

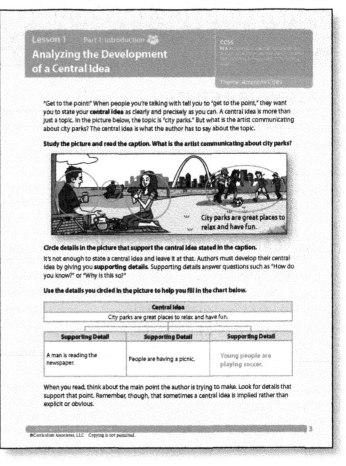

- Point out that sometimes the central idea is implied rather than explicit, and students must infer what the central idea is. Describe an informational text that you have read recently. Explain how you used details to infer the central idea.

Genre Focus

Informational Texts: Historical Account

Tell students that an informational text is any nonfiction text—printed or electronic—that is written to inform the reader about a topic or explain a concept or process. Examples include nonfiction books; magazine, newspaper, or encyclopedia articles; and instructions. Ask students to name other types of informational texts. (*biographies and autobiographies*)

Explain that one type of informational text is a historical account. A historical account is often based on historical documents or other primary sources. It may describe a place, event, trend, community, or individual from a specific time period. It provides readers with facts, examples, and other details about the past.

Based on these characteristics, have students give examples of historical accounts they have read. What was the topic of the account? What was the time period? How did reading a historical account add to their understanding of events in that era?

Tell students that in this lesson they will read historical accounts about three very different American cities: San Antonio, Texas; New York, New York; and Chapel Hill, North Carolina.

AT A GLANCE

Students identify the central idea in an informational text and explain how the author uses details to develop and support the central idea.

STEP BY STEP

- Invite volunteers to tell what they learned on the previous page about analyzing the relationship between a central idea and supporting details. Tell students that in this lesson they will learn to identify central ideas and supporting details when they read a historical account about San Antonio.

- Read "San Antonio's Remarkable History." Then read the questions: "What is the central idea? How does the author use details to develop the central idea?"

- Tell students you will perform a Think Aloud to demonstrate a way to answer the questions.

Think Aloud: I see from the title that the topic of this account is the history of the city of San Antonio. In the first sentence, the author says San Antonio is a large "modern-day metropolis." I think that's one important idea. As I continue reading, I see that the author tells some interesting facts about the city's early history. I think the central idea is not directly stated. It is a combination of these two ideas.

- Direct students to the questions on the second half of the page. Explain that the questions will help students figure out the central idea and how it is developed with supporting details.

- Have students answer the first question. (*Sample response: San Antonio is a modern-day metropolis with a remarkable history.*)

Think Aloud: Now I will look for details to support this central idea. The second paragraph is all about the history of San Antonio in the 1800s. The author gives the events in order, using actual dates. These are supporting details about the city's remarkable history.

- Have students answer the second question. (*Sample response: Details include facts about events that happened on specific dates.*)

- Ask students to answer the last question. Invite volunteers to share their answers with the class. (*Sample response: The details are connected by being told in sequence. Each event leads to the next.*)

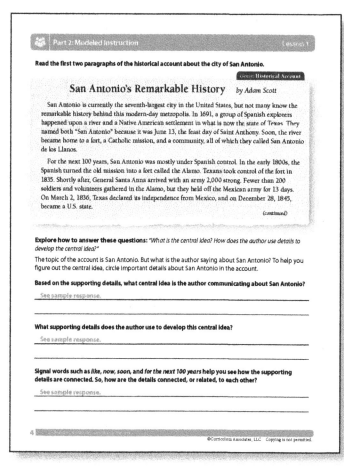

Part 2: Modeled Instruction Lesson 1

Read the first two paragraphs of the historical account about the city of San Antonio.

Genre: Historical Account

San Antonio's Remarkable History   *by Adam Scott*

San Antonio is currently the seventh-largest city in the United States, but not many know the remarkable history behind this modern-day metropolis. In 1691, a group of Spanish explorers happened upon a river and a Native American settlement in what is now the state of Texas. They named both "San Antonio" because it was June 13, the feast day of Saint Anthony. Soon, the river became home to a fort, a Catholic mission, and a community, all of which they called San Antonio de los Llanos.

For the next 100 years, San Antonio was mostly under Spanish control. In the early 1800s, the Spanish turned the old mission into a fort called the Alamo. Texans took control of the fort in 1835. Shortly after, General Santa Anna arrived with an army 2,000 strong. Fewer than 200 soldiers and volunteers gathered in the Alamo, but they held off the Mexican army for 13 days. On March 2, 1836, Texas declared its independence from Mexico, and on December 28, 1845, became a U.S. state.

(continued)

Explore how to answer these questions: *"What is the central idea? How does the author use details to develop the central idea?"*

The topic of the account is San Antonio. But what is the author saying about San Antonio? To help you figure out the central idea, circle important details about San Antonio in the account.

Based on the supporting details, what central idea is the author communicating about San Antonio?

See sample response.

What supporting details does the author use to develop this central idea?

See sample response.

Signal words such as *like, now, soon,* and *for the next 100 years* help you see how the supporting details are connected. So, how are the details connected, or related, to each other?

See sample response.

4

©Curriculum Associates, LLC   Copying is not permitted.

ELL Support: Multiple-Meaning Words

Explain that many English words have more than one meaning. These words are called multiple-meaning words. Tell students that when they find one of these words in their reading, using context—the meanings of the words and phrases surrounding the word—can help them determine which meaning of the word is being used.

- Point out the word *happened* in paragraph 1. Ask students what the word means, such as when someone asks, "What happened to your arm?" (*"came about, occurred"*)

- Tell students that *happened* has a slightly different meaning in the passage. Discuss the context: the founding of San Antonio in 1691 by Spanish explorers who had never been there before. Given this context, ask students what they think *happened* means here. (*"came upon unexpectedly or by chance, discovered"*) **(RI.8.4; L.8.4a)**

AT A GLANCE

Students continue reading about San Antonio. They answer a multiple-choice question and analyze how each paragraph helps to develop the central idea.

STEP BY STEP

- Tell students they will continue reading about San Antonio.

- The Close Reading helps students connect the supporting details to the central idea. The Hint will help them identify the answer that summarizes the central idea.

- Have students read the final paragraph and underline supporting details, as directed by the Close Reading.

- Ask volunteers to share the details they underlined and explain what central idea they support.

- Have students circle the answer to the question.

- If partners need help with the final activity, have them go back and reread all the details in the account they circled or underlined. Remind them that the central idea combines two main ideas—that San Antonio is a modern, thriving city and it has a rich history. Have partners think about how the city's history contributed to its growth into a modern city. That will help them see how all the ideas in the account connect to each other.

ANSWER ANALYSIS

Choice A is incorrect. The question asks for the central idea. That San Antonio prospered after the Civil War is a supporting detail about the city's transformation into a modern metropolis.

Choice B is incorrect. The siege of the Alamo is one event that supports the account's central idea.

Choice C is incorrect. Market Square is an example of how San Antonio is a thriving city, not the central idea.

Choice D is correct. It is the only choice that sums up the central idea and supporting details in the account.

ERROR ALERT: Students who did not choose D may be confusing central idea and details. Review that the central idea is the main point of a text and captures the important ideas in a summarizing statement. One detail alone cannot represent the ideas of a text.

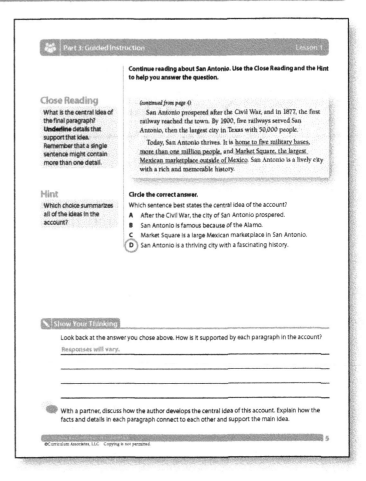

Tier Two Vocabulary: *Prospered*

- Read paragraph 1. Ask students what the paragraph is mostly about. (*how the coming of the railroad contributed to San Antonio's growth in the decades after the Civil War*)

- Direct students to the word *prospered* in the first sentence. Tell students that when people prosper, they don't just grow, they are successful, and they do well financially. In the context of a city's growth, ask students what *prospered* means. (*"expand in a successful way, thrive"*)

- Ask what other words would make sense in place of *prospered*. (*thrived, flourished*) **(RI.8.4; L.8.4a)**

AT A GLANCE

Students read a historical account about New York City twice. After the first reading, you will ask three questions to check your students' understanding of the text.

STEP BY STEP

- Have students read the text silently without referring to the Study Buddy or the Close Reading text.

- Ask the following questions to ensure students' comprehension of the text:

  What two cities would the Brooklyn Bridge join? *(Brooklyn and New York)*

  Why do you think the author included information about railroads, steamships, the telephone, and engineering feats in paragraphs 2 and 3? *(These details provide historical context by describing other innovations that were developed during this period and moved society forward.)*

  How would the Brooklyn Bridge benefit Brooklynites and New Yorkers? *(It would open up new markets for Brooklyn goods. It would help relieve overcrowding in New York City.)*

- Then ask students to reread paragraph 1 and look at the Study Buddy think aloud. What does the Study Buddy help them think about?

Tip: The Study Buddy reminds students to consider the title and look for details about New York in 1869. Point out that this date must be significant since it is in the title. Encourage students to determine what it represents and why it is central to the article.

- Have students read the rest of the text. Tell them to follow the directions in the Close Reading.

Tip: Point out that 1869 seems to represent a turning point from the author's point of view. Ask students to explain what the city is on the verge of. Recognizing this supporting detail will help students understand the article's central idea.

- Finally, have students answer the questions on page 7. Use the Answer Analysis to discuss correct and incorrect responses.

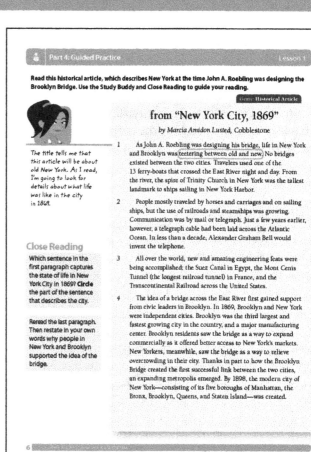

Tier Two Vocabulary: *Teetering*

- Point out the word *teetering* in paragraph 1. Tell students that *teeter-totter* is another word for *seesaw*. Have a volunteer demonstrate how a teeter-totter works.

- Based on the meaning of *teeter-totter*, ask students what image comes to mind when they hear the word *teetering*? *(something going up and down repeatedly)*

- Read the first sentence of the article. Discuss what the author means by "life in New York and Brooklyn was teetering between old and new." *(The cities were on the verge of leaving the old behind and entering the modern age.)*

- Based on what they know, ask students what *teetering* means. *("to swing unsteadily from one thing or position to another")* **(RI.8.4; L.8.4a)**

STEP BY STEP

- Have students read questions 1–3, using the Hints to help them answer the questions.

Tip: Remind students to identify the main point of each paragraph and see how the author connects them to develop the central idea of the whole article.

- Discuss with students the Answer Analysis below.

ANSWER ANALYSIS

1 The correct choice is A. It states a central idea. Choices B and C are incorrect. They state details from paragraphs 2 and 3. Choice D is incorrect. It is a supporting detail, not a central idea. It supports the idea of New York's transition from old modes of transportation to new.

2 The correct choice is C. It explains how the Brooklyn Bridge helped create modern-day New York City. Choices A and B are incorrect. They develop the idea that people wanted to build the bridge, not why it helped create modern-day New York City. Choice D is incorrect. Although it may be true, it does not support how New York City became the city that it is today.

3 Sample response: The final paragraph summarizes the significance and impact of the Brooklyn Bridge. The author explains how the bridge united two independent cities, and "an expanding metropolis emerged." The final paragraph also concludes that the Brooklyn Bridge created "the modern city of New York," tying together the ideas of life "teetering between old and new" in paragraph 1 and the world becoming more modern in paragraphs 2 and 3.

RETEACHING

Use a chart to verify the correct answer to question 2. Draw the chart below, and work with students to fill in the boxes. Sample responses are provided.

Central Idea The Brooklyn Bridge helped create modern-day New York City.	
Detail	**Detail**
united two independent cities	conveys sudden and dramatic growth

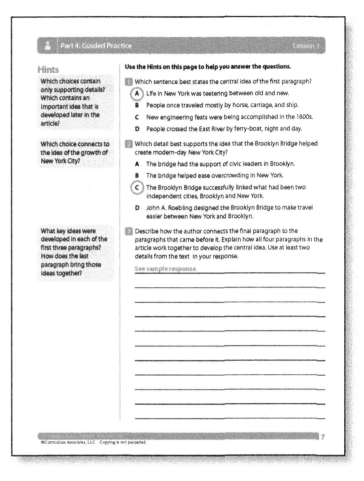

Integrating Standards

Use these questions to further students' understanding of "New York City, 1869."

1 What are other examples the author includes of the technologies being implemented and the engineering feats taking place in the second half of the nineteenth century? *(RI.8.3)*

Railroads and steamships were fast becoming common modes of transportation. A telegraph cable had been laid across the Atlantic Ocean. Other engineering marvels such as the Suez Canal and the Monte Cenis Tunnel were also being built.

2 Apart from Roebling's vision and design, explain the factors that contributed to the success of the Brooklyn Bridge. *(RI.8.1)*

The people of Brooklyn and New York saw the advantages of a bridge. Civic leaders and residents wanted it. Brooklyn was a manufacturing center. Linking the cities would relieve overcrowding.

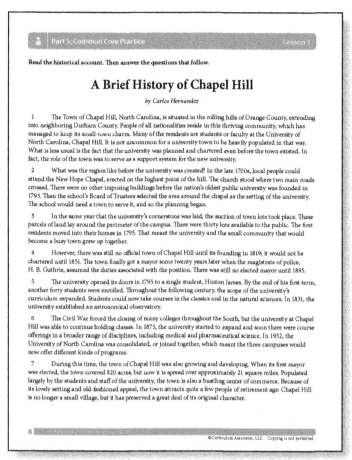

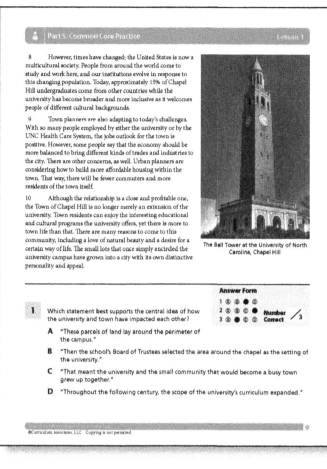

AT A GLANCE

Students independently read a longer account and answer questions in a format that provides test practice.

STEP BY STEP

- Tell students to use what they have learned about reading closely and tracing the development of a central idea to read the account on pages 8 and 9.

- Remind students to circle or underline important ideas or supporting details.

- Tell students to answer the questions on pages 9 and 10. For questions 1–3, they should fill in the correct circle on the Answer Form.

- When students have finished, use the Answer Analysis to discuss correct responses and the reasons for them. Have students fill in the Number Correct on the Answer Form.

ANSWER ANALYSIS

1   Choice C is correct. The question asks about the relationship between the university and the town. Choice C is the only choice that connects the two entities by referring to the fact that the school and the town were planned together and grew up together. Choice A is a supporting detail about how the town was originally populated, and Choice B is a detail about how the site for the university was chosen. Choice D also relates only to the university. **(DOK 2)**

Theme Connection

- How do all the accounts in this lesson relate to the theme of American cities?

- What is one fact or idea about growing American cities that you learned from each account in this lesson?

©Curriculum Associates, LLC   Copying is not permitted.

ANSWER ANALYSIS

2 Choice D is correct. This statement connects the "lovely setting" of Chapel Hill to attracting retired people, making it "more than just a college town." Choice A mentions the town's location, but that in itself does not support the statement. Choices B and C have to do with events that made Chapel Hill even more of a college town. **(DOK 2)**

3 Choice B is correct. It is a fact that shows that many nationalities are represented in Chapel Hill. Choice A is incorrect. Being a center of commerce might attract people from different countries, but that is not supported with facts. Choices C and D are evidence of the town's efforts to deal with economic growth, not of its diverse population. **(DOK 2)**

4 Sample response: The town has its businesses and the university has its courses and cultural life, but they have always been closely connected by the services the town provides the university. More and more, they have become two domains that thrive from exchange with one another. The author writes, "Although the relationship is a close and profitable one, the Town of Chapel Hill is no longer merely an extension of the university." Each offers something important. **(DOK 3)**

> **Part 5: Common Core Practice**   Lesson 1
>
> **2** One reason Chapel Hill has developed into more than just a college town is its location. Which sentence from the passage best supports this analysis?
>
> **A** "In the late 1700s, local people could attend the New Hope Chapel, erected on the highest point of the hill."
>
> **B** "In 1831, the university established an astronomical observatory."
>
> **C** "In 1932, the University of North Carolina was consolidated, or joined together, which meant the three campuses would now offer different kinds of programs."
>
> **D** "Because of its lovely setting and old-fashioned appeal, the town attracts quite a few people of retirement age."
>
> **3** According to the account, "People of all nationalities reside in this thriving community." Which detail from the account best supports this idea?
>
> **A** The town of Chapel Hill is a center of commerce.
>
> **B** About 15% of Chapel Hill's undergraduates come from other countries.
>
> **C** Town planners are adapting to modern challenges.
>
> **D** The economy needs to be more balanced to encourage business growth.
>
> **4** Explain how the relationship between the town and the university of Chapel Hill changed over time. Use at least **two** details from the account to support your explanation.
>
> _See sample response._
>
> _____
>
> _____
>
> _____
>
> _____
>
> _____
>
> _____
>
> _____
>
> ✔ **Self Check** Go back and see what you can check off on the Self Check on page 2.
>
> 10   ©Curriculum Associates, LLC   Copying is not permitted.

Integrating Standards

Use these questions and tasks as opportunities to interact with "A Brief History of Chapel Hill."

1 Why do you think the area around New Hope Chapel was chosen as the site of the new university? Cite details from the text to support your inference. **(RI.8.1)**

The account says that a chapel existed at the site, which was the highest point of the hill, and that two roads crossed there. A university built on a hill would be an imposing sight, and since people were used to traveling the two roads to the chapel, the school would be in a familiar and easy-to-reach location.

2 In paragraph 8 the author describes the university today as "broader and more inclusive." Tell what you think the word *inclusive* means. **(RI.8.4; L.8.4a, L.8.4b)**

This paragraph tells that the university has more students from other countries and cultural backgrounds. The account says that it "welcomes" these new students. Also, the prefix in- can mean "in,

into," as in include. *Given these clues, I think* inclusive *means "including everyone or everything," "encompassing."*

3 Write a brief summary of the account, including details that support the central idea. **(RI.8.2; W.8.4)**

Summaries may vary but should include details about Chapel Hill's unique relationship with the university and how it changed over time, creating two separate but vibrant, growing, and diverse entities.

4 Discuss in small groups: What is the central idea of this account? How does each paragraph in this account help to develop this central idea? **(SL.8.1)**

Discussions will vary. After students have agreed upon the account's central idea, have them take turns describing the role of each paragraph in this idea's development. Encourage students to elaborate on each other's ideas. Remind them to be sure to discuss each paragraph the author includes.

Writing Activities

You Were There (W.8.3)

- Challenge students to think about what Chapel Hill was like in 1795 based on details in "A Brief History of Chapel Hill." What is the story behind the facts of the town's and university's founding?

- Have students write a short story of the founding of the town from the viewpoint of either one of the first residents to move into the thirty parcels of land or a member of the Board of Trustees who had to "sell" the idea of a university to the other board members and the original inhabitants of the area.

Participial Phrases (L.8.1a)

- Tell students that a participle is a word that is formed from a verb but is used as an adjective. Point out the clause "our institutions evolve in response to this changing population" in paragraph 8 of "A Brief History of Chapel Hill." Tell students that *changing*, formed from the verb *change*, is a participle modifying *population*.

- Explain that sometimes other words accompany a participle. This is a participial phrase. Point out the phrase "extending into neighboring Durham County" in this account's first sentence.

- Ask students to find the participial phrase in paragraph 2. (*"erected on the highest point of the hill"*) Ask what noun it modifies. (*New Hope Chapel*)

LISTENING ACTIVITY (SL.8.6)

Listen Closely/Conduct an Interview

- Invite students to interview an adult about how the place where she or he grew up has changed over the years.

- Suggest that students write interview questions covering details similar to the ones in "A Brief History of Chapel Hill," such as changes to the landscape, population, and buildings.

- Remind students to listen carefully and record the interviewee's responses.

MEDIA ACTIVITY (RI.8.7)

Be Creative/Make a Video

- Invite partners or groups to make a video of their city or town. What will their central idea of the video be? What supporting details will they include in the dialogue or images to develop this central idea? Encourage students to write a plan before making their videos.

- Have volunteers play their videos for the class.

- Discuss with students how viewing a video of a place compares with reading an account about one.

DISCUSSION ACTIVITY (SL.8.1)

Talk in a Group/Compare and Contrast Cities

- Have students review what they learned about San Antonio, New York City, and Chapel Hill from this lesson's passages.

- Have students form small groups to compare and contrast the histories of these cities. What was similar about how they evolved over time? What was different? How are the cities similar to and different from each other today?

- Allow 10 to 15 minutes for discussion. Then have each group share its results with the class.

RESEARCH ACTIVITY (W.8.7; SL.8.4, SL.8.5)

Research and Present/Give a Presentation

- Tell students that John A. Roebling was a civic engineer. Have them use the facts in "New York City, 1869" to plan a presentation on Roebling.

- Students should research additional information on the engineer and write a brief report on some aspect of his life or work to present orally.

- Students should include architectural drawings, actual photographs, or their own or another artist's rendering of one of Roebling's works.

- Have students present their findings to the class.

Summarizing Informational Texts

LESSON OBJECTIVES

- Identify the central ideas in an informational text and the important details that support these ideas.
- Summarize an informational text by restating in one's own words the central ideas and important details.
- Provide an objective summary free of personal opinions or judgments.

THE LEARNING PROGRESSION

- **Grade 7:** CCSS RI.7.2 requires students to determine and analyze the development of two or more central ideas over the course of a text and provide an objective summary.
- **Grade 8: CCSS RI.8.2 builds on the Grade 7 standard by emphasizing how students should summarize texts objectively in their own words by using central ideas and supporting details.**
- **Grade 9:** CCSS RI.9.2 has students analyze the development of a central idea, including how it emerges and is shaped and refined by specific details and requires them to provide an objective summary of the text.

PREREQUISITE SKILLS

- Identify central ideas and details that support them.
- Recognize how ideas develop over the course of a text.
- Understand the connections between ideas in a text.
- Summarize information concisely and objectively.

TAP STUDENTS' PRIOR KNOWLEDGE

- Tell students that they will be working on a lesson about summarizing informational texts. Remind them that summaries are brief restatements of the most important information and ideas of a text.
- Ask students if they have ever told a friend about a movie they just saw or a book they just read. Explain that if they retell the story objectively, they explain major events in the story without giving their opinions or judgments.
- Ask volunteers to summarize a movie or book without giving any clues as to whether or not they liked it.
- Point out that a brief, concise summary is more helpful than a convoluted one because it's easier to follow and understand. Explain that summarizing an informational text is a very similar process.
- As needed, review how to determine the central idea of a text when it is not stated. (*Think about the important idea that the supporting details are trying to explain or describe.*)
- Point out that readers should restate the most important ideas in their own words. Being able to summarize the central ideas of a text will help students to better understand and retain the information they read.

Ready *Teacher Toolbox*

teacher-toolbox.com

	Prerequisite Skills	RI.8.2
Ready Lessons	✓	✓
Tools for Instruction	✓	✓
Interactive Tutorials		✓

CCSS Focus

RI.8.2 … provide an objective summary of the text.

ADDITIONAL STANDARDS: RI.8.1, RI.8.3, RI.8.4, RI.8.7; L.8.1, L.8.1a, L.8.4a, L.8.4b, L.8.5; W.8.2, W.8.4, W.8.8; SL.8.1, SL.8.4, SL.8.6 (See page A39 for full text.)

AT A GLANCE

By reading an informational text, students practice the process of summarizing in an objective manner.

STEP BY STEP

- Read the introductory paragraph that includes the definitions of *summary* and *objective*. Then have students read the text about the influence of the Roman Empire in early Europe.

- Once they have finished reading, have students underline any important pieces of information in the text that would be important to include in a summary of this text.

- Explain that the chart demonstrates how to summarize an informational text without including opinions or judgments.

- Ask volunteers to read the central idea, important details, and summary in the chart. Ask students if they would include any other pieces of information based on the text they underlined.

- Stress that when students summarize text, they should restate ideas using their own words. Ask volunteers to briefly summarize the text about the influence of the Roman Empire.

- Then read the paragraph below the chart. Reinforce the idea that summaries give a brief restatement of the most important ideas and help students to be sure they comprehend a text's most important points.

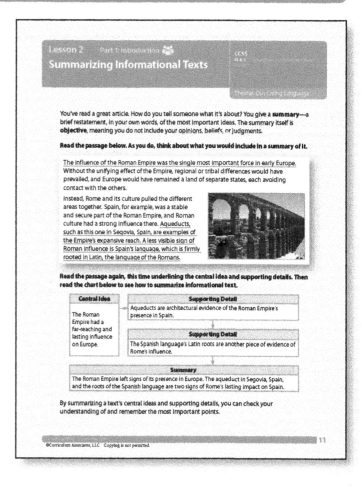

Genre Focus

Informational Texts: Report

Tell students that in this lesson they will read informational texts. One type of informational text is a report. A report is an informational text written to inform about a topic. Reports explain information and facts about a certain topic in an objective fashion. Point out that students have written reports for several types of classes, including science, history, and social studies.

Reports often include photos and captions to help readers understand the information. The writer of a report often ends by giving a bibliography telling where he or she found the information.

Explain that the short selection they just read comes from a report about the Roman Empire. It required research and used facts to explain important ideas.

Based on their previous schoolwork, ask students to name reports they have written for other classes. What classes have they written reports for? What topics have they written reports about?

Tell students that in this lesson they will also read another report, "The Signs of Language." It tells about deaf children in Nicaragua who invented their own sign language. Additionally, students will read two other passages. One is an essay about word etymology, or the history of words. The other is an article describing how languages change over time.

AT A GLANCE

Students read the beginning of an essay about etymology and determine what information should be included in a summary of this part of the essay.

STEP BY STEP

- Invite volunteers to tell what they learned on the previous page about summarizing a text's central idea and key supporting details.

- Tell students that on this page they will determine what information should be included in the summary of the beginning of an essay.

- Read "Understand English Word Origins." Then read the question: "What information should be included in a summary of this portion of the essay?"

- Tell students you will use a Think Aloud to demonstrate a way to answer the question.

Think Aloud: This passage gives two examples of words and their backgrounds. In the first sentence, the author says, "Some names of objects originate from the object's appearance." In the first sentence of paragraph 2, the author says that some word origins "tell us what an object used to be." These seem to be the two important details that should be included as part of a summary.

- Direct students to the chart and ask where they've seen it before. Remind them that it shows the process of summarizing an informational text.

- Ask students to write important details in the chart.

Think Aloud: Based on the idea that all of the details relate to, I can use the important details I identified to state the central idea that is implied by the text.

- Have students write the central idea in the chart.

- Then have a volunteer read aloud the summary at the bottom of the chart, and encourage students to compare it to the central idea and important details they recorded.

- Finally, have students discuss the prompt at the bottom of the page. Invite volunteers to share their answers with the class. (*Sample response: I would remove the words that show an opinion, such as* fascinating *and* great.)

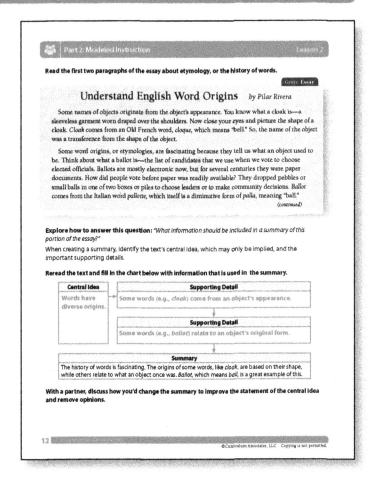

ELL Support: Possessives

- Explain to students that possessives are words that show who or what owns something. To make a singular noun a possessive noun, add an apostrophe and *s*. To make a plural noun a possessive noun, add only an apostrophe.

- Direct students to the phrase *object's appearance* in paragraph 1. Have them identify the possessive noun and tell whether it is singular or plural. (*object's; singular*) Then ask students what belongs to the object. (*its appearance*)

- Also tell students that some pronouns such as *my, your, his, her,* and *its* show possession. Have students identify an example of a possessive pronoun in this essay and what ownership it shows. (*your; eyes that belong to you*) **(L.8.1)**

AT A GLANCE

Students continue reading the essay about etymology. They answer a multiple-choice question and analyze the best summary of the text on this page.

STEP BY STEP

- Tell students that they will continue reading the essay about etymology.

- The Close Reading helps students recognize that the text does not always directly state the central idea. Remind students that a careful reading of the text will help them figure out the central focus. The Hint will help them read the question and answer choices carefully in order to select the best answer.

- Have students read the passage and jot down their ideas regarding the central idea of this part of the text, as directed by the Close Reading.

- Ask volunteers to share their ideas for the central idea of this part of the essay. If necessary, ask students to sum up this part of the text in a sentence.

- Have students respond to Show Your Thinking. Ask them to give reasons why they chose the summary they did. Then have students work in pairs to summarize the entire essay.

ANSWER ANALYSIS

Choice A is incorrect. It is not supported by facts in the text.

Choice B is incorrect. It provides some information regarding the origins of money words, but it does not explain the central idea.

Choice C is correct. It incorporates the central idea of this part of the text, which is the origin of money words. It also gives the main supporting details.

Choice D is incorrect. It contains an opinion, which makes this a poor summary.

ERROR ALERT: Students who did not choose C might not have a clear picture of what makes a good summary. Remind them that a good summary is a brief restatement. Only C gives a concise restatement without being too general or including an opinion.

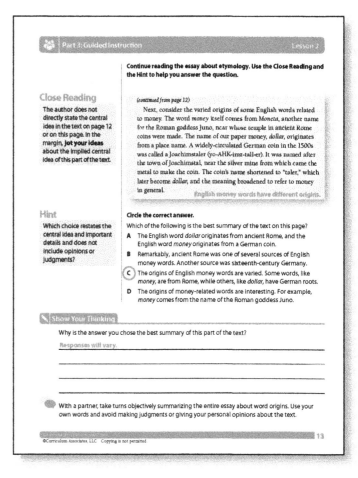

Tier Two Vocabulary: *Broadened*

- Direct students to the word *broadened* in the last sentence. Help them use context clues to figure out the meaning. (*"widened something, extended"*) **(RI.8.4; L.8.4a)**

- Ask students what words could be used in place of *broadened*. (*expanded, widened, enlarged*)

- Then have students name other phrases or uses of the word *broadened* they may know. (*broadened your horizon, broadened the coverage*)

AT A GLANCE

Students read a passage twice about sign language developed by children in Nicaragua. After the first reading, you will ask three questions to check your students' understanding of the passage.

STEP BY STEP

- Have students read the passage silently without referring to the Study Buddy or the Close Reading text.

- Ask the following questions to ensure students' comprehension of the text:

  According to the author, when and where did deaf children in Nicaragua make up their own sign language? (*In the early 1980s, 500 children at a school for the deaf began developing their own sign language.*)

  What does the author mean when he says, "no one 'spoke' sign language"? (*He means that deaf people communicated with gestures, not signs for words.*)

  Why is Nicaraguan Sign Language considered a new language? (*It has developed from simple gestures into a communication tool that uses complex signs and rules about combining signs into sentences. It is being taught in other schools and is being written down.*)

- Then ask students to reread paragraph 1 and look at the Study Buddy think aloud. What does the Study Buddy help them think about?

Tip: The Study Buddy tells students to underline the first sentence. Learning to identify the central idea of a text is an important part of understanding a report or any informational text.

- Have students read the rest of the passage. Tell them to follow the directions in the Close Reading.

Tip: The Close Reading guides students to identify the details that support the most important ideas in paragraph 2. Tell students that when they look for the main idea in a paragraph, they should also look for the points that support the central idea of the text. Encourage students to use this strategy as they look for central ideas that are not clearly stated.

- Finally, have students answer the questions on page 15. Use the Answer Analysis to discuss correct and incorrect responses.

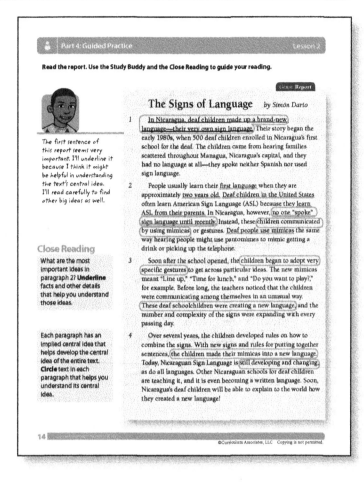

Tier Two Vocabulary: *Complexity*

- Point out the word *complexity* in paragraph 3. Have students identify the base word (*complex*) and the suffix (*-ity*). Elicit from students that the suffix *-ity* means "state or condition of." Then have students use the meaning of the suffix as well as the context of the sentence to determine the meaning of *complexity*. ("*state or condition of being complicated or advanced*") **(RI.8.4; L.8.4a, L.8.4b)**

- Have students explain what the text means when it says that the "number and complexity of the signs were expanding with every passing day." (*the signs were becoming more numerous and advanced*)

STEP BY STEP

- Have students read questions 1–3, using the Hints to help them answer the questions.

Tip: The first Hint reminds students that a summary is a brief restatement in their own words that does not include an opinion. Any words that convey a feeling or reaction toward the text should not be included in a summary.

- Discuss with students the Answer Analysis below.

ANSWER ANALYSIS

1   The correct choice is D. It contains only the facts and gives a concise summary of the sign language developed by deaf children in Nicaragua. Choices A and C use words that connote opinion. Choice B is a fact, but it lacks a central idea.

2   The correct choice is C. It states the facts from paragraph 2. Choice A takes a casual tone that doesn't focus on the facts. Choice B passes judgment. Choice D is also judgmental and does not include accurate facts from the report.

3   Sample response: At a school in Nicaragua in the early 1980s, deaf children who neither spoke nor used sign language turned a simple system of gestures into an entirely new language. Over time, the language continued to change and develop. Nicaraguan Sign Language is now taught at other Nicaraguan schools for deaf children.

RETEACHING

Use a chart to verify the correct answer to question 3. Draw the chart below, and work with students to fill in the boxes. Sample responses are provided.

Central Idea: Deaf children in Nicaragua made up their own new sign language.		
Detail: Deaf Nicaraguan children communicated with gestures.	**Detail:** Children adopted specific gestures to stand for specific ideas.	**Detail:** Nicaraguan Sign Language is still developing.
Summary: At a Nicaraguan school in the 1980s, deaf children who didn't speak nor use sign language turned a system of gestures into a new language. The language is still developing and is taught at other schools.		

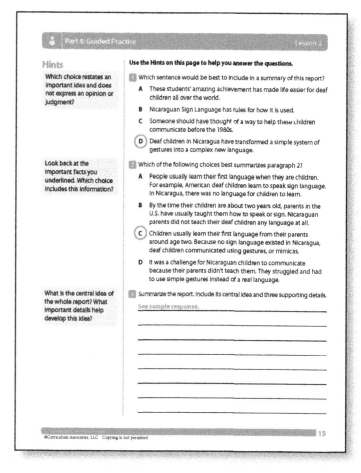

Integrating Standards

Use these questions to further students' understanding of "The Signs of Language."

1   How is Nicaraguan Sign language similar to other languages? **(RI.8.3)**

It uses specific gestures to get across particular ideas; the deaf children use it to communicate among themselves; it uses a complex system of signs and rules for putting together sentences; it is being taught in other schools and is becoming a written language.

2   How does the author explain *mimicas*? **(RI.8.1)**

The author defines mimicas as gestures and explains that deaf people use them the same way hearing people use pantomimes.

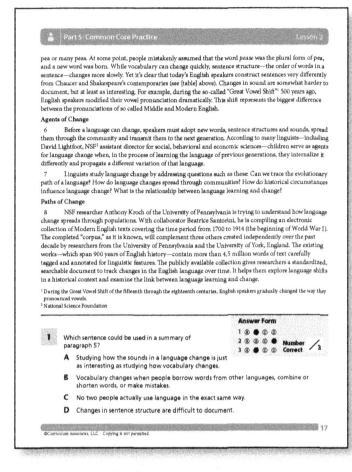

Read the social studies article. Then answer the questions that follow.

from "Language Change"

by Nicole Mahoney, National Science Foundation online

1 In some ways, it is surprising that languages change. After all, they are passed down through the generations reliably enough for parents and children to communicate with each other. Yet linguists find that all languages change over time—albeit at different rates. For example, Japanese has changed relatively little over 1,000 years. English, on the other hand, evolved rapidly in just a few centuries. Many present-day speakers find Shakespeare's sixteenth century texts difficult and Chaucer's fourteenth century *The Canterbury Tales* nearly impossible to read.

FROM *THE CANTERBURY TALES*	TRANSLATION
WHAN that Aprille with his shoures soote The droghte of Marche hath perced to the roote, And bathed every veyne in swich licour, Of which vertu engendred is the flour. . . .	When April with its showers sweet Has pierced the drought of March to the root And bathed every vein with that liquid By whose power is produced the flower. . . .

Why They Change

2 Languages change for a variety of reasons. Large-scale shifts often occur in response to social, economic and political pressures. History records many examples of language change fueled by invasions, colonization and migration. Even without these kinds of influences, a language can change dramatically if enough users alter the way they speak it.

3 Frequently, the needs of speakers drive language change. New technologies, industries, products and experiences simply require new words. Plastic, cell phones and the Internet didn't exist in Shakespeare's time, for example. By using new and emerging terms, we all drive language change. But the unique way that individuals speak also fuels language change. That's because no two individuals use a language in exactly the same way. The vocabulary and phrases people use depend on where they live, their age, education level, social status and other factors. Through our interactions, we pick up new words and sayings and integrate them into our speech. Teens and young adults for example, often use different words and phrases from their parents. Some of them spread through the population and slowly change the language.

4 No two individuals use a language in exactly the same way. The vocabulary and phrases people use are linked to where they live, their age, education level, social status and sometimes to their membership in a particular group or community.

Types of Change

5 Three main aspects of language change over time: vocabulary, sentence structure and pronunciations. Vocabulary can change quickly as new words are borrowed from other languages, or as words get combined or shortened. Some words are even created by mistake. As noted in the Linguistic Society of America's publication *Is English Changing?*, *pea* is one such example. Up until about 400 years ago, *pease* referred to either a single

16 ©Curriculum Associates, LLC Copying is not permitted.

pea or many peas. At some point, people mistakenly assumed that the word *pease* was the plural form of pea, and a new word was born. While vocabulary can change quickly, sentence structure—the order of words in a sentence—changes more slowly. Yet it's clear that today's English speakers construct sentences very differently from Chaucer and Shakespeare's contemporaries (see [table] above). Changes in sound are somewhat harder to document, but at least as interesting. For example, during the so-called "Great Vowel Shift"[1] 500 years ago, English speakers modified their vowel pronunciation dramatically. This shift represents the biggest difference between the pronunciations of so called Middle and Modern English.

Agents of Change

6 Before a language can change, speakers must adopt new words, sentence structures and sounds, spread them through the community and transmit them to the next generation. According to many linguists—including David Lightfoot, NSF[2] assistant director for social, behavioral and economic sciences—children serve as agents for language change when, in the process of learning the language of previous generations, they internalize it differently and propagate a different variation of that language.

7 Linguists study language change by addressing questions such as these: Can we trace the evolutionary path of a language? How do language changes spread through communities? How do historical circumstances influence language change? What is the relationship between language learning and change?

Paths of Change

8 NSF researcher Anthony Kroch of the University of Pennsylvania is trying to understand how language change spreads through populations. With collaborator Beatrice Santorini, he is compiling an electronic collection of Modern English texts covering the time period from 1700 to 1914 (the beginning of World War I). The completed "corpus," as it is known, will complement three others created independently over the past decade by researchers from the University of Pennsylvania and the University of York, England. The existing works—which span 900 years of English history—contain more than 4.5 million words of text carefully tagged and annotated for linguistic features. The publicly available collection gives researchers a standardized, searchable document to track changes in the English language over time. It helps them explore language shifts in a historical context and examine the link between language learning and change.

[1] During the Great Vowel Shift of the fifteenth through the eighteenth centuries, English speakers gradually changed the way they pronounced vowels.
[2] National Science Foundation

1 Which sentence could be used in a summary of paragraph 5?

A Studying how the sounds in a language change is just as interesting as studying how vocabulary changes.

B Vocabulary changes when people borrow words from other languages, combine or shorten words, or make mistakes.

C No two people actually use language in the exact same way.

D Changes in sentence structure are difficult to document.

Answer Form
1 Ⓐ ● Ⓒ Ⓓ
2 Ⓐ Ⓑ Ⓒ ●   Number Correct ___/3
3 Ⓐ ● Ⓒ Ⓓ

©Curriculum Associates, LLC Copying is not permitted. 17

AT A GLANCE

Students independently read a longer passage and answer questions in a format that provides test practice.

STEP BY STEP

- Tell students to use what they have learned about reading closely and summarizing to read the passage on pages 16 and 17.

- Remind students to underline or circle important points they would include in a summary.

- Tell students to answer the questions on pages 17 and 18. For questions 1–3, they should fill in the correct circle on the Answer Form.

- When students have finished, use the Answer Analysis to discuss correct responses and the reasons for them. Have students fill in the Number Correct on the Answer Form.

ANSWER ANALYSIS

1 The correct choice is B. It gives facts about vocabulary, which is one of the three main aspects of language change as covered in paragraph 5. Choice A is incorrect because it makes a judgment by calling the study of the changing sounds in language interesting. Choice C is mentioned in an earlier paragraph, and is not addressed in paragraph 5. Choice D is incorrect because it is a misquoted fact. The author notes that changes in sound, not sentence structure, are harder to document. **(DOK 2)**

Theme Connection

- How do all the texts in this lesson relate to the theme of our living language?

- What is the most surprising fact that you learned about language from the texts in this lesson? What makes it surprising?

©Curriculum Associates, LLC Copying is not permitted.

ANSWER ANALYSIS

2 The correct choice is D. The author does not state children are the best and most effective agents of language change. Choices A, B, and C all reflect important information from paragraphs 6 and 7, so each could be included in a summary of this section of the article. **(DOK 2)**

3 The correct choice is B. The author mentions collections of English texts that have been tagged and made available for study, showing how researchers use texts to understand changes in language. Choices A, C, and D are incorrect. Each gives supporting details related to the study of language but does not state a central idea. **(DOK 2)**

4 Sample response: Individual speakers are a major influence on language change. This is because no two individuals use language in exactly the same way. Every individual speaker has his or her own unique way of speaking. Many factors affect how an individual uses language, including location, age, education, and social status. When individuals interact with other individuals, they often spread new words and ways of saying things. If enough people start using a new word, for example, it eventually becomes part of the language. **(DOK 2)**

Part 5: Common Core Practice Lesson 2

2 Which sentence should not be used in a summary of paragraphs 6 and 7?
   A Linguists study language by asking how language changes spread.
   B Language changes must be adopted by a community and passed on to other generations.
   C Children change language by using it differently from previous generations.
   D Children are the best and most effective agents of language change.

3 Look at paragraph 8. What central idea do the sentences in this paragraph support?
   A Researchers study language changes in different communities.
   B Researchers are compiling vast collections of texts that will help them explore shifts in language.
   C Researchers use language to understand English history.
   D Researchers have discovered a link between language learning and change.

4 Summarize the relationship between individual speakers and language change. Use at least two details from the text in your response.
   See sample response.

✓ **Self Check** Go back and see what you can check off on the Self Check on page 2.

18

©Curriculum Associates, LLC   Copying is not permitted.

Integrating Standards

Use these questions and tasks as opportunities to interact with "Language Change."

1 Review the lines from *The Canterbury Tales*. Without reading the translation, what lines can you figure out on your own? Why? **(RI.8.1)**

Responses will vary. Students might recognize words such as Aprille, shours, droghte, *and* roote *because they have spellings close to those used now.*

2 What are some reasons why languages change, according to paragraph 2? **(RI.8.3)**

Reasons languages change include "social, economic and political pressures." Historically, languages changed because of invasions, colonization, and migration. Also, if enough people alter the way a language is spoken, the language will change.

3 In paragraph 3, what does the word *fuels* mean? **(RI.8.4; L.8.5)**

Here, fuels *means "drives." The unique way that people speak drives, or impacts, language changes.*

3 Reread paragraph 4. Write to explain the central idea of this paragraph. Then give an additional example that illustrates how vocabulary or the phrases used differ due to differences in people's location, age, or membership in a particular group or community. **(W.8.2, W.8.4)**

Answers will vary. Students should state that the central idea of the paragraph is that no two individuals use language in exactly the same way. Examples may include regional phrases or words, slang, jargon, or other differences in dialect.

4 Discuss in small groups: Reread the first sentence of the article: "In some ways, it is surprising that languages change." Based on details in the entire article, do you agree that it is surprising that languages change? Why or why not? Cite evidence from the text to support your opinion. **(SL.8.1)**

Discussions will vary. Students should refer to the article for evidence for their responses. Remind them to follow discussion rules.

Writing Activities

Write an Informative Summary (W.8.2, W.8.4)

• Ask students to review all the passages in this lesson. Then briefly review what students have learned about creating a good summary.

• Ask students to imagine that this lesson is a short book needing a description for a book jacket or online profile. Have students write a summary of the entire lesson. Remind them to be objective and to include information about each passage using their own words. Challenge them to keep their summaries brief.

Verbals (L.8.1a)

• Explain to students that infinitives and participles are two types of verbals. An infinitive includes the word *to* followed by a verb, such as *to help*. It functions as a noun in a sentence. A participle is a verb with the ending *-ing* such as *speaking skills*. It functions as an adjective in a sentence.

• Direct students to paragraph 8 of "Language Change." Point out the infinitive *to understand* in sentence 1 and the participle *existing works* in sentence 4. Discuss the function of each example.

• Ask students to write a brief paragraph about the importance of being able to summarize an informational text. Challenge them to include at least one infinitive and at least one participle in their writing.

LISTENING ACTIVITY (SL.8.4)

Listen Closely/Connect Ideas

• Have small groups review the central idea and important details in "Language Change."

• Have one student restate the central idea of paragraph 1. Then have students take turns telling important details that support the central idea.

• Each student listens closely, repeating the central idea and details that were already stated before adding another supporting detail from the text.

DISCUSSION ACTIVITY (SL.8.1)

Talk in a Group/Discuss the Role of Children

• Have students review the "Agents of Change" section in "Language Change."

• Pose a question to the class for discussion: Why do you think children are recognized as agents of change when it comes to language?

• Spark conversation by asking what students have noticed about the way younger siblings or other children use language. Do they mispronounce certain words or make up new ones? Encourage students to bring up any stories about language experiences to contribute to the discussion.

MEDIA ACTIVITY (RI.8.7; SL.8.6)

Be Creative/"Whan that Aprille"

• Play an audio recording of the well-known "Whan that Aprille" text excerpted in "Language Change."

• Then have students take turns reading the selection from *The Canterbury Tales* as it appears in the "Language Change."

• Students should listen to the varying ways they each pronounce unfamiliar words and refer to the recorded performance for correct pronunciations. Have students evaluate the advantages and disadvantages of listening to the audio and reading the written text.

RESEARCH ACTIVITY (W.8.8; SL.8.4)

Research and Present/Give a Presentation

• Have students work individually or form small groups and reread "Understand English Word Origins." Have each student or group present the etymology of a word of their choosing.

• Students should research the word using a dictionary, thesaurus, and other reference sources. Suggest the inclusion of interesting facts and first uses to make the presentation more engaging.

Citing Evidence to Make Inferences

LESSON OBJECTIVES

- Use explicitly stated details in an informational text, along with background knowledge, as evidence to make inferences about the topic of the text.

THE LEARNING PROGRESSION

- **Grade 7:** CCSS RI.7.1 requires students to cite several pieces of textual evidence to support an inference.

- **Grade 8: CCSS RI.8.1 builds on the Grade 7 standard by having students cite textual evidence that most strongly supports an analysis of inferences drawn from the text.**

- **Grade 9:** CCSS RI.9.1 requires students to cite strong and thorough textual evidence to support analysis of inferences drawn from the text.

PREREQUISITE SKILLS

- Recognize and understand explicit statements within a text.

- Draw inferences based on implicit information within a text.

- Recognize how authors use textual evidence to support claims.

- Cite specific evidence that supports a particular explicit claim or inference.

TAP STUDENTS' PRIOR KNOWLEDGE

- Tell students they will be working on a lesson about citing evidence to make inferences. Remind students that an inference is an educated guess that is based on facts and details in a text, along with their own background knowledge about the topic.

- Ask students why it is important to make inferences while reading. (*Sometimes an author doesn't say everything explicitly. Readers need to make inferences to understand something completely.*)

- Have students think about a nonfiction passage they read recently. Did the author describe every aspect of the topic completely? Did they have to make an inference? Have students provide examples of inferences they have made when reading and explain how they combined text evidence with their own knowledge to make the inference.

- Help students think of types of text evidence from which they can make inferences. (*specific words used to describe objects or events; direct quotes that provide additional information*)

- Explain to students that they should always pay attention to details that describe various aspects of an article's topic. These details help them not only understand what the article is about but also make inferences to understand what the author means but doesn't say directly.

Ready *Teacher Toolbox*

teacher-toolbox.com

	Prerequisite Skills	RI.8.1
Ready Lessons	✓	✓
Tools for Instruction		✓ ✓
Interactive Tutorials		✓

CCSS Focus

RI.8.1 Cite the textual evidence that most strongly supports an analysis of what the text says explicitly as well as inferences drawn from the text.

ADDITIONAL STANDARDS: *RI.8.2, RI.8.3, RI.8.4, RI.8.5, RI.8.7, RI.8.9; L.8.1, L.8.2b, L.8.4a; W.8.1, W.8.2, W.8.8; SL.8.1, SL.8.2, SL.8.4 (See page A39 for full text.)*

AT A GLANCE

By studying a photo and its caption, students practice making an inference based on evidence and what they already know.

STEP BY STEP

- Read the first paragraph and review the meaning of *evidence*, along with relevant examples. Explain that careful readers make inferences based on evidence as they read because it helps them understand a text and the information in it better.

- Have students study the photo and read the caption. Then have them think about the evidence in the image and the caption and whether it supports or disproves the idea that the photo shows an alien spacecraft.

- Explain to students that the chart will help them organize and analyze evidence from the photo and its caption, in addition to information they already know, in order to make a logical inference.

- Read the evidence in the chart, and have students compare it to the evidence they identified. Then have them add another piece of evidence.

- Next, read the Background Knowledge column, and guide students to suggest any additional background knowledge that is relevant.

- Finally, review the entire strategy and discuss why the inference in the chart is accurate.

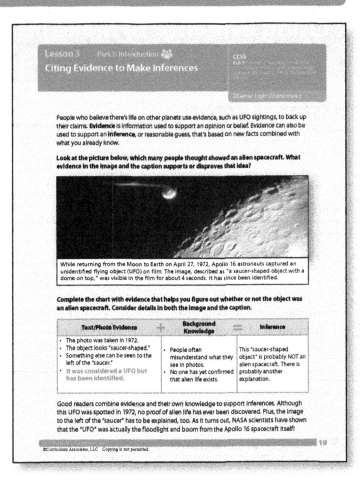

Genre Focus

Informational Texts: Scientific Account

Tell students that in this lesson, they will read three scientific articles. Explain that a scientific account is a type of informational text that provides timely information about a scientific topic. Remind students that the purpose of an informational text is to inform or explain. Scientific accounts are usually written about new discoveries or about topics that have recently changed. They provide detailed information and an explanation of this new information.

The opening of a scientific account usually engages the reader's attention, and the body of the article gives facts, examples, and details. It answers the questions *who, what, when, where, why,* and *how.* Articles may also contain subheadings, which signal what's coming next. Scientific accounts also contain technical scientific terms that may be unfamiliar to readers.

Explain that scientific accounts can be about many different topics, but they usually provide a great deal of information. For example, an article about space might be an informational article, but an article about the physics of space travel would be a scientific account. An article about pandas might be an informational article, but an article examining the stages of development in the life cycle of pandas would be a scientific account.

AT A GLANCE

Students read an scientific account about auroras and then use evidence from the account and what they already know to make an inference.

STEP BY STEP

- Invite volunteers to tell what they learned on the previous page about making inferences.

- Tell students that in this lesson they will read an account about auroras. They will make an inference about details they read in a text.

- Read "What Are Auroras?"

- Then read the question: "What inference can you make about why auroras fascinate people?"

- Tell students you will use a Think Aloud to demonstrate a way of answering the question.

Think Aloud: The author doesn't directly say why people find auroras fascinating, so I'll need to find clues in the account to figure out the answer. I'll need to make an inference. In the first paragraph, the author asks me to imagine a "brilliant laser light show in the sky" with "ribbons of green, red, or violet." I've never seen that before, so I think I would find that fascinating.

- Direct students to the chart and ask where they've seen a similar chart before. Review that it helps them use text evidence to make an inference.

- Point out the text evidence in the chart. Have students record other evidence in the first column.

Think Aloud: When I read about the laser light show, I realized that I had never seen that, so I thought it would be interesting. I'll bet many people think the same thing. I used background knowledge to help me identify the important evidence.

- Ask students to add their own background knowledge to the chart.

Think Aloud: Now that I've found some important clues, I can make an inference that answers the question. I think auroras are beautiful and rare.

- Have students complete the chart.

- Finally, have students work in pairs to respond to the prompt at the bottom of the page. Invite volunteers to share their responses with the class.

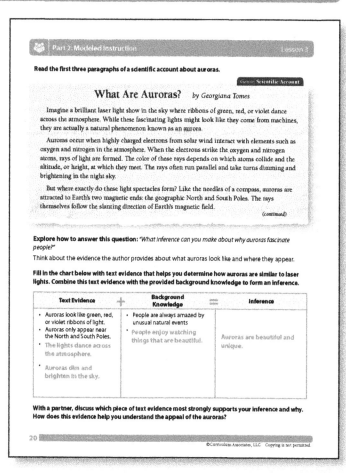

Tier Two Vocabulary: *Interact*

- Direct students to the word *interact* in paragraph 2. Write the word *interact* on the board, and underline the prefix *inter-*. Explain that this prefix means "between or among." Have students explain the meaning of *interact*. ("*to act in a way that affects something else*") **(RI.8.4; L.8.4a)**

- Write the words *interactive* and *interaction* on the board. Have students use the meaning of *interact* to suggest meanings for these words.

- Then have them brainstorm a list of things that can be interactive and examples of when they might engage in interaction. Encourage students to use the words in sentences that demonstrate an understanding of their meanings.

AT A GLANCE

Students continue reading the account about auroras. They answer a multiple-choice question and identify evidence that was used to make an inference.

STEP BY STEP

- Tell students they will continue reading the account about auroras.

- The Close Reading helps students identify specific evidence that helps them understand one aspect of auroras. The Hint will help them narrow down the answer choices to the one that is most reasonable.

- Have students read the account and underline two sentences that provide evidence explaining where people view auroras, as directed by the Close Reading.

- Ask volunteers to share the sentences they underlined. Discuss why this evidence is important. If necessary, ask, "Where do the auroral ovals occur? Which continents are near the magnetic poles?"

- Then have students respond to the prompt in Show Your Thinking. Place students into pairs and encourage them to share the evidence they identified. Point out that many pieces of evidence can support an idea, but some are stronger than others.

ANSWER ANALYSIS

Choice A is correct. The account specifically describes auroras that occur in "high northern latitudes" and "high southern latitudes." It also says the auroral ovals only surround the magnetic poles.

Choice B is incorrect. It shows some places where the Aurora borealis can be seen, but it is not enough evidence to make the inference.

Choice C is incorrect. It shows some places where the Aurora australis can be seen, but it is not enough evidence to make the inference.

Choice D is incorrect. It does not help someone make the inference about where auroras are not visible.

ERROR ALERT: Students who did not choose A might have been confused because all the choices include text evidence. They should be mindful, however, that they need to find evidence that supports the student's inference in the question.

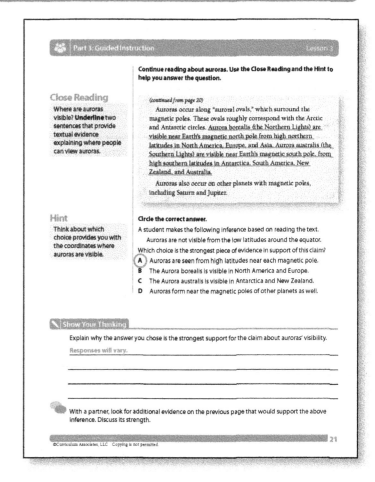

ELL Support: Regular Plural Nouns

- Explain to students that nouns name people, places, or things. Students can usually look at the endings of nouns to know how many.

- Direct students to the words *auroras*, *ovals*, and *poles* in the article. Write the words, along with their singular forms, on the board. Tell students these are all regular plural nouns because an -s is added to the end of the singular noun to form the plural.

- Have students find other regular plural nouns in this article. (*circles, lights, latitudes, planets*) **(L.8.1)**

AT A GLANCE

Students read a newspaper article about UFOs twice. After the first reading, you will ask three questions to check your students' comprehension of the article.

STEP BY STEP

- Have students read the article silently without referring to the Study Buddy or Close Reading text.

- Ask the following questions to ensure students' comprehension of the text:

  Where did the airline employees see something in the sky? (*They reported seeing it sitting motionless over Concourse C at O'Hare International Airport.*)

  What did airline officials think the object was? (*They had no knowledge of the event, and none of the officials saw the object.*)

  What did the Federal Aviation Administration think the object was? (*The FAA suggested it was a weather phenomenon during which airport lights made people see something strange in low clouds.*)

- Ask students to reread paragraph 1 and look at the Study Buddy think aloud. What does the Study Buddy help them think about?

Tip: The Study Buddy refers students to specific evidence in paragraph 1. It then models a think aloud that shows how to read with specific evidence or information in mind. It helps students understand how to read with a purpose.

- Have students read the rest of the article. Tell them to follow the directions in the Close Reading.

Tip: This article contains a lot of information that can be used as evidence. It is important for students to be able to differentiate the evidence and make logical inferences based on selected information.

- Finally, have students answer the questions on page 23. Use the Answer Analysis to discuss correct and incorrect responses.

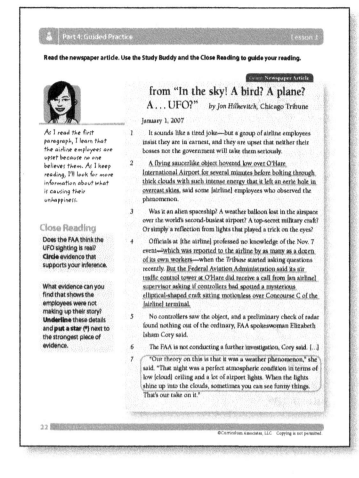

Tier Two Vocabulary: *Earnest*

- Direct students to the word *earnest* in paragraph 1. Point to the *-est* ending and explain that this does not indicate a superlative adjective here. Have students use context clues to determine the meaning of the word. (*"serious, sincere"*) **(RI.8.4; L.8.4a)**

- Have students describe people or situations that are earnest. Challenge students to think of synonyms or antonyms. (*serious, sincere, frivolous, lighthearted*)

STEP BY STEP

- Have students read questions 1–3, using the Hints to help them answer those questions.

Tip: Question 3 requires students to identify evidence and select which is most relevant to a specific inference. Have students identify all the evidence that supports the inference and then decide which information provides the strongest support.

- Discuss with students the Answer Analysis below.

ANSWER ANALYSIS

1 The correct choice is C. The article says the employees are upset because their bosses and the government will not "take them seriously." The evidence in Choice C supports this fact. Choices A, B, and D are all facts from the article, but none of them explains why the employees are upset.

2 The correct choice is D. Paragraph 6 says the FAA is not conducting a further investigation. The statement in Choice D provides a realistic alternative to and believable explanation for the sighting. Choices A, B, and C are all examples of evidence in the mystery and lead to more questions rather than answer any.

3 Sample response: Witnesses saw a flying saucerlike object in the sky that seemed to have intense energy and left a hole in the clouds. This occurrence was seen by many people (12), and the air traffic control tower even received a call about a craft hovering above Concourse C. The fact that so many people saw this "UFO" is strong evidence that it was real.

RETEACHING

Use a chart to answer question 3. Draw the chart below, and work with students to fill in the boxes. Sample responses are provided.

Text Evidence	Background Knowledge	Inference
flying saucerlike object with intense energy; many people saw it	When many people see the same thing, it usually means it's real.	The fact that so many people saw this "UFO" is strong evidence that it was real.

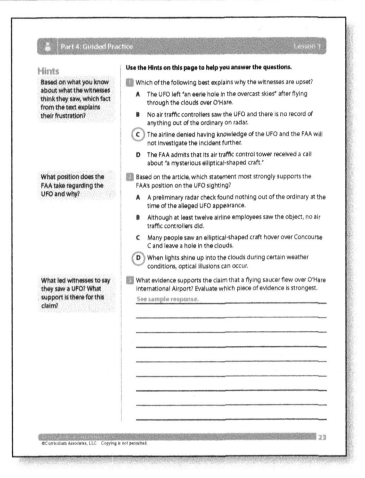

Integrating Standards

Use these questions to further students' understanding of "In the sky! A bird? A plane? A . . . UFO?"

1 What is the central idea of this article? Which details support this idea? **(RI.8.2)**

The central idea is that several people witnessed a UFO over an airport, but their bosses and the government would not believe them. Rather, these people had other explanations for the event.

2 What distinctions are made between the airline employees and the government? **(RI.8.3)**

The airline employees saw something they didn't recognize and thought it was a UFO. They had no background knowledge about the object or event. The FAA spokeswoman said, "When the lights shine up into the clouds, sometimes you can see funny things." She had knowledge that led to a different explanation.

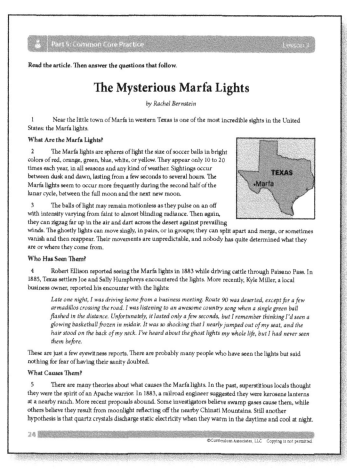

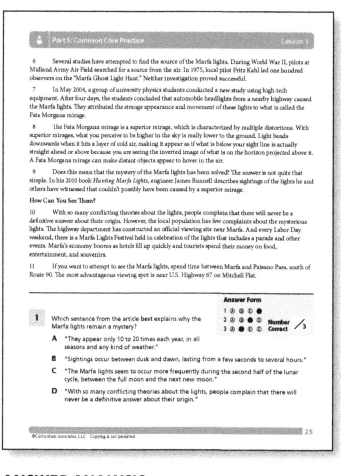

AT A GLANCE

Students independently read a longer article and answer questions in a format that provides test practice.

STEP BY STEP

- Tell students to use what they have learned about reading closely and citing evidence to make inferences to read the article on pages 24 and 25.

- Remind students to circle or underline facts and details that lead them to make inferences.

- Tell students to answer the questions on pages 25 and 26. For questions 1–3, they should fill in the correct circle on the Answer Form.

- When students have finished, use the Answer Analysis to discuss correct responses and the reasons for them. Have students fill in the Number Correct on the Answer Form.

ANSWER ANALYSIS

1 Choice D is correct. There are many different theories about what causes the lights, and many of them conflict with one another. People believe different things, and it is unlikely everyone will believe the same thing. Even when the physics students provided a strong scientific explanation, not everyone believed it. Choices A, B, and C describe when the Marfa lights appear. It is true that the lights don't appear very often, so they are difficult to see, but none of these choices is the best explanation for why the lights remain a mystery. **(DOK 2)**

Theme Connection

- How do all the articles in this lesson relate to the theme of light phenomena?

- What is one fact or idea you learned about light phenomena from each article in this lesson?

2 Choice C is correct. The sentences say people feared their sanity would be doubted. This supports the idea that people who see and report strange phenomena are usually not believed. People who don't see the phenomena generally don't believe those who do. Choice A does not explain the rarity of reports. Even if the reports were ignored, there would still be reports. Choices B and D do not explain the rarity of eyewitness reports. **(DOK 2)**

3 Choice B is correct. The article says that the Marfa lights were seen as far back as 1883, before cars and headlights were invented. There must be another explanation. Choices A and C might make some believe that headlights are not responsible for the lights, but they are not definitive proof. Choice D sums up the article's main point, but it does not point to a possible explanation of the Marfa lights other than headlights. **(DOK 2)**

4 Sample response: There are few complaints about the lights because the local population has used them as a way of attracting people to visit and spend money in Marfa. This is best supported by this sentence: "Marfa's economy booms as hotels fill up quickly and tourists spend their money on food, entertainment, and souvenirs." **(DOK 3)**

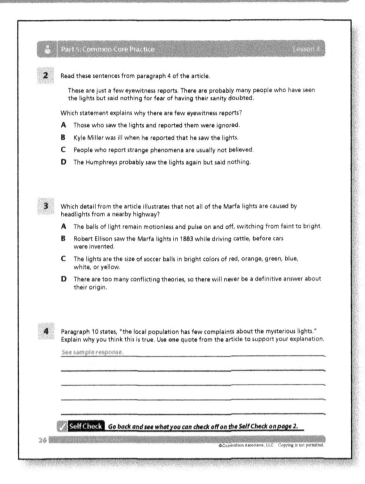

Integrating Standards

Use these questions and tasks as opportunities to interact with "The Mysterious Marfa Lights."

1 What is the central idea of this article? How is this idea developed throughout the text? **(RI.8.2)**

The central idea is that there are as many explanations for the Marfa lights as there are eyewitnesses. At the beginning of the article, the author describes some of the earliest sightings, which took place in the 1880s. Then, in the "What Causes Them?" section, many different explanations from then until now are discussed. The article goes on to describe the scientific explanation put forth in 2004, but it also says some people still have other ideas.

2 What is the meaning of *superior* in the scientific term *superior mirage*? **(RI.8.4; L.8.4a)**

The word superior *can have several different meanings. In the scientific term* superior mirage, *it means "farther above" or "higher in position." A superior mirage is a mirage that "you perceive to be higher in the sky [but] is really lower to the ground."*

3 How do the italicized sentences in paragraph 4 help develop a key concept of the article? **(RI.8.5)**

The sentences are a quote from an eyewitness. They provide a first-hand account of the Marfa lights, which lends credibility to their existence. They also highlight how difficult it is to see the lights, because the speaker says he was all alone "except for a few armadillos" and the lights lasted only a few seconds.

4 Write an objective summary of "The Mysterious Marfa Lights." Be sure to include relevant evidence from the text. **(RI.8.2; W.8.2)**

Summaries will vary. Sample response: The Marfa lights are mysterious, colorful balls of light. Despite scientific explanations, people still disagree on how to explain this phenomenon.

5 Discuss in small groups: What are your thoughts about the cause of the Marfa lights? **(SL.8.1)**

Discussions will vary. Remind students to use details from the text to support their ideas.

Writing Activities

Write an Argument (W.8.1)

- Have students think about the purpose of scientific accounts. Are they useful? Based on evidence in "The Mysterious Marfa Lights," not everyone believes scientific explanations.

- Ask students to write an argument that supports a claim about the role and purpose of scientific accounts, particularly as they relate to unexplained phenomena. Students can take either side of the issue, but they should support their claims with clear reasons and relevant evidence.

Punctuation (L.8.2b)

- Remind students that punctuation can serve many purposes. Explain that some forms of punctuation indicate a pause or break.

- Direct students to the ellipsis in paragraph 6 on page 22. Remind students that this passage is an excerpt from a longer newspaper article. Point out that the ellipsis indicates missing words. This passage is not complete, and a section of the original article that appeared here was omitted.

- Have students find other examples of punctuation that indicates a pause or break in this lesson's articles, such as dashes or commas. Then have students write a paragraph with two or three relevant examples.

LISTENING ACTIVITY (SL.8.2)

Listen Closely/Interpret Information

- Have small groups of students study and describe the photo on page 19 and one of the articles from this lesson.

- Students must listen closely to the descriptions and group discussion. They should interpret information and explain how it contributes to their understanding of light phenomena.

DISCUSSION ACTIVITY (RI.8.9; SL.8.1)

Talk in a Group/Compare Articles

- Ask students to compare and contrast information provided in this lesson's articles.

- Have students form small groups to compare and contrast information presented on light phenomena. Do any of the facts contradict one another? Is any of the information open to interpretation? Why do they think there is conflicting information?

- Appoint one member of each group to take notes. Allow 10 to 15 minutes for discussion, and then have each group share its results with the class.

MEDIA ACTIVITY (RI.8.7)

Be Creative/View Video of Light Phenomena

- Direct students to video presentations of various light phenomena, including those discussed in the lesson's articles if possible. Have them choose one to watch.

- Students should compare and contrast the experience of reading about the phenomenon with viewing it for themselves. How does what they see and hear contribute to their understanding? How does it differ from reading about these phenomena in the text?

RESEARCH ACTIVITY (W.8.8; SL.8.4)

Research and Present/Write a Report

- Ask students to research more information about one of the light phenomena described in this lesson's articles. They should gather relevant information from print and digital sources.

- Remind students to assess the credibility of each source they choose and quote or paraphrase their conclusions.

- Students should present their findings orally to the class. Have them make a bibliography or references list that includes all of their sources.

Analyzing Comparisons and Analogies

LESSON OBJECTIVES

- Analyze how ideas, individuals, and events in informational text are connected and how the interactions between them are related.

- Identify the distinctions between ideas, individuals, and events and the strategies authors use to make those distinctions, such as comparisons and analogies.

- Identify the similarities between ideas, individuals, and events and the strategies the authors use to make those distinctions, such as comparisons and analogies.

THE LEARNING PROGRESSION

- **Grade 7:** CCSS RI.7.3 requires students to build connections by analyzing how key individuals, events, and ideas interact and influence one another.

- **Grade 8: CCSS RI.8.3 builds on the Grade 7 standard by requiring students to identify both connections and distinctions among these text elements and to identify the strategies authors use to describe those relationships, such as comparisons and analogies.**

- **Grade 9:** CCSS RI.9.3 requires students to analyze how the author unfolds an analysis or series of ideas or events.

PREREQUISITE SKILLS

- Identify the ideas, individuals, events, etc., present in a text.

- Understand that these different elements impact one another within a text.

- Analyze how these interactions function.

TAP STUDENTS' PRIOR KNOWLEDGE

- Tell students they will be working on a lesson about analyzing comparisons and analogies, and the strategies authors use to make those distinctions. Review that a comparison shows a similarity or difference between things. An analogy is a way of explaining or describing something by pointing out a feature it has in common with something else. When you make a distinction, you are showing the differences between two or more things.

- Explain that students can analyze a comparison by examining the relationship between things. Share this comparison: *Blood cells carry nutrients to the body like trucks delivering groceries.* Ask students what is being compared and what it helps them understand. *(blood cells and delivery trucks; it helps me visualize how blood cells work)*

- Explain that an analogy might describe the working of the circulatory system by comparing it to the interstate highway system, using various features of each to extend the comparison. For example, veins and arteries could be compared to opposing lanes.

- Point out that comparisons and analogies help readers see new relationships between parts of a text. Sometimes the relationships are explicit, and sometimes they must be inferred by the reader.

Ready *Teacher Toolbox*

teacher-toolbox.com

	Prerequisite Skills	RI.8.3
Ready Lessons	✓	✓
Tools for Instruction	✓	
Interactive Tutorials		✓

CCSS Focus

RI.8.3 Analyze how a text makes connections among and distinctions between individuals, ideas, or events (e.g., through comparisons [and] analogies . . .).

ADDITIONAL STANDARDS: **RI.8.1, RI.8.2, RI.8.4, RI.8.7; L.8.1, L.8.1c, L.8.4a, L.8.4d; W.8.2, W.8.6, W.8.7; SL.8.1, SL.8.4, SL.8.6** (See page A39 for full text.)

AT A GLANCE

Students study an image that contains a comparison. They learn to analyze the comparison being made in order to better understand the meaning.

STEP BY STEP

- Read the introductory paragraph and the definition of *analogies*. Discuss what it means to analyze comparisons and analogies. Then have students study the image and think about the sign and the message it is sending about oranges.

- Explain that the chart helps students see how the sign compares two different things to show how they are alike and to make an important point. Read the chart and discuss that the purpose of the message on the sign is to get consumers to purchase oranges.

- Ask students to discuss other real-life situations when they have seen comparisons, such as in advertising or media.

- Reinforce how using comparisons and analogies is a way to help the reader connect with the meaning of what is being read.

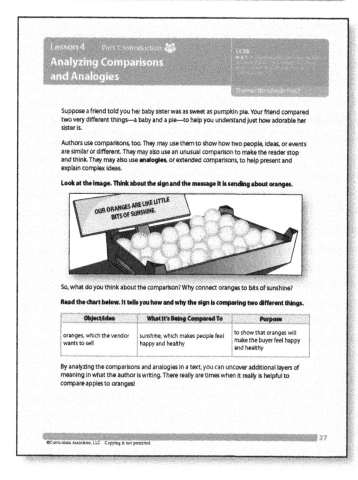

Genre Focus

Informational Texts: Economic Account

Tell students that in this lesson they will read informational texts. Review that an informational text is a piece of writing that provides information about a topic. The purpose of an informational text is to inform or to explain. The text often answers the questions *who, what, when, where, why,* and *how* about the topic.

Tell students that one type of informational text is an economic account. An economic account usually contains information about things related to the economy, such as money, statistical facts, and figures.

Based on these characteristics, ask students to name economic accounts they have read. What kinds of information did they learn from reading this text? Discuss with students when it might be useful to read this type of text.

Explain that "The Egg Business Lays an Egg" is an economic account that traces the history and ultimate failure of a small business in India.

Tell students that "A Delicious Taste of History" and "The Many Faces of Nigerian Food" are historical and social studies accounts, respectively, that describe the reasons behind the diversity of foods eaten in two different countries.

AT A GLANCE

Students read an account about the history of food in Puerto Rico. They then analyze the author's analogy between dinner and history.

STEP BY STEP

- Invite volunteers to tell what they learned on the previous page about how and why writers use comparisons and analogies.

- Tell students that they will now read about the history of food in Puerto Rico.

- Read "A Delicious Taste of History." Then read the questions: "What does the author mean when she compares dinner to a history lesson? How is this analogy developed throughout this part of the account?"

- Tell students you will use a Think Aloud to demonstrate a way to answer the questions.

Think Aloud: The author of this account compares dinner to a history lesson. I know that I can analyze the author's comparison by thinking about how these two things are similar and different and how the author connects the two ideas.

- Remind students that the chart helps them to analyze a comparison and to focus on its purpose.

Think Aloud: The second sentence helps me understand the comparison. It states, "The history of Puerto Rico . . . is reflected in its dishes—everything from pineapples to *arroz con pollo* . . . is influenced by the story of the island's residents and visitors."

- Point out in the chart that dinner is being compared to history. Ask students to think about connections between a country's history, people, and food.

Think Aloud: I think the connection between dinner and history is that the ingredients in the foods served in Puerto Rico have cultural history behind them.

- Have students complete the chart. Then have them answer the question at the bottom of the page. Invite volunteers to share their responses with the class. *(Sample response: Europeans and Africans influenced Puerto Rican food when they came to the island. Some Puerto Rican dishes came about after these people arrived. This continues the analogy that Puerto Rican foods reflect the cultural history.)*

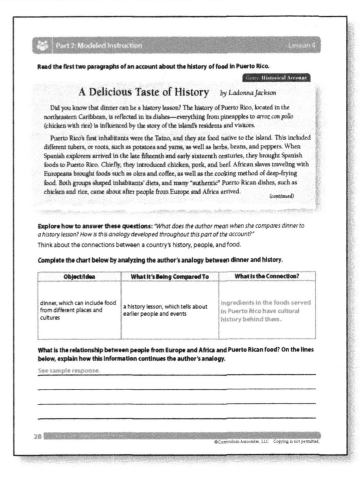

ELL Support: Regular Plural Nouns

- Explain to students that nouns name people, places, or things. Students can look at the endings of nouns to know *how many*. Explain that to form the plural of a regular noun, you add either *-s* or *-es*.

- Point out the regular plural nouns *dishes*, *residents*, and *visitors* in paragraph 1. Work with students to identify how each plural was formed (*dishes*: add *-es*; *residents* and *visitors*: add *-s*) and to tell how many (*more than one*).

- Then point out the word *centuries* in paragraph 2. Have students identify the singular form of this noun and explain how the spelling changes to form the plural. (century: *change y to i and add -es*) **(L.8.1)**

AT A GLANCE

Students continue reading about the history of food in Puerto Rico. They answer a multiple-choice question and describe the distinctions the author made.

STEP BY STEP

- Tell students they will continue reading about the history of food in Puerto Rico.

- The Close Reading helps students identify a detail that continues the author's analogy. The Hint will help them think about the connections the author makes.

- Have students read the rest of the account and underline details that show how becoming a U.S. territory affected the food of Puerto Rico, as directed by the Close Reading.

- Ask volunteers to share the details they underlined. Discuss the connections the author has made.

- Have students respond to the Show Your Thinking and Pair/Share activities. *(Sample response for Pair/ Share: The author distinguishes the Spanish, African, and American influences by describing which foods these cultures brought to Puerto Rico.)*

ANSWER ANALYSIS

Choice A is correct. It supports the author's central idea, which is that different cultural groups influenced Puerto Rican food.

Choice B is incorrect. Americans brought in corn oil and lard, which were less expensive than olive oil, rather than more expensive.

Choice C is incorrect. The author does compare different cooking oils, but this is only a minor detail in this paragraph.

Choice D is incorrect. The author is not comparing food from Puerto Rico to food in the United States.

ERROR ALERT: Students who did not choose A might not understand how to make connections between ideas. Point out that the account talks about different cultures bringing food to Puerto Rico. Only Choice A describes how this paragraph is similar to the previous paragraphs.

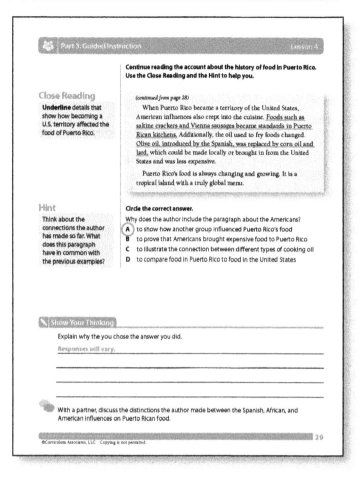

Tier Two Vocabulary: *Standards*

- Direct students to the word *standards* in paragraph 1. Point out that the word can have several meanings, including "levels of quality," "used or accepted as normal or common," or "code of behavior." Ask students to tell what *standards* means in this sentence. (*"used or accepted as normal or common"*) Guide students to point out context clues that help them understand this meaning. (*"influences crept into the cuisine"*)

- Have students consult a thesaurus to determine words that could be used in place of *standards* in this context. (*staples, essentials, constants*) **(RI.8.4; L.8.4a)**

AT A GLANCE

Students read about food in Nigeria. After the first reading, you will ask three questions to check your students' understanding of the account.

STEP BY STEP

- Have students read the account silently without referring to the Study Buddy or Close Reading text.

- Ask the following questions to ensure students' comprehension of the text:

  What is the name of one of the most common dishes in both Nigeria and western Africa? (*jollof rice*)

  What is used to make a popular stew? (*peanuts or groundnuts*)

  How do most Nigerian dishes taste? (*spicy*)

- Then ask students to reread the title and look at the Study Buddy think aloud. What does the Study Buddy help them think about?

Tip: The Study Buddy tells students to think about the meaning of the title and to look for details that help explain the analogy. Paying attention to the analogy in a text will help students understand the author's purpose for writing.

- Have students read the rest of the account. Tell them to follow the directions in Close Reading.

Tip: The Close Reading guides students to identify the distinctions and analogy the author makes. Being able to compare and contrast concepts presented in a text will help students to evaluate and synthesize information.

- Finally, have students answer the questions on page 31. Use the Answer Analysis to discuss correct and incorrect responses.

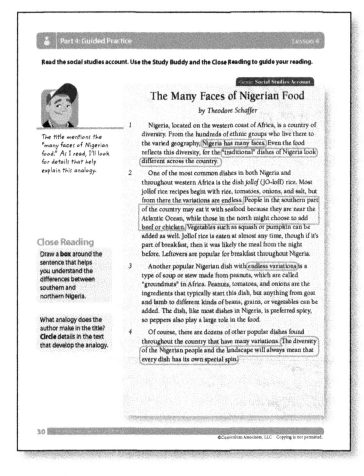

Tier Two Vocabulary: *Diversity*

- Have students find the word *diversity* in paragraph 1. Point out the suffix *-ity* and explain that it means "the state of." Ask students to identify the base word. (*diverse*) Given the context and what they know, ask students to tell what *diversity* means. ("*the state of being varied*")

- Encourage students to use a dictionary or thesaurus to verify this meaning. (**RI.8.4; L.8.4a, L.8.4d**)

STEP BY STEP

- Have students read questions 1–3, using the Hints to help them answer the questions.

Tip: The Hints remind students to look back at the text to analyze comparisons. This will help them to better understand the author's meaning. If students have trouble answering the questions, have them work in pairs to review their marked texts.

- Discuss with students the Answer Analysis below.

ANSWER ANALYSIS

1 The correct choice is B. The author compares the many variations of the rice dish and the stew. Choice A is incorrect. Only the groundnut stew is directly described as spicy. Choice C is incorrect. Only the jollof rice is mentioned as being eaten for breakfast. Choice D is incorrect because it states a distinction. Jollof contains rice, while groundnut stew contains peanuts.

2 The correct choice is C. The people in southern parts of Nigeria add seafood to their jollof because they live near the Atlantic Ocean. Choice A is incorrect. The author doesn't say how much chicken people in the southern parts of the country eat. Choice B is incorrect. Jollof is eaten throughout Nigeria. Choice D is incorrect because the author states that the groundnut stew is popular in Nigeria, but he doesn't name a specific part of the country.

3 Sample response: The analogy means that Nigerian dishes differ as much as people's faces. The author mentions the country's many ethnic groups and varied geography, which are also "faces" of Nigeria. He also discusses the variations in jollof rice recipes and in groundnut soup ingredients. Each version of these dishes is as unique as the face of its cook.

RETEACHING

Use a chart to verify the correct answer to question 1. Draw the chart below, and work with students to fill in the boxes. Sample responses are provided.

Object/Idea	What It's Being Compared to	What Is the Connection?
jollof	groundnut stew	Both have many variations.

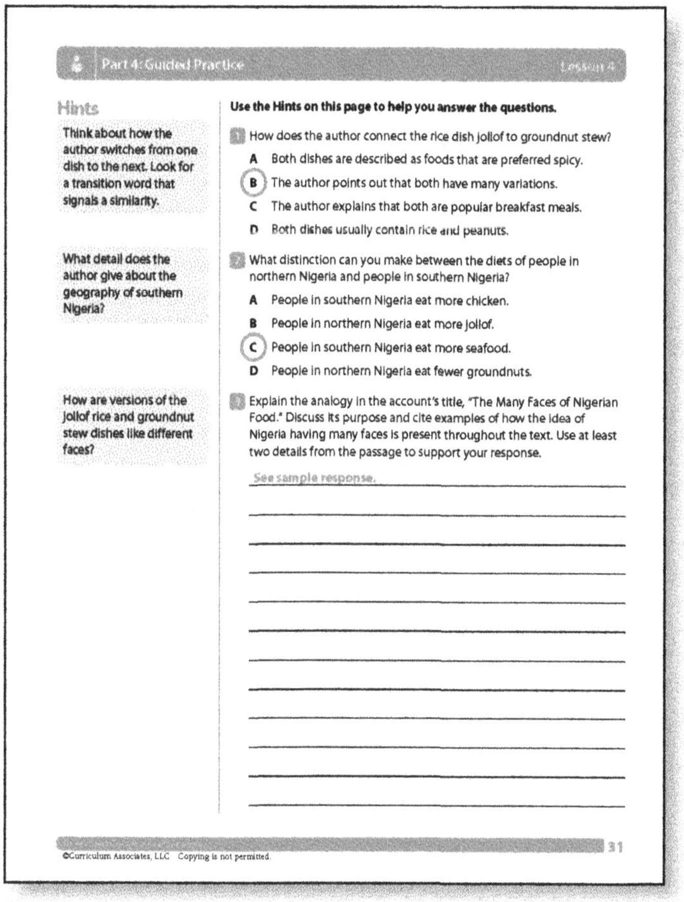
Part 4: Guided Practice Lesson 4

Hints

Think about how the author switches from one dish to the next. Look for a transition word that signals a similarity.

What detail does the author give about the geography of southern Nigeria?

How are versions of the jollof rice and groundnut stew dishes like different faces?

Use the Hints on this page to help you answer the questions.

1 How does the author connect the rice dish jollof to groundnut stew?

A Both dishes are described as foods that are preferred spicy.
B The author points out that both have many variations.
C The author explains that both are popular breakfast meals.
D Both dishes usually contain rice and peanuts.

2 What distinction can you make between the diets of people in northern Nigeria and people in southern Nigeria?

A People in southern Nigeria eat more chicken.
B People in northern Nigeria eat more jollof.
C People in southern Nigeria eat more seafood.
D People in northern Nigeria eat fewer groundnuts.

3 Explain the analogy in the account's title, "The Many Faces of Nigerian Food." Discuss its purpose and cite examples of how the idea of Nigeria having many faces is present throughout the text. Use at least two details from the passage to support your response.

See sample response.

©Curriculum Associates, LLC Copying is not permitted. 31

Integrating Standards

Use these questions to further students' understanding of "The Many Faces of Nigerian Food."

1 How does the author's use of the word *diversity* in paragraphs 1 and 4 make a connection to the title of the account? ***(RI.8.4)***

The author uses the word diversity *to convey the message that there are many different types of food served in Nigeria, and that is directly related to the many different ethnic groups who live there.*

2 What can you infer about the ingredients that people in different parts of Nigeria choose to put in their jollof rice? ***(RI.8.1)***

I can infer that people from different parts of the country put ingredients in the rice that are readily available to them. The text says people in the southern part of the country add seafood because they are near the ocean, where seafood comes from.

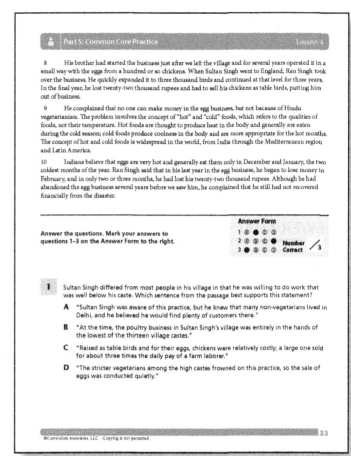

AT A GLANCE

Students independently read a longer article and answer questions in a format that provides test practice.

STEP BY STEP

- Tell students to use what they have learned about reading closely and analyzing comparisons and analogies to read the article on pages 32 and 33.

- Remind students to underline or circle important points.

- Tell students to answer the questions on pages 33 and 34. For questions 1–3, they should fill in the correct circle on the Answer Form.

- When students have finished, use the Answer Analysis to discuss correct responses and the reasons for them. Have students fill in the Number Correct on the Answer Form.

ANSWER ANALYSIS

1   Choice B is correct. Before Singh, a member of a high caste, started his egg operation, the poultry business in his village "was entirely in the hands of the lowest of the thirteen village castes." No one in his village had ever done anything like what he was doing. Choice A tells how many people in Delhi were different from people in Singh's village, but there's no comparison to Singh himself. Choice C compares the cost of eggs to the work required to pay for them, but it does not compare people in any way. Choice D mentions a view of high caste members about Singh's chosen business but does not highlight how unusual his actions were. ***(DOK 2)***

Theme Connection

- How do all the passages in this lesson relate to the theme of worldwide food?

- What is one fact or idea you learned about worldwide food from each account in this lesson?

ANSWER ANALYSIS

2 Choice D is correct. The expansion of the egg business had little effect on people in the area. It didn't matter to them that eggs were more available or probably more affordable. Their beliefs, especially about the "hot" quality of eggs, kept them from buying more eggs. Choice A is incorrect because many people would not buy the eggs during most of the year even if they had the money. Choice B is not supported by anything in the article. Choice C is incorrect because Ran Singh's business would have been seen as a failure, even by people who questioned the caste system. **(DOK 2)**

3 Choice A is correct. Sultan Singh was much more cautious with the egg business than Ran. Choice B is incorrect. Both brothers were thinking about the future. Choice C is incorrect. Ran Singh ran the business similarly to Sultan. Choice D is incorrect. The article doesn't discuss Ran's career prior to taking over the egg business. **(DOK 2)**

4 Sample response: Not all residents of Delhi were vegetarians, so there was a market for eggs. However, eggs are "hot foods," which are only eaten during December and January. The short season for "hot" foods led to the failure of the egg business. The brothers had been mindful of Hindu vegetarianism, but had failed to realize that the egg's status as a "hot" food would affect the sales. **(DOK 3)**

Panel (reproduced worksheet):

> **Part 5: Common Core Practice** — Lesson 4
>
> **2** When Ran Singh took over his brother's egg business, he expanded the operation from about 100 chickens to more than 3,000. Which statement accurately describes the impact this event had on the people in the area?
>
> **A** It had little effect because people could not afford the eggs.
>
> **B** It made eggs a more important part of people's daily diet.
>
> **C** It helped people see the value of working below your caste.
>
> **D** It had almost no effect due to people's beliefs about eating eggs.
>
> **3** Which statement accurately compares Sultan Singh and Ran Singh?
>
> **A** Sultan Singh managed his business with caution, but Ran Singh was overly ambitious.
>
> **B** Sultan Singh was old-fashioned, but Ran Singh had a keen eye for future opportunities.
>
> **C** Sultan Singh honored the caste system tradition, but Ran Singh had little respect for it.
>
> **D** Sultan Singh had a successful career outside of the egg business, but Ran Singh did not.
>
> **4** The authors draw a clear connection between Hindu vegetarianism and the concept of "hot" and "cold" foods. Describe how this comparison explains why the Singh brothers' business failed. Use at least **two** details from the text to support your answer.
>
> *See sample response.*
>
> ✓ **Self Check** Go back and see what you can check off on the Self Check on page 2.
>
> 34
>
> ©Curriculum Associates, LLC Copying is not permitted.

Integrating Standards

Use these questions and tasks as opportunities to interact with "The Egg Business Lays an Egg."

1 What is Sultan Singh's professional background outside of his egg business? Cite evidence from the text. **(RI.8.1)**

He ran a farm and had another job that is not named: He was "a well-educated man with a good job outside his farm . . . ."

2 Explain how Sultan Singh's egg business changed after he went to England. **(RI.8.1)**

When Sultan Singh went to England, his brother took over the business. He quickly expanded it from around a hundred chickens to three thousand and ran the business at that level for three years.

3 Write a paragraph about the difference between "hot" and "cold" foods. **(W.8.2)**

Many Indians believe hot foods produce heat in the body and generally eat them during the cold season; cold foods are believed to produce coolness in the body and are more appropriate for the hot months.

4 Discuss in small groups: What is the central idea of this text? How is it developed over the course of the text through supporting details? **(RI.8.2; SL.8.1)**

Discussions will vary. Encourage groups to agree on a central idea of the text before determining which ideas in the text support it. Review that a paragraph may have a main idea that helps to develop the text's overall central idea. Encourage students to analyze each individual paragraph and to follow discussion rules.

Writing Activities

Write an Informative Essay (W.8.2)

- Have students think about what they learned about worldwide foods. How do foods become a tradition in a country or region? What is the cultural and economic importance of foods?

- Ask students to write an informative essay about worldwide foods. Encourage them to include specific pieces of evidence from each of this lesson's articles in their writing. Remind them to include a clear introduction, develop their ideas with specific details, and provide a concluding statement.

- Have students share their essays with the class and discuss which arguments are the most convincing.

Indicative Mood (L.8.1c)

- Direct students to the first sentence of paragraph 2 in "A Delicious Taste of History": *Puerto Rico's first inhabitants were the Taino, and they ate food native to the island.* Point out that this sentence is an example of the indicative mood. It states a fact.

- Work with students to identify other examples of the indicative mood in this article. Then have students write a paragraph in which they make a comparison and use the indicative mood throughout their writing.

LISTENING ACTIVITY (SL.8.4)

Listen Closely/Analyze Word Choice

- Have students work in pairs to discuss the authors' comparisons in "The Egg Business Lays an Egg."

- One student selects a comparison the authors make. The other student listens closely and identifies what the connection is.

- Students reverse roles and repeat the activity.

DISCUSSION ACTIVITY (SL.8.1)

Talk in a Group/Talk About Worldwide Foods

- Have students think about the worldwide foods they read about in this lesson. How are all of the foods in the different countries similar? How are they different?

- Have students form small groups to discuss the similarities and differences of the foods they read about and their impact on the country's culture and economy. Students may also compare and contrast these foods to others with which they are familiar.

- Appoint one member of each group to take notes. Allow 10 to 15 minutes for discussion. Then have each group share their ideas with the class.

MEDIA ACTIVITY (RI.8.7)

Be Creative/Evaluate Media Formats

- Direct students to the image of an advertisement for oranges on page 27. Review that the sign makes a comparison.

- Then ask students to find television or online advertisements about food and compare them to this image. What are some advantages and disadvantages of each medium? How do comparisons impact the effectiveness of each advertisement's message?

RESEARCH ACTIVITY (W.8.6, W.8.7; SL.8.6)

Research and Present/Use Technology

- Have students choose one of the topics from this lesson that they would like to learn more about. Then have them ask themselves questions about the topic and use multiple digital and print sources to find the answers.

- Have students use technology to publish research reports. Make students' reports available to the class. Then have students review and comment on one another's reports using features of the chosen technology, such as commenting tools.

Analyzing Categories

LESSON OBJECTIVES

- Analyze how ideas, individuals, and events in informational text are connected and interrelated.

- Identify similarities and distinctions between ideas, individuals, and events and the devices used by authors to make those distinctions, including comparisons and categories.

THE LEARNING PROGRESSION

- **Grade 7:** CCSS RI.7.3 focuses on building connections by analyzing interactions between individuals, events, and major ideas in a text.

- **Grade 8: CCSS RI.8.3 builds on the Grade 7 standard by focusing on specific strategies authors use to make connections among and distinctions between text elements.**

- **Grade 9:** CCSS RI.9.3 requires students to analyze how an author introduces, develops, and connects a series of ideas or events.

PREREQUISITE SKILLS

- Identify the ideas, individuals, and events present in a text.

- Analyze how different elements influence and interact with one another within a text.

- Analyze how authors develop text structure and techniques such as comparisons, analogies, and categories within a text.

TAP STUDENTS' PRIOR KNOWLEDGE

- Tell students they will be working on a lesson about analyzing categories. Ask what a category is. (*a group of things that have something in common*)

- Ask students to imagine they are going shopping to buy a new DVD player. They go to a large store that sells things such as televisions, computers, clothing, furniture, linens, toys, books, and so on. Ask what students can do to find the DVD players in the store. (*They can ask a salesperson or look at a store directory to find out where electronics are sold. Elicit the idea that the products in the store are arranged in categories: electronics, food, clothing, hardware, linens, etc.*)

- Ask: Why is it important to arrange things in categories? (*You can find them easily.*)

- Remind students that authors may organize informational texts to compare and contrast individuals, ideas, or events. Authors may use categories to make the connections or distinctions clear to readers. Sometimes the categories are concrete, and sometimes they are abstract. Analyzing connections and distinctions by thinking about categories is important because it helps readers better understand the relationships among concepts in a text.

Ready *Teacher Toolbox*

teacher-toolbox.com

	Prerequisite Skills	RI.8.3
Ready Lessons	✓	✓
Tools for Instruction		✓
Interactive Tutorials		✓

CCSS Focus

RI.8.3 Analyze how a text makes connections among and distinctions between individuals, ideas, or events (e.g., through . . . categories).

ADDITIONAL STANDARDS: RI.8.1, RI.8.2, RI.8.4, RI.8.7; L.8.4a, L.8.4b, L.8.4c; W.8.1, W.8.2, W.8.4, W.8.7, W.8.8; SL.8.1, SL.8.4, SL.8.6 (*See page A39 for full text.*)

Part 1: Introduction **Lesson 5**

AT A GLANCE

By studying photos of electronic devices, students are introduced to the way authors organize informational text into categories to show connections among and distinctions between ideas, individuals, and events.

STEP BY STEP

- Read the paragraph and discuss the definition of *categories*.

- Direct students to study the technologies shown in the photographs. Have students decide how they might categorize the technologies by shared characteristics.

- Explain that the graphic organizer shows a way to organize the technologies into categories. Read the two listed in the chart. Point out that all the items may fit in at least one category, but some may belong in more than one category.

- Direct students to the technology items listed in the second column. Discuss why cell phones and email belong in a category about keeping in touch with friends.

- Work with students to complete the chart.

- Review the entire chart, guiding students to understand that it shows one way to categorize the items shown in the photos.

- Have students give real-life examples of when they categorize things, such as organizing a collection.

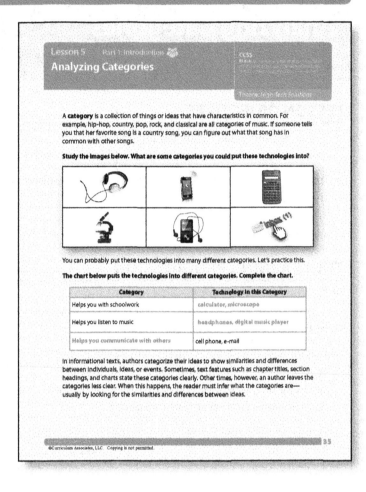

Genre Focus

Informational Texts: Technical Account

Tell students that in this lesson, they will read informational texts that are technical accounts. Explain that a technical account is written to inform or explain how scientific knowledge has been used for practical purposes in everyday life. It may explain a process or structure or may describe features of a specific device. Often, a technical account uses precise language and content-specific terms. These words might be unfamiliar if readers are reading about a topic new to them. For example, the word *interface* might be used in a technical account that explains how computers work.

Based on these characteristics, ask students to share examples of technical accounts they have read. What was the nature of the text? What technical terms do they recall? Did the text successfully explain how to operate something, such as an electrical appliance? Was the information easy or difficult to follow? Why?

Explain that the texts in this lesson provide different technical accounts. "Data Dilemma: Analog vs. Digital" compares different types of phone technology. "High-Tech Runner" describes a new kind of prosthetic technology. "Cool Jobs: Wide World of Robots" tells more about ways that technology is working to help people who have diseases or physical disabilities.

38 L5: Analyzing Categories

©Curriculum Associates, LLC   Copying is not permitted.

AT A GLANCE

Students read about phone technology. They analyze how the author compares and contrasts two types of telephone operating systems.

STEP BY STEP

- Invite volunteers to tell what they learned on the previous page about categorization.

- Tell students that in this lesson they will learn how to analyze connections among and distinctions between ideas and then categorize them.

- Read "Data Dilemma: Analog vs. Digital." Then read the question: "What are some of the advantages and disadvantages of each type of phone?"

- Tell students you will use a Think Aloud to demonstrate a way to answer the question.

Think Aloud: The title gives me a clue that the author is going to make comparisons between analog and digital phones. As I reread the text, I can look for advantages and disadvantages of each type of phone.

- Direct students to the table. Review that it shows a way of organizing the characteristics of the two phones. Point out the *Analog* row, and have students label the other row as *Digital*.

- Next, point out the categories—Advantages and Disadvantages. Then describe the characteristics of analog phones to add to each category in the first row of the table.

Think Aloud: I read that analog phones are less expensive and produce a richer sound than digital phones. These are advantages of analog phones. However, analog phones are tied to a base and have a limited range. These are disadvantages.

- Point out the disadvantages of analog phones in the table. Have students complete the row by listing advantages of these phones according to the text.

- Then have students read the advantages of digital phones. Ask them to list the disadvantages to complete the table.

- Finally, have students discuss the prompt at the bottom of the page. Discuss their responses.

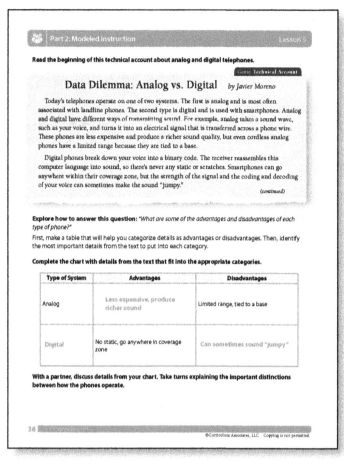

ELL Support: Compound Words

- Explain to students that a compound word is made up of two smaller words. Often, readers can look at the two smaller words to figure out the meaning of the compound word.

- Direct students to the word *landline* in the second sentence. Talk about the meaning of the smaller words *land* ("the solid ground of Earth") and *line* ("a conducting wire or cable"). Then ask students what they think the word *landline* means ("a phone that uses a telephone cable instead of cellular or satellite services to transmit signals").

- Have students identify other compound words in the passage (*smartphones, anywhere, sometimes*) and discuss their meanings. **(RI.8.4; L.8.4a)**

AT A GLANCE

Students continue reading the article about phone technology. They answer a multiple-choice question and analyze how the information was categorized.

STEP BY STEP

- Tell students they will continue reading the article about phone technology.

- The Close Reading helps students focus on the characteristics of each type of phone. The Hint will help them focus on the categories and select the best answer for the question.

- Have students read the article and label the phones' characteristics, as directed by the Close Reading.

- Ask volunteers to share the characteristics they labeled for each type of phone. Discuss how the text makes connections between the two types of phones through comparisons and categories.

- Have students circle the answer to the question, using the Hint to help. Then have them respond to the question in Show Your Thinking. (*Sample response: The author compares how the phones send and receive calls and their reliability, sound, and functionality.*)

ANSWER ANALYSIS

Choice A is incorrect. The text does not say anything about accessories.

Choice B is incorrect. The text gives examples of applications but does not categorize them.

Choice C is incorrect. The text refers to one type of user (a user who wants more functionality from his or her phone), but it does not categorize the types of users.

Choice D is correct. The author makes distinctions between the phones by categorizing their features and functions.

ERROR ALERT: Students who did not choose D may have chosen an answer not supported by the text. Each choice describes a way to categorize information about the two phones, but only D describes how they are categorized in this text.

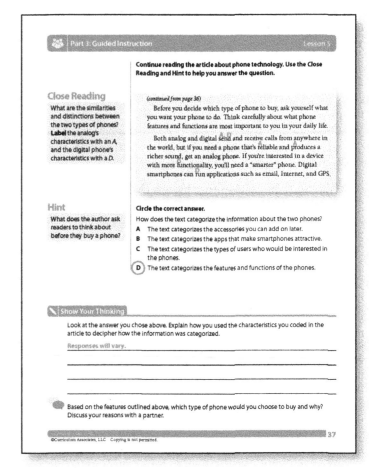

Part 3: Guided Instruction

Lesson 5

Continue reading the article about phone technology. Use the Close Reading and Hint to help you answer the question.

Close Reading

What are the similarities and distinctions between the two types of phones? **Label** the analog's characteristics with an *A*, and the digital phone's characteristics with a *D*.

(continued from page 36)

Before you decide which type of phone to buy, ask yourself what you want your phone to do. Think carefully about what phone features and functions are most important to you in your daily life.

Both analog and digital send and receive calls from anywhere in the world, but if you need a phone that's reliable and produces a richer sound, get an analog phone. If you're interested in a device with more functionality, you'll need a "smarter" phone. Digital smartphones can run applications such as email, Internet, and GPS.

Hint

What does the author ask readers to think about before they buy a phone?

Circle the correct answer.

How does the text categorize the information about the two phones?

A The text categorizes the accessories you can add on later.

B The text categorizes the apps that make smartphones attractive.

C The text categorizes the types of users who would be interested in the phones.

D The text categorizes the features and functions of the phones.

Show Your Thinking

Look at the answer you chose above. Explain how you used the characteristics you coded in the article to decipher how the information was categorized.

Responses will vary.

Based on the features outlined above, which type of phone would you choose to buy and why? Discuss your reasons with a partner.

37

Tier Two Vocabulary: *Functionality*

- Direct students to the word *functionality* in paragraph 2. Have students think about the context of the paragraph. (*It's about the functions of analog and digital telephones.*) Then work with students to determine that *functionality* means "the sum of what a product can do for a user" in this context.

- Explain that *functionality* can also mean "quality of being functional" or "capability of serving a purpose well."

- As needed, explain that the Latin root *functio* means "to perform." Discuss other words with this root: *function, functional.* (*RI.8.4; L.8.4a, L.8.4b*)

AT A GLANCE

Students read a text twice about how technology helped a young woman move beyond a personal tragedy. After the first reading, you will ask three questions to check your students' understanding of the text.

STEP BY STEP

- Have students read the text silently without referring to the Study Buddy or Close Reading text.

- Ask the following questions to ensure students' comprehension of the text:

  What tragic events happened that changed Jami Goldman's life? (*A car accident in a snowstorm caused Jami to be stranded for 11 days. By the time she was found, frostbite had set in and Jami's legs had to be amputated below the knees.*)

  How did Jami's grandfather influence her life after the accident? (*Jami's grandfather inspired her to make the most of her life, no matter what.*)

  How has technology helped Jami improve her life? (*A new type of prosthetic enabled Jami to become a runner with the U.S. Paralympic Track and Field Team. She has set world records, won gold medals, and become an inspirational figure for others.*)

- Then ask students to reread paragraphs 1 and 2 and look at the Study Buddy think aloud. What does the Study Buddy help them think about?

> **Tip:** The Study Buddy reminds students to pay attention to how the author categorizes details to give a text structure. Remind students that text structure is the way an author organizes ideas. A chronological structure describes events in order.

- Have students read the rest of the text. Tell them to follow the directions in the Close Reading.

> **Tip:** The Close Reading helps students identify details that can help them recognize the connections between events in Jami's life. Learning to analyze how an author connects ideas can help readers understand relationships in a text.

- Finally, have students answer the questions on page 39. Use the Answer Analysis to discuss correct and incorrect responses.

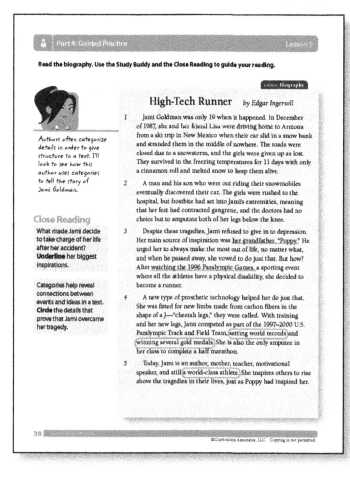

Tier Two Vocabulary: *Contracted*

- Have students find the word *contracted* in paragraph 2. Ask: In this context, does *contracted* mean "entered into a formal agreement" or "became affected with"? (*"became affected with"*) Have students point out context clues that helped them determine this meaning. (*"rushed to the hospital," "frostbite had set into Jami's extremities"*)

- Have students use a dictionary or thesaurus to find synonyms of *contracted* in this context. (*acquired, became afflicted with, became infected with*) **(RI.8.4; L.8.4a, L.8.4c)**

STEP BY STEP

- Have students read questions 1–3, using the Hints to help them answer the questions.

Tip: If students have trouble answering question 1, point out that the question asks which detail is *not* something that inspired Jami to change her life. Have students consider each choice and ask themselves whether this detail helped inspire Jami.

- Discuss with students the Answer Analysis below.

ANSWER ANALYSIS

1 The correct answer is C. The man and his son who saved Jami did not inspire her to change her life. Choices A and D are incorrect. Jami's grandfather inspired her to overcome her tragedy. Choice B is incorrect. The 1996 Paralympics inspired Jami.

2 The correct answer is B. The details explain how technology enabled Jami to become a runner. Choices A, C, and D do not describe the connection between the details.

3 Sample response: The text details are grouped into a structure that follows the chronological order of her story. The first set of details all relate to her accident and the amputation of her legs. The next set of details relates to the category of sources for her inspiration to become a runner. The next group of details describes how technology enabled her to succeed as a runner on the U.S. Paralympic Track and Field Team. The final set of details describes how she works to inspire others.

RETEACHING

Use a chart to verify the correct answer to question 3. Draw the chart below, and work with students to fill in the boxes. Sample responses are provided.

Category	Before	After
Events	car accident, is rescued, frostbite in extremities, doctors amputate, vows to follow Poppy's advice, watches Paralympics	new prosthetic legs, trains and competes in Paralympics, sets records, becomes inspirational figure

---

Part 4: Guided Practice — Lesson 5

Hints

Which answer choice is not identified in the biography as one of Jami's inspirations?

Reread paragraph 4 and look carefully at each detail the author mentions.

Consider how each paragraph in the biography focuses on a different aspect of Jami's experience.

Use the Hints on this page to help you answer the questions.

1 Which event would not be included in the category "Events that inspired Jami to change her life"?

- A Jami took a vow after her grandfather passed away.
- B Jami watched the 1996 Paralympic Games.
- **C** A man and his son eventually found Jami's car.
- D Poppy urged her to make the most of life.

2 What is the connection among all of the details in paragraph 4?

- A The details show all of the problems and challenges that Jami had to overcome.
- **B** The details all help explain how Jami achieved her goal of becoming a runner.
- C The details show the importance of the Paralympic Games.
- D The details illustrate how Jami's cheetah legs work.

3 Explain how you would categorize the details in this biography and how they give a structure to Jami's story. Use at least three details from the text to support your response.

See sample response.

_____

Integrating Standards

Use these questions to further students' understanding of "High-Tech Runner."

1 How do you know that Jami was determined to overcome the tragedies that resulted from her car accident? Cite text evidence. **(RI.8.1)**

"Despite these tragedies, Jami refused to give in to depression." Also, she decided to become a runner after viewing the athletes at the Paralympic Games.

2 Summarize the biography. **(RI.8.2)**

Sample response: Jami Goldman was in a car accident and had to have both legs amputated. Her grandfather's inspirational words and the Paralympic Games motivated Jami to become a runner. Prosthetic technology enabled her to compete with the U.S. Paralympic Track and Field Team, set world records, and win gold medals. She continues to work to inspire others.

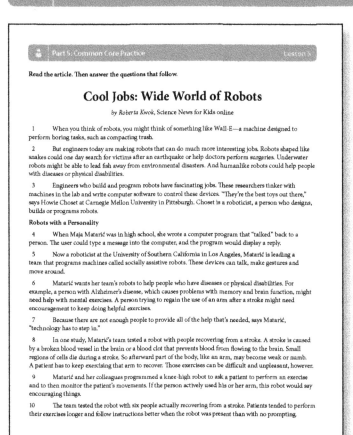

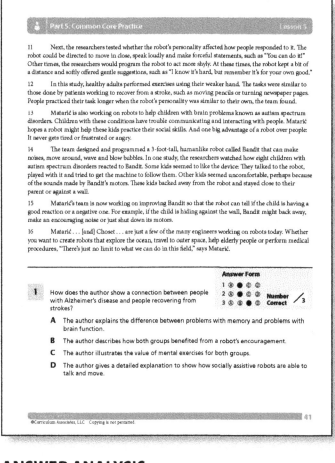

AT A GLANCE

Students independently read a longer article and answer questions in a format that provides test practice.

STEP BY STEP

- Tell students to use what they have learned about reading closely and analyzing categories to read the passage on pages 40 and 41.

- Remind students to underline or circle important points.

- Tell students to answer the questions on pages 41 and 42. For questions 1–3, they should fill in the correct circle on the Answer Form.

- When students have finished, use the Answer Analysis to discuss correct responses and the reasons for them. Have students fill in the Number Correct on the Answer Form.

ANSWER ANALYSIS

1   Choice B is correct. In paragraph 6, the author makes a connection between a person with Alzheimer's and people recovering from strokes by categorizing them as people who can use encouragement from robots. Choice A is incorrect. It tells the difference between the problems Alzheimer's and strokes cause, but not a connection between people with these problems. Choice C is incorrect. The author illustrates the value of mental exercises for people with Alzheimer's disease, not stroke victims. Choice D is incorrect. In paragraph 5, the author says robots are able to talk and move but never explains how they do this. **(DOK 2)**

Theme Connection

- How do all the passages in this lesson relate to the theme of high-tech solutions?

- What is one fact or idea you learned from each passage?

ANSWER ANALYSIS

2 Choice B is correct. The author makes comparisons between the positive and negative reactions to explain why some autistic children played with Bandit and some moved away. Choice A is incorrect. The author does not describe how adults reacted to Bandit. Choice C is incorrect. The author tells how Matarić's team is working on improving Bandit, so it can be used in situations that make children uncomfortable. Choice D is incorrect because it is not the best choice to answer the question. **(DOK 3)**

3 Choice C is correct. The text says socially assistive robots "can talk, make gestures and move around," which are human characteristics. Choice A is incorrect. The text does not address the level of programming. Choice B is incorrect. The text doesn't say assistive robots are used only for therapy and rehabilitation. Choice D is incorrect. The text doesn't say the robots can experience emotions. **(DOK 2)**

4 Sample response: Socially assistive robots talk with the people they serve. For example, robots made to help stroke victims give encouragement to patients doing exercises designed to help them recover. Studies show that people respond best to a robot with a "personality" similar to their own. For example, a gentle person responds best to a robot that speaks in gentle terms, while a forceful person appreciates a robot that speaks forcefully. The

results a robot gets often depend on the personality it's been given, making this feature an important part of its development. **(DOK 3)**

Part 5: Common Core Practice — Lesson 5

2 Why does the author describe both the positive and negative reactions of autistic children to the robot Bandit?

  A The author wants to show the differences between how children and adults reacted to Bandit.

  B The author wants to explain why some children played with Bandit and some seemed uncomfortable and moved away.

  C The author hopes to prove that the robot cannot be used in certain situations.

  D The author is suggesting why and how Bandit can be improved.

3 Which statement **best** describes the distinction between socially assistive robots and other sophisticated robots?

  A Socially assistive robots require more complex programming.

  B Socially assistive robots can only be used for therapy and rehabilitation.

  C Socially assistive robots are designed to have characteristics that are more humanlike.

  D Socially assistive robots both experience and react to emotions.

4 An important part of developing socially assistive robots is giving the robot what we could call a "personality." Write a paragraph that supports this conclusion. Use at least **two** details from the article in your response.

  See sample response.

  _____

  _____

  _____

  _____

  _____

  _____

  _____

  ✓ **Self Check** Go back and see what you can check off on the Self Check on page 2.

  42 ©Curriculum Associates, LLC Copying is not permitted.

Integrating Standards

Use these questions and tasks as opportunities to interact with "Cool Jobs: Wide World of Robots."

1 Besides socially assistive robots, what other examples of robots are mentioned? **(RI.8.1)**

"Robots shaped like snakes could one day search for victims after an earthquake or help doctors perform surgeries. Underwater robots might be able to lead fish away from environmental disasters."

2 What is the central idea of this article, and how does the author develop it? **(RI.8.2)**

The central idea is that engineers are currently building all kinds of robots, and the possibilities of what they can do are limitless. The author provides details about how researchers are developing robots to help people with diseases and physical disabilities.

3 According to the author, what advantage is there

to having robots help children with autism spectrum disorders? **(RI.8.1)**

Robots never get tired or frustrated as people do.

4 Write a paragraph about one way socially assistive robots help people. **(W.8.2, W.8.4)**

Sample response: Socially assistive robots can help people recovering from a stroke who may be trying to regain the use of an arm. Robots can be programmed to ask a patient to perform an exercise and to then monitor the patient's movement.

5 Have students take turns reading sections of the article and summarizing each section's central idea and important details. **(SL.8.1)**

Discussions will vary. Encourage students to provide objective summaries free from opinions.

---

44 L5: Analyzing Categories

Writing Activities

Write a Compare and Contrast Essay *(W.8.1)*

- Challenge students to synthesize the information they read in "High-Tech Runner" and "Cool Jobs: Wide World of Robots" to write an informative essay about ways technology can be used to improve people's health and quality of life.

- Remind students to introduce the topic clearly, develop it with relevant information using precise language and domain-specific vocabulary, and provide a concluding statement.

- Allow students to share their writing with the class.

Latin Roots *(L.8.4b)*

- Direct students to the words *amputate* and *amputee* on page 38.

- Remind students that words are made up of word parts such as prefixes, suffixes, and root words. Explain that the Latin root *amputare* means "to cut away." Discuss how knowing the meaning of this root helps to understand the meaning of the words *amputate* and *amputee*.

- Have students write a sentence using a word that contains the root *amputare*.

LISTENING ACTIVITY *(SL.8.6)*

Listen Closely/Pacing

- Have partners take turns describing advantages and disadvantages of some of the electronic devices shown on page 35.

- One student names an advantage for one device. The other names a disadvantage for the same device, followed by another advantage. They continue until they have exhausted ideas.

DISCUSSION ACTIVITY *(SL.8.1)*

Talk in a Group/Discuss Vocabulary

- Have students form small groups to discuss domain-specific vocabulary encountered in one of the passages in this lesson.

- Students skim the passage, select several words, and have one group member write down the words. Tell students to discuss their own definitions of the words, based on the reading. Then allow them to look up the words in a print or online dictionary to verify the meanings as used in the passage's context.

- Allow 10 to 15 minutes for discussion. Then have each group share the results with the class.

MEDIA ACTIVITY *(RI.8.7)*

Be Creative/Create a Commercial

- Have students review what they learned about telephones in "Data Dilemma: Analog vs. Digital."

- Tell students to create a commercial designed to "sell" one of these two telephone systems.

- Have students write a script for their commercial and add drawings.

- Allow time for students to share their commercials with the class.

RESEARCH ACTIVITY *(W.8.7, W.8.8; SL.8.4)*

Research and Present/Give a Presentation

- Have students use "High-Tech Runner" and "Cool Jobs: Wide World of Robots" as a starting point to research how technology can be used to improve the quality of life for people with disabilities.

- Ask students to use print and digital sources to research information about assistive technology, such as TTY for people who are deaf.

- Students should take notes and write a brief report for an oral presentation. If possible, they should include a visual display, such as photographs downloaded from the Internet.

SCORING GUIDE AND ANSWER ANALYSIS

Informational Passage Answer Analysis

1A ● Ⓑ Ⓒ Ⓓ   3 Ⓐ ● Ⓒ Ⓓ
1B Ⓐ Ⓑ Ⓒ ●   4 Ⓐ Ⓑ Ⓒ ●
2 Ⓐ Ⓑ ● Ⓓ

1 Part A: Choice A is correct. States like Wyoming gave women voting rights, while other states withheld them. Choice B is incorrect because, the article says, "states in the South and the North were reluctant" to allow women to vote. Choice C is incorrect because some Western states allowed suffrage. Choice D is not supported by the text. **(RI.8.1; DOK 3)**

Part B: Choice D is correct. This statement shows that certain states granted suffrage, regardless of what other states allowed. Choices A and B describe the arguments surrounding suffrage, but not whether states were free to enact it independently. Choice C introduces the idea of a single state having an effect on the debate, but the sentence does not support Part A on its own. **(RI.8.1; DOK 3)**

2 Choice C is correct. The fact that forty men attended the women's rights convention supports the inference that at least some men supported women's rights.

Choice A is incorrect. White men had the vote in the early nineteenth century, but it does not support the idea that many men supported women's suffrage. Choice B is incorrect. It explains that some men believed women should not be involved in politics, so it does not support the idea that some men supported women's suffrage. Choice D is also incorrect. It shows that there were disagreements about the Fifteenth Amendment, but does not say anything about men supporting the women's movement. **(RI.8.1; DOK 3)**

3 Choice B is correct. It correctly states that the central idea of the paragraph is that many Americans changed their opinions about women's roles because of World War I.

Choice A is incorrect. It explains that women helped during World War I, but it does not state the central idea of the paragraph. Choice C is incorrect. Paragraph 13, not paragraph 12, is about the Nineteenth Amendment. Choice D is incorrect. The fact that the major political parties supported suffrage after the war is a detail from the paragraph, but it does not state the central idea of the paragraph. **(RI.8.2; DOK 2)**

4 Choice D is correct. The disagreement over the contents of the Fifteenth Amendment is introduced at the end of paragraph 5. Paragraph 6 continues this topic and shows how it led to a divide in the women's suffrage movement.

Choice A is incorrect. Stone and Howe are discussed in paragraph 6, but the cooperation between these two women is not important to both paragraphs. Choice B is incorrect. While the Civil War is discussed in paragraph 6, this event is not important to both paragraphs. Choice C is also incorrect. Although Douglass and Anthony are discussed in paragraph 5, their partnership is not the idea that connects the two paragraphs. **(RI.8.3; DOK 2)**

SAMPLE RESPONSES

Short Response

5   After the Civil War, the Fifteenth Amendment was proposed to give African-American men the right to vote. Some members of the women's suffrage movement believed that a new amendment should give the right to vote to all citizens, including women. Other members felt that the proposed amendment was a step in the right direction. These members reasoned that once African-American men got the right to vote it would be easier for women to get the right. Two separate women's groups formed as a result of this disagreement. **(RI.8.2; DOK 2)**

6   In the section "The Great Divide," the author shows that even though women suffragists were fighting for the same thing—the right to vote—they did not always agree with one another on certain issues. They argued over whether or not to support the Fifteenth Amendment, which would give African American men the right to vote. This divided the women into two groups that went about achieving their goals in different ways. Eventually, the two sides did put aside their differences and united as one group. **(RI.8.2; DOK 3)**

7   The author explains that women's suffragists and abolitionists were fighting for the same thing—securing the right to vote for every United States citizen. The author strengthens this connection by explaining that several suffragists, including Lucretia Mott and Elizabeth Cady Stanton, supported the abolitionist movement. In turn, some famous abolitionists, including Frederick Douglass, supported the women's suffrage movement. This support led to the formation of the American Equal Rights Association in 1866. **(RI.8.3; DOK 3)**

8   Women were considered citizens but they were not allowed to vote. This meant that though they lived in the United States and obeyed the laws, they had no say in who ran the government. They had no effect on anyone around them. In this analogy, they are being compared to someone who sits in a boat without any oars. Without oars, you can't control where you're headed—you just float. **(RI.8.3; DOK 3)**

Performance Task

9   The author discusses several women who fought for the right to vote. Many of these women differed in their approaches to achieving this goal. Some worked through organizations, while others took individual stands.

Some women fought for suffrage by organizing large-scale conventions or organizations. Elizabeth Cady Stanton and Lucretia Mott brought attention to the issue by setting up the first women's rights convention. Organizations also helped spread the word, but not all the organizations attempted to secure the vote in the same manner. The National Woman Suffrage Association, established by Stanton and Susan B. Anthony, worked to change voting laws at the federal level. On the other hand, the American Woman Suffrage Association, started by Lucy Stone, tried to get states to amend their constitutions to allow women to vote.

Individuals also tried to use certain laws to argue that women should have the right to vote. Virginia Louisa Minor and Victoria Woodhull believed that under the Fourteenth Amendment, which granted citizenship to all persons born in the United States, women should be able to vote. However, their attempts to argue this point in court were defeated. No matter how they went about trying to secure the vote, all these women were connected in their belief that women should have the same rights as men. **(RI.8.3; DOK 3)**

SCORING RUBRICS

Short-Response Rubric

2 points   The response is accurate, complete, and fulfills all requirements of the task. Text-based support and examples are included. Any information that goes beyond the text is relevant to the task.

1 point   The response is partially accurate and fulfills some requirements of the task. Some information may be inaccurate, too general, or confused. Support and examples may be insufficient or not text-based.

0 points   The response is inaccurate, poorly organized, or does not respond to the task.

Performance Task Rubric

4 points   The response
- Fulfills all requirements of the task
- Uses varied sentence types and some sophisticated vocabulary
- Includes relevant and accurate details from the texts as well as text-based inferences
- Demonstrates a thorough understanding of the texts
- Maintains a clear focus and organization
- Is fluent and demonstrates a clear voice
- Uses correct spelling, grammar, capitalization, and punctuation

3 points   The response
- Fulfills all requirements of the task
- Uses simple sentences and grade-level vocabulary
- Includes relevant and accurate details from the texts
- Demonstrates a mainly literal understanding of the texts
- Maintains a mostly clear focus and organization
- Is fluent and demonstrates some sense of voice
- Uses mostly correct spelling, grammar, capitalization, and punctuation

2 points   The response
- Fulfills some requirements of the task
- Uses simple sentences, some fragments, and grade-level vocabulary
- Includes some relevant and accurate details from the texts
- Demonstrates some misunderstandings or gaps in understanding of the texts
- Attempts to maintain a clear focus and organization
- Is difficult to read, includes some inaccuracies, and demonstrates little or no sense of voice
- Contains some inaccurate spelling, grammar, capitalization, and punctuation that may hinder understanding

1 point   The response
- Fulfills few requirements of the task
- Uses sentence fragments and below-grade-level vocabulary
- Includes no details or irrelevant details to support the response
- Demonstrates very little understanding of the texts
- Does not establish a clear focus or organization
- Is difficult to read, contains many inaccuracies, and demonstrates no sense of voice
- Uses incorrect spelling, grammar, capitalization, and punctuation to an extent that impedes understanding

0 points   The response is irrelevant, poorly organized, or illegible.

Citing Evidence to Support Inferences

LESSON OBJECTIVES

- Use textual evidence, along with background knowledge, to make reasonable inferences about a literary text.

- Evaluate textual evidence to identify the pieces that most strongly support an inference drawn from the text.

THE LEARNING PROGRESSION

- **Grade 7:** CCSS RL.7.1 requires students to cite several pieces of textual evidence to support an analysis of what the text says explicitly as well as inferences drawn from the text.

- **Grade 8: CCSS RL.8.1 requires students to deepen their understanding of how to cite textual evidence that most strongly supports an analysis of what the text says explicitly as well as inferences drawn from the text.**

- **Grade 9:** CCSS RL.9.1 requires students to cite strong and thorough textual evidence to support an analysis of what the text says explicitly as well as inferences drawn from the text.

PREREQUISITE SKILLS

- Recognize and understand explicit statements within a text.

- Draw inferences based on implicit information within a text.

- Cite textual evidence to support inferences.

- Quote details and examples accurately from a text when making inferences.

TAP STUDENTS' PRIOR KNOWLEDGE

- Tell students they will be working on a lesson about citing text evidence to support inferences. Ask students what an inference is. (*an informed or logical guess based on details in the text and on what the reader already knows from his or her own experiences*)

- Ask students what they would think if they were viewing an action movie in which a person was flying high in the air. (*The person is flying with the help of visual effects, wires, or 3D imagery.*) Point out that no one directly told them this. Students used clues and their own experience to figure it out.

- Discuss how students can use what they already know to help them understand what they read. For example, if students are reading about a nail-biting moment in a football game, they might use their experiences with team sports to help them understand the excitement of the moment. Encourage students to give other examples.

- Then ask students what text evidence is. (*facts, clues, examples, details, descriptions, and other information from the text*) Ask students how text evidence can be used to make inferences. Have students consider suspenseful stories they have read and the inferences they made while reading.

- Point out that making inferences as they read will help students to better appreciate a literary text.

⬛ Ready *Teacher Toolbox*		*teacher-toolbox.com*
	Prerequisite Skills	*RL.8.1*
Ready Lessons	✓	✓
Tools for Instruction		✓ ✓
Interactive Tutorials		✓

CCSS Focus

RL.8.1 Cite the textual evidence that most strongly supports an analysis of what the text says explicitly as well as inferences drawn from the text.

ADDITIONAL STANDARDS: **RL.8.2, RL.8.3, RL.8.4, RL.8.7; L.8.1, L.8.3, L.8.4a, L.8.4b, L.8.4d; W.8.4, W.8.7; SL.8.1, SL.8.4, SL.8.5**
(*See page A39 for full text.*)

AT A GLANCE

By studying characters in a familiar setting, students are introduced to the idea of making inferences in everyday life. They learn that citing textual and visual evidence can help them make inferences about a text.

STEP BY STEP

- Read aloud the introductory paragraph about text evidence and inferences. Ask students to study the photo and draw arrows to the evidence that helps them figure out how the family feels about moving.

- Explain that the chart shows the process of a making an inference. Read the first column and ask students to compare the evidence listed to the items they arrowed. Ask volunteers to tell what other evidence in the photo they saw. Have students add the evidence to the chart. (*The family members are smiling.*)

- Next, read the background knowledge, and guide students to suggest other relevant background knowledge. Finally, review the entire strategy and discuss why it is reasonable to draw the inference based on the evidence and background knowledge.

- Ask students how making inferences is like solving a mystery. Discuss why authors do not reveal everything in a text.

- To reinforce how using text evidence to make inferences is a valuable reading strategy, share how you used this process with a book or a movie.

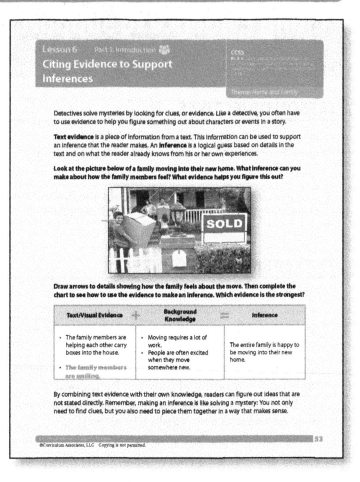

Genre Focus

Literary Texts: Lyric Poetry

Tell students that in this lesson they will read a poem. Review that a poem is a piece of writing that uses language in an unusual way to express emotions, ideas, or experiences. Poems often use language that is descriptive and speaks to the senses.

One type of poem is a lyric poem, which expresses personal thoughts and feelings. Lyric poems often include the following characteristics:

- They are brief.
- They are written in the first person.
- The expression of emotion may be song-like.

- Themes address broad personal topics such as love or loyalty.

Many lyric poems may include stanzas, or groups of lines that form a pattern. They also sometimes contain rhyme, which is the use of repeated sounds at the ends of words. Have students share any lyric poems they have read and describe the theme or message of the poem.

Tell students that in this lesson they will read a lyric poem called "Dusting." Explain that "A Smart Cookie" is an excerpt from a novel about a young girl and her mother. *Maud Martha* is a story about an important moment in a family's life.

AT A GLANCE

Students make an inference about a lyric poem and use text evidence to support their inference.

STEP BY STEP

- Invite volunteers to tell what they learned on the previous page about making inferences.

- Tell students that in this lesson they will learn how to cite evidence to make inferences when they read.

- Read aloud the beginning of the poem "Dusting."

- Then read the question: "What inference can you make about how the speaker feels about the everyday task of dusting?"

- Now, tell students you will use a Think Aloud to demonstrate a way of answering the question.

Think Aloud: As I read, I see that the speaker does not directly say how she feels about dusting. She and her mother dust "each morning." The speaker writes her name on the furniture with her finger. The word *scrawled* makes it seem like she does it quickly and sloppily.

- Direct students to the chart. Remind them that it shows the process of making an inference, and point out the first piece of text evidence.

- Tell students to add more evidence to the first column of the chart.

Think Aloud: I know that people usually use rags or feather dusters when dusting. I also know that when people do the same task every day, especially a chore, they sometimes find it boring.

- Point out the background knowledge in the chart. Have students add any additional background knowledge they think is relevant. Remind them that combining evidence with their own experience can help them make inferences.

- Then ask students to complete the inference in the third column. Invite volunteers to share their responses with the class.

- Finally, have students discuss the question at the bottom of the page. (*Sample response: The strongest piece of evidence is that the speaker writes her name in the dust on the furniture. Rather than using traditional methods of dusting, she makes it creative.*)

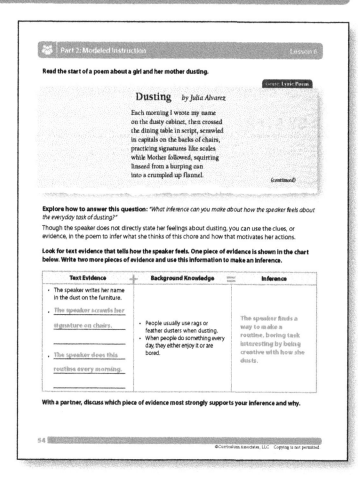

Tier Two Vocabulary: *Scrawled*

- Point out the word *scrawled* in line 3. Given the context and what they know, ask students to tell what *scrawled* means. ("*to write carelessly*") Encourage students to use a dictionary or thesaurus to help them verify this meaning.

- Have students suggest other words that would make sense in place of *scrawled*. (*scribbled, wrote quickly, drew*) (**RL.8.4; L.8.4a, L.8.4d**)

AT A GLANCE

Students continue reading the poem about dusting. They answer a multiple-choice question and analyze the evidence that helped them select the correct answer.

STEP BY STEP

- Tell students that they will continue reading the poem about dusting.

- The Close Reading helps students identify and remember important evidence. The Hint will help them understand the question by rephrasing it.

- Have students read the poem and underline two pieces of evidence that help them make an inference about the speaker, as directed by the Close Reading.

- Ask volunteers to share the details they underlined. Discuss what inference students can make about the speaker based on this evidence.

- Have students respond to the question in Show Your Thinking. (*Sample response: By refusing to be "anonymous," the speaker states that she wants to be important and wants people to remember her.*)

- Then have partners complete the Pair/Share activity. (*Sample response: The speaker and her mother work together on their chores but have different styles. The speaker does not want to be like her mother. She says she "refused with every mark / to be like her.")*

ANSWER ANALYSIS

Choice A is incorrect. The speaker does help her mother, but this is not the strongest piece of evidence.

Choice B is incorrect. The speaker does scribble her name in the dust, but it doesn't show how she wants to make her mark on the world.

Choice C is incorrect. The mother erases the speaker's name and fingerprints. This doesn't show how the speaker wants to make her mark on the world.

Choice D is correct. Refusing to be "anonymous" shows that the speaker wants to be important in the world.

ERROR ALERT: Students who did not choose D may have misunderstood the speaker's meaning in the first five and last two lines of the poem. Explain what *anonymous* means. Have students restate the speaker's thoughts in their own words.

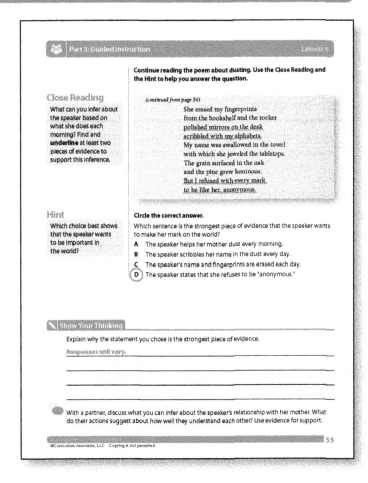

Continue reading the poem about dusting. Use the Close Reading and the Hint to help you answer the question.

Close Reading

What can you infer about the speaker based on what she does each morning? Find and **underline** at least two pieces of evidence to support this inference.

(continued from page 54)

She erased my fingerprints
from the bookshelf and the rocker
polished mirrors on the desk
scribbled with my alphabets.
My name was swallowed in the towel
with which she jeweled the tabletops.
The grain surfaced in the oak
and the pine grew luminous.
But I refused with every mark
to be like her, anonymous.

Hint

Which choice best shows that the speaker wants to be important in the world?

Circle the correct answer.

Which sentence is the strongest piece of evidence that the speaker wants to make her mark on the world?

A The speaker helps her mother dust every morning.
B The speaker scribbles her name in the dust every day.
C The speaker's name and fingerprints are erased each day.
D The speaker states that she refuses to be "anonymous."

Show Your Thinking

Explain why the statement you chose is the strongest piece of evidence.

Responses will vary.

With a partner, discuss what you can infer about the speaker's relationship with her mother. What do their actions suggest about how well they understand each other? Use evidence for support.

©Curriculum Associates, LLC   Copying is not permitted.   55

Tier Two Vocabulary: *Luminous*

- Direct students to the word *luminous*. Ask them to tell what *luminous* means in this sentence. ("*bright and shiny*") Guide students to point out context clues that help them understand this meaning. ("*polished," "jeweled*")

- Explain that *luminous* contains the Latin root *lumen*, meaning "light." Ask students to explain how knowing the meaning of this root helps them understand the meaning of *luminous*. (*Something that is luminous is full of light.*) **(RL.8.4; L.8.4a, L.8.4b)**

AT A GLANCE

Students read a story about a mother and her child twice. After the first reading, you will ask three questions to check your students' comprehension of the text.

STEP BY STEP

- Have students read the story silently without referring to the Study Buddy or Close Reading text.

- Ask the following questions to ensure students' comprehension of the text:

  What does the mother mean when she says, "I could've been somebody"? (*She means she could have finished school, had a good job, or done something important in life.*)

  Why do you think the mother has trouble knowing which subway train to take downtown? (*It can be inferred that she may be worldly in some ways, such as knowing two languages, but she is sheltered in others, such as knowing how to get around her own city.*)

  How do you know the mother still has a very powerful desire to learn and grow as a person? (*She is artistic in her sewing, she would like to go to the ballet or a play, and she borrows opera records.*)

- Then ask students to reread paragraph 1 and look at the Study Buddy think aloud. What does the Study Buddy help them think about?

Tip: The Study Buddy guides students through the process of making an inference. It encourages them to identify the strongest evidence to support their inference. Explain that many details may support an inference, but some are stronger than others.

- Have students read the text. Tell them to follow the directions in the Close Reading.

Tip: The Close Reading helps students identify explanations and examples that can be used as text evidence. Learning to analyze evidence will help students make strong inferences. Ask them if the mother is still able to do all the things she loves.

- Finally, have students answer the questions on page 57. When students have finished, use the Answer Analysis to discuss correct and incorrect responses.

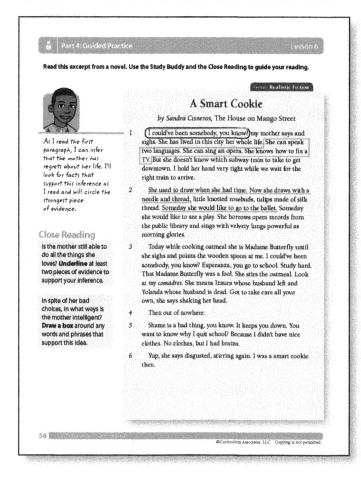

ELL Support: Possessives

- Explain to students that possessives are words that show who or what owns something. Tell them that pronouns are words that stand for a noun. Like nouns, pronouns can show possession. Work with students to list possessive pronouns, such as *my, his, her, their,* and *its.*

- Point out the word *my* in paragraph 1. Tell students that this word shows that the mother belongs to the speaker of the passage.

- Have students identify other possessive pronouns in this passage. Ask them to identify the ownership that each pronoun shows. (*"her whole life," the life belonging to the mother; "her hand," the hand of the mother*) **(L.8.1)**

STEP BY STEP

- Have students read questions 1–3, using the Hints to help them answer those questions.

Tip: Point out to students that sometimes they will begin with text evidence and then make an inference based on what they read. At other times, they will analyze an inference and then find the text evidence to support it.

ANSWER ANALYSIS

1 The correct choice is B. The mother wants her daughter to stay in school, unlike she did. Choice A tells how the mother has substituted sewing for her love of art, but this detail does not show that the mother wants the daughter to turn out differently. Choice C is a detail that shows the mother's talent and love of culture. Choice D relates a reason the mother dropped out of school.

2 The correct choice is C. The fact that the mother cannot catch the train by herself shows that she must depend on others to get around the city. Choice A is a detail that supports the fact that the mother is smart and loves culture. Choices B and D are details that show the mother's talents.

3 Sample response: The mother refers to herself as a "smart cookie" sarcastically. She really believes that she was not smart for quitting school. Evidence includes the fact that the author says the mother is "disgusted" when she talks about dropping out because she was ashamed of her clothes. She also tells her daughter to stay in school, which suggests she now believes school is important.

RETEACHING

Use a graphic organizer to verify the correct answer to question 1. Draw the graphic organizer below, leaving the boxes blank. Work with students to fill in the boxes. Sample responses are provided.

Text Evidence	What I Know	Inference
"'Esperanza, you go to school. Study hard.'"	Most parents want their children to do as well as or better than they did.	The mother wants her daughter to turn out differently.

Part 4: Guided Practice — Lesson 6

Hints

Which choice explains what the mother wants for her daughter?

What is something the daughter can do, but the mother can't?

Explain why you think the mother refers to herself as a "smart cookie."

Use the Hints on this page to help you answer the questions.

1. Read the following inference about the mother in "Smart Cookie."

   The mother doesn't want her daughter to turn out like she did.

   Which piece of evidence best supports this inference?

   A The mother used to draw, but now draws with a needle and thread.

   B The mother tells her daughter to go to school and study hard.

   C The mother sings along to music from borrowed opera records.

   D The mother admits that she used to be ashamed of her clothes.

2. Which of the following sentences best supports the inference that the mother is trapped in her situation?

   A She dreams of going to the ballet and a play someday.

   B She sings while she cooks oatmeal for her daughter.

   C She doesn't know which train to take to get downtown.

   D She can speak two languages and knows how to fix a TV.

3. Explain why it's reasonable to think that the mother may really have been a "smart cookie." Support your inference with at least two pieces of evidence from the text.

   See sample response.

   _____

   _____

   _____

   _____

   _____

   _____

   _____

   _____

   _____

©Curriculum Associates, LLC   Copying is not permitted.   57

Integrating Standards

Use these questions to further students' understanding of "A Smart Cookie."

1 What words and phrases reveal the daughter's view of her mother's talents? How do these help convince readers with their vividness? **(RL.8.4)**

Phrases such as "little knotted rosebuds, tulips made of silk thread" and "sings with velvety lungs powerful as morning glories" show the daughter is touched by the power of her mother's talents. These details make the mother's loss of educational opportunities even more touching and real.

2 Summarize the text. **(RL.8.2)**

A mother and daughter are waiting for a subway train to arrive. The daughter recalls the talents her mother has and recalls the advice her mother gave her while she was making oatmeal earlier that day, as well as the reason her mother gave for why she quit school.

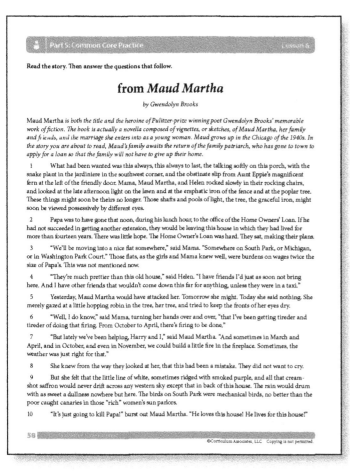

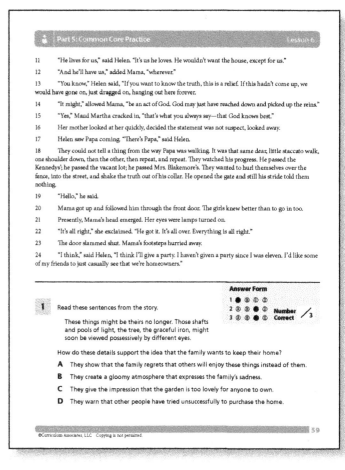

AT A GLANCE

Students independently read another story and answer questions in a format that provides test practice.

STEP BY STEP

- Tell students to use what they have learned about reading closely and citing text evidence to make inferences. Have them read the story on pages 58 and 59.

- Remind students to underline or circle important text evidence.

- Tell students to answer the questions on pages 59 and 60. For questions 1–3, they should fill in the correct circle on the Answer Form.

- When students have finished, use the Answer Analysis to discuss correct responses and the reasons for them. Have students fill in the Number Correct on the Answer Form.

ANSWER ANALYSIS

1 Choice A is correct. The phrase "different eyes" refers to the others who will enjoy these things instead of the family. Choice B inaccurately describes the sentences as gloomy. They are full of graceful beauty and regret. Choice C is inaccurate because the family wants to remain the owners of the garden. Choice D inaccurately describes the sentences as giving a warning that other people have unsuccessfully tried to purchase the home. **(DOK 2)**

Theme Connection

- How do all the passages in this lesson relate to the theme of home and family?

- What is one fact or idea you learned about home and family from each of the passages in this lesson?

2 Choice C is correct. Helen and Maud Martha know Mama is trying to make them feel better. Choice A is incorrect. It describes what the family members are thinking as they sit on the porch. Choice B mentions places Mama talks about moving to, but this does not support the assertion. Choice D reflects Helen's efforts to support her mother's forced positive attitude. **(DOK 3)**

3 Choice C is correct. Maud Martha does not respond to what Helen and Mama say about the advantages of moving, but their talk upsets her. When she gazes at the robin hopping in "her tree," it shows her attachment to her home. When she tries "to keep the front of her eyes dry," it shows she is upset by the talk of moving. Choices A and B are incorrect. These are the things said by Mama and Helen that Maud Martha does not believe are really true. Choice D describes Maud Martha's response when she herself talks about staying in the house. **(DOK 3)**

4 Sample response: Their house represents comfort and togetherness. Even though with more money they could have lived in a fancier neighborhood, all of the characters want to keep their old home. Although only Maud Martha declares this feeling, Mama, Helen, and Papa all feel that the house and yard are "what had been wanted . . . always." **(DOK 3)**

The following is a reproduction of the student page:

Part 5: Common Core Practice   Lesson 6

2 When Mama talks about moving into a nice apartment somewhere, she is really just trying to make Helen and Maud Martha feel better about moving. Which sentence from the passage best supports this assertion?

A "These things might soon be theirs no longer."

B "'Somewhere on South Park, or Michigan, or in Washington Park Court.'"

C "Those flats, as the girls and Mama knew well, were burdens on wages twice the size of Papa's."

D "'And I have other friends that wouldn't come down this far for anything, unless they were in a taxi.'"

3 Maud Martha does not believe at all that moving might be a good thing, as Helen and Mama suggest. Which sentence from the passage best supports this inference?

A "'We'll be moving into a nice flat somewhere,' said Mama."

B "'I have friends I'd just as soon not bring here.'"

C "She merely gazed at a little hopping robin in the tree, her tree, and tried to keep the fronts of her eyes dry."

D "She knew from the way they looked at her, that this had been a mistake."

4 Explain what you can infer about what the house represents to the characters in this story. Use at least two pieces of direct evidence from the story to support your answer.

See sample response.

✓ **Self Check**   *Go back and see what you can check off on the Self Check on page 52.*

60   ©Curriculum Associates, LLC   Copying is not permitted.

Integrating Standards

Use these questions and tasks as opportunities to interact with *Maud Martha*.

1 What is the setting in this story? How does it reflect the theme of the importance of home and family? **(RL.8.2)**

The front porch of the family's home is the setting. It reveals the importance of home and family because the porch is obviously a traditional gathering place for the family. It represents the heart of the family and comfort in an anxious time.

2 How does Maud Martha's dialogue help reveal the family's real feelings about losing the house? **(RL.8.3)**

The other family members are trying to put a brave face on the possibility of losing their home. They are covering up their feelings. Only Maud Martha occasionally breaks through and expresses the family's true feelings. The difference creates a tension in the story that builds over the course of the plot.

3 Look at the word *staccato* in paragraph 18. *Staccato* is a word often used in music to indicate a quick, abrupt beat. How does the Latin root meaning "shortened, regular" relate to the text? **(RL.8.4; L.8.4b)**

The father's gait is described as that "dear, little staccato walk." The meaning "shortened and regular" describes the rhythmic pattern of the father's walk. This adds to the story's suspense because the characters and the readers cannot tell from the father's walk whether or not he got the loan.

4 Discuss in small groups: What inferences can you make about why the family talks about other flats they might move to and about getting tired of starting the fire? What evidence most strongly supports your inference? **(SL.8.1)**

Discussions will vary. Remind students to cite direct evidence to support their inferences and to follow discussion rules.

Writing Activities

Write a Lyric Poem *(W.8.4)*

- Have students review the lyric poem "Dusting." Review how the speaker reveals her thoughts about making her mark on the world through this routine chore she completes with her mother. Remind them that a lyric poem expresses thoughts and feelings about a broad topic.

- Challenge students to write a lyric poem that conveys an idea related to the theme of family or friends. Tell them to include relevant descriptive details and sensory language. Encourage them to use similes, metaphors, and other figurative language.

- Allow time for students to share their poems with the class.

Sentence Patterns *(L.8.3)*

- Have students reread "A Smart Cookie." Work with students to identify the different sentence patterns the author uses to vary the sentence structure. How does this story's sentence structure differ from others? Discuss how this varied structure helps keep readers interested and reflects the vivid characters.

- Ask students to write their own paragraphs that use varied sentence structures. Have them exchange paragraphs with a partner and talk about what they did to keep the writing interesting.

LISTENING ACTIVITY *(SL.8.1)*

Listen Closely/Connecting Topics

- After reading the excerpt from *Maud Martha,* have students form small groups.

- Have each student write one or two questions about the topic of home and family that can be answered using evidence from the text.

- Then ask students to take turns answering each other's questions. Students must listen closely to the question before answering it with evidence from the text.

DISCUSSION ACTIVITY *(SL.8.1)*

Talk in a Group/Compare and Contrast

- Have students form small groups to compare and contrast two of the characters they read about.

- Provide the following prompts: How are the characters alike? How are they different? What points of view about home and family do the characters share?

- Appoint one member of each group to take notes. Allow 10 to 15 minutes for discussion. Then have each group share its results with the class.

MEDIA ACTIVITY *(RL.8.7)*

Be Creative/Make a Scrapbook

- Have students review the family photograph on page 53. Remind students that they had to make an inference about the photo.

- Invite students to create a scrapbook page that shows two photographs from a magazine that require the viewer to make an inference.

- Have students exchange scrapbook pages and explain how they inferred the meaning of their partner's photographs.

RESEARCH ACTIVITY *(W.8.7; SL.8.4, SL.8.5)*

Research and Present/Give a Presentation

- Have students create a biographical presentation about Gwendolyn Brooks, the author of *Maud Martha.*

- Ask students to research information to include, such as details about Brooks' life and other literary texts she wrote.

- Students should produce a visual display with photographs and book covers of the author's work.

- Students should take notes and write a brief report for their oral presentations.

Analyzing Dialogue and Incidents in Stories and Drama

Theme: *Doers and Dreamers*

LESSON OBJECTIVES

- Analyze how specific lines of dialogue within the plot of a story or drama propel the action, reveal aspects of a character, and provoke a decision.

THE LEARNING PROGRESSION

- **Grade 7:** CCSS RL.7.3 requires students to analyze how particular elements of a story or drama interact (e.g., how setting shapes the characters or plot).

- **Grade 8: CCSS RL.8.3 builds on the Grade 7 standard by requiring students to analyze specific lines of dialogue or incidents to see how they propel the action, reveal aspects of a character, or provoke a decision.**

- **Grade 9:** CCSS RL.9.3 requires students to analyze how complex characters (e.g., those with multiple or conflicting motivations) develop over the course of a text, interact with other characters, and advance the plot or develop the theme.

PREREQUISITE SKILLS

- Identify setting, character, and plot.
- Recognize dialogue in stories and drama.
- Identify causes and effects in stories and drama.
- Explain how elements of a story or drama interact.

TAP STUDENTS' PRIOR KNOWLEDGE

- Tell students they will be working on a lesson about analyzing how particular lines of dialogue or incidents in a story or drama propel the action, reveal aspects of a character, or provoke a decision. Remind them that dialogue is a conversation between two or more characters in a story or drama.

- Ask students to think about how they get to know people in real life. (*They notice what people say and how they act.*) Then ask students how they get to know characters in stories. (*by noticing what characters say and how they act*) Point out to students that sometimes writers state directly what characters are like, but more often they reveal what characters are like through their words and actions.

- Review with students that in plays, movies, and books, dialogue is a crucial element of characterization. Have students give examples of information dialogue can reveal about a character. (*how smart characters are, whether they are shy or outgoing, how they feel about other characters*)

- Explain that one way to analyze lines of dialogue or incidents in a story is to notice whether or not the characters' words match their actions. Making connections between what is said and what is done helps the reader better understand the characters and events.

Ready *Teacher Toolbox*

teacher-toolbox.com

	Prerequisite Skills	RL.8.3
Ready Lessons	✓	✓
Tools for Instruction	✓	
Interactive Tutorials	✓	✓

CCSS Focus

RL.8.3 Analyze how particular lines of dialogue or incidents in a story or drama propel the action, reveal aspects of a character, or provoke a decision.

ADDITIONAL STANDARDS: **RL.8.1, RL.8.2, RL.8.4, RL.8.7; L.8.1a, L.8.4a, L.8.4b, L.8.4c; W.8.1, W.8.7; SL.8.1, SL.8.4** (*See page A39 for full text.*)

AT A GLANCE

By studying a cartoon, students are introduced to the idea of how dialogue reveals information about the characters and events. Students learn to recognize connections between the dialogue and the action.

STEP BY STEP

- Read aloud the introductory paragraph and the definition of *dialogue*.

- Have students study the cartoon and think about how the dialogue helps them understand the characters and the situation. Ask them to circle details that reveal important information about the characters and events.

- Explain that the chart shows how to analyze what dialogue reveals about the characters and how it affects the story. Point out the dialogue in the chart. Have students compare it to the details they circled.

- Now have students complete the chart. Discuss the fact that this dialogue is what causes the man to take his yarn back from the cat. The dialogue affects the story because it shows that the man realizes the cat, not his knitting, is the problem.

- Ask students to discuss real-life situations in which they have paid close attention to dialogue, such as when conversing with friends or family members.

- Reinforce that paying attention to dialogue can help students understand more of what's happening in a story or drama.

Genre Focus

Literary Texts: Drama

Tell students that in this lesson they will read a type of literature called drama. A drama, or play, is a story to be acted out on a stage. A drama has a script with dialogue and stage directions.

A drama's script tells each character, or actor, what to say. The dialogue is presented with the character's name followed by a colon. The text after the colon contains the words that the character speaks. A script may include a monologue, or a speech that one character says to other characters. Or it may include a soliloquy, which is a speech that a character directs to the audience that reveals the character's feelings.

Stage directions are often shown in a separate format, such as in an italicized font. The stage directions describe the setting and tell the actors how to speak, move, or behave on the stage.

Ask students to name dramas they have read. What were the plays about? What did they learn about the characters, setting, and plot events from the dialogue and stage directions? Students may mention plays such as *Oliver!*

Explain that "The Ascent of Man" is a play about a prehistoric man and the doctor who created him in a lab. *The Comical History of Don Quixote* is a play about a man who thinks a windmill is a giant.

The right side of the page shows a reproduction of the student lesson page:

Lesson 7   Part 1: Introduction

Analyzing Dialogue and Incidents in Stories and Drama

Theme: Doers and Dreamers

At some point, you've probably put a television show on mute. You could still see what was happening on the screen, but you couldn't hear what the actors were saying. Yet understanding the **dialogue**, or the conversation between characters, is just as important as watching the events taking place on the screen. Similarly, analyzing the events and dialogue in a story or drama will deepen your understanding of the setting, characters, and plot.

Study these scenes. What does the dialogue tell you about the characters and the situation?

Circle any details that give you important information about the characters and events.

Use your observations about the scenes above to fill out the chart below.

Dialogue	What This Reveals About the Characters
"It's taking me a long time to make this scarf." "Maybe you should ask the cat about that."	The man is not paying attention to his surroundings, but the woman is.

	How This Affects the Story
	The man realizes that it's the cat, not his knitting, that is the problem!

When you talk with people, you probably consider whether their words match their actions. When you read dialogue, look for connections between what characters say and what they do. These connections will give you important clues about the main characters and key events.

©Curriculum Associates, LLC   Copying is not permitted.   61

AT A GLANCE

Students read a play and analyze what the dialogue reveals about the main character.

STEP BY STEP

- Invite volunteers to tell what they learned on the previous page about the importance of analyzing dialogue in a story or drama.

- Tell students that in this lesson they will learn how to analyze dialogue to learn about a character.

- Read aloud "The Ascent of Man."

- Then read the question: "What does the dialogue reveal about Tor?"

- Tell students you will use a Think Aloud to demonstrate a way to answer the question.

Think Aloud: I know that dialogue is the words characters speak. As I read the play, I will think about what each character says. I will also pay attention to what the characters say about each other.

- Direct students to the chart and ask where they've seen a similar chart before. Point out the lines of dialogue from the play.

Think Aloud: When talking about Tor, Brett says, "So, this is the famous caveman, eh?" Olivia replies, "You know he's not a caveman, Brett." This dialogue tells me that Tor may be a caveman, or he acts like one and is simple. This helps me better understand Tor's character.

- Have students analyze what the first two lines of dialogue reveal about Tor and record their answers in the chart.

Think Aloud: Tor's dialogue shows me that he can't pronounce Olivia's name correctly, and he uses the verb *eat* instead of the noun *food* to talk about going to dinner. This suggests he doesn't speak English well and may be unfamiliar with modern customs.

- Ask students to complete the chart with the information that each line of dialogue reveals about Tor.

- Finally, have students share their completed charts with a partner, as directed at the bottom of the page. Have them discuss what they learned about Tor from each line of dialogue.

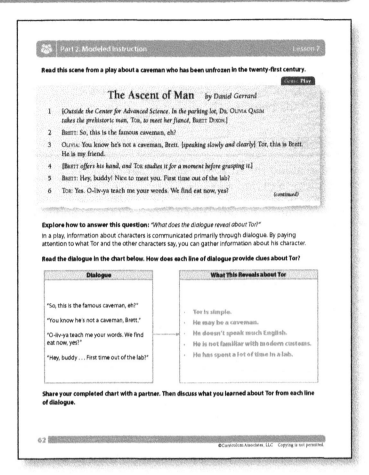

ELL Support: Prefixes

- Explain to students that many English words have prefixes. A prefix is a group of letters added to the beginning of a word to change its meaning.

- Point out the word *prehistoric* in line 1. Ask students if they can identify the prefix and the base word. (*pre-; historic*) Explain that the prefix *pre-* means "before."

- Tell students that adding the prefix *pre-* to *historic* has changed the meaning to "before history was written."

- Tell students to be careful when identifying prefixes. The word *uniform*, for example, has the prefix *uni-*, which means "one," rather than the prefix *un-*, which means "not." **(RL.8.4; L.8.4b)**

AT A GLANCE

Students continue reading the play "The Ascent of Man." They answer a multiple-choice question and analyze how an incident can create the plot's conflict.

STEP BY STEP

- Tell students they will continue reading the play "The Ascent of Man."

- The Close Reading helps students identify an incident that propels the plot forward. The Hint will help them make connections between an incident and a character.

- Have students read the rest of the play and circle one incident in this scene that may lead to a larger problem, as directed by the Close Reading. Ask volunteers to share what they circled. If necessary, ask, "What is the conflict in this scene? What causes this conflict?"

- Have students answer the question, using the Hint to help them. Then have students respond to the Show Your Thinking. *(Sample response: The incident of Brett opening the car door causes Tor to think Brett is trying to feed Olivia to an animal.)*

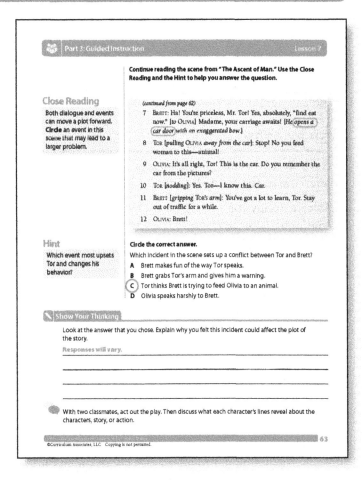

ANSWER ANALYSIS

Choice A is incorrect. Brett does make fun of Tor, but that is not what sets up the conflict.

Choice B is incorrect. By the time Brett grabs Tor's arm, the conflict has already started between the two characters.

Choice C is correct. Tor mistakenly thinks the car is an animal. This incident sets up a conflict between Tor and Brett.

Choice D is incorrect. When Olivia speaks harshly to Brett, it is in reaction to the conflict that has been set up between Tor and Brett.

> **ERROR ALERT:** Students who did not choose C might not understand how to analyze dialogue. Point out that while the other choices are plausible, the conflict between Tor and Brett is set up when Tor thinks Brett is trying to feed Olivia to an animal.

Tier Two Vocabulary: *Exaggerated*

- Direct students to the word *exaggerated* in paragraph 7. Given the context and their background knowledge, ask students what *exaggerated* means. (*"increased beyond what is normal"*) Encourage students to use a dictionary or thesaurus to help them verify this meaning.

- Have students suggest other words that would make sense in place of *exaggerated*. (*overemphasized, dramatized*) **(RL.8.4; L.8.4a, L.8.4c)**

AT A GLANCE

Students read a science fiction story about a time machine twice. After the first reading, you will ask three questions to check your students' understanding of the passage.

STEP BY STEP

- Have students read the passage silently without referring to the Study Buddy or Close Reading text.

- Ask the following questions to ensure students' comprehension of the text:

  Why is the Time Traveller so hungry? (*He has been time travelling.*)

  Who most wanted the Time Traveller to tell his story? (*the Editor*)

  How long does the Time Traveller claim to have been gone? (*eight days*)

- Then ask students to reread paragraph 1 and look at the Study Buddy think aloud. What does the Study Buddy help them think about?

Tip: The Study Buddy tells students to pay attention to how the dialogue provides clues about the main character and what has happened to him. Encourage students to look at each line of dialogue carefully and put themselves in the main character's place. Have them ask themselves what each line of dialogue reveals about how the character feels and why. Remind them that sometimes dialogue reveals information about a different character.

- Have students read the rest of the text. Tell them to follow the directions in the Close Reading.

- Finally, have students answer the questions on page 65. Use the Answer Analysis to discuss correct and incorrect responses.

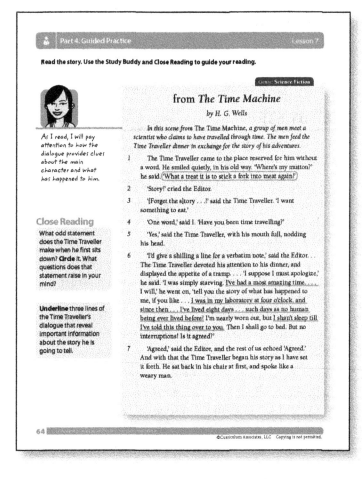

Tier Two Vocabulary: *Verbatim*

- Direct students to the word *verbatim* in paragraph 6. Have students think about the context of the paragraph. (*It's about the Editor saying he would pay for a note.*) Then work with students to determine that *verbatim* means "word for word."

- As needed, explain that the Latin root *verbum* means "word." Discuss how knowing this Latin root helps students understand the meaning of *verbatim*. **(RL.8.4; L.8.4a, L.8.4b)**

STEP BY STEP

- Have students read questions 1–3, using the Hints to help them answer the questions.

Tip: If students have trouble answering question 1, have them eliminate choices that do not reveal how the Traveller feels about what has happened to him. Eliminating incorrect choices will help students select the correct answer.

- Discuss with students the Answer Analysis below.

ANSWER ANALYSIS

1 The correct choice is B. The Traveller is expressing that he has had unique experiences in his travels. Choices A and C are incorrect. They show the Traveller is hungry after what happened, not how he feels about what happened. Choice D shows that the Traveller is tired but will tell his story. It doesn't reveal how he feels about what happened to him.

2 The correct choice is B. The men are eager to hear the story and agree to the Traveller's demand not to interrupt. Choice A is incorrect. The story gives no such details. Choice C is incorrect. The men ask if the Traveller has been traveling, but they don't ask for proof. Choice D is incorrect. The Traveller agrees to tell his story before he has slept.

3 Sample response: The way the Traveller speaks about his experience shows that he is passionate and determined. He says, "I've had a most amazing time." His agreement to share his story shows he is a fair-minded, committed scientist.

RETEACHING

Use a chart to verify the correct answer to question 3. Draw the chart below, and work with students to fill in the boxes. Sample responses are provided.

Dialogue	What This Reveals About the Traveller
• "I've lived eight days... such days as no human being ever lived before!" • "I've had a most amazing time..." • "I'm nearly worn out, but I shan't sleep till I've told this thing over to you."	• He has had unique experiences while time traveling. • He did enjoy his travels. Though he is tired from his travels, he still wants to share his story.

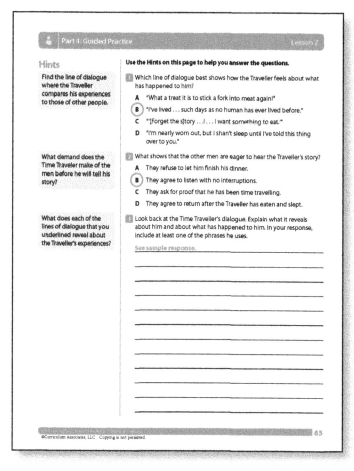

Integrating Standards

Use these questions to further students' understanding of the excerpt from *The Time Machine*.

1 Describe the points of view of the Time Traveller and the reader. How do these points of view differ and create a sense of suspense? **(RL.8.2)**

The Time Traveller is weary, excited, and hungry from his journey. He lingers over his food, delaying the telling of his adventure. The reader's point of view is closer to that of the Editor, who is eager to hear the story. The waiting creates suspense.

2 What details support the inference that the men in the story believe that the scientist has been time traveling? **(RL.8.1)**

The narrator asks, "One word. . . . Have you been time travelling?" Then the Editor says he would pay to hear exactly what happened. Because the men accept the Time Traveller's answer without proof, they most likely believe he has been time traveling.

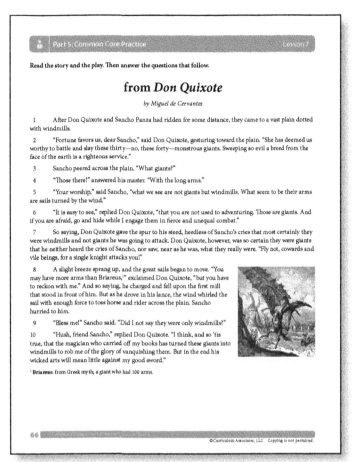

Read the story and the play. Then answer the questions that follow.

from *Don Quixote*

by Miguel de Cervantes

1   After Don Quixote and Sancho Panza had ridden for some distance, they came to a vast plain dotted with windmills.

2   "Fortune favors us, dear Sancho," said Don Quixote, gesturing toward the plain. "She has deemed us worthy to battle and slay these thirty—no, these forty—monstrous giants. Sweeping so evil a breed from the face of the earth is a righteous service."

3   Sancho peered across the plain. "What giants?"

4   "Those there!" answered his master. "With the long arms."

5   "Your worship," said Sancho, "what we see are not giants but windmills. What seem to be their arms are sails turned by the wind."

6   "It is easy to see," replied Don Quixote, "that you are not used to adventuring. Those are giants. And if you are afraid, go and hide while I engage them in fierce and unequal combat."

7   So saying, Don Quixote gave the spur to his steed, heedless of Sancho's cries that most certainly they were windmills and not giants he was going to attack. Don Quixote, however, was so certain they were giants that he neither heard the cries of Sancho, nor saw, near as he was, what they really were. "Fly not, cowards and vile beings, for a single knight attacks you!"

8   A slight breeze sprang up, and the great sails began to move. "You may have more arms than Briareus,[1] exclaimed Don Quixote, "but you have to reckon with me." And so saying, he charged and fell upon the first mill that stood in front of him. But as he drove in his lance, the wind whirled the sail with enough force to toss horse and rider across the plain. Sancho hurried to him.

9   "Bless me!" Sancho said. "Did I not say they were only windmills?"

10   "Hush, friend Sancho," replied Don Quixote. "I think, and so 'tis true, that the magician who carried off my books has turned these giants into windmills to rob me of the glory of vanquishing them. But in the end his wicked arts will mean little against my good sword."

[1] **Briareus:** from Greek myth; a giant who had 100 arms.

from *The Comical History of Don Quixote*

by Thomas d'Urfey

end of ACT I, SCENE I

1   DON QUIXOTE: See you that giant, Sancho? [*points offstage*]

2   SANCHO [*confused*]: Giant, sire?

3   DON QUIXOTE: That monstrous giant, with arms almost two leagues long! See how he swings 'em about, and fans himself to cool his head.

4   SANCHO: I see no giant, sire. I see a windmill, its sails turning.

5   DON QUIXOTE: Idiot! They may look like sails to you, but I know they are the arms of giants. Go and hide, if you are afraid. I will enter into cruel and unequal battle with the beasts. [*Exit*]

6   SANCHO: Are you blind? Your brains will be dashed out by the sails! [*Exit SANCHO . . . curtain falls*]

beginning of ACT I, SCENE II

[*Curtain rises upon the interior of an inn. Two friends of DON QUIXOTE, NICHOLAS and PEREZ, sit at a table, picking at plates of uneaten food.*]

7   NICHOLAS: Those two mad fools have gone knight erranting.[2]

8   PEREZ: It troubles me that a man who had such good sense should be so strangely bewitched by the idea of knight errantry.

9   NICHOLAS: 'Tis indeed a strange infatuation.

10   PEREZ [*brightening*]: But I think I have used my time well. While you have been searching for the whimsical knight, his housekeeper and I have been burning his books.

11   NICHOLAS: I have no doubt that will help cure him. Those tales of knighthood have upended his sense—but look! Here comes our host.

[*Enter VINCENT, laughing*]

12   NICHOLAS: Innkeeper! What makes you so merry this morning?

13   VINCENT [*laughing*]: Oh, my ribs! Don Quixote, Don Quixote.

14   PEREZ: Why? What of him?

15   VINCENT: The mad fool has charged a windmill, swearing it was a giant! The sails spun him about like a rat in a wheel until, at last, Fortune let him keep the few brains he has left and tossed him into a fish pond. [*shaking with laughter*] Oh, I shall burst!

[2] **Erranting:** from old French; wandering in search of adventure

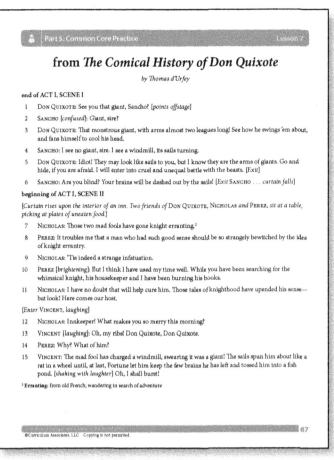

AT A GLANCE

Students independently read a story and a play and answer questions in a format that provides test practice.

STEP BY STEP

• Tell students to use what they have learned about reading closely and analyzing dialogue and incidents to read the passages on pages 66 and 67.

• Remind students to underline or circle important dialogue and incidents.

• Tell students to answer the questions on page 68. For questions 1–3, they should fill in the correct circle on the Answer Form.

• When students have finished, use the Answer Analysis to discuss correct responses and the reasons for them. Have students fill in the Number Correct on the Answer Form.

ANSWER ANALYSIS

1   Choice B is correct. Sancho addresses Don Quixote as "your worship," which is a term of great respect. Choice A is incorrect. While Sancho does tell Don Quixote that the "giants" are windmills, that is not a sign of respect. Choice C is incorrect. Sancho does not try to convince Don Quixote not to fight. He tries to tell Don Quixote that the windmills are not giants. Choice D is incorrect. While Sancho does hurry to Don Quixote to see if he is hurt, this shows he wants to help him. It is not necessarily a sign of respect. **(DOK 2)**

Theme Connection

• How do all the passages in this lesson relate to the theme of doers and dreamers?

• What is one fact or idea you learned about doers and dreamers from each passage in this lesson?

ANSWER ANALYSIS

2 Choice D is correct. Don Quixote is convinced the windmills are giants. "Deemed us worthy to battle" shows he thinks he must fight them. Choice A is incorrect. Don Quixote does not realize that what he sees are windmills. Choice B is incorrect. "Fortune favors us" means they are fortunate, not that Don Quixote wants to make his fortune. Choice C is incorrect. Don Quixote thinks he must rid the earth of the windmills, not that he needs to go out and rid the earth of other evil. *(DOK 2)*

3 Choice A is correct. Quixote's friends are concerned and want to try to help him. Choice B is incorrect. Vincent, not Perez and Nicholas, thinks Don Quixote is a fool. Choice C is incorrect. The friends plot to help "cure" Don Quixote, but they don't think he is dangerous. Choice D is incorrect. The Innkeeper is making fun of Don Quixote. Perez and Nicholas do not seek the Innkeeper's advice. *(DOK 2)*

4 Sample response: Sancho respects Don Quixote and tries to help him. Sancho calls Quixote "your worship" and warns that "what we see are not giants but windmills." Vincent thinks Don Quixote is silly and laughable. He calls Don Quixote a "mad fool" and laughs until he feels like he will burst. *(DOK 4)*

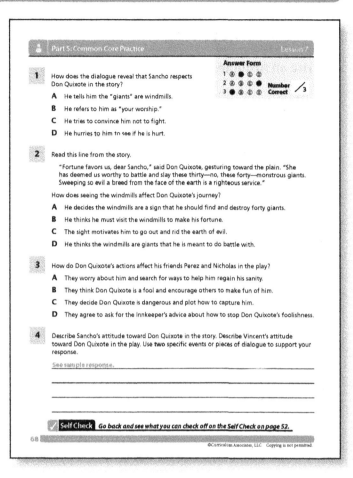

Integrating Standards

Use these questions and tasks as opportunities to interact with *Don Quixote* and *The Comical History of Don Quixote*.

1 What does Don Quixote think the windmills are? How does he describe them in the story? *(RL.8.1)*

Don Quixote thinks the windmills are giants. He describes them as "monstrous" with "long arms."

2 Summarize in your own words what Don Quixote thinks happens to the giants at the end of the story. *(RL.8.2)*

Don Quixote thinks a magician turned the giants into windmills.

3 In paragraph 9 of the play, what does *infatuation* mean? What is Don Quixote's infatuation? Use a dictionary to help you. *(RL.8.4; L.8.4a, L.8.4c)*

Infatuation means "an extreme focus on something." Don Quixote's infatuation is with the idea of knight errantry, or the search for adventure, that he reads in books about knighthood.

4 How does Don Quixote's allusion to Briareus impact the meaning and tone of the story? Cite evidence from the text to explain your answer. *(RL.8.4)*

Sample response: Don Quixote is determined to have an adventure and insists that the windmills are giants. By having Quixote describe the windmills as having "more arms than Briareus," Cervantes emphasizes that Quixote sees only what he wants to see, even to the point of wild exaggeration. This description also contributes to the humorous tone.

5 Discuss in small groups: What do you learn about Don Quixote from the story and play? How does reading both texts increase your understanding of this character and the events? *(SL.8.1)*

Discussions will vary. Encourage students to cite specific connections between the events and the characters in the story and the play. Students should analyze the information that is revealed about Don Quixote to explain why he behaves the way he does.

Writing Activities

Write an Argumentative Essay (W.8.1)

- Review with students that dialogue reveals information about characters and helps to propel the action of a story or drama. Challenge students to determine criteria for what makes dialogue effective and successful based on the dialogue they read in this lesson.

- Have students use their criteria to evaluate the dialogue in this lesson's passages. Which story or drama achieved the criteria well, and why? Remind them to introduce their claim, support it with text evidence, and provide a concluding statement.

- Allow students to share their essays with the class.

Gerunds (L.8.1a)

- Explain to students that a gerund is a verb that ends in -*ing* and functions as a noun in a sentence. Direct them to paragraph 4 of *The Time Machine*. Point out the gerund, *travelling*. Discuss its function.

- Have students locate another gerund in this passage. (*Sample response: starving*)

- Then guide students to write a paragraph about time travel, using at least two gerunds.

LISTENING ACTIVITY (SL.8.1)

Listen Closely/Summarize

- Have partners take turns reading aloud paragraphs from the story *Don Quixote*.

- One student reads aloud the paragraph and then summarizes it in his or her own words. The other student provides feedback on whether the partner provided an objective summary.

- Partners switch roles and continue the activity until they've summarized the entire story.

DISCUSSION ACTIVITY (SL.8.1)

Talk in a Group/Discuss Characters

- Have students form small groups to discuss the three main characters from this lesson's passages: Tor, the Time Traveller, and Don Quixote.

- Provide the following prompts to inform the discussion: How do all of these characters relate to the theme of doers and dreamers? In what other ways are the characters similar? How are the characters unique, and what distinguishes them from one another?

- Allow 10 to 15 minutes for discussion. Then have each group share its results with the class.

MEDIA ACTIVITY (RL.8.7)

Be Creative/Watch a Film Production

- Direct students to a film version of *Don Quixote* or *The Time Machine*.

- Have students watch the entire film or just the scene that they read about in this lesson.

- Then have students discuss how closely the film followed the text they read. Encourage students to evaluate the effectiveness of the choices the director made in the film version.

RESEARCH ACTIVITY (W.8.7; SL.8.4)

Research and Present/Give a Presentation

- Have students research another scene from *The Time Machine* or *Don Quixote*. The scene should have ample dialogue to use as the basis for an oral report.

- Ask students to present their chosen excerpt and give a detailed analysis of how the dialogue and incidents in the scene reveal information about the characters and propel the plot forward.

- After students give their reports, allow time for listeners to ask the presenter questions about the analysis.

Determining Theme

LESSON OBJECTIVES

- Recognize broader messages in works of literature as themes.

- Identify how characters' thoughts, feelings, and actions point to a story's theme.

- Understand how a character's development can reveal a story's theme.

THE LEARNING PROGRESSION

- **Grade 7:** CCSS RL.7.2 requires students to determine a theme of a text and analyze its development over the course of the text.

- **Grade 8: CCSS RL.8.2 builds on the Grade 7 standard by having students analyze the theme's development over the course of the text, including its relationship to the characters, setting, and plot.**

- **Grade 9:** CCSS RL.9.2 requires students to analyze in detail a theme's development over the course of the text, including how it emerges and is shaped and refined by specific details.

PREREQUISITE SKILLS

- Recognize literary elements such as characters, setting, and plot.

- Recognize how details help support larger ideas.

- Explain how details and literary elements contribute to the theme of a text.

TAP STUDENTS' PRIOR KNOWLEDGE

- Tell students they will be working on a lesson about theme. First, ask students what the theme of a story is. (*a message or lesson that an author wants to convey*) Ask for examples of common literary themes. (*Stealing is wrong; Stand up for your beliefs; Hard work always pays off.*)

- Explain that most stories have some kind of theme and that theme is an important element of fiction. The theme enables readers to connect a story to their own lives and to relate to the characters. Without a theme, readers might lose interest in a story.

- Ask students to tell you the main plot events of a familiar story. (*King Midas wishes that everything he touches would turn to gold, and his wish is granted, although he is no longer able to touch food or people.*) Challenge them to use the main events to come up with a theme, and emphasize that there might be more than one theme. (*A theme from the story of King Midas is: Be careful what you wish for.*)

- Ask students to share examples of stories with which they connected. Encourage them to explain why they identified with the story's characters or events. Challenge them to describe the story's theme. Point out that identifying the theme of a story will help them to better appreciate what they read.

Ready *Teacher Toolbox*

teacher-toolbox.com

	Prerequisite Skills	RL.8.2
Ready Lessons	✓	✓
Tools for Instruction	✓	✓
Interactive Tutorials		✓

CCSS Focus

RL.8.2 Determine a theme or central idea of a text and analyze its development over the course of the text, including its relationship to the characters, setting, and plot . . . .

ADDITIONAL STANDARDS: **RL.8.1, RL.8.3, RL.8.4, RL.8.7; L.8.1, L.8.4a, L.8.4d, L.8.5a, L.8.5b; W.8.3, W.8.4, W.8.8; SL.8.1**
(*See page A39 for full text.*)

AT A GLANCE

Students study a photograph and its caption, think about the story it tells, and practice determining a theme, or a lesson about life.

STEP BY STEP

- Read the first paragraph and review the meaning of *theme*. Explain that careful readers are mindful of theme since it helps them better understand a story's events and characters' motivations.

- Have students study the photograph and its caption. Encourage them to think about the story being told and the message being conveyed. Ask students to circle details in the image and caption that suggest a message or life lesson.

- Explain to students that the chart shows how to analyze details in order to help them determine a theme. Read the character, setting, and action details in the chart, and have students compare these details to the details they circled in the photo and caption.

- Then read the theme in the chart and discuss how it is supported by all the details. Review that this statement is a message or lesson about life that is being conveyed. Have students discuss other possible themes of the photo and caption.

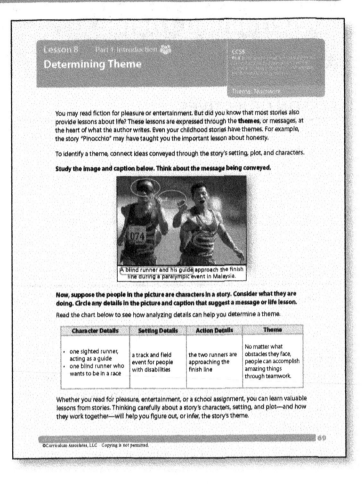

Genre Focus

Literary Texts: Realistic Fiction

Tell students that they will be reading examples of realistic fiction in this lesson. Review with students that a realistic fiction story has characters, settings, and situations that are believable and could really exist, although the story is made up by the author.

Realistic fiction stories usually take place in the present. Contemporary readers can easily identify with the characters and situations. For example, the realistic stories in this lesson deal with a boy's relationship with his grandfather and a girl who feels overwhelmed by a school project.

Have students talk about realistic fiction stories they have read. Familiar examples may include *Hatchet*, *The Breadwinner*, *HUSH*, and *Because of Winn-Dixie*.

The first two stories in this lesson are examples of realistic fiction. The third story is a Native American legend. Unlike realistic fiction a legend is handed down through generations, not made up by a particular author. It takes place in the distant past and may include characters and events that are not totally realistic. Still, students should be able to relate to all the stories in this lesson and use their own experiences to better understand the themes.

AT A GLANCE

Students read a realistic story and identify the theme that is being developed.

STEP BY STEP

- Invite volunteers to tell what they learned on the previous page about determining the theme of a text.

- Tell students that in this lesson they will read a story about a boy named Holden and his grandfather.

- Read aloud the story "Holden and Pops."

- Then read the question "What do the details in this part of the story suggest about how people sometimes judge others?"

- Tell students you will use a Think Aloud to demonstrate a way of answering the question.

Think Aloud: This part of the story is about Holden and his mother, so I'm going to focus on details that describe their actions and feelings. These story details should reveal the theme or central idea of this part of the story. At the beginning of the story, Holden remarks that his grandfather wouldn't be interested in video games. Holden also says, "You know how he is about big, scary technology."

- Direct students to the chart and review that it will help them to analyze the details from the story in order to determine this part of the story's theme.

- Point out Holden's comments about Pops.

Think Aloud: Holden's mother asks Holden if he has ever tried showing Pops one of his video games. She tells Holden, "Pops might surprise you."

- Point out Mom's comments about Pops in the chart.

Think Aloud: Holden seems to think Pops would never be interested in video games because Holden thinks Pops doesn't understand technology. Mom's words suggest that she feels Holden's grandfather is more interesting than Holden thinks he is.

- Have students read Mom's attitude toward Pops in the chart and then complete the chart to describe Holden's attitude.

- Finally, have students respond to the prompt at the bottom of the page. Invite volunteers to share their responses with the class. (*Sample response: People might surprise you if you keep an open mind.*)

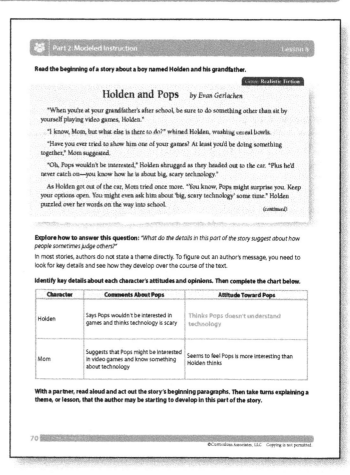

ELL Support: Contractions

- Direct students to the words *you're* in paragraph 1 and *you'd* in paragraph 3. Explain that these are contractions, two words that have been joined together and shortened. When the words are joined, letters are dropped and an apostrophe is added to take the place of any dropped letters.

- Work with students to identify the two words in each contraction (*you are; you would*) and write them on the board. Have volunteers read each sentence aloud with the two words in place of the contraction. Point out that writers use contractions to make their characters' speech sound natural.

- Have students find another contraction on this page and identify the two words in it. (*he'd, he would*) **(L.8.1)**

AT A GLANCE

Students continue reading the story about Holden and Pops. They answer a multiple-choice question and analyze details from the story to determine the theme.

STEP BY STEP

- Tell students they will continue reading the story about Holden and Pops.

- Close Reading helps students identify the point in the story at which Holden's feelings and actions change. The Hint will help students recognize how a character's change in attitude relates to the theme.

- Have students read the story and circle words that tell how Holden's feelings change, as directed by Close Reading.

- Ask volunteers to share the words they circled. Discuss why they chose these words. If necessary, ask, "How does Holden react to Pops at first? How does Holden respond to Pops's comment about the Tomahawk?"

- Have students circle the answer to the question, using the Hint to help them. Then have them respond to Show Your Thinking. If students have trouble identifying additional life lessons, ask them to think about what Holden learns from Mom and Pops.

ANSWER ANALYSIS

Choice A is incorrect. Holden and Pops developed a bond over the video game, but the story never suggests family bonds can *only* be developed through shared interests.

Choice B is incorrect. It suggests how Holden feels at the beginning of the story, not how his attitude changes.

Choice C is incorrect. Holden did learn from his mother's advice, but that is not the main theme of this story.

Choice D is correct. Holden assumed Pops wouldn't be interested in his video game, but that was incorrect. Holden didn't know that Pops flew an airplane in 1941.

ERROR ALERT: Students who did not choose D might not have understood that a theme reflects the beginning, middle, and end of a story. Point out that some details support each choice, but the entire story and how Holden changes support only D.

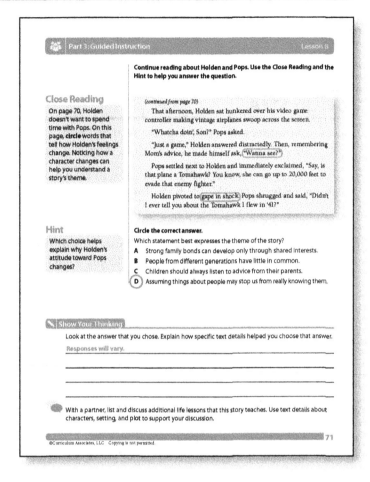

Tier Two Vocabulary: *Hunkered*

- Direct students to the word *hunkered* in paragraph 1. Have students use context clues from the story to suggest a meaning. ("crouched" or "bent over something")

- Ask students to use a thesaurus to help them identify synonyms that would make sense in place of *hunkered* in the story: *hunched, huddled, curled up.* **(RL.8.4; L.8.4a, L.8.4d)**

AT A GLANCE

Students read a realistic story about a student's preparations for a school career fair. After the first reading, you will ask three questions to check your students' comprehension of the story.

STEP BY STEP

- Have students read the story silently without referring to the Study Buddy or Close Reading text.

- Ask the following questions to ensure students' comprehension of the text:

  Why is Angie reluctant to ask others for help? (*Angie thinks she is the only person who can get everything right.*)

  What advice does Karim give to Angie? (*Karim tells Angie to delegate and ask her friends for help.*)

  How does Angie feel at the end of the story? (*Angie is very happy and pleased with the way the career fair has turned out, especially the introductory video. She is glad that she learned to delegate.*)

- Ask students to reread paragraph 1 and look at the Study Buddy text. What does the Study Buddy help them think about?

Tip: The Study Buddy models identifying details that show how a character's feelings change over the course of a story. Recognizing differences between a character at the beginning and at the end of a story will help students understand the theme.

- Then have students read the rest of the story. Tell them to follow the directions in Close Reading.

Tip: In this story, the theme is evident in the ways that the main character changes throughout the story and the lesson she learns. Remind students to pay attention to character development, as it can have a significant impact on the theme and on the story as a whole.

- Finally, have students answer the questions on page 73. Use the Answer Analysis to discuss correct and incorrect responses.

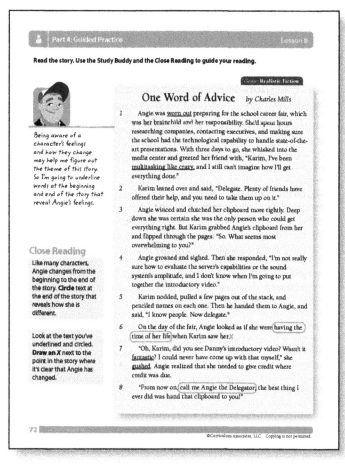

Tier Two Vocabulary: *Capability*

- Direct students to the word *capability* in paragraph 1. Point to the *-ity* ending and explain that this ending forms nouns from other parts of speech.

- Point out the base word *capable* and ask students to define it (*"having the ability to do something"*) Then have them use word parts and context to define *capability*. (*"the extent of someone's ability to do something"*) Discuss what it means for the school to have "technological capability." **(RL.8.4; L.8.4b)**

STEP BY STEP

- Have students read questions 1–3, using the Hints to help them answer those questions.

Tip: Question 3 requires students to identify two details supporting the correct answer to question 2. Point out the connection between these questions.

- Discuss with students the Answer Analysis below.

ANSWER ANALYSIS

1 The correct choice is C. Paragraph 3 states that Angie "was certain she was the only person who could get everything right." *Competent* means "having the ability to do something." Choice A is incorrect. Karim says that several friends already offered to help. Choice B is incorrect. Angie did not ask Karim for help. Choice D is incorrect. There is no team at the beginning of the story.

2 The correct choice is B. The events of the story teach Angie the value of trusting others to do as good of a job as she could do herself. Choices A and C are incorrect. They reflect Angie's attitude at the beginning, when she thinks she must do everything herself. Choice D is incorrect, and the theme it states is not supported by the story. Karim gives great advice, and he also lends a hand.

3 The correct choices are 4 and 6. These excerpts show how Angie's attitudes about and approach to leadership change after Karim convinces her to delegate tasks. Choice 4 is what Angie says about Danny's video. Choice 6 is what she says to Karim at the end of the story. Both statements show Angie learning to trust in the skills of others. Choices 1–3 are incorrect; they reflect Angie's attitudes and frustrations at the beginning of the story and do not support the theme given in question 2. Choice 5 is also incorrect. It is part an admission by Angie that she is not up to all the tasks that confront her.

RETEACHING

Use a chart to model how to answer question 2.

	Comments	Attitude
Beginning	can't imagine how she'll get it all done	overwhelmed, not trusting of others
End	thankful	pleased, trusting

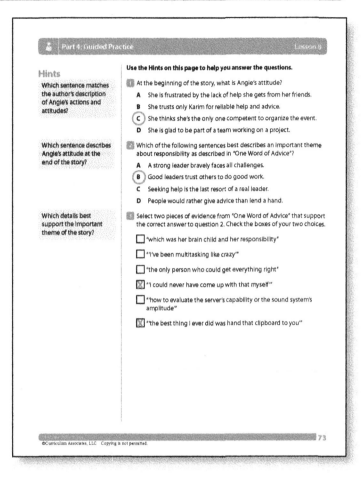

Integrating Standards

Use these questions to further students' understanding of "One Word of Advice."

1 How do you know that trusting others is difficult for Angie? **(RL.8.1)**

When Karim tells Angie to delegate and to ask friends for help, Angie "winced and clutched her clipboard more tightly." Her reaction to the suggestion is one of fear. She doesn't think anyone else can do what she's doing, and she's not willing to let go of her responsibility.

2 What is the meaning of "give credit where credit was due" in paragraph 7? **(RL.8.4; L.8.5a)**

It means that people should be recognized for their hard work. Angie is surprised and pleased with Danny's introductory video. Therefore, she is willing to recognize him for his efforts and congratulate him on a job well done.

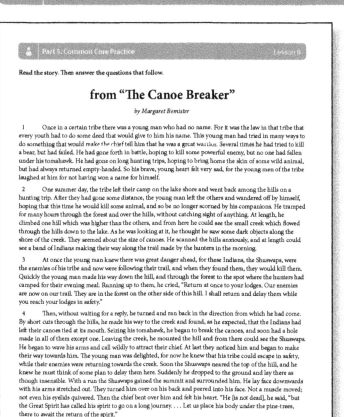

Read the story. Then answer the questions that follow.

from "The Canoe Breaker"

by Margaret Bemister

1   Once in a certain tribe there was a young man who had no name. For it was the law in that tribe that every youth had to do some deed that would give to him his name. This young man had tried in many ways to do something that would make the chief tell him that he was a great warrior. Several times he had tried to kill a bear, but had failed. He had gone forth in battle, hoping to kill some powerful enemy, but no one had fallen under his tomahawk. He had gone on long hunting trips, hoping to bring home the skin of some wild animal, but had always returned empty-handed. So his brave, young heart felt very sad, for the young men of the tribe laughed at him for not having won a name for himself.

2   One summer day, the tribe left their camp on the lake shore and went back among the hills on a hunting trip. After they had gone some distance, the young man left the others and wandered off by himself, hoping that this time he would kill some animal, and so be no longer scorned by his companions. He tramped for many hours through the forest and over the hills, without catching sight of anything. At length, he climbed one hill which was higher than the others, and from here he could see the small creek which flowed through the hills down to the lake. As he was looking at it, he thought he saw some dark objects along the shore of the creek. They seemed about the size of canoes. He scanned the hills anxiously, and at length could see a band of Indians making their way along the trail made by the hunters in the morning.

3   At once the young man knew there was great danger ahead, for these Indians, the Shuswaps, were the enemies of his tribe and now were following their trail, and when they found them, they would kill them. Quickly the young man made his way down the hill, and through the forest to the spot where the hunters had camped for their evening meal. Running up to them, he cried, "Return at once to your lodges. Our enemies are now on our trail. They are in the forest on the other side of this hill. I shall return and delay them while you reach your lodges in safety."

4   Then, without waiting for a reply, he turned and ran back in the direction from which he had come. By short cuts through the hills, he made his way to the creek and found, as he expected, that the Indians had left their canoes tied at its mouth. Seizing his tomahawk, he began to break the canoes, and soon had a hole made in all of them except one. Leaving the creek, he mounted the hill and from there could see the Shuswaps. He began to wave his arms and call wildly to attract their chief. At last they noticed him and began to make their way towards him. The young man was delighted, for now he knew that his tribe could escape in safety, while their enemies were returning towards the creek. Soon the Shuswaps neared the top of the hill, and he knew he must think of some plan to delay them here. Suddenly he dropped to the ground and lay there as though insensible. With a run the Shuswaps gained the summit and surrounded him. He lay face downwards with his arms stretched out. They turned him over on his back and peered into his face. Not a muscle moved; not even his eyelids quivered. Then the chief bent over him and felt his heart. "He [is not dead]," he said, "but the Great Spirit has called his spirit to go on a long journey. . . . Let us place his body under the pine-trees, there to await the return of the spirit."

74   ©Curriculum Associates, LLC Copying is not permitted.

5   The Indians lifted the body of the young man, carried it to a clump of pine-trees and laid it down. Then they walked some yards away and held a council.

6   As soon as they were a safe distance away, the young man jumped up. He ran down the hill, and reaching the canoes, jumped into the unbroken one and began to paddle down the creek.

7   The Shuswaps turned and saw him. With fierce cries, they began to race down the hillside, and when they arrived at the spot where they had left their canoes, and saw what had happened, they filled the air with their angry yells. The young man was now out on the lake in the canoe, and they were unable to follow him, as all the other canoes were wrecked. They ran angrily along the lake shore, thinking he would land on their side, but instead, he made his way across the lake to the other side.

8   When the young man reached the shore, he again seized his tomahawk, and this time broke the canoe with which he had saved his life. The defeated Shuswaps, standing on the shore, saw him do this, and again they filled the air with their angry yells. There was nothing for them to do but to return to their camp, while the young man made his way along the lake shore to the village of his tribe. When he reached there, he found that he was no longer a man without a name. His brave deed had won for him the name of Kasamoldin—the canoe breaker—and ever afterwards in his tribe, and to others, he was known by this name.

Answer the questions. Mark your answers to questions 1–3 on the Answer Form to the right.

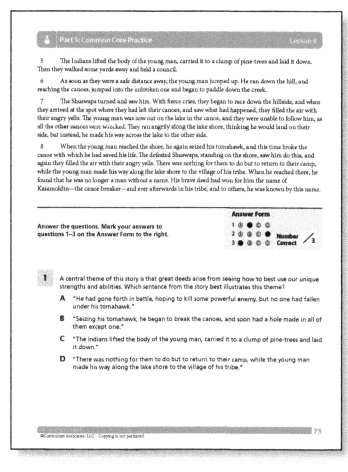

Answer Form

1 Ⓐ Ⓑ ● Ⓓ
2 Ⓐ Ⓑ ● Ⓓ   **Number Correct** /3
3 ● Ⓑ Ⓒ Ⓓ

1   A central theme of this story is that great deeds arise from seeing how to best use our unique strengths and abilities. Which sentence from the story best illustrates this theme?

A   "He had gone forth in battle, hoping to kill some powerful enemy, but no one had fallen under his tomahawk."

B   "Seizing his tomahawk, he began to break the canoes, and soon had a hole made in all of them except one."

C   "The Indians lifted the body of the young man, carried it to a clump of pine-trees and laid it down."

D   "There was nothing for them to do but to return to their camp, while the young man made his way along the lake shore to the village of his tribe."

75   ©Curriculum Associates, LLC Copying is not permitted.

AT A GLANCE

Students independently read a longer story and answer questions in a format that provides test practice.

STEP BY STEP

• Tell students to use what they have learned about reading closely and determining theme to read the story on pages 74 and 75.

• Remind students to circle or underline important details in the story.

• Tell students to answer the questions on pages 75 and 76. For questions 1–3, they should fill in the correct circle on the Answer Form.

• When students have finished, use the Answer Analysis to discuss correct responses and the reasons for them. Have students fill in the Number Correct on the Answer Form.

ANSWER ANALYSIS

1   Choice B is correct. The young man tried to perform a "great deed" that would earn him a name by imitating the successes of others, only to fail again and again. When he makes the brave choice to protect his people against the enemy tribe, he chooses actions within his own range of strength and abilities. Choice A is incorrect. It describes one of the young man's failed attempts to be like others. Choice C shows the young man's bravery, but it does not illustrate a moment of insight and action as Choice B does. Choice D describes the aftermath of the young man's actions, but does not directly support the theme. **(DOK 2)**

Theme Connection

• How do all the stories in this lesson relate to the theme of teamwork?

• What is one fact or idea you learned about teamwork from each story in this lesson?

2 Choice D is correct. The young man was unable to earn a name by performing the actions that other people in his tribe traditionally did to get names. He finally earns a name by performing a brave, but unique, deed. Choice A is incorrect. The young man does not decide his own name. Choice B is incorrect. The Shuswaps are the enemies of the young man's tribe. Choice C is incorrect because the young man never becomes a "great warrior." ***(DOK 2)***

3 Choice A is correct. The young man shows incredible courage in his encounter with the Shuswaps. This personal strength shows how the character changes, and it best supports the story's theme. Choices B, C, and D are incorrect. The young man does show physical strength, determination, and fear, but these details don't show how the young man changes. ***(DOK 2)***

4 Sample response: The author develops the theme of finding your own strengths and abilities through the conflict the young man faces. The young man wants to earn his name but fails by traditional means, such as killing a bear. But when he sees his tribe in danger, he comes up with his own unique way to save them by breaking the enemy's canoes. This earns him a name meaning "canoe breaker." ***(DOK 3)***

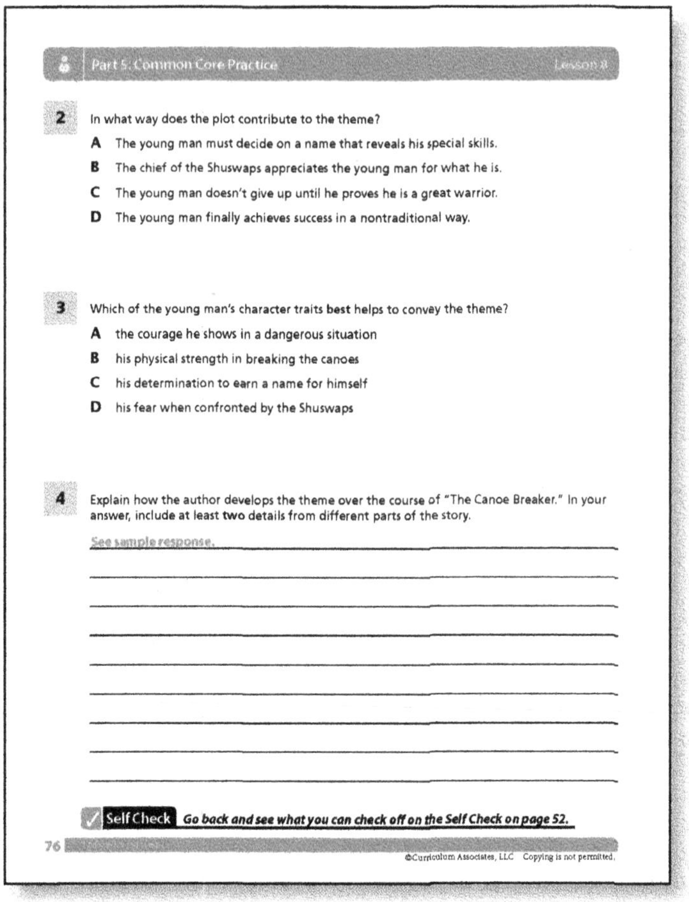
Part 5: Common Core Practice Lesson 8

2 In what way does the plot contribute to the theme?

A The young man must decide on a name that reveals his special skills.
B The chief of the Shuswaps appreciates the young man for what he is.
C The young man doesn't give up until he proves he is a great warrior.
D The young man finally achieves success in a nontraditional way.

3 Which of the young man's character traits **best** helps to convey the theme?

A the courage he shows in a dangerous situation
B his physical strength in breaking the canoes
C his determination to earn a name for himself
D his fear when confronted by the Shuswaps

4 Explain how the author develops the theme over the course of "The Canoe Breaker." In your answer, include at least **two** details from different parts of the story.

See sample response.

Self Check *Go back and see what you can check off on the Self Check on page 52.*

76

©Curriculum Associates, LLC Copying is not permitted.

Integrating Standards

Use these questions and tasks as opportunities to interact with "The Canoe Breaker."

1 What details from the beginning of the story help you determine the young man's feelings? **(RL.8.1)**

After so many unsuccessful attempts to earn his name through brave deeds, the young man's "heart felt very sad." In addition, "the young men of the tribe laughed at him for not having won a name for himself." The young man felt sad, upset, and probably embarrassed about his failures.

2 How do certain events reveal aspects of the young man's character? **(RL.8.3)**

Sample response: When the young man spots enemies of his tribe, he springs into action, warns his tribe of the danger, and smashes the enemy's canoes. This event reveals the young man's true character.

3 What does the phrase *filled the air* mean in paragraph 8? What does this descriptive detail contribute to the story? ***(RL.8.4; L.8.5a)***

According to the story, the defeated Shuswaps "filled the air with their angry yells." They are not literally putting anything into the air. Rather, they are making so much noise that the air seems thick with their voices. This detail helps readers visualize the scene.

4 Write a brief summary of this story. **(W.8.4)**

Summaries will vary. Sample response: A young man has not earned a name. He tries traditional ways but fails. Then one day he sees an enemy tribe nearby and alerts his tribe of the danger. He then breaks the enemy's canoes and pretends to be unconscious to distract them. Finally, he gets away in a canoe and has helped save his tribe. This brave deed earns him a name.

5 Discuss in small groups: What are additional lessons this story teaches? Use details about the characters, setting, and events to support your discussion. ***(SL.8.1)***

Discussions will vary. Have students think about what the characters learn from the events.

Writing Activities

Narrative Writing: New Story/Same Theme (W.8.3)

- Have students review the themes of the stories in this lesson. Ask students to identify ways in which the author of each story developed the theme. What details about character, setting, and plot did they use?

- Ask students to choose one of the themes from this lesson and write a new story with the same theme. Their stories should not be too similar to the story from this lesson, but it should convey the same theme.

- Encourage students to read aloud their stories, and have the class identify the theme.

Connotations and Denotations (L.8.5c)

- Review the definitions of and differences between a word's connotation and denotation. Remind students that words with similar denotations can have different connotations.

- Direct students to the words *winced*, *groaned*, and *sighed* in "One Word of Advice." Have students discuss or look up the meaning of each.

- Then have students reread the story and determine the connotation of each word. What is the difference between the words? Encourage students to find other words in this lesson's stories with similar denotations and different connotations.

LISTENING ACTIVITY (SL.8.1)

Listen Closely/Make Inferences

- Have partners reread "The Canoe Breaker." Ask each student to write an inference they made about the characters, setting, or events based on evidence in the text.

- As one student shares his or her inference, the other student must listen closely. He or she then provides evidence from the text that supports the inference.

- Students then switch roles and repeat the activity.

DISCUSSION ACTIVITY (SL.8.1)

Talk in a Group/Compare Characters

- Ask students to compare and contrast two of the characters in this lesson's stories.

- Have students form small groups to compare and contrast each character's traits, the character's problem, and the lesson he or she learns.

- Appoint one member of each group to take notes. Allow 10 to 15 minutes for discussion, and then have each group share its results with the class.

MEDIA ACTIVITY (RL.8.7)

Be Creative/Listen to a Storyteller

- Direct students to video recordings by Native American storytellers, such as those available at www.watchknowlearn.org or www.pbs.org.

- Students should compare and contrast the experience of watching and listening to a storyteller to the experience of reading a similar story. In which case is the theme more evident?

RESEARCH ACTIVITY (W.8.8; SL.8.4)

Research and Present/Give a Presentation

- Have students review the photo on page 69. Ask students to research the Paralympics and some of its events. Which events require teamwork? How are these events different from their Olympic counterparts? What obstacles do the athletes face?

- Have students present their findings to the class. Remind them to use appropriate eye contact, adequate volume, and clear pronunciation.

- Encourage students to include a multimedia component in their presentations, if possible. They should use these components to clarify their findings and emphasize important points.

Summarizing Literary Texts

Theme: *Views of Other Worlds*

LESSON OBJECTIVES

- Summarize a literary text by restating in one's own words the main characters, setting, and key events in sequence.
- Provide an objective summary free of personal opinions or judgments.

THE LEARNING PROGRESSION

- **Grade 7:** CCSS RL.7.2 requires students to analyze the development of a theme across a text as well as to summarize the text objectively.
- **Grade 8: CCSS RL.8.2 builds on the Grade 7 standard by requiring students to focus more directly on the interaction between characters, setting, and plot in developing themes and creating a summary that is objective, brief, and in students' own words.**
- **Grade 9:** CCSS RL.9.2 requires students to further analyze how a theme emerges and is shaped and refined as well as to summarize the text objectively.

PREREQUISITE SKILLS

- Identify characters, setting, and important details in a literary text.
- Use one's own words to summarize a text.
- Avoid including personal opinions or judgments when providing an objective summary of a text.

TAP STUDENTS' PRIOR KNOWLEDGE

- Tell students they will be working on a lesson about summarizing. They will learn how to summarize a story in a way that is objective, or free of opinions or judgments.
- Ask students what kind of information they would include in a story summary. (*the setting, main characters, conflict; important plot details*)
- Read these two plot summaries:

  (1) On a cool autumn day, a family of three bears goes for a walk in the woods. While they are gone, a young girl comes to their house. She eats their porridge, sits in their chairs, and then falls asleep. When the bears come home, they find the girl sleeping.

  (2) This is an unbelievable story! It is about three bears that go for a walk while they wait for their breakfast to cool. You won't believe what happens while they're gone!

- Ask: Which summary is better and why? (*The first because it includes the setting, main characters, and important events. The second summary doesn't give the setting or enough information about the plot, and it's not objective.*)
- Explain to students that being able to summarize a story will help them understand and remember what they read.

Ready *Teacher Toolbox* teacher-toolbox.com

	Prerequisite Skills	RL.8.2
Ready Lessons	✓	✓
Tools for Instruction		✓
Interactive Tutorials	✓	✓

CCSS Focus

RL.8.2 … provide an objective summary of the text.

ADDITIONAL STANDARDS: **RL.8.1, RL.8.3, RL.8.4, RL.8.5, RL.8.6; L.8.1, L.8.4a, L.8.4c, L.8.4d, L.8.5a; W.8.3, W.8.4, W.8.7, W.8.8; SL.8.1, SL.8.4** (*See page A39 for full text.*)

AT A GLANCE

Students study two images and think about what details to include in a summary of the events pictured. They learn to concentrate on the most essential details, such as setting, characters, and important events, without interjecting their own opinions.

STEP BY STEP

- Read the paragraph and discuss the definitions of *summarize* and *objective*. Then direct students to the two images. Have them study the images and look for details about the character, setting, and events.

- Explain that the graphic organizer shows a way to organize these details and use them to create a summary. Read aloud the details provided for characters, setting, and important events, and ask students to compare them to the details they noticed. Then read the summary and discuss how it highlights the most important points in a clear, concise way and does not include any opinions.

- Ask students to suggest real-life situations when it has been important for them to be able to summarize an event.

- Share an example of how you have summarized a literary text when reading. Explain how using this skill helped you better understand the text and remember important plot details.

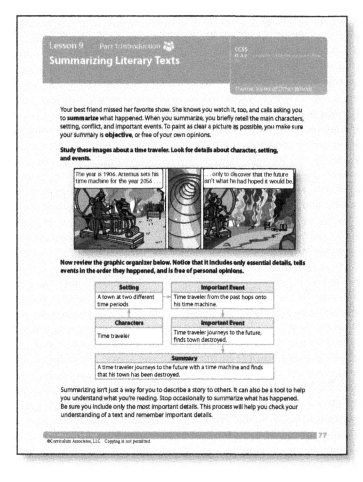

Genre Focus

Literary Texts: Science Fiction

Tell students that in this lesson they will read a kind of literary text called science fiction. Explain that science fiction is a fiction story that explores the possible impact of a scientific theory or advance on humans and societies. Science fiction stories usually share these characteristics:

- usually set in a different time and place, often in the future

- may be based on known scientific data and theories, as well as creative imagination

- setting, events, and characters may be fantastic, or they may seem believable and familiar

Based on these characteristics, ask students to share examples of science fiction they have read. What were the stories about? Were they set in the past or the future? What scientific theories or technology did the story include? Was the story set on Earth or on another planet?

Explain that all three passages in this lesson are science fiction. "Touchdown on Spectra Omicron 8" is about a mission to begin transforming a planet to support human life. "Prime Contact" is about an encounter with an alien. The excerpt from *The War of the Worlds* is about an invasion from Martians.

AT A GLANCE

Students read the beginning of a science fiction story and evaluate a summary, crossing out opinions and judgments. Then they work to improve the summary.

STEP BY STEP

- Invite volunteers to tell what they learned on the previous page about summarizing events.

- Tell students that in this lesson they will learn how to analyze a summary and then they will improve the summary while keeping it objective.

- Read aloud "Touchdown on Spectra Omicron 8."

- Then read the question: "How can you best summarize this part of the story?"

- Tell students you will use a Think Aloud to demonstrate a way to answer the question.

- Read the sample summary of the story.

Think Aloud: I know a summary should not include opinions and judgments, which are words that reflect the summarizer's personal feelings. I'll reread the summary and look for words that give opinions. The first sentence says the Ulysses "sets off on a really dangerous mission." The words "really dangerous" sound like an opinion. I see that they are not in the story, so they express the opinion of the writer. Those words don't belong in the summary.

- Work with students to identify and cross out the words that reflect opinions in the first two sentences. Discuss how these words show opinions, not details from the story.

Think Aloud: The last sentence starts with "The most interesting part…" This is a judgment and does not belong in a summary.

- Have students cross out the judgment in the last sentence and restate it more objectively. Then tell them to read the summary with the words crossed out to themselves.

- Finally, allow partners time to add to and improve the summary as directed at the bottom of the page. (*Sample response: Captain Jane Young and the Ulysses crew travel six years through space to land on Spectra Omicron 8, where they plan to begin terraforming.*)

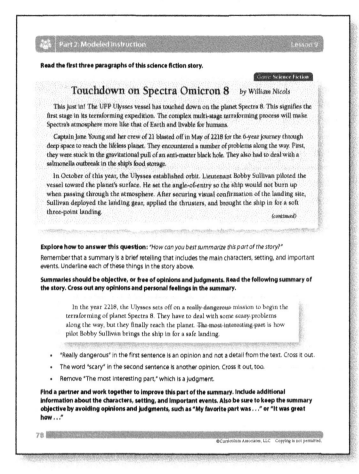

Tier Two Vocabulary: *Deployed*

- Have students find the word *deployed* in paragraph 3. Based on the context and what they know, ask students to tell what *deployed* means. (*"to move into position"*) Encourage students to use a dictionary to verify this meaning.

- Have students suggest other words that would make sense in place of *deployed*. (*positioned, set out, extended*) **(RL.8.4; L.8.4a, L.8.4d)**

AT A GLANCE

Students continue reading the science fiction story. They answer a multiple-choice question and then work with a partner to summarize the entire story.

STEP BY STEP

- Tell students they will continue reading the science fiction story.

- Remind them to use the features in the left margin. The Close Reading helps students focus on details about characters, setting, and events that will be important to the summary. The Hint will help them avoid words and phrases that are not objective.

- Tell students to read the rest of the story and mark details about characters, setting, and events, as directed by the Close Reading. Ask volunteers to share the words they marked. Discuss why these details, and not others in the text, are important when summarizing.

- Have students circle the answer to the question, using the Hint to help them avoid choices that are not objective. Then have them discuss the Show Your Thinking. Use the Answer Analysis below to support the discussion of correct and incorrect choices.

- Finally, have students work in pairs to summarize the entire story. Allow time for pairs to share and evaluate each other's summaries.

ANSWER ANALYSIS

Choice A is correct. It objectively summarizes the story and includes the main character, setting, and important events.

Choice B is incorrect. The word *strong* expresses a personal feeling about Captain Young that is not part of the text.

Choices C and D are incorrect. They are unimportant details, not important events in the story.

ERROR ALERT: Students who did not choose A may not have understood that the question asked for a summary. Remind them that a summary is objective and includes only the main characters, setting, and important events.

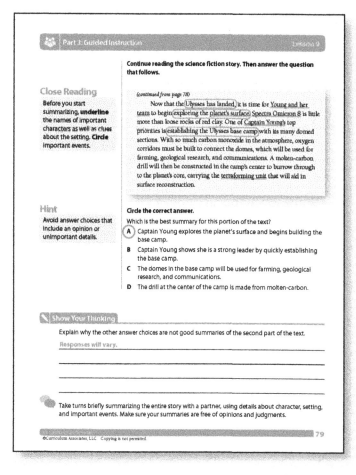

Continue reading the science fiction story. Then answer the question that follows.

Close Reading
Before you start summarizing, **underline** the names of important characters as well as clues about the setting. **Circle** important events.

(continued from page 78)

Now that the Ulysses has landed, it is time for Young and her team to begin exploring the planet's surface. Spectra Omicron 8 is little more than loose rocks of red clay. One of Captain Young's top priorities is establishing the Ulysses base camp with its many domed sections. With so much carbon monoxide in the atmosphere, oxygen corridors must be built to connect the domes, which will be used for farming, geological research, and communications. A molten-carbon drill will then be constructed in the camp's center to burrow through to the planet's core, carrying the terraforming unit that will aid in surface reconstruction.

Hint
Avoid answer choices that include an opinion or unimportant details.

Circle the correct answer.

Which is the best summary for this portion of the text?

A Captain Young explores the planet's surface and begins building the base camp.

B Captain Young shows she is a strong leader by quickly establishing the base camp.

C The domes in the base camp will be used for farming, geological research, and communications.

D The drill at the center of the camp is made from molten-carbon.

Show Your Thinking

Explain why the other answer choices are not good summaries of the second part of the text.

Responses will vary.

_____

_____

_____

Take turns briefly summarizing the entire story with a partner, using details about character, setting, and important events. Make sure your summaries are free of opinions and judgments.

©Curriculum Associates, LLC Copying is not permitted. 79

Tier Two Vocabulary: *Burrow*

- Direct students to the word *burrow* in the last sentence. Ask students to tell what *burrow* means in this sentence. (*"to make a hole or tunnel"*) Guide students to point out context clues that help them understand this meaning. (*"drill," "through to the planet's core"*)

- Point out that in this sentence *burrow* is a verb. Explain that as a noun *burrow* can mean "a hole or tunnel dug by a small animal, such as a rabbit or chipmunk, to make a home."

- Have students write two sentences using the word *burrow* as a verb in one sentence and as a noun in the other. (**RL.8.4; L.8.4a**)

AT A GLANCE

Students read a passage twice about a meeting with an alien. After the first reading, you will ask three questions to check your students' understanding.

STEP BY STEP

- Have students read the passage silently without referring to the Study Buddy or the Close Reading text.

- Ask the following questions to ensure students' comprehension of the text:

  Who is telling the story? (*the Imperator*)

  Why did the Imperator meet with Allya? (*so that Allya could tell the Imperator about where she traveled and her encounter with an alien race.*)

  What is the alien who returned with Allya? (*a cat*) What clues helped you to know? (*e.g., "purring sound," "Meow," "licking its paws"*)

- Then ask students to reread paragraphs 1–3 and look at the Study Buddy think aloud. What does the Study Buddy help them think about?

Tip: The Study Buddy reminds students to stop while reading to summarize key details. Remind students that stopping to summarize not only helps them describe the story to others but also is a way of helping them understand what they are reading.

- Have students read the rest of the passage. Tell them to follow the directions in the Close Reading.

Tip: The Close Reading helps students identify the main characters and important details in the story's plot. This is the information that they will want to include in a summary of the story.

- Finally, have students answer the questions on page 81. Use the Answer Analysis to discuss correct and incorrect responses.

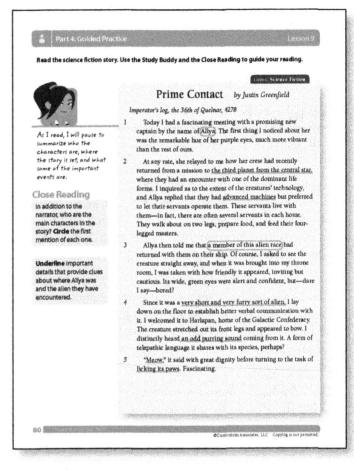

ELL Support: Irregular Past-Tense Verbs

- Explain that verbs are action words. The past tense of a verb tells that the action has already happened. The past tense of a regular verb ends in *-ed*. The past tense of an irregular verb does not.

- Have students find the word *brought* in paragraph 3. Explain that the present tense verb *bring* was changed to the past tense verb *brought*. Irregular verbs have special forms in the past tense, so their past tense form needs to be remembered.

- Have students locate other irregular past tense verbs in this passage and identify each present tense verb that was changed. (*said*: changed from *say*; *heard*: changed from *hear*) **(L.8.1)**

STEP BY STEP

- Have students read questions 1–3, using the Hints to help them answer the questions.

Tip: If students have trouble answering question 1, remind them that a summary should not include opinions or unimportant details. Have them identify the choice that is both important and objective.

- Discuss with students the Answer Analysis below.

ANSWER ANALYSIS

1 The correct answer is B. It tells an important event objectively. Choice A is incorrect. "It's very funny" suggests an opinion. Choice C is incorrect. It is a detail from the story but not an important event. Choice D is incorrect. It is an unimportant detail.

2 The correct answer is D. It is an objective statement that gives important information about the surprise end of the story. Choice A is incorrect because it does not tell about the ending of the story. Choices B and C are incorrect because they give opinions.

3 The correctly numbered list of events:

2   An alien creature boards Allya's ship.

4   Captain Allya tells how the servants care for their masters.

7   The Imperator lies down on the floor.

3   The Imperator meets with Captain Allya.

1   Allya and her crew visit another planet.

6   The Imperator notices the alien's confidence.

8   The alien makes a strange purring sound.

5   The Imperator asks to meet the alien.

RETEACHING

For question 3, students may have had difficulty distinguishing between the order of events as presented in the story and the order of events in which they actually happened in the world of the story. Draw a time line on the board to represent the chronological order of events, and ask volunteers to discuss when events happened.

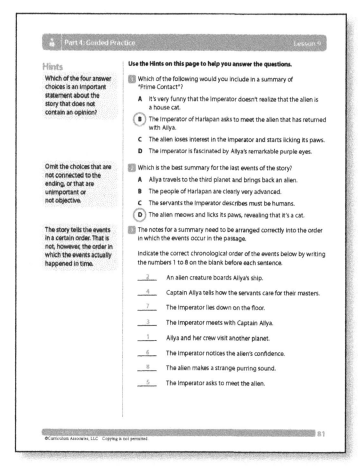

Integrating Standards

Use these questions to further students' understanding of "Prime Contact."

1 What assumption do both Allya and the Imperator make that affects future story events? **(RL.8.3)**

Both assume that the "member of the alien race" is the dominant life form on the third planet and is master over its "two legged servants." They base their assumptions on the limited observations of the mission crew and don't realize their mistake.

2 How does the author manipulate the reader's point of view to create the surprise ending? **(RL.8.6)**

The author gives clues to help readers infer that the alien creature is really a cat and deliberately uses the joke that cats are masters of the house, not their owners. The story characters, however, don't realize their mistake, so these different points of view produce a humorous ending.

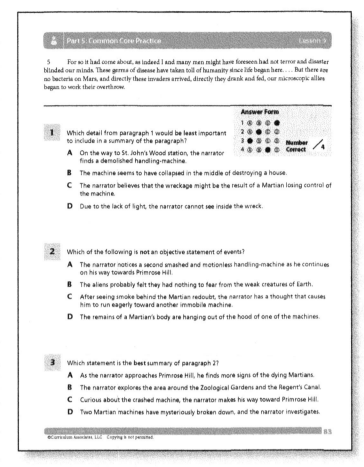

AT A GLANCE

Students independently read a longer science fiction story and answer questions in a format that provides test practice.

STEP BY STEP

- Tell students to use what they have learned about reading closely and summarizing literary text to read the science fiction story on pages 82 and 83.

- Remind students to underline or circle important details about the characters, setting, and events.

- Tell students to answer the questions on pages 83 and 84. For questions 1–4, they should fill in the correct circle on the Answer Form.

- When students have finished, use the Answer Analysis to discuss correct responses and the reasons for them. Have students fill in the Number Correct on the Answer Form.

ANSWER ANALYSIS

1   Choice D is correct. The question asks which detail is least important, and it's not important that the narrator can't see inside the wreck. The information provided in the other sentences is more important: information about finding the wreck, where it was found, and what might have caused it. **(DOK 2)**

2   Choice B is correct. It is not an objective statement because "weak creatures" reflect an opinion or personal feelings. Choices A, C, and D are incorrect. Each choice is an objective statement of events in the story. None of the statements contain opinions or personal feelings. **(DOK 2)**

Theme Connection

- How do all the stories in this lesson relate to the theme of views of other worlds?

- Which of the science fiction stories in the lesson did you enjoy most? What did you like best about it?

ANSWER ANALYSIS

3 Choice A is correct. The narrator is heading toward the hill when he sees another "motionless" Martian vehicle. Choice B omits important details about what the narrator sees. Choice C simply restates the first sentence of the paragraph. Choice D is not objective because it contains the word *mysteriously*. **(DOK 2)**

4 Choice C is correct. It gives details about the characters and the events including an explanation of why they happened. Choice A is incorrect. Where the narrator has to stand is not as important as details about the devastation he saw and what caused it. Choice B is incorrect. It is an unimportant detail about the setting. Choice D is incorrect. It gives an opinion and is not objective. **(DOK 2)**

5 Sample response: The narrator sees two ruined handling-machines and thinks they might have malfunctioned. Then the narrator sees smoke behind a Martian redoubt, but this time he sees remains of the dead Martian inside. From the peak of the redoubt, the narrator views overturned machines and dead Martians scattered all about. The Martians have been defeated because they have no natural defenses against Earth's bacteria. **(DOK 2)**

Part 5: Common Core Practice Lesson 9

4 Which statement relating to paragraphs 4 and 5 would be **most** important to include in a summary of the end of the story?

A The narrator has to stand on the crest of the Martian fortification in order to see the scene in its interior.

B On the other side of the redoubt is a huge space with odd areas of shelter.

C The Martians are conquered by simple disease bacteria to which their bodies are not immune.

D The people of Earth should have recognized the importance of bacteria in defeating the Martians.

5 Write a brief and objective summary of this story. Remember to include the most important events, as well as at least **three** key details about characters and setting.

See sample response.

_____

✔ **Self Check** Go back and see what you can check off on the Self Check on page 52.

84

©Curriculum Associates, LLC   Copying is not permitted.

Integrating Standards

Use these questions and tasks as opportunities to interact with the excerpt from *The War of the Worlds*.

1 What words does the author use in paragraph 1 that tell you the narrator thinks the wreckage is the result of a Martian losing control of his machine? **(RL.8.1)**

"It seemed to me then that this might have happened by a handling-machine escaping from the guidance of its Martian."

2 In paragraph 1, what does the narrator mean by saying that he sees a "mechanical Samson" lying among the ruins? **(RL.8.4)**

The narrator is comparing one of the Martian's destructive machines to Samson, a Biblical hero. Samson was a strong man who killed many enemies and caused a lot of destruction.

3 Based on the text, what can you infer about the narrator's traits? **(RL.8.1, RL.8.3)**

Sample response: The narrator is brave, fearless, and curious. In the midst of all the ruins and devastation, he's not afraid to keep investigating.

4 In paragraph 4, what does the author mean when he says, "slain, all after man's devices had failed, by the humblest things . . . upon this earth"? **(RL.8.4; L.8.5a)**

The author is suggesting that sometimes the smallest, meekest thing (bacteria) can bring down the biggest thing (the "monster" that was the Martians and their powerful machines).

5 Discuss in small groups: How is this story similar to "Prime Contact"? How is it different? **(RL.8.5; SL.8.1)**

Discussions will vary. Students should recognize similarities in point of view (narrators) and characters (aliens and Martians), and differences in setting (outer space, Earth) and in tone (one humorous, one serious). Both stories have a surprise ending, although of a very different nature.

Writing Activities

Rewrite a Story as a Play *(W.8.3)*

- Challenge students to think about how they could rewrite "Touchdown on Spectra Omicron 8" or "Prime Contact" as a play instead of a story. Will they use a narrator? How will they adapt the narrative into lines for each character? What stage directions will they write?

- Have students write one of the two stories as a play.

- Allow time for students to share their plays with the class. If possible, have students perform one of the plays as a Reader's Theater.

Consult Reference Materials *(L.8.4c)*

- Direct students to the word *terraforming* in paragraph 1 of "Touchdown on Spectra Omicron 8."

- Tell students they can use a print or online dictionary to clarify the precise meaning of a word. Have students find the definition of *terraforming* and tell its meaning. (*"to transform a planet to resemble Earth, especially to support human life"*)

- Ask students to look up other unfamiliar words from this lesson's passages to determine their meanings.

LISTENING ACTIVITY *(SL.8.4)*

Listen Closely/Conduct a News Interview

- Have student pairs use the details in this scene from *The War of the Worlds* to create a news interview announcing the discovery of the dead Martians.

- One student is the interviewer from a news station while the other student is an eyewitness.

- Students must listen carefully to each other as they ask and answer questions. Encourage them to be creative, while still basing their discussion on the story.

DISCUSSION ACTIVITY *(SL.8.1)*

Talk in a Group/Discuss Science Fiction

- Help students recall the characteristics of science fiction. Ask them to discuss in small groups how the stories in this lesson conform to the genre.

- Using these stories, as well as other examples of science fiction they have read, have groups discuss what makes a good science fiction story.

- Appoint one member of each group to take notes. Allow 10 to 15 minutes for discussion. Then have each group share its discussion with the class.

MEDIA ACTIVITY *(RL.8.3; W.8.4)*

Be Creative/Create a Poster

- Select one story in this lesson and discuss some of the images the author creates in the reader's mind.

- Tell students to imagine one of the stories is going to be made into a TV show and their job is to design a poster to advertise it. Invite students to create a visual to appear on the poster.

- Have small groups discuss how their visuals represent images created in the story.

RESEARCH ACTIVITY *(W.8.7, W.8.8; SL.8.4)*

Research and Present/Give a Presentation

- Point out that H. G. Wells, the author of *The War of the Worlds*, is credited with being one of the fathers of science fiction.

- Have students research information to use in an oral presentation about this author or another influential author of science fiction, such as Jules Verne, Isaac Asimov, or Ray Bradbury. Students may wish to read a novel written by the author and include information about it as well.

- Students should take notes and write a brief report for their presentations.

SCORING GUIDE AND ANSWER ANALYSIS

Literary Passage Answer Analysis

1 ● Ⓑ Ⓒ Ⓓ   4 Ⓐ Ⓑ Ⓒ ●
2 ● Ⓑ Ⓒ Ⓓ   5 Ⓐ ● Ⓒ Ⓓ
3 Ⓐ ● Ⓒ Ⓓ

1 Choice A is correct. If children are afraid to ride Olly, the horse is not useful to Pops in his business of giving riding lessons.

Choice B is incorrect. It supports the idea that Ted can't afford Olly, but it does not support why Olly is not useful to Pops. Choice C is incorrect. The detail that the horse is a full-time proposition shows how difficult it is to board a horse, but it does not indicate why the horse is not useful to Pops. Choice D is also incorrect. Ted's outburst that Olly might not belong to him much longer shows what might happen to Olly because he isn't useful to Pops, but it does not support the idea of why Olly is not useful to Pops. **(RL.8.1; DOK 2)**

2 Choice A is correct. Mom demonstrates her wisdom as a judge by accurately summarizing both sides of the argument between her husband and her son.

Choice B is incorrect. While it is probably appropriate that Mom interrupts the argument after some time, she most clearly shows that she is a wise judge by summarizing the argument between Pops and Ted. Choice C is incorrect. When Mom shakes her head, she is most likely feeling that the debate has continued for too long. Choice D is also incorrect. Mom makes a good suggestion, but her wisdom is best shown in the way she summarizes both sides of the argument. **(RL.8.3; DOK 2)**

3 Choice B is correct. Olly's behavior supports the idea that the boy and horse belong together.

Choice A is incorrect. The fact that Olly isn't suitable for children to ride doesn't support the idea that he belongs with Ted. The best evidence is that Olly behaves with Ted as though this boy were his favorite person. Choice C is incorrect. Ted's canter on Olly suggests he gets pleasure from riding the horse but does not prove that Olly truly belongs with Ted. Choice D is also incorrect. Mrs. Saunders' approval of Olly is not the best evidence that Olly belongs with Ted. **(RL.8.1; DOK 2)**

4 Choice D is correct. Mrs. Saunders listens to Ted's story about how hard he is trying to find a way to keep the horse. She notes that he is an early riser and seems able. This shows that she is motivated by her belief that Ted will work hard.

Choice A is incorrect. Mrs. Saunders judges Olly to be a fine horse, but her decision to offer Ted a job is most likely motivated by her belief that Ted will work hard to keep his horse. Choice B is incorrect. Since Mrs. Saunders knows Ted's family, she would be aware that Pops is a practical man who would not keep a horse he could not use; however, her most likely motivation is her belief that Ted will work hard to keep Olly. Choice C is also incorrect. Mrs. Saunders may have fond memories of Ted as a small child, but this is not the most likely reason she offers him a job. She has recent evidence that he will work hard; that is her most likely motivation. **(RL.8.3; DOK 2)**

5 **Part A:** Choice B is correct. When Ted hears Pops wants to get rid of Olly, he decides to find a way to keep him. Finding work is a challenge for Ted, but his willingness to take any work that comes his way eventually leads to success.

Choice A is incorrect. Ted is respecting his father's wishes in finding a way to help pay for Olly's food. Choice C has some truth in the context of the story, but it doesn't get at the most important message of the story. Choice D is almost the opposite of how Ted thinks, which is: If you really want something, you find a way to get it. **(RL.8.2; DOK 3)**

Part B: Choices 3, 4, and 7 best support the correct answer to Part A. Choice 3 describes how Ted visited "every local store" in search of work that would help him support Olly. Choice 4 tells how he looks for work among his neighbors. Choice 7 shows Ted's willingness to perform any job.

Choice 1 is Ted's dad explaining the problem he sees with keeping Olly. Choice 2 is Ted's mom giving him some advice. Both choices lead to Ted's efforts, but they do not directly support the theme. Choice 6 is simply a description from the meeting between Mrs. Saunders and Ted, which relates to the events of the story, but not the theme. **(RL.8.2; DOK 3)**

SAMPLE RESPONSES

Short Response

6 Mrs. Saunders asks about how the stable is doing, which shows that she is interested in the business aspect of things. She sees that Olly is important to Ted and realizes that she can make a business deal with Ted. She is in need of help around the orchard and Ted needs a way to earn money. She suggests a deal that will help Ted keep his horse while providing her with the help she needs in the orchard. **(RL.8.1; DOK 3)**

7 The correctly numbered list of events:

5   Ted tells Mrs. Saunders about his efforts to keep Olly.

3   Ted visits local stores looking for work.

1   Pops tells Ted he wants to get rid of Olly.

6   Mrs. Saunders offers Ted a job at the apple orchard.

2   The family debates the issue of keeping Olly.

4   Ted rides Olly by the orchard early on a Saturday morning. **(RL.8.2; DOK 2)**

8 Ted argues with his father about keeping the horse although Pops has already stated that the horse has to go. Ted tries to find work to earn enough money to pay for his horse's needs. He spends weeks searching for work without finding anything. But he shows his determination when he says that he won't give up. Finally, he agrees to give up his early mornings to work for Mrs. Saunders in order to take care of Olly. These events show that Ted is very determined. **(RL.8.1, RL.8.3; DOK 3)**

Performance Task

9 There are a number of events and details in the story that reveal Ted's character and how he solves his problem. In the beginning of the story, the author shows the affection between Ted and Olly as Ted pats the horse and Olly nuzzles him. Ted proves his enthusiasm and his loyalty to Olly by declaring that he is a "good horse," although Pops argues that Olly is just trouble for the stable. Because Pop has the power to make the decision about Ted's horse, Ted is upset.

After Mom suggests that Ted ask around for paying work, Ted tries to do this but no one is hiring. He spends several weeks searching and does not give up. This shows how persistent he is and that he really is trying to take responsibility for Olly's care.

Ted's real pleasure is riding Olly. He gets up extra early to get in a ride across the fields, even though he works at the stable on Saturdays and isn't going to get much rest. This shows how precious his time with Olly is—Ted is willing to give up some sleep to be with his favorite horse.

It is easy to put yourself in Ted's place when he pours out his troubles to Mrs. Saunders. He probably would not have confided in someone he did not know very well unless he was feeling desperate. The fact that he immediately agrees to get up very early in the morning three times a week to work in the orchard proves how much he cares about Olly. With hard work and determination, Ted resolves his problem. **(RL.8.3; DOK 3)**

SCORING RUBRICS

Short-Response Rubric

2 points   The response is accurate, complete, and fulfills all requirements of the task. Text-based support and examples are included. Any information that goes beyond the text is relevant to the task.

1 point   The response is partially accurate and fulfills some requirements of the task. Some information may be inaccurate, too general, or confused. Support and examples may be insufficient or not text-based.

0 points   The response is inaccurate, poorly organized, or does not respond to the task.

Performance Task Rubric

4 points   The response
- Fulfills all requirements of the task
- Uses varied sentence types and some sophisticated vocabulary
- Includes relevant and accurate details from the texts as well as text-based inferences
- Demonstrates a thorough understanding of the texts
- Maintains a clear focus and organization
- Is fluent and demonstrates a clear voice
- Uses correct spelling, grammar, capitalization, and punctuation

3 points   The response
- Fulfills all requirements of the task
- Uses simple sentences and grade-level vocabulary
- Includes relevant and accurate details from the texts
- Demonstrates a mainly literal understanding of the texts
- Maintains a mostly clear focus and organization
- Is fluent and demonstrates some sense of voice
- Uses mostly correct spelling, grammar, capitalization, and punctuation

2 points   The response
- Fulfills some requirements of the task
- Uses simple sentences, some fragments, and grade-level vocabulary
- Includes some relevant and accurate details from the texts
- Demonstrates some misunderstandings or gaps in understanding of the texts
- Attempts to maintain a clear focus and organization
- Is difficult to read, includes some inaccuracies, and demonstrates little or no sense of voice
- Contains some inaccurate spelling, grammar, capitalization, and punctuation that may hinder understanding

1 point   The response
- Fulfills few requirements of the task
- Uses sentence fragments and below-grade-level vocabulary
- Includes no details or irrelevant details to support the response
- Demonstrates very little understanding of the texts
- Does not establish a clear focus or organization
- Is difficult to read, contains many inaccuracies, and demonstrates no sense of voice
- Uses incorrect spelling, grammar, capitalization, and punctuation to an extent that impedes understanding

0 points   The response is irrelevant, poorly organized, or illegible.

Analyzing Word Meanings

LESSON OBJECTIVES

- Determine the figurative, connotative, and technical meanings of words and phrases as they are used in an informational text.

THE LEARNING PROGRESSION

- **Grade 7:** CCSS RI.7.4 requires students to determine the meanings of words and phrases in a text, including figurative, connotative, and technical meanings.

- **Grade 8: CCSS RI.8.4 builds on the Grade 7 standard by requiring students to use analytical skills to determine word meanings, including the meanings of figurative, connotative, and technical language.**

- **Grade 9:** CCSS RI.9.4 emphasizes determining the meaning of words and phrases in a text, including figurative, connotative, and technical meanings.

PREREQUISITE SKILLS

- Identify unfamiliar words.
- Use context to determine meaning.
- Analyze examples of figurative language.
- Analyze words that have technical meanings.
- Understand that words have connotative as well as denotative meanings.
- Recognize that authors choose words carefully and for a certain purpose and effect.

TAP STUDENTS' PRIOR KNOWLEDGE

- Tell students that they will be working on a lesson about word meanings, which includes figurative meanings, connotations, and technical meanings.

- Ask students why authors use figurative language such as metaphors, similes, and personification. (*to create interesting or unusual effects that help the reader create mental images*)

- Tell students that connotations help to clarify the feelings associated with a word in a positive, negative, or neutral way. An example is "that crowd is rowdy" versus "that crowd is excited." Which has the more negative connotation? (*rowdy*)

- Explain to students that technical words are commonly seen in texts that cover specific subjects or topics. Understanding technical words is essential when reading science texts or other works that use a specialized vocabulary.

- Point out to students that analyzing the meanings of words in a text will help them to better comprehend and think critically about what they read.

▦ Ready *Teacher Toolbox*   teacher-toolbox.com

	Prerequisite Skills	RI.8.4
Ready Lessons	✓	✓
Tools for Instruction	✓ ✓	✓ ✓
Interactive Tutorials	✓	✓

CCSS Focus

RI.8.4 Determine the meaning of words and phrases as they are used in a text, including figurative, connotative, and technical meanings...

ADDITIONAL STANDARDS: **RI.8.1, RI.8.2, RI.8.3, RI.8.5, RI.8.6, RI.8.7, RI.8.8; L.8.4a, L.8.4d, L.8.5a; W.8.1, W.8.6, W.8.7; SL.8.1, SL.8.5** (*See page A39 for full text.*)

AT A GLANCE

By reading a short magazine article, students explore figurative language, strong connotations, and technical words. They learn how authors make choices about words and that these words convey specific meanings.

STEP BY STEP

- Read aloud the paragraph and the definitions of *figurative meaning, connotations,* and *technical meanings.*

- Direct students to the magazine article and ask them to circle an example of figurative language, underline words with strong connotations, and put a box around any technical words.

- Ask students to share the words they marked and explain how these words impacted their reading of the text.

- Explain that the chart shows the three types of language, an example of each, and its effect on meaning. Read aloud the Example column and have students compare these examples to the text they marked in the article. Then read the last column of the chart. Discuss with students the effect of each example on the meaning of the text.

- Ask students to give examples of times when they, as writers, have chosen specific figurative language, words with connotations, or technical terms to convey meaning and feeling in their writing.

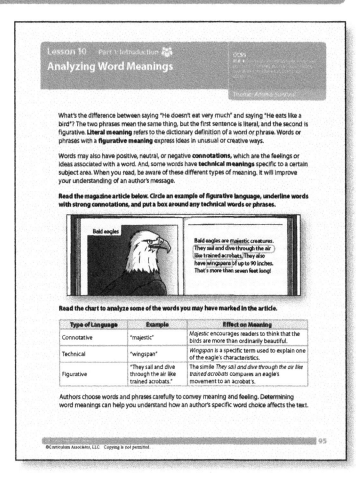

Genre Focus

Informational Texts: Article

Tell students that in this lesson they will read informational texts. One type of informational text is an article, which is a piece of nonfiction writing that provides details about a topic.

The purpose of an article is to inform or to explain. Articles are often written for magazines, newspapers, or online publications.

The opening of an article usually engages the reader's attention, and the body of the article gives facts, examples, reasons, and descriptions. The article answers the questions *who, what, when, where, why,* and *how.*

Articles, such as the one shown on this page about bald eagles, often include photographs and captions to help readers understand the information.

Ask students what other types of articles they have read. Mention that most areas of interest have magazines or publications devoted strictly to that topic. For example, some popular magazines feature fashion, music, cars, boats, fishing, and the news.

Ask students to name any magazines, newspapers, or web sites they read to find out about subjects that interest them. Tell students that in this lesson they will read informational texts on mollusks, armadillos, and animal regeneration.

AT A GLANCE

Students read a scientific account about mollusks and determine how the author's word choices helped them understand the author's intended meaning.

STEP BY STEP

- Invite volunteers to tell what they learned on the previous page about figurative, connotative, and technical language.

- Tell students that in this lesson they will identify these types of language in a scientific account about mollusks.

- Read aloud "The Mollusk Family."

- Then read the question: "How do the word choices in the scientific account help you understand the author's intended meaning?"

- Tell students you will use a Think Aloud to demonstrate a way to answer the question.

Think Aloud: I will read the account and look for examples of figurative language, words with strong connotations, and technical words. In the second paragraph, the author compares the function of the mantle to "a suit of armor." This phrase is figurative language. It helps me understand that the mantle is tough and durable, like a knight's suit of armor.

- Direct students to complete the first row of the chart. Remind them that the chart helps them analyze the effects of language on the meaning of the text.

Think Aloud: Now I will look for words that have a strong connotation. I'll ask myself which words the author uses that have a strong positive, neutral, or negative feeling. One example is the word *amazing* in the first paragraph. It tells readers how the author feels about mollusks. He thinks they are amazing, which has a very positive connotation.

- Have students complete the second row of the chart.

Think Aloud: This account is about mollusks, so I'll look for technical terms related to this topic. The word *octopods* is an example. It is the plural form of *octopus*, and it is an example of an animal that is a mollusk.

- Have students complete the third row of the chart.

- Then have students discuss their completed charts with a partner as directed at the bottom of the page.

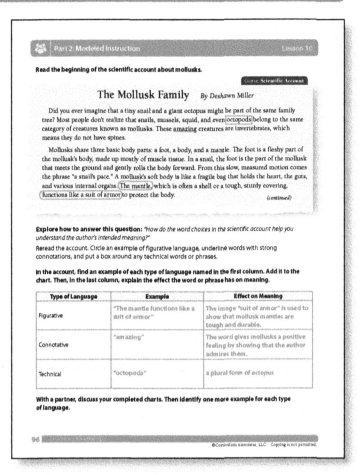

ELL Support: Idioms

- Direct students to the phrase *a snail's pace* in paragraph 2. Point out that the author identifies the origin of the phrase *a snail's pace* as the "slow, measured motion" of the mollusk. Explain that *A snail's pace* is an example of an idiom. An idiom is a phrase that is made up of words that mean something different when they are used together in a phrase than what the words mean individually.

- Work with students to understand that *a snail's pace* is often used to describe things that move at a very slow rate. Have students use this idiom in a sentence. (*The bus is moving at a snail's pace.*)

- Some other common idioms are *miss the boat, see eye to eye,* and *costs an arm and a leg.* (**RI.8.4; L.8.5a**)

AT A GLANCE

Students continue reading about mollusks. They answer a multiple-choice question and analyze how different types of language are used in the account.

STEP BY STEP

- Tell students they will continue reading about the mollusk family.

- The Close Reading helps students to select two phrases that assist in the comprehension of the technical term *defense mechanisms*. The Hint will help them consider the connotations, or feelings, that the words in the question suggest.

- Have students read the passage and circle the two phrases that help them understand *defense mechanism*, as directed by Close Reading.

- Ask volunteers to share the phrases they circled.

- Have students circle the answer to the question, using the Hint to help. Then have them respond to the question in Show Your Thinking. Remind students that words may have a positive, neutral, or negative connotation.

ANSWER ANALYSIS

Choice A is incorrect. The author is writing to inform readers, not to warn them.

Choice B is correct. The author uses these words to heighten the understanding of different types of mollusks and their defense mechanisms.

Choice C is incorrect. The author is not explaining a mystery.

Choice D is incorrect. The author is not focusing only on unusual shells grown by the mollusk family. Other defense mechanisms are utilized.

> **ERROR ALERT:** Students who did not choose B may not have read the question carefully. Point out that the question asks for the statement that best explains why the author chose certain language. How do the mollusks compare? How does the author use language to make it clear that different mollusks have different defense mechanisms?

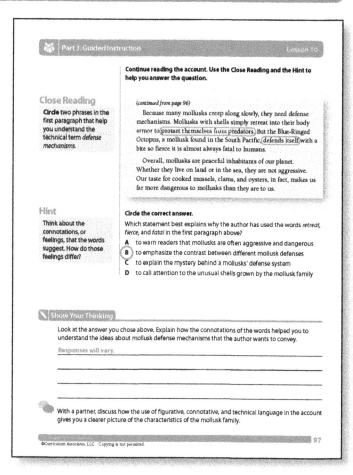

Tier Two
Vocabulary: *Inhabitants*

- Direct students to the word *inhabitants* in paragraph 2. Ask students where mollusks live according to this sentence. (*"our planet"*) Then ask students to identify other context clues that help them figure out the meaning of *inhabitants*. (*"live on land or in the sea"*) Now ask students what *inhabitants* means. (*"those who live permanently in a place"*)

- Ask students what other words would make sense in place of *inhabitants*. (residents, dwellers) **(RI.8.4; L.8.4a)**

AT A GLANCE

Students read a passage about armadillos twice. After the first reading, you will ask three questions to check your students' understanding of the passage.

STEP BY STEP

- Have students read the passage silently without referring to the Study Buddy or Close Reading text.

- Ask the following questions to ensure students' comprehension of the text:

  What is the origin of the word *armadillo*? (*It comes from a Spanish word meaning "little armored one."*)

  Name some of the animals that armadillos are related to. (*sloths, anteaters, dinosaurs, glyptodonts*)

  How do armadillos find food? (*They use their sense of smell.*)

- Then ask students to reread paragraph 1 and look at the Study Buddy think aloud. What does the Study Buddy help them think about?

Tip: As students read and identify connotative, figurative, and technical language, explain to them that examples of these language types often stand out from other words. They are the words that make writing engaging and more interesting to read.

- Have students read the rest of the passage. Tell them to follow the directions in the Close Reading.

Tip: Remind students to take special notice of descriptive words and words that seem more specific or particular to the subject. As instructed in the Close Reading, students should underline examples of figurative language and circle words that are used to describe armadillos.

- Finally, have students answer the questions on page 99. Use the Answer Analysis to discuss correct and incorrect responses.

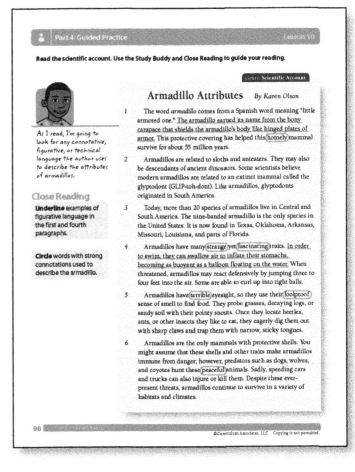

Part 4: Guided Practice
Lesson 10

Read the scientific account. Use the Study Buddy and Close Reading to guide your reading.

Genre: Scientific Account

Armadillo Attributes   *By Karen Olson*

As I read, I'm going to look for any connotative, figurative, or technical language the author uses to describe the attributes of armadillos.

Close Reading

Underline examples of figurative language in the first and fourth paragraphs.

Circle words with strong connotations used to describe the armadillo.

1   The word *armadillo* comes from a Spanish word meaning "little armored one." The armadillo earned its name from the bony carapace that shields the armadillo's body like hinged plates of armor. This protective covering has helped this homely mammal survive for about 55 million years.

2   Armadillos are related to sloths and anteaters. They may also be descendants of ancient dinosaurs. Some scientists believe modern armadillos are related to an extinct mammal called the glyptodont (GLIP-toh-dont). Like armadillos, glyptodonts originated in South America.

3   Today, more than 20 species of armadillos live in Central and South America. The nine-banded armadillo is the only species in the United States. It is now found in Texas, Oklahoma, Arkansas, Missouri, Louisiana, and parts of Florida.

4   Armadillos have many strange yet fascinating traits. In order to swim, they can swallow air to inflate their stomachs, becoming as buoyant as a balloon floating on the water. When threatened, armadillos may react defensively by jumping three to four feet into the air. Some are able to curl up into tight balls.

5   Armadillos have terrible eyesight, so they use their foolproof sense of smell to find food. They probe grasses, decaying logs, or sandy soil with their pointy snouts. Once they locate beetles, ants, or other insects they like to eat, they eagerly dig them out with sharp claws and trap them with narrow, sticky tongues.

6   Armadillos are the only mammals with protective shells. You might assume that these shells and other traits make armadillos immune from danger; however, predators such as dogs, wolves, and coyotes hunt these peaceful animals. Sadly, speeding cars and trucks can also injure or kill them. Despite these ever-present threats, armadillos continue to survive in a variety of habitats and climates.

98

©Curriculum Associates, LLC   Copying is not permitted.

Tier Two Vocabulary: *Descendants*

- Have students find the word *descendants* in paragraph 2. Given the context and what they know, ask students what *descendants* means. (*"persons, plants, or animals that come from a particular ancestor"*) Encourage students to use a dictionary or thesaurus to help them verify this meaning. **(RI.8.4; L.8.4a, L.8.4d)**

- Ask what other words would make sense in place of *descendants*. (relatives, kin)

STEP BY STEP

- Have students read questions 1–3, using the Hints to help them answer the questions.

Tip: The descriptive words in paragraph 5 help portray the armadillo's appearance. Paying close attention to descriptive language helps the reader to formulate a clear perspective of the subject.

- Discuss with students the Answer Analysis below.

ANSWER ANALYSIS

1   Choice B is correct. Traits rendering armadillos "immune from danger" make them unaffected by threats. Choice A is incorrect. Being immune from something may involve a defense against it, but that's not the same as being "defensive." Choice C, "threatened," plays off "danger," but it's not a meaning of "immune." Choice D, "unaware," hints the armadillo's shell might make it unaware of danger, but that's not the same as "immune."

2   Choice C is correct. The fact that armadillos can be injured or killed by something gives a clue to the meaning of "immune." If armadillos were truly immune to danger, they would be unaffected by threats in their environment. Choice A plays off the notion of immunity as a defense, but that's not the same as reacting defensively. Choices B and D are incorrect. Both phrases support the description of armadillos, but neither helps define "immune."

3   Sample response: The word choices reveal that the author wants readers to admire the armadillo and see it as an unusual and complex creature. *Homely, strange,* and *terrible* show that the author finds even the negative traits of the armadillo interesting. *Foolproof, fascinating,* and *peaceful* have positive connotations that reveal the armadillo's qualities.

RETEACHING

Use a chart to verify the correct answer to question 3. Draw the chart below, and work with students to fill in the boxes. Sample responses are provided.

Words	Connotation
homely, strange, terrible	negative
foolproof, fascinating, peaceful	positive

Part 4: Guided Practice — Lesson 10

Hints

Find this word in paragraph 6.

Use the Hints on this page to help you answer the questions.

1   What does the word "immune" mean as it is used in the passage?

A   defensive

B   unaffected

C   threatened

D   unaware

Look for context clues in paragraph 6 that might help you understand the meaning of "immune."

2   Which of the phrases from the passage best helps the reader understand the meaning of "immune"?

A   "may react defensively"

B   "these peaceful animals"

C   "can also injure or kill them"

D   "in a variety of habitats and climates"

Look back at the descriptive words you circled. Which words have a positive connotation? Which words have a negative connotation?

3   Explain why the author uses words like *homely, strange, fascinating, terrible, foolproof,* and *peaceful* to describe armadillos. Write a paragraph about what these word choices reveal about how the author would like readers to feel about armadillos. Use at least three specific details from the text in your response.

See sample response.

_____

99

Integrating Standards

Use these questions to further students' understanding of "Armadillo Attributes."

1   Why do you think the author begins the article with an explanation of the word *armadillo*? **(RI.8.5)**

This explanation is a good introduction and lets the reader know that the armadillo is an interesting animal that has been around for a long time.

2   What is the central idea of this article? How is this idea developed through supporting details? **(RI.8.2)**

The central idea is that armadillos have many characteristics that make them unique and able to survive in their habitats. Supporting details include information about the armadillo's sense of sight and smell, as well as facts about where armadillos live.

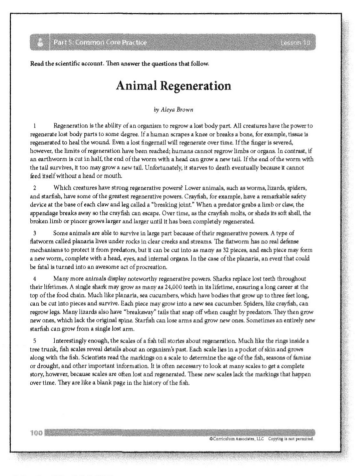

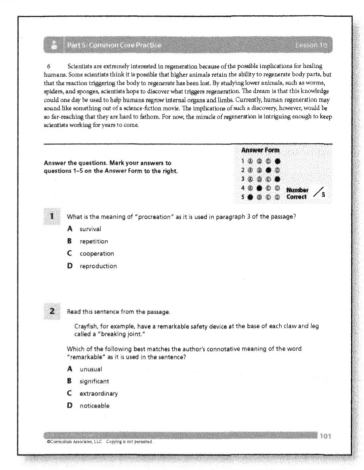

AT A GLANCE

Students independently read a longer scientific account and answer questions in a format that provides test practice.

STEP BY STEP

- Tell students to use what they have learned about reading closely and analyzing word meanings to read the scientific account on pages 100 and 101.

- Remind students to underline or circle important word choices.

- Tell students to answer the questions on pages 101 and 102. For questions 1–5, they should fill in the correct circle on the Answer Form.

- When students have finished, use the Answer Analysis to discuss correct responses and the reasons for them. Have students fill in the Number Correct on the Answer Form.

ANSWER ANALYSIS

1 Choice D is correct. "Procreation" refers to the flatworm's ability to reproduce itself. Choice A is incorrect. The worm's ability is related to its survival, but the word does not mean "procreation." Choice B, "repetition," may touch on the flatworm's ability to multiply itself, but it's incorrect. Choice C is also incorrect. The flatworm's "awesome act" doesn't require the cooperation of another flatworm. **(DOK 2)**

2 Choice C is correct. The author shows amazement at the crayfish's ability to grow back body parts. When he refers to the crayfish's "breaking joint," it is with a sense of wonder. Choices A, B, and D are incorrect. All might mean "remarkable," but they have a far more neutral tone than "extraordinary." **(DOK 2)**

Theme Connection

- How do all the passages in this lesson relate to the theme of animal survival?

- What is one fact or idea you learned about animal survival from each passage in this lesson?

ANSWER ANALYSIS

3 Choice D is correct. The author uses the word *powers* to describe different animal abilities. Choices A, B, and C are incorrect. *Powers* may mean "influence," "authority," or "forcefulness" in other contexts, but none of these definitions matches the author's intended meaning. **(DOK 2)**

4 Choice B is correct. An appendage is a body part attached to the larger, main body of a creature. A limb or claw is an example of an appendage on a crayfish. Choices A, C, and D all come from descriptions of a crayfish, but none of the phrases, contribute to an understanding of *appendage*. **(DOK 2)**

5 Choice A is correct. In the passage, "hope" best matches the meaning of "dream." The account establishes that one reason that scientists study regeneration in animals is they will be able to use what they learn to someday help humans regenerate body parts. Choices B, C, and D are all possible meanings of "dream," but none are correct in this context. Discoveries related to human regeneration may be far off, but it is not a "fantasy" (Choice B) or an "illusion" (Choice D). Nothing in the account suggests that current research constitutes anything as definite as a "plan" (Choice C). **(DOK 2)**

Part 5: Common Core Practice   Lesson 10

3 As used in paragraphs 2, 3, and 4 of the passage, the word *powers* is **closest** in meaning to

  A influence

  B authority

  C forcefulness

  D abilities

4 Which of the phrases from the passage best helps the reader understand the meaning of the word "appendage"?

  A "have a remarkable safety device"

  B "grabs a limb or claw"

  C "sheds its soft shell"

  D "grows larger and larger"

5 Read this sentence from the passage.

  The dream is that this knowledge could one day be used to help humans regrow internal organs and limbs.

  Which word best matches the meaning of "dream" as it is used in this sentence?

  A hope

  B fantasy

  C plan

  D illusion

✓ Self Check *Go back and see what you can check off on the Self Check on page 94.*

102   ©Curriculum Associates, LLC   Copying is not permitted.

Integrating Standards

Use these questions and tasks as opportunities to interact with "Animal Regeneration."

1 Name two animals with regenerative powers and explain why regeneration helps them to survive. **(RI.8.1)**

Sharks regenerate teeth. The growth of new teeth allows sharks to catch food for years and years. Earthworms can grow new tails if they are cut off. By growing new tails, they can continue to live.

2 Give an example of a "lower animal" and a "higher animal" and explain what you think the difference is. **(RI.8.3)**

Worms are lower animals. Humans are higher animals. Lower animals are more simple creatures in terms of physical makeup. Worms have less complex systems than humans and other higher animals have.

3 Why do some scientists believe that human regeneration may be possible? **(RI.8.8)**

They believe that the reaction that triggers

regeneration has been lost. By studying lower animals such as worms, scientists may be able to discover what triggers regeneration and make human regeneration possible.

4 Why do you think the author believes that regeneration will keep scientists studying for years to come? **(RI.8.6)**

The author seems to be very interested in the study of regeneration and understands that it is a complicated science, which seems to have a long way to go. Based on this point of view about regeneration, the author thinks that scientists will continue to study it.

5 Discuss is small groups: How would this article be different if the author had a different point of view about regeneration? What types of language might the author use instead? **(SL.8.1)**

Discussions will vary. Have students consider how the figurative language, words with connotations, and technical terms reveal the author's point of view.

Writing Activities

Write a Scientist's Speech (W.8.1)

- Have students write a speech from the point of view of a scientist who studies human regeneration.

- Students should use the examples of other animals that regenerate in a speech about the hopes and possibilities for human regeneration. Encourage them to cite specific evidence from "Animal Regeneration" in their writing.

- Allow time for students to present their speeches to the class.

It's All in the Context (L.8.4a)

- Have students reread the scientific account on page 97. Review that context clues are words in the surrounding text that help them understand the meaning of a term. Point out that context clues can be especially helpful in understanding the technical language an author uses. Have students identify context clues that help them understand what *defense mechanisms* are. Ask students to give a definition for *defense mechanisms*. ("*adaptations that help an animal protect itself*")

- Ask students to write their own sentence with context clues to clarify a technical word of their choice from one of this lesson's passages.

LISTENING ACTIVITY (SL.8.1)

Listen Closely/Ask and Answer Questions

- Have students review "Animal Regeneration." As they reread, have them write questions that can be answered using information from the account.

- Have students work in pairs. One student poses his or her questions while the other student cites evidence from the text to provide an answer.

- Students then switch roles and repeat the activity.

DISCUSSION ACTIVITY (SL.8.1)

Talk in a Group/Discuss Animal Survival

- Have students review what they learned about animal survival from each of this lesson's passages.

- Have students form small groups to discuss animal survival. To promote discussion, provide the following prompts: What are examples of animal survival? What language would you use to describe each example to show your point of view about it?

- Have groups present their examples of figurative, connotative, and technical language to the class.

MEDIA ACTIVITY (RI.8.7; W.8.6)

Be Creative/Caption Action

- Have students review the magazine article on page 95. Remind them that the text added important facts that could be not derived from the image alone.

- Invite students to create their own magazine articles. Students should select an image to accompany one of this lesson's other passages. They then use the passage to add a caption that provides additional information about the image.

- Students should use a word processing program or other software to help them create a two-page article that includes both the image and the text.

RESEARCH ACTIVITY (W.8.7; SL.8.5)

Research and Present/More on Mollusks

- Ask students to use the information in "The Mollusk Family" to research and present a slide show of information about different mollusks.

- Both the images and the verbal portion of the presentation should include the topics covered in the scientific account.

- Have students present their slide shows.

Analyzing Word Choice

LESSON OBJECTIVES

- Analyze the impact of specific word choices on meaning and tone.

- Analyze the impact of analogies or allusions to other texts on meaning and tone.

THE LEARNING PROGRESSION

- **Grade 7:** CCSS RI.7.4 requires students to analyze the impact of a specific word choice on meaning and tone.

- **Grade 8: CCSS RI.8.4 builds on the Grade 7 standard by requiring students to analyze the impact of word choices on meaning and tone. Students demonstrate greater sophistication and knowledge of craft by considering analogies and allusions to other texts.**

- **Grade 9:** CCSS RI.9.4 emphasizes analyzing the cumulative impact of specific word choices on meaning and tone.

PREREQUISITE SKILLS

- Identify unfamiliar words.

- Use context to determine meaning.

- Understand tone.

- Recognize the relationship between word choice and the overall meaning or tone of a text.

TAP STUDENTS' PRIOR KNOWLEDGE

- Tell students they will be working on a lesson about analyzing word choice.

- Remind students that they often analyze word choice in their own life, such as when considering the impact of their words on a particular audience.

- Explain that authors carefully choose words to express their ideas in the best way possible. One way authors express their ideas is through allusions. An allusion is a reference that one text makes to another work.

- Have students consider what they would think if a teacher or parent told them: "Don't act like the boy who cried wolf!" What does this allusion mean? Why is this word choice effective? (*It means the speaker doesn't want the person to whom he or she is talking to say something is wrong when it really isn't. It is an effective word choice because it is descriptive and refers to a story that is familiar to most people.*)

- Point out to students that analyzing an author's word choice will help them to better understand the author's intended meaning and tone.

Ready *Teacher Toolbox* teacher-toolbox.com

	Prerequisite Skills	RI.8.4
Ready Lessons	✓	✓
Tools for Instruction	✓ ✓	✓
Interactive Tutorials	✓	✓

CCSS Focus

RI.8.4 … analyze the impact of specific word choices on meaning and tone, including analogies or allusions to other texts.

ADDITIONAL STANDARDS: RI.8.1, RI.8.3, RI.8.6, RI.8.7; L.8.1b, L.8.4a, L.8.4b, L.8.4d; W.8.1, W.8.4, W.8.6, W.8.7; SL.8.1, SL.8.4, SL.8.6 (*See page A39 for full text.*)

AT A GLANCE

Students read a response to a history assignment. They learn to consider word choice and explore how authors use analogies and allusions to express their ideas.

STEP BY STEP

- Read aloud the first two paragraphs, including the definitions of *analogy* and *allusion*. Then encourage students to study the response to a history assignment and think about what the student's word choice tells them about the pioneers' journey. Ask them to underline the analogy and the allusion that the student includes.

- Explain that the chart shows how word choice affects the text's meaning. Read the word choices and have students compare them to the text they underlined. Then read the Impact on Meaning column of the chart and discuss how each type of language affects the reader's understanding of the pioneers' journey.

- Ask students to discuss other real-life situations when they have used an analogy or an allusion.

- Reinforce that authors use analogies and allusions to help readers connect with the meaning of the text. Provide an example by reading the second sentence of the text as "You set out in a wagon, traveling westward across the land." Ask students to share how the change in word choice affected the mental image that was created.

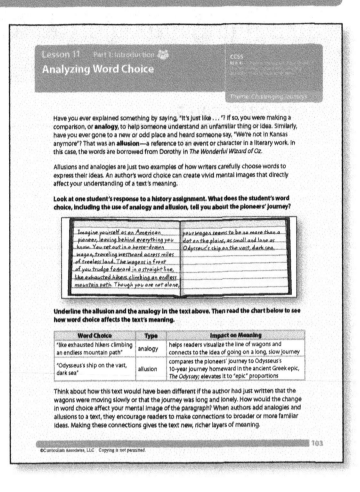

Genre Focus

Informational Texts: Biography

Tell students that in this lesson they will read informational texts. One type of information text is a biography, which tells the story of a person's life. Biographies usually address the following:

- when and where the person was born

- what special events happened during the lifetime of the person

- why the person is important

Based on these characteristics, ask students to name biographies they have read. Who have they read about, and what did they like about the biographies?

Students may be familiar with biographies of famous Americans including Martin Luther King, Jr., George Washington, and Cesar Chavez.

Explain that the article "Amelia Earhart: First in Flight" is a biography about a brave young woman who was known for her great accomplishments in air travel.

Tell students that the articles "The Trans-Pacific Passage Toward the Gold Fields" and "Dust Bowl Migrants" are historical accounts of challenging journeys that occurred in the past.

AT A GLANCE

Students read a biography about Amelia Earhart and think about the author's word choice in order to analyze meaning and tone.

STEP BY STEP

- Invite volunteers to tell what they learned on the previous page about analyzing an author's word choice and its effects on meaning and tone.

- Tell students that in this lesson they will learn how to think about an author's word choice in order to analyze the meaning and tone.

- Read "Amelia Earhart: First in Flight."

- Then read the question: "Select one word and one phrase from this biography. What is the impact of both the word and the phrase on the biography's meaning and tone?"

- Tell students you will use a Think Aloud to demonstrate a way to answer the question.

Think Aloud: In the first paragraph, I see that the word *excel* is used more than once. *Excel* means "to do exceptionally well," so I think this word helps me know that Earhart did exceptionally well. This word also has a positive tone, suggesting the author admires Earhart.

- Direct students to the chart and review that it helps them to analyze the impact of a word choice on the text's meaning and tone.

- Point out the information for *excel* in the chart.

Think Aloud: I also notice the word choice "as ardently as Olympic athletes pursue their goals." I wonder why the author chose to make this comparison. I think it means that Earhart is similar to Olympians, who are very successful people. *Ardently* means "enthusiastic or passionate," which adds to the text's positive tone.

- Have students complete the second row of the chart.

- Finally, have students work in pairs to discuss the prompt at the bottom of the page. Invite volunteers to share their answers. *(Sample response: Someone who is obsessed with something thinks about nothing else. The word has negative connotations because it implies an imbalance or a lack of good judgment. The tone of the text would have been negative or critical if the author had used that word.)*

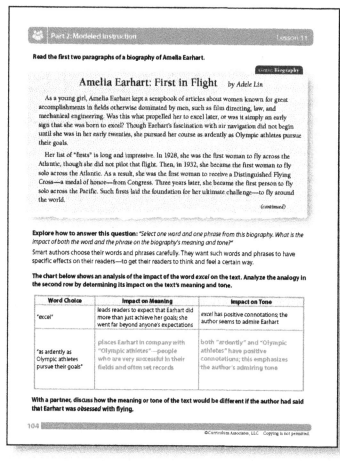

Tier Two Vocabulary: *Propelled*

- Direct students to the word *propelled* in paragraph 1. Based on the context, have students determine the meaning of *propelled* as it is used in this sentence. *("drove, moved forward")* Have students use a dictionary to check this meaning.

- Ask what other words would make sense in place of *propelled*. (pushed, drove)

- On the board, write the related words *propel* and *propelled*. Discuss with students some contexts in which these words might appear: *I had to use my feet to propel my bike up the hill. The jet ski was propelled by the waves from the boats on the lake.* **(RI.8.4; L.8.4a, L.8.4d)**

AT A GLANCE

Students continue reading about Amelia Earhart. They answer a multiple-choice question and explain how an allusion affects the text's tone.

STEP BY STEP

- Tell students they will continue reading about Amelia Earhart.

- The Close Reading helps students identify and remember an allusion that suggests the text's tone. The Hint will help them think about how word choice conveys the author's attitude.

- Have students read the article and underline an allusion and words or phrases that suggest tone, as directed by the Close Reading.

- Ask volunteers to share the allusion and the words or phrases they underlined. Discuss the author's word choice and how it relates to the tone. Also ask students to discuss the author's attitude toward Earhart, and how the comparison to Icarus complements it.

- Place students in pairs to discuss the question at the bottom of the page. (*Sample response: The use of negative language creates sympathy for Earhart's struggles. This is a continuation of the author's earlier tone.*)

ANSWER ANALYSIS

Choice A is incorrect. It does not reflect the author's tone in the text.

Choice B is incorrect. The allusion and the author's tone do not emphasize failure.

Choice C is incorrect. The allusion does not indicate a mystery.

Choice D is correct. The author's tone shows she admires Earhart, and the allusion compares Earhart to Icarus, who is a legendary figure.

> **ERROR ALERT:** Students who did not choose D might not understand how to analyze the author's tone. Point out that the article talks about many of the things listed in the other answer choices, but only choice D accurately reflects the author's tone.

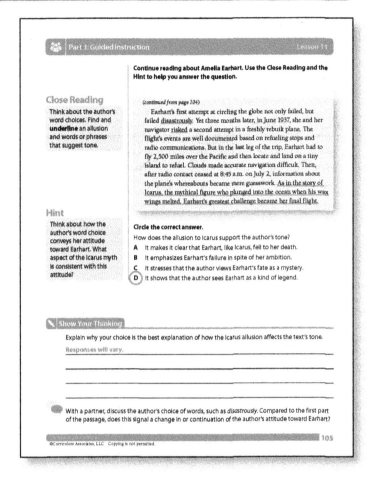

ELL Support: Suffixes

- Explain to students that many English words have suffixes. A suffix is a group of letters added to the end of a word to change its meaning. Work with students to show how the meaning of a word changes with a suffix.

- Point out the word *disastrously*. Help students identify the suffix (*-ous*), word ending (*-ly*), and the base word (*disaster*). Explain to students that the suffix *-ous* means "having the characteristics of" and the ending *-ly* changes a word to an adverb. Tell students that adding *-ously* to the base word *disaster* changed the meaning to "having the characteristics of a disaster."

- Repeat the activity with the word *navigator* ("one who navigates") and *mythical* ("relating to mythology"). **(RI.8.4; L.8.4b)**

AT A GLANCE

Students read a historical account about the gold rush of 1849 twice. After the first reading, you will ask three questions to check your students' understanding of the text.

STEP BY STEP

- Have students read the passage silently without referring to the Study Buddy or Close Reading text.

- Ask the following questions to ensure students' comprehension of the text:

  What happened to the population of California as a result of the gold rush? (*The population of California more than doubled several times.*)

  From what other country did people come to try to find gold? (*People came from China.*)

  What made a ship's voyage difficult for working-class passengers? (*They had to travel in the hold of the ship where it was dark. They didn't have sanitation. Conditions may have been fatal for some.*)

- Then ask students to reread paragraph 1 and look at the Study Buddy think aloud. What does the Study Buddy help them think about?

Tip: The Study Buddy tells students to pay close attention to words that create strong images or make comparisons to help them recognize the tone. Students who have difficulty grasping the tone of a text may need help with recognizing that words have shades of meaning. Review with students that many words are synonyms, or words that mean nearly the same thing. However, some create a stronger image than others. For example, the words *happy* and *jubilant* have similar meanings but *jubilant* has a much stronger positive connotation. Students may use references such as dictionaries to help them recognize these subtle differences in meaning and how they impact the tone of a text.

- Have students read the rest of the passage. Tell them to follow the directions in the Close Reading.

- Finally, have students answer the questions on page 107. Use the Answer Analysis to discuss correct and incorrect responses.

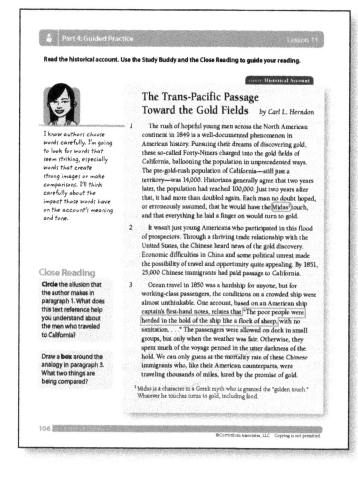

Tier Two
Vocabulary: *Phenomenon*

- Point out the word *phenomenon* in paragraph 1. Given the context and what they know, ask students what *phenomenon* means. (*"a rare event"*) Ask them which words and phrases in the text helped them figure out this meaning. (*"charged into the gold fields," "ballooning the population"*)

- Explain to students that the word *phenomenon* comes from a Greek root word meaning "to show." Have students discuss how this Greek root gives them a clue about the meaning of *phenomenon*. **(RI.8.4; L.8.4a, L.8.4b)**

STEP BY STEP

- Have students read questions 1–3, using the Hints to help them answer the questions.

> **Tip:** The Hints remind students to look back at the text to analyze word choice. This will help them to better understand the author's meaning and tone, and it will assist them in answering the questions.

- Discuss with students the Answer Analysis below.

ANSWER ANALYSIS

1. The correct choice is B. The word choices suggest a sudden movement or growth. Choice A is incorrect. The phrase *charged into* is not used to suggest the Forty-Niners were reckless. Choice C is incorrect. The word *ballooning* does give the idea of growth but it does not suggest that the idea of breaking easily in this context. Choice D is incorrect. The word *unprecedented* indicates that this event never happened before, not that it isn't well understood.

2. The correct choice is D. The allusion to Midas gives a bittersweet tone because this story involves both happiness, turning things to gold, and sadness, turning even food to gold. Choice A is incorrect. The story of Midas doesn't suggest foolishness. Choice B is incorrect. The story of Midas doesn't suggest being unprepared. Choice C is incorrect. Midas may have ended up richer, but this doesn't best describe the allusion's impact.

3. Sample response: The analogy compares the Chinese passengers to a flock of sheep as they are "herded" into the hold of the ship and "penned" in darkness. The analogy makes the passengers seem helpless and at the mercy of the people running the ship. The image also suggests sympathy for the passengers and adds to the compassionate tone.

RETEACHING

Use a chart to verify the correct answer to question 1. Draw the chart below, and work with students to fill in the boxes. Sample responses are provided.

Word Choice	Type	Impact on Meaning
"charged into the gold fields…ballooning the population"	analogy	conveys sudden and dramatic growth

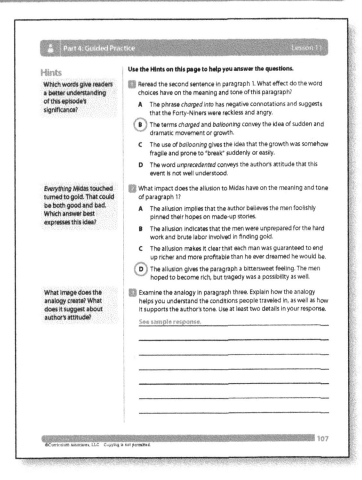

Integrating Standards

Use these questions to further students' understanding of "The Trans-Pacific Passage Toward the Gold Fields."

1. Why do you think the author states "historians generally agree" when describing the population growth from 1849 to 1851? **(RI.8.1)**

   It must be difficult to count how many people actually lived in the area, so the author probably qualified the population growth with "historians generally agree" because the actual number isn't known for certain.

2. What factors caused thousands of Chinese to decide to travel to California? **(RI.8.3)**

   Economic difficulties and political unrest in China caused thousands of Chinese to immigrate to California. They left their homes for the appeal of travel and opportunity.

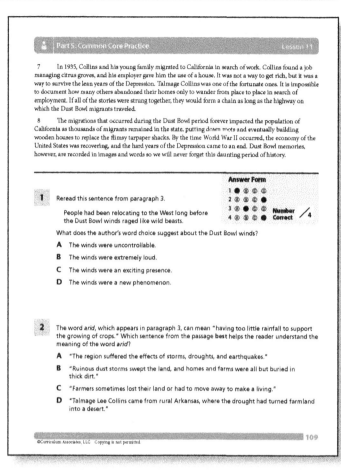

AT A GLANCE

Students independently read a longer article and answer questions in a format that provides test practice.

STEP BY STEP

- Tell students to use what they have learned about reading closely and analyzing word choice to read the article on pages 108 and 109.

- Remind students to underline or circle analogies, allusions, and other words or phrases that suggest meaning and tone.

- Tell students to answer the questions on pages 109 and 110. For questions 1–4, they should fill in the correct circle on the Answer Form.

- When students have finished, use the Answer Analysis to discuss correct responses and the reasons for them. Have students fill in the Number Correct on the Answer Form.

ANSWER ANALYSIS

1. Choice A is correct. The comparison "raged like wild beasts" shows the winds were uncontrollable. Choice B is incorrect. The winds were probably loud, but *raged* does not refer to noise. Choice C is incorrect. A wild beast is not necessarily exciting. Choice D is incorrect. The winds were a phenomenon but a wild beast is not. **(DOK 3)**

2. Choice D is correct. It describes conditions in rural Arkansas, "where the drought had turned farmland into a desert." Choices A and B don't help the reader understand the word *arid*. Choice C describes the effects of arid conditions on farmers. **(DOK 2)**

Theme Connection

- How do all the passages in this lesson relate to the theme of challenging journeys?

- What is one fact you learned about challenging journeys from each passage in this lesson?

ANSWER ANALYSIS

3 Choice B is correct. "Like you'd taken a bulldozer and bulldozed it" suggests the dust storms were strong. Choice A is incorrect. The phrase does not suggest that leveling a field is difficult. Choice C is incorrect. The phrase doesn't suggest inexperienced farmers have problems. Choice D is incorrect. The phrase is not referring to preparing the soil. **(DOK 3)**

4 Choice D is correct. Comparing the stories with the links of "a chain as long as the highway" suggests the great number of people whose lives were changed by the Dust Bowl. Choice A mistakenly equates the "chain" with a connection to the places left. Similarly, Choice B mistakenly suggests that a "chain" of stories made for a bond among travelers. Choice C offers an image of travelers along the nation's roads, but that's an incorrect interpretation. **(DOK 3)**

5 Sample response: The migrants were farmers whose land had been destroyed by the Dust Bowl. They knew California had a mild climate, good farmland, and jobs. To the migrants, it was a place that held the promise of giving them back "the good life" they'd lost at home. It was a place where they might once again work, grow food, and not go hungry. It was the place, they imagined, that would save them. **(DOK 3)**

Part 5: Common Core Practice   Lesson 11

3 Reread these sentences from paragraph 6.

> I'd plant the seed. You'd plant it down in the furrow where it'd be leveled over like you'd taken a bulldozer and bulldozed it. . . ."

How does the analogy contribute to the meaning of the article?

A It describes the difficulty of leveling a field.

B It suggests the great force of the dust storms.

C It describes the problems of inexperienced farmers.

D It explains the careful preparation of the prairie soil.

4 Read this sentence from the passage.

> If all of the stories were strung together, they would form a chain as long as the highway on which the Dust Bowl migrants traveled.

How does the figurative language in this sentence contribute to the meaning of the passage?

A It indicates that the migrants always remained connected to the places they had left.

B It explains how storytelling helped create a strong bond among traveling migrants.

C It describes the once steady stream of migrants seen traveling the nation's highways.

D It suggests the great number of migrants who each survived a difficult time.

5 The author uses the phrase "the Promised Land" to describe how California appeared to Dust Bowl migrants. Explain what this phrase reveals about the problems and hopes of the migrants. Use at least **one** detail from the text to support your response.

See sample response.

✓ **Self Check** *Go back and see what you can check off on the Self Check on page 94.*

110

©Curriculum Associates, LLC   Copying is not permitted.

Integrating Standards

Use these questions and tasks as opportunities to interact with "Dust Bowl Migrants."

1 Reread paragraph 1. What can you infer about topsoil and its importance? **(RI.8.1)**

Sample response: Topsoil is important for the growth of crops. The text states that the winds "stripped away the topsoil, and farming became difficult or impossible." Since farming became nearly impossible, topsoil must be important for crops to grow.

2 What are two examples of evidence the author includes to help support his point of view that the time of the Dust Bowl was a "daunting period of history"? **(RI.8.6)**

Sample response: The author includes details about how "millions of people found themselves enduring poverty." He also describes the many hardships of Talmage Lee Collins and his family. This evidence shows that the time period was extremely difficult and disheartening.

3 Write a paragraph about Thompson and Collins, whom the author uses as examples in this article. How does the author connect them? **(RI.8.3; W.8.4)**

Sample response: The author uses Thompson to show how her family was affected by Dust Bowl migrants in California during the Depression. Collins' experience illustrates how Dust Bowl migrant families suffered through the Depression.

4 Discuss in small groups: What were some causes of the Dust Bowl and reasons the migrants left the area in the 1930s and 1940s? What were some of the effects of these events? How did the Depression impact this challenging time? **(SL.8.1)**

Discussions will vary. Encourage students to find specific causes and effects that the author provides, and have them explain how one event led to its result. Remind students to elaborate on and respond to one another's ideas.

Writing Activities

Write an Argumentative Essay (W.8.1)

• Have students think about each challenging journey they read about in this lesson's passages. Which journey was the most challenging of all? Why?

• Ask students to write an essay in which they convince their audience that their chosen journey was the most challenging. Encourage them to include possible opposing viewpoints about why another journey might be considered more challenging, and to provide evidence to disprove those claims. Remind them to choose their words and phrases carefully and to maintain a formal writing style.

• Have students share their essays with the class and discuss which arguments are the most convincing.

Passive and Active Voice (L.8.1b)

• Direct students to this sentence in paragraph 4 of "Dust Bowl Migrants": "Many of the smaller farms had been taken over by giant corporations." Point out that this is the passive voice.

• Work with students to rephrase the sentence in the active voice. (*Giant corporations took over many of the smaller farms.*) Then have students work in pairs to practice writing sentences in the passive voice and revising them to use the active voice. Encourage them to discuss when each type of voice is effective to use in writing.

LISTENING ACTIVITY (SL.8.4)

Listen Closely/Analyze Word Choice

• Have students work in pairs to discuss the author's word choices in "Dust Bowl Migrants."

• One student selects a word or phrase that is striking, makes a comparison, or is an allusion and describes its impact on meaning and tone. The listener then paraphrases the description in his or her own words to reinforce understanding.

• Students reverse roles and repeat the activity.

DISCUSSION ACTIVITY (SL.8.1)

Talk in a Group/Talk about Journeys

• Have students think about the journeys they read about in this lesson. How are all of the journeys similar? How are they different?

• Have students form small groups to discuss the similarities and differences of the journeys they read about. Students may also wish to compare and contrast these journeys to others with which they are familiar.

• Appoint one member of each group to take notes. Allow 10 to 15 minutes for discussion. Then have each group share their ideas with the class.

MEDIA ACTIVITY (RI.8.7)

Be Creative/Evaluate Media Formats

• Direct students to a brief video about the California gold rush. As students watch the video, have them keep in mind the video's tone and meaning as conveyed through various film techniques including sound and lighting.

• Then ask students to compare this video to the article they read about this topic. What are some advantages and disadvantages of each medium? How do word choice and film techniques impact the tone of their respective media?

RESEARCH ACTIVITY (W.8.6, W.8.7; SL.8.6)

Research and Present/Use Technology

• Have students choose one of the topics from this lesson that they would like to learn more about. Then have them ask themselves questions about the topic and use multiple digital and print sources to find the answers.

• Have students use technology to publish research reports. Make students' reports available to the class. Then have students review and comment on one another's reports using features of the chosen technology, such as commenting tools.

Analyzing the Structure of Paragraphs

Theme: *The Civil Rights Movement*

LESSON OBJECTIVES

- Analyze the structure of individual paragraphs in an informational text.

- Determine the function of particular sentences within a paragraph in developing a key concept about a topic in informational text.

THE LEARNING PROGRESSION

- **Grade 7:** CCSS RI.7.5 requires students to analyze how major sections of a text contribute to the whole, helping students understand how authors organize ideas through the structure of a text.

- **Grade 8: CCSS RI.8.5 requires students to take a more fine-grain approach to text structure by examining how individual sentences in a paragraph work together to build and refine a key concept about the topic of an informational text.**

- **Grade 9:** CCSS RI.9.5 requires students to analyze how individual sentences and larger sections work to develop and refine an author's ideas or claims.

PREREQUISITE SKILLS

- Identify text structures and organizational patterns.

- Identify main ideas and supporting details.

- Recognize how individual sections of text help shape and develop ideas.

TAP STUDENTS' PRIOR KNOWLEDGE

- Remind students they've learned how paragraphs in an informational text work together to develop the author's overall message about a topic. Explain that in this lesson, students will analyze the structure of single paragraphs to figure out how the author has organized the information and developed ideas.

- Point out that one way to think about paragraph structure is to consider the purpose a paragraph serves. For instance, suppose an author wants to explain the causes of the Great Depression. What paragraph structure would be reflected in his or her sentences? (*cause and effect*) Review other common paragraph structures: main idea and supporting details, comparison and contrast, problem and solution, and chronology (sequence).

- Next, explain that students can also think of paragraph structure as the way an author organizes sentences to develop and support a specific idea about a topic. Using a paragraph from a science or history textbook, discuss the details provided in individual sentences. Point out how the sentences work together to develop the more important idea, known as the key concept.

- Note that being able to analyze the purpose of a paragraph as well as the role played by individual sentences will help students become critical readers.

■ Ready *Teacher Toolbox*   *teacher-toolbox.com*

	Prerequisite Skills	*RI.8.5*
Ready Lessons	✓	✓
Tools for Instruction		✓ ✓
Interactive Tutorials		✓

CCSS Focus

RI.8.5 Analyze in detail the structure of a specific paragraph in a text, including the role of particular sentences in developing and refining a key concept.

ADDITIONAL STANDARDS: **RI.8.1, RI.8.2, RI.8.3, RI.8.4, RI.8.7; L.8.2b, L.8.4a, L.8.4b; W.8.2, W.8.4, W.8.8; SL.8.1, SL.8.4, SL.8.5, SL.8.6** (*See page A39 for full text.*)

AT A GLANCE

By studying details in a photograph, students are introduced to the concept of how sentences in a paragraph contribute to the paragraph's key concept.

STEP BY STEP

- Read aloud the paragraph and the definition of *key concept*. Then direct students to study the photograph closely. Have students circle details that help them understand what is happening.

- Invite volunteers to share details they circled and explain how the details help the viewer understand what is happening in the photograph.

- Explain that the chart shows the relationship between details in the photo and a paragraph that an author might write to describe it. Read sentence 1, its role, and the key concept. Then discuss how the sentence relates to the photo and the key concept.

- Discuss the role of sentence 2 and its relation to the key concept. Ask students to add a sentence to describe the crowd's reaction. If necessary, ask: What feelings are revealed in the faces of the crowd?

- Read and discuss sentence 3, its role, and its relationship to the key concept.

- Read and discuss the last paragraph. Then ask volunteers to describe how this skill might help them determine key concepts in textbooks, primary sources, and other types of informational text.

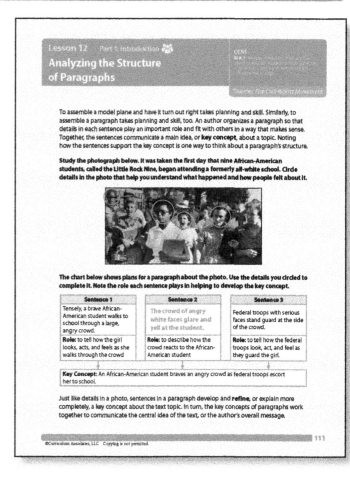

Genre Focus

Informational Texts: Public Document

Tell students that in this lesson, they will read informational texts that are public documents. Explain that a public document is a text that is issued or published for public knowledge or information. Public documents may share these characteristics:

- provide information or guidelines

- provide explanations for actions taken

- generally published by an official or a government source

Based on these characteristics, ask students to share examples of public documents they have read or know about. These may include laws, proclamations (such as the Emancipation Proclamation), transcripts of court decisions or government hearings, official transcripts of public meetings, or pamphlets about historical sites. Have students describe what they read about and what they learned.

Explain that two of the passages in this lesson are public documents. In *Brown v. Board of Education*, students will read an excerpt from the official transcript of a decision made by the United States Supreme Court. In "The Little Rock Nine," they will read an excerpt of a public document about a historic event. Students will also read an informational text, "A Landmark Case for Civil Rights," which provides important background about events in the struggle for racial equality.

AT A GLANCE

Students read a historical account. They also determine the key concept of a paragraph and analyze how specific sentences help to develop the concept.

STEP BY STEP

- Invite volunteers to tell what they learned on the previous page about identifying details in a photograph to help them figure out a key concept. Tell students that they will now learn how to analyze the way individual sentences give details and fit together in a paragraph to develop its key concept.

- Read aloud "A Landmark Case for Civil Rights."

- Then read the question: "What role do the sentences play in helping to develop the key concept of this paragraph?"

- Tell students you will use a Think Aloud to demonstrate a way to answer the question.

Think Aloud: I know that sentences in a paragraph work together to build the key concept, or the most important idea the author wants to convey. Sometimes the concept might be stated in the first or last sentence, but not here. Instead, sentence 1 names a court case that is important in the fight for civil rights. Then sentence 2 goes back in time to describe the purpose of the 14th Amendment and how the states were ignoring it. I wonder what role the other sentences play in describing the struggle for civil rights.

- Direct students to the chart, and ask where they've seen a similar one. Review that it shows how individual sentences help to develop and explain more completely the key concept of the paragraph.

- Guide students in discussing details in sentences 2, 5, and 7 and the role they play in the paragraph.

Think Aloud: Sentence 5 describes a court ruling that allowed states to supply separate but equal facilities. Then sentences 6 and 7 tell how the states provided separate but inferior services and facilities. The details in the sentences help to develop an important idea: the states continued to allow unequal treatment of people of color. That's the key concept.

- Have students complete the chart by writing in the key concept of the paragraph. Invite volunteers to share their answers.

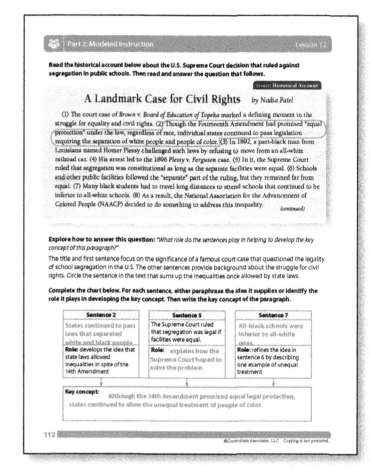

Tier Two Vocabulary: *Inferior*

- Direct students to the word *inferior* in sentence 7. Ask students to tell what *inferior* means in this sentence ("*poorer quality,*" "*of less merit,*" "*functioning below*"). Have them tell which context clues helped them determine the meaning.

- Ask students to think of other words that mean about the same as *inferior* (*mediocre, substandard*). Then ask students to suggest words that mean the opposite of *inferior* (*superior, extraordinary*). **(RI.8.4; L.8.4a)**

AT A GLANCE

Students continue reading about the landmark court ruling. They answer a multiple-choice question and describe the key concept of the paragraph.

STEP BY STEP

- Tell students they will continue reading the historical account about the court ruling.

- The Close Reading helps students look for a sentence that most closely states the key concept and two details that develop it. The Hint will help them think about how each sentence develops the key concept.

- Have students read the paragraph, circle the sentence that most closely states the key concept, and then underline two details that help develop this concept, as directed by the Close Reading.

- Ask volunteers to share the sentence they circled. Discuss why the sentence is a close restatement of the key concept. Ask volunteers to share the sentences they underlined. Discuss how details in the sentences play a role in developing the concept.

- Have students respond to the question in Show Your Thinking. (*Sample response: The Supreme Court ruling that public schools could no longer be segregated struck down the earlier "separate but equal" court decision. The Justices determined that school segregation was illegal. Now African-Americans and other minorities had the right to attend the same schools as white people.*)

ANSWER ANALYSIS

Choice A is incorrect. The differences in opinions may be inferred but were not directly discussed in the text.

Choice B is incorrect. The purpose of the paragraph was not to compare and contrast events related to the case.

Choice C is correct. The majority of sentences describe events that led to the court case and changes in the law.

Choice D is incorrect. Only the last two sentences give broad hints about subsequent events.

> **ERROR ALERT:** Students who did not choose C may not understand the meaning of *turning point*. Explain that a *turning point* is a time at which a significant change occurs, as when a law is overturned.

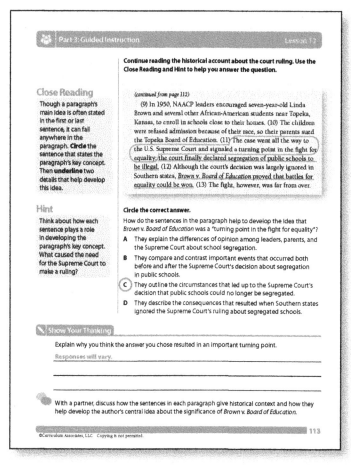

Tier Two Vocabulary: *Admission*

- Direct students to the word *admission* in sentence 10. Ask students to tell what *admission* means in this context. (*"the process of being allowed to enter a place"*) Have them describe which context clues helped them determine the meaning.

- Ask students to use *admission* in this context in their own sentences. (*Sample responses: It costs ten dollars for admission to the museum. There is no admission to the park after sundown. This coupon is good for five dollars off the price of admission.*) **(RI.8.4; L.8.4a)**

AT A GLANCE

Students read a passage twice from the official transcript of a decision made by the United States Supreme Court. After the first reading, you will ask three questions to check your students' understanding of the text.

STEP BY STEP

- Have students read the passage silently without referring to the Study Buddy or Close Reading text.

- Ask the following questions to ensure students' comprehension of the text:

  What question did the Supreme Court have to decide in *Brown v. Board of Education*? (*Do segregated schools provide an equal education, and are they legal under the Fourteenth Amendment?*)

  According to the transcript, what are some ways that society demonstrates our recognition of the importance of education? (*State and local governments have compulsory school attendance laws and spend a great amount of money on education.*)

  As described in the transcript, what are some of the benefits of getting an equal education? (*the ability to carry out basic responsibilities, the foundation of good citizenship, an appreciation of cultural values, preparation for later training*)

- Then ask students to reread the first paragraph and look at the Study Buddy think aloud. What does the Study Buddy help them think about?

Tip: The Study Buddy reminds students to pay attention to each sentence in a paragraph. Review how each sentence contributes to the key concept, and how each paragraph develops and builds on the central idea of the entire text. Also remind students that not all paragraphs have the same structure. In some, the first or last sentence may state the key concept. In other paragraphs, the key concept must be inferred from ideas in the sentences, and readers need to figure out how ideas are related.

- Have students reread the remaining paragraphs and follow the directions in the Close Reading.

- Finally, have students answer the questions on page 115. Use the Answer Analysis to discuss correct and incorrect responses.

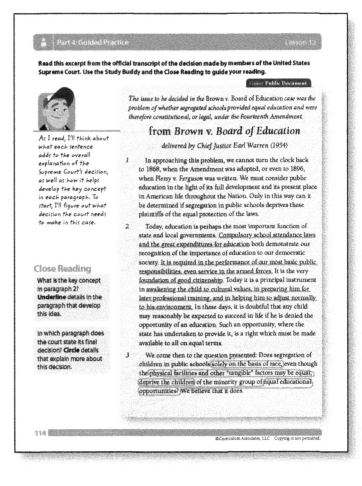

ELL Support: Suffixes

- Explain to students that many English words have suffixes. A suffix is a group of letters added to the end of a word to change the word's meaning.

- Direct students to the word *education* in paragraph 1. Ask students to identify the suffix (*-tion*) and the base word (*educate*). Tell students that *-tion* means "act or process of." Adding the suffix *-tion* to the word *educate* changes its meaning to "the process of educating." Point out that sometimes the spelling of the base word changes when you add a suffix.

- Repeat the activity with *segregation* in paragraph 1 and *recognition* in paragraph 2. (*RI.8.4; L.8.4b*)

STEP BY STEP

- Have students read questions 1–3, using the Hints to help them answer the questions.

  Tip: If students have trouble answering question 2, have them consider each answer choice and ask themselves whether or not it expresses the key concept or only a detail from a single sentence.

- Discuss with students the Answer Analysis below.

ANSWER ANALYSIS

1 The correct choice is C. It stresses that the court needed to take into account the importance of education in its ruling. Neither choice A nor D is correct, since neither point is supported by the text. Choice B is incorrect; the text states that the court also considered the importance of education.

2 The correct choice is B. The key concept in paragraph 2 is that a good education is crucial to both individuals and society. Choices A, C, and D each describe a detail that develops the key concept.

3 Sample response: Paragraph 2 makes claims about the importance of a good education in today's world. It details the way education is the means to developing responsible, well-adjusted citizens and preparing children for later professional training. The transcript concludes that, since education plays such an important role, "it is doubtful that any child may reasonably be expected to succeed in life if he is denied the opportunity of an education" and that this right "must be made available to all on equal terms."

RETEACHING

To verify the correct answer to question 3, work with students to complete a chart like the one below. Help them tell *why* details in the sentences in paragraph 2 support the key concept. Sample responses are given.

Key Concept: A chance for a good education is a right that must be made available to everyone on equal terms .		
Sentence 1	**Sentence 3**	**Sentence 5**
Education is the most important function of government.	People need an education to carry out basic public responsibilities.	Education teaches cultural values and prepares students for later training.

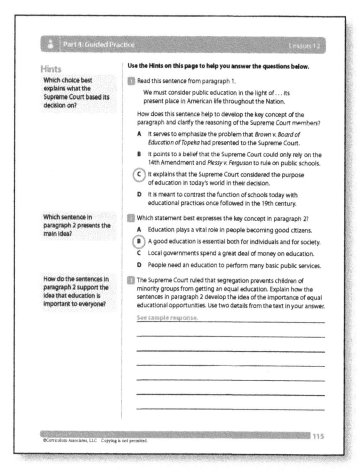

Integrating Standards

Use these questions to further students' understanding of *Brown v. Board of Education.*

1 Why was it so important that the Supreme Court hear and rule on a court case originating from Topeka, Kansas? **(RI.8.3)**

The Constitution gave the Supreme Court the power to make final decisions on cases about federal laws. Their ruling about the legality of segregation would affect all public schools across the nation.

2 What connections does the text make to events in history that preceded *Brown v. Board of Education*? What does this tell you about the fight for equal rights? **(RI.8.3)**

In paragraph 1, the text refers to the Fourteenth Amendment, adopted in 1868, and Plessy v. Ferguson, written in 1896. This shows that the struggle for equal rights was long and difficult.

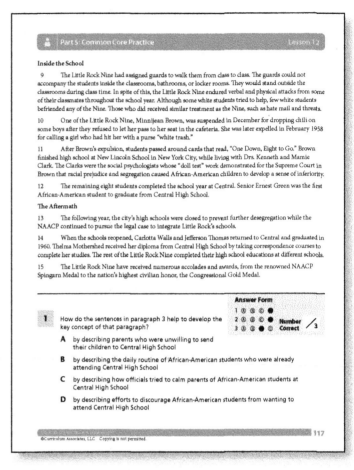

Part 5: Common Core Practice Lesson 12

Read the public document. Then answer the questions that follow.

from "The Little Rock Nine"

from The National Park Service

Who Are the Little Rock Nine?

1   In 1957, nine ordinary teenagers walked out of their homes and stepped up to the front lines in the battle for civil rights for all Americans. The media coined the name "Little Rock Nine," to identify the first African-American students to desegregate Little Rock Central High School.

The End of Legal Segregation

2   In 1954, the *Brown v. Board of Education of Topeka* Supreme Court decision outlawed segregation in public education. Little Rock School District Superintendent Virgil Blossom devised a plan of gradual integration that would begin at Central High School in 1957. The school board called for volunteers from all-black Dunbar Junior High and Horace Mann High School to attend Central.

3   Prospective students were told they would not be able to participate in extracurricular activities if they transferred to Central—such as football, basketball, or choir. Many of their parents were threatened with losing their jobs, and some students decided to stay at their own schools.

The First Day of School

4   On September 3, 1957, the Little Rock Nine arrived to enter Central High School, but they were turned away by the Arkansas National Guard. Governor Orval Faubus called out the Arkansas National Guard the night before to, as he put it, "maintain and restore order . . . " The soldiers barred the African-American students from entering.

5   The students arrived at Central alone on the first day. By prior arrangement, they gathered at the 16th Street entrance with several local ministers who accompanied them. Elizabeth Eckford arrived at the other end of the block by herself. She was met by a mob screaming obscenities and threats, chanting, "Two, four, six, eight, we ain't gonna integrate!"

6   More than two weeks went by before the Little Rock Nine again attempted to enter Central High School. On September 23, 1957, the Little Rock Nine entered the school. Outside, rioting broke out and the Little Rock police removed the Nine for their safety.

The President Becomes Involved

7   On September 24, 1957, President Dwight D. Eisenhower ordered units of the U.S. Army's 101st Airborne Division—the "Screaming Eagles"—into Little Rock and federalized the Arkansas National Guard. In a televised speech delivered to the nation, President Eisenhower stated, "Mob rule cannot be allowed to override the decisions of the courts."

8   On September 25, 1957, under federal troop escort, the Little Rock Nine made it inside for their first full day of school. The 101st Airborne left in October and the federalized Arkansas National Guard troops remained throughout the year.

116   ©Curriculum Associates, LLC   Copying is not permitted.

Inside the School

9   The Little Rock Nine had assigned guards to walk them from class to class. The guards could not accompany the students inside the classrooms, bathrooms, or locker rooms. They would stand outside the classrooms during class time. In spite of this, the Little Rock Nine endured verbal and physical attacks from some of their classmates throughout the school year. Although some white students tried to help, few white students befriended any of the Nine. Those who did received similar treatment as the Nine, such as hate mail and threats.

10   One of the Little Rock Nine, Minnijean Brown, was suspended in December for dropping chili on some boys after they refused to let her pass to her seat in the cafeteria. She was later expelled in February 1958 for calling a girl who had hit her with a purse "white trash."

11   After Brown's expulsion, students passed around cards that read, "One Down, Eight to Go." Brown finished high school at New Lincoln School in New York City, while living with Drs. Kenneth and Mamie Clark. The Clarks the social psychologists whose "doll test" work demonstrated for the Supreme Court in Brown that racial prejudice and segregation caused African-American children to develop a sense of inferiority.

12   The remaining eight students completed the school year at Central. Senior Ernest Green was the first African-American student to graduate from Central High School.

The Aftermath

13   The following year, the city's high schools were closed to prevent further desegregation while the NAACP continued to pursue the legal case to integrate Little Rock's schools.

14   When the schools reopened, Carlotta Walls and Jefferson Thomas returned to Central and graduated in 1960. Thelma Mothershed received her diploma from Central High School by taking correspondence courses to complete her studies. The rest of the Little Rock Nine completed their high school educations at different schools.

15   The Little Rock Nine have received numerous accolades and awards, from the renowned NAACP Spingarn Medal to the nation's highest civilian honor, the Congressional Gold Medal.

1   How do the sentences in paragraph 3 help to develop the key concept of that paragraph?

Answer Form
1 Ⓐ Ⓑ Ⓒ ●
2 Ⓐ Ⓑ Ⓒ ●   **Number** / 3
3 Ⓐ Ⓑ ● Ⓓ   **Correct**

   A   by describing parents who were unwilling to send their children to Central High School

   B   by describing the daily routine of African-American students who were already attending Central High School

   C   by describing how officials tried to calm parents of African-American students at Central High School

   D   by describing efforts to discourage African-American students from wanting to attend Central High School

©Curriculum Associates, LLC   Copying is not permitted.   117

AT A GLANCE

Students independently read a longer passage and answer questions in a format that provides test practice.

STEP BY STEP

- Tell students to use what they have learned about reading closely and analyzing the structure of paragraphs to read the passage on pages 116 and 117.

- Remind students to underline or circle important points.

- Tell students to answer the questions on pages 117 and 118. For questions 1–3, they should fill in the correct circle on the Answer Form.

- When students have finished, use the Answer Analysis to discuss correct responses and the reasons for them. Have students fill in the Number Correct on the Answer Form.

ANSWER ANALYSIS

1   Choice D is correct. The third paragraph describes efforts to deter the African American students from attending Central High School: they were told they could not participate in extracurricular activities, and their parents were threatened with losing their jobs. Choices A, B, and C are incorrect because they are not supported by the text. Paragraph 3 does not say anything about parents being unwilling to send their children to Central High School; it does not describe anyone's routine; and it does not describe officials trying to calm parents. **(DOK 2)**

Theme Connection

- How do all the passages in this lesson relate to the theme of the civil rights movement?

- What is one fact or idea you learned about the civil rights movement from each passage in this lesson?

©Curriculum Associates, LLC   Copying is not permitted.

ANSWER ANALYSIS

2 Choice D is correct. It describes the mob's negative reaction to any effort to integrate the high school. Choice A tells how the students arrived, not how they had trouble entering. Choice B describes only where the students met. Choice C describes Elizabeth Eckford's arrival but doesn't tell about her entering the school. **(DOK 2)**

3 Choice C is correct. The fact that verbal and physical attacks were made on the Little Rock Nine shows the guards were not effective. Choice A is incorrect. The quote does not suggest that the guards were a practical solution. Choice B is incorrect. The text does not suggest that the guards ever allowed the students to be mistreated. Choice D is incorrect. The quote only implies that the Little Rock Nine were subject to frequent attacks. **(DOK 2)**

4 Sample response: The key concept of paragraph 14 is that the Little Rock Nine made a variety of choices about their education when the schools reopened. The sentences in the paragraph support this idea by giving examples of how the various members of the group pursued their education in different ways. **(DOK 3)**

> **Part 5: Common Core Practice**   Lesson 12
>
> **2** Which sentence from paragraph 5 best helps to develop the idea that the Little Rock Nine had trouble even entering the school?
>
> **A** "The students arrived at Central alone on the first day."
>
> **B** "By prior arrangement, they gathered at the 16th Street entrance. . . ."
>
> **C** "Elizabeth Eckford arrived at the other end of the block by herself."
>
> **D** "She was met by a mob screaming obscenities and threats. . . ."
>
> **3** Reread paragraph 9. Then read this sentence.
>
> > In spite of this, the Little Rock Nine endured verbal and physical attacks from some of their classmates throughout the school year.
>
> How does the sentence above help to develop the key concept of paragraph 9?
>
> **A** It explains why guards were a practical solution to keeping the Little Rock Nine safe once inside the school.
>
> **B** It illustrates the part the guards played in allowing some high school students to mistreat the Little Rock Nine.
>
> **C** It shows that the guards were not effective in protecting the Little Rock Nine from all threats.
>
> **D** It describes an eventful day for the Little Rock Nine while under guard at school.
>
> **4** Reread the section titled "The Aftermath," which describes what happened to the Little Rock Nine in later years. Then describe the key concept of paragraph 14 and how the sentences in that paragraph develop that concept. Include **one** detail from the paragraph in your response.
>
> See sample response.
>
> _____
>
> _____
>
> _____
>
> _____
>
> ✔ **Self Check** _Go back and see what you can check off on the Self Check on page 94._
>
> 118   ©Curriculum Associates, LLC   Copying is not permitted.

Integrating Standards

Use these questions and tasks as opportunities to interact with the excerpt from "The Little Rock Nine."

1 How did the Little Rock school district plan to comply with the *Brown v. Board of Education* decision? Cite evidence from the text. (**RI.8.1**)

The District Superintendent "devised a plan of gradual integration that would begin at Central High School in 1957. The school board asked volunteers … to attend Central."

2 The last sentence in paragraph 1 refers to the Little Rock Nine as the first students "to desegregate Little Rock Central High School." What does *desegregate* mean? (**RI.8.4; L.8.4b**)

The prefix de- means "reversal of something," so desegregate *means "to reverse the policy of segregation."*

3 Cite two details from the text that show how the federal government intervened in Little Rock's attempt at desegregation. (**RI.8.3**)

President Eisenhower ordered U.S. Army troops to protect the students and federalized the Arkansas National Guard, putting them under his command. In a speech, he stated, "Mob rule cannot be allowed to override the decisions of the courts."

4 Write an informative paragraph about September 3, 1957, at Little Rock Central High School. (**W.8.2**)

Students' paragraphs will vary. Sample response: The first real test of the Brown v. Board of Education *decision was on September 3, 1957, when nine African-American students arrived to enter Little Rock Central High School. The students were met by angry mobs and turned away by the Arkansas National Guard.*

5 Discuss in small groups: Take turns reading sections of the document and summarizing the important ideas in each section. (**RI.8.2; SL.8.1**)

Discussions will vary. Encourage students to be objective in their summaries.

Writing Activities

Write a Newspaper Article *(W.8.2, W.8.4)*

- Have students review "The Little Rock Nine." Then ask them to imagine it is 1957 and they are "on the scene" in Little Rock.

- Using information from the public document, challenge students to write a newspaper article about the events. Remind them to answer the questions *who, what, when, where, why,* and *how* in their article.

- Allow students to share their writing with the class.

Ellipsis *(L.8.2b)*

- Have students reread paragraph 4 of "The Little Rock Nine." Call attention to the phrase "maintain and restore order . . .," and write it on the board.

- Explain that the three dots are called an ellipsis. An ellipsis is usually used to indicate text where has been omitted, such as when an author uses a quotation and wants to skip over part of it. An ellipsis may also be used to indicate faltering or interrupted speech, or a pause.

- Ask students to explain why an ellipsis is used in this paragraph. *(to indicate on omission in a quotation)*

LISTENING ACTIVITY *(SL.8.4, SL.8.6)*

Listen Closely/Conduct a News Interview

- Have pairs of students use information in *Brown v. Board of Education* to create a news interview following the Supreme Court's decision.

- One student is the news interviewer while the other student is Chief Justice Earl Warren.

- Students must listen carefully to each other as they ask and answer questions. Encourage them to be objective while basing their interview on information from the official transcript.

DISCUSSION ACTIVITY *(SL.8.1)*

Talk in a Group/Talk about Inequality

- Have students use what they read about the Civil Rights Movement to reflect on inequalities that exist today.

- Have small groups discuss the following: Do inequalities exist in your school community now? If so, what are they and what can be done to remedy them? If not, what do you know about inequalities that currently exist elsewhere?

- Allow 15 minutes for discussion. Then have students share their ideas with the class.

MEDIA ACTIVITY *(RI.8.7)*

Be Creative/Watch a Video

- Direct students to videos on the Internet about the Little Rock Nine.

- Discuss how the experience of reading about the events compares with listening to and watching actual footage of what occurred.

- Ask students to tell how what they see and hear on the video contributes to their understanding of the events. have them tell how the experience differs from just reading about the same events.

RESEARCH ACTIVITY *(W.8.8; SL.8.5)*

Research and Present/Write a Report

- Have students use the information in this lesson as a springboard for a written report on segregation from the Civil War to the present.

- Ask students to research additional information, such as information about the Jim Crow Laws and the 13th, 14th, and 15th Amendments. Students should take notes and write a brief report.

- Suggest that students use primary sources, such as the actual text of the amendments. Encourage students to include photographs or videos.

Determining Point of View

LESSON OBJECTIVES

- Determine an author's point of view and purpose about a topic in informational text.

- Cite evidence to explain how an author's point of view is conveyed in text.

THE LEARNING PROGRESSION

- **Grade 7:** CCSS RI.7.6 requires students to determine an author's point of view or purpose in a text.

- **Grade 8: CCSS RI.8.6 builds on the grade 7 standard by strengthening students' understanding of how to determine an author's point of view or purpose in a text.**

- **Grade 9:** CCSS RI.9.6 requires students to determine an author's point of view or purpose at a more sophisticated level.

PREREQUISITE SKILLS

- Identify an author's purpose, perspective, and point of view.

- Recognize descriptive statements and word choices that make clear the text is expressing the author's point of view.

- Analyze different points of view on the same topic.

TAP STUDENTS' PRIOR KNOWLEDGE

- Tell students they will be working on a lesson about identifying the author's purpose and point of view. Ask what an author's purpose is. (*the author's main reason for writing, such as to entertain, inform, or persuade*) Ask what an author's point of view is. (*what the author thinks or believes*)

- Ask students to think about the author's purpose and point of view as you read aloud the following paragraph:

  Do you wish there were a healthy snack that tasted like a treat? Then try a Yippee Bar. It's full of honey and dried fruit, but it's also covered in chocolate. Each Yippee Bar has only 100 calories, but it tastes like 1,000! You can eat a Yippee Bar and feel like you've had a real treat.

- Ask: What is the author's purpose in writing this paragraph? (*to persuade people to eat Yippee Bars*) What does the author believe about Yippee Bars? (*They are a healthful snack.*)

- Tell students that recognizing an author's purpose and point of view will help them understand the meaning of a text and evaluate the contents.

Ready *Teacher Toolbox* teacher-toolbox.com

	Prerequisite Skills	RI.8.6
Ready Lessons	✓	✓
Tools for Instruction	✓	
Interactive Tutorials		✓

CCSS Focus

RI.8.6 Determine an author's point of view or purpose in a text . . .

ADDITIONAL STANDARDS: RI.8.1, RI.8.2, RI.8.4, RI.8.5, RI.8.7; L.8.4a, L.8.4b, L.8.4c; W.8.2, W.8.5, W.8.7, W.8.8; SL.8.1, SL.8.2, SL.8.4, SL.8.6 (*See page A39 for full text.*)

AT A GLANCE

By reading an excerpt of an essay, students build an understanding of how to analyze textual evidence to recognize the author's point of view.

STEP BY STEP

- Read aloud the first paragraph. Discuss the definitions of *author's purpose* and *author's point of view*. Point out that an author's tone is his or her attitude toward a topic.

- Direct students to the excerpt. Have them read the excerpt twice, the second time underlining phrases that express key points.

- Ask what the topic of the excerpt is. Invite volunteers to share the phrases they underlined. Ask: What key point does the author make with each phrase?

- Convey that the chart shows the process of analyzing a text to determine an author's point of view.

- Read aloud the details in the chart. Have students compare the textual evidence in column 2 to the phrases they underlined. Discuss the ideas expressed in column 3 and how they lead to recognizing the author's point of view.

- Share an example of a persuasive text you've read, such as book or movie review. Explain how recognizing the author's purpose and point of view gave you a better understanding of the text. Explain whether you agreed with the author or developed your own point of view.

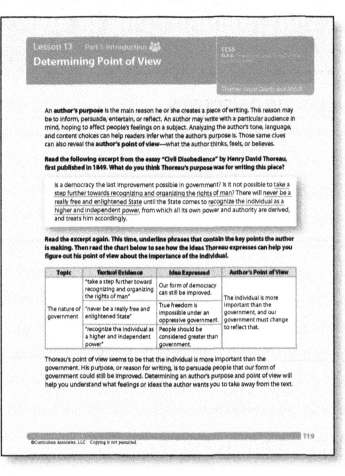

Genre Focus

Informational Texts: Speech

Tell students that in this lesson they will read a speech. Explain that a speech is written remarks, spoken and delivered to an audience.

Speeches have an introduction, a body, and a conclusion. In the body, facts and details are usually included to support the opinions or ideas of the speaker. In the conclusion, the speaker's opinions may be repeated to reinforce the ideas to the listener.

Speeches can have different purposes. They might be delivered in order to persuade the audience of an opinion, inform about a topic, or simply entertain. Some speeches are very influential.

Have students share speeches that they have read or heard. You may also wish to share how or why a speech you once heard had an impact on you.

Explain that the excerpt from "The Hypocrisy of American Slavery, July 4, 1852" is a speech that was given by Frederick Douglass, a former American slave, on the occasion of the Fourth of July. Addressing a community in Rochester, NY, he spoke about how wrong it was to celebrate freedom while slaves were not free. Douglass began with a series of powerful questions and punctuated his speech with further questions that he answered to make his point.

Mention that the other passages students will read in this lesson include editorials and an essay.

AT A GLANCE

Students read an editorial about Edith Wilson. They analyze text evidence to infer the author's point of view.

STEP BY STEP

- Invite volunteers to tell what they learned on the previous page about analyzing an author's purpose and point of view. Tell students they will continue to do so during this lesson.

- Read aloud "The First Female President."

- Then read the question: "What text evidence helps you infer the author's point of view about Edith Wilson?"

- Tell students you will use a Think Aloud to demonstrate a way to answer the question.

Think Aloud: The editorial is about Edith Wilson, wife of President Woodrow Wilson. I know that an editorial expresses the author's opinion. The text doesn't state the author's opinion directly, so I'll look for and underline words and phrases that signal his attitude toward Edith Wilson. In the first paragraph, the author says her contributions to the presidency are "a testament to this remarkable woman's strength and intelligence." This positive language suggests the author thinks Edith was an amazing woman.

- Direct students to the chart and ask where they've seen a similar chart. Review that it shows a way of analyzing the text to determine the author's point of view. Point out the first piece of textual evidence and the idea it expresses.

Think Aloud: I'll continue reading to look for other descriptive words and phrases that signal what the author thinks about Edith Wilson.

- Help students locate other textual evidence and have them add it to complete column 2 on the chart. Then discuss the ideas expressed and have students complete column 3.

Think Aloud: Now I'll review the ideas expressed and see what they reveal about the author's attitude toward Edith Wilson. That will help me figure out the author's point of view.

- Have students complete the chart. Invite volunteers to share their answers with the class.

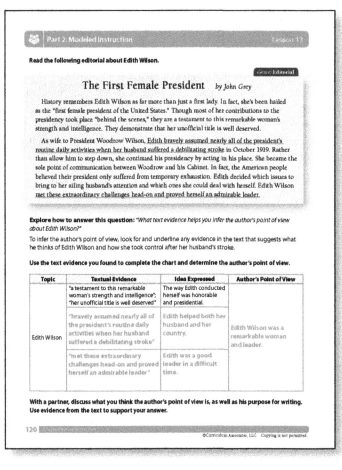

Tier Two Vocabulary: *Testament*

- Direct students to the word *testament* in paragraph 1. Ask students to tell what *testament* means in this sentence. (*"strong evidence for something"*) Have them tell which context clues helped them determine the meaning.

- Suggest that students look up *testament* in a dictionary or thesaurus to find synonyms. Ask: What are some words that could be used in place of *testament*? (evidence, proof, confirmation) **(RI.8.4; L.8.4a, L.8.4c)**

AT A GLANCE

Students read another editorial about Edith Wilson. They answer a multiple-choice question and analyze how to best state the author's point of view.

STEP BY STEP

- Tell students they will read another editorial about Edith Wilson.

- The Close Reading helps students find evidence that shows how the author feels about Edith Wilson. The Hint will help them think about the author's feelings.

- Have students read the editorial and underline words and phrases that convey the author's thoughts, feelings, or beliefs, as directed by the Close Reading.

- Ask students to complete the multiple-choice question. Discuss students' answers.

- Have students respond to the Show Your Thinking. (*Sample response: The author expresses his point of view through negative words and phrases that accuse Edith Wilson of wrongdoing. He calls her plan an "elaborate deception" and says that she "purposefully misled Congress." He describes her as "dishonest," and argues, "history must not look favorably" upon what she did.*)

ANSWER ANALYSIS

Choice A is incorrect. The author describes what Edith Wilson did as "hijacking the government." This does not suggest the author thinks she did the right thing.

Choice B is incorrect. The author says that remembering Edith Wilson as the first female president would be ignoring the "elaborate deception she orchestrated."

Choice C is incorrect. The author says history "must not look favorably" on what Edith Wilson did, which is the opposite of deserving praise.

Choice D is correct. The author describes what Edith Wilson did as an "elaborate deception."

ERROR ALERT: Students who did not choose D may not have recognized the negative tone the author used and its relation to his point of view. Point out some of the words and phrases that illustrate the author's negative feelings about Edith Wilson.

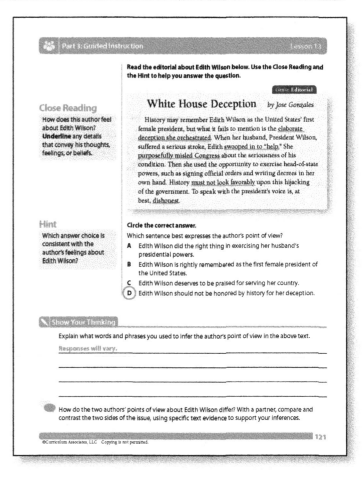

ELL Support: Prefixes

- Explain to students that many English words have prefixes. A prefix is a group of letters added to the beginning of a word to change the word's meaning.

- Direct students to the word *misled* in sentence 3. Help students identify the prefix (*mis-*) and the base word (*led*). Tell students that *mis-* means "wrongly." Ask what *misled* means. (*"led in the wrong direction"*)

- Direct students to the word *dishonest* in the last sentence. Help students identify the prefix (*dis-*) and the base word (*honest*). Tell students that *dis-* means "not" or "opposite of." Ask what *dishonest* means. (*"not honest"*) **(RI.8.4; L.8.4b)**

AT A GLANCE

Students read an essay about Betsy Ross twice. After the first reading, you will ask three questions to check your students' comprehension of the text.

STEP BY STEP

- Have students read the passage silently without referring to the Study Buddy or Close Reading text.

- Ask the following questions to ensure students' comprehension of the text:

  What role do most people believe Betsy Ross played in the American Revolution? (*She sewed the first American flag.*)

  What do some modern flag historians claim regarding Betsy Ross? (*They claim that Betsy Ross was not involved in any way in the creation of the first flag.*)

  Why do most people still believe that Betsy Ross sewed the first flag? (*The flag historians who are trying to discredit the story have failed to provide any evidence that it is not true.*)

- Then ask students to reread paragraph 1 and look at the Study Buddy think aloud. What does the Study Buddy help them think about?

Tip: The Study Buddy reminds students to determine the author's purpose to help figure out the author's point of view. Point out that authors do not always state their point of view. Students need to infer the author's feelings based on text evidence.

- Have students read the rest of the passage. Tell them to follow the directions in the Close Reading.

Tip: Close Reading helps students identify positive words and phrases that can be used as text evidence to determine the author's opinion and feelings. Learning to identify and analyze text evidence will help students infer the author's point of view.

- Finally, have students answer the questions on page 123. Use the Answer Analysis to discuss correct and incorrect responses.

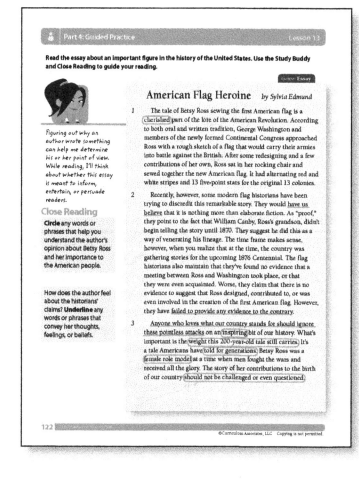

Tier Two Vocabulary: *Cherished*

- Have students find the word *cherished* in paragraph 1. Guide them to identify the base word (*cherish*), and then ask: If you cherish something do you treasure it or not care about it? (*treasure it*) Ask students to name something they cherish. (*freedom, family, a possession*)

- Point out the inflected ending *-ed* and have students tell how it affects the meaning of the base word. (*It changes the verb to the past tense.*)

- Have students tell what is described as being cherished. (*the tale of Betsy Ross sewing the first American flag*) Then ask students to tell the meaning of *cherished*. ("*treasured, held dear*") **(RI.8.4; L.8.4a)**

STEP BY STEP

- Have students read questions 1–3, using the Hints to help them answer the questions.

Tip: If students have trouble answering question 2, have them consider the words they circled and underlined in the Close Reading on the previous page. Point out that these words can be used to help them make an inference.

- Discuss with students the Answer Analysis below.

ANSWER ANALYSIS

1 The correct choice is B. The essay says the story of Betsy Ross "should not be challenged." Choice A is incorrect. The essay doesn't address facts about Ross's life. Choice C is incorrect. Historians haven't proven the story is a myth. Choice D is incorrect. There is no proof Canby fabricated the story.

2 The correct choice is D. The fact that Americans still love to tell the story supports the author's point of view. Choices A and B are incorrect. They describe beliefs of flag historians. Choice C is incorrect. The author says Betsy Ross made "a few contributions of her own," not many contributions.

3 Sample response: The author wrote this essay to persuade people that Betsy Ross was a great historical figure and that flag historians' arguments should be ignored. The author uses positive language to describe Ross's contributions, such as "cherished part of the lore" and "female role model." She also states that people should ignore the "pointless attacks" that flag historians make.

RETEACHING

Use a chart to verify the correct answer to question 2. Draw the chart below, and work with students to fill in the boxes. Sample responses are provided.

Topic: Betsy Ross

Evidence	Idea	Point of View
"cherished part of the lore"; "female role model"	great historical figure	Betsy Ross was an inspirational woman whose story should not be questioned
"pointless attacks"; "should not be challenged"	contributions should not be questioned	

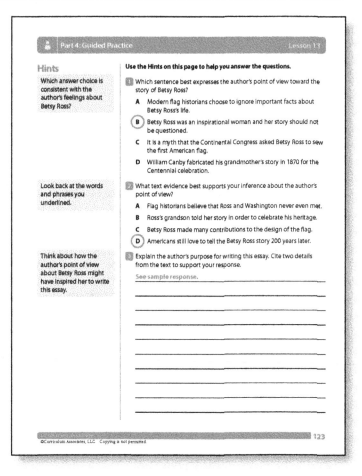

Integrating Standards

Use these questions to further students' understanding of "American Flag Heroine."

1 What is the key concept of paragraph 2? Cite a sentence that helps develop that concept. **(RI.8.5)**

The key concept is that some flag historians are trying to discredit the Betsy Ross story: "The flag historians . . . found no evidence that a meeting between Ross and Washington took place, or that they were even acquainted."

2 The author uses the words *elaborate fiction* to describe what flag historians think of the Betsy Ross story. Why do you think the author chose these words? **(RI.8.4)**

Sample response: Fiction is a made-up story; something that is elaborate is detailed and well planned. The author used "elaborate fiction" to emphasize that the historians believe the story is more than untrue—they think it is a hoax.

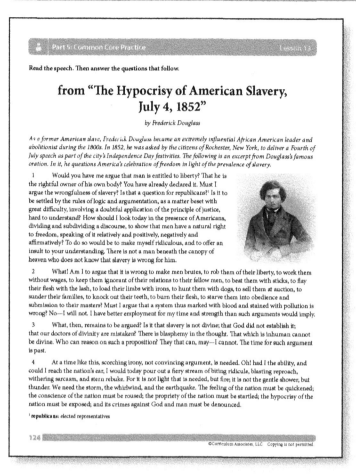

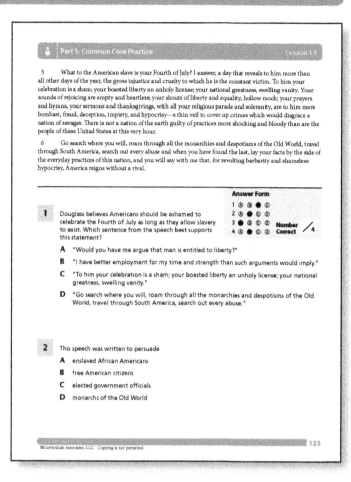

AT A GLANCE

Students independently read a speech and answer questions in a format that provides test practice.

STEP BY STEP

- Tell students to use what they have learned about reading closely and determining point of view to read the speech on pages 124 and 125.

- Remind students to underline or circle important points.

- Tell students to answer the questions on pages 125 and 126. For questions 1–4, they should fill in the correct circle on the Answer Form.

- When students have finished, use the Answer Analysis to discuss correct responses and the reasons for them. Have students fill in the Number Correct on the Answer Form.

ANSWER ANALYSIS

1 Choice C is correct. In this sentence, Douglass takes issue with Americans of his time celebrating July 4, boasting of liberty and "national greatness" even though many people still owned slaves. Choices A and B are incorrect because neither refer to the holiday. Choice D is part of Douglass' efforts to instill shame in his listeners, but it does not support the statement in question as strongly as Choice C. **(DOK 2)**

2 Choice B is correct. The speech was delivered to citizens of New York who were free people. Choices A and C are incorrect. The speech was not delivered to slaves or government officials. Choice D is incorrect. Douglass mentions monarchs to point out abuses that have occurred in history. **(DOK 3)**

Theme Connection

- How do all the passages in this lesson relate to the theme of great deeds and minds?

- How do the lesson's passages change your point of view about these legendary figures?

ANSWER ANALYSIS

3 Choice A is correct. Douglass questions how Americans can celebrate their freedom when they deny freedom to slaves. Choice B is incorrect. Douglass cites the practices of South America and Old World nations as a way of comparing them to slavery. Choice C is incorrect. Douglass's intent is to provoke his listeners to recognize their hypocrisy. Choice D is incorrect; Douglass does not reflect on the significance of the U.S. declaring independence. **(DOK 3)**

4 Choice B is correct. This statement shows that the immoral nature of slavery is obvious to everyone. Choice A is incorrect because it does not support the idea that argument is not needed. Choice C provides a different reason for not making the argument. Choice D goes against the inference because it actually does argue against slavery. **(DOK 2)**

5 Sample response: I analyzed the author's word choices and tone to determine that he feels strongly that it's hypocritical to celebrate the nation's independence when slaves are not free. Douglass says that this day more than any other reveals "the gross injustice and cruelty" of slavery. The "shouts of liberty and equality [are] hollow mock." He ends with an accusation that the nation is even bloodier on this day because of what it represents. **(DOK 3)**

Part 5: Common Core Practice — Lesson 13

3 What does Douglass hope to accomplish in "The Hypocrisy of American Slavery"?

  A He wants to convince his audience that it is wrong to celebrate independence while denying freedom to slaves.

  B He would like to give his audience information about the terrible practices of South American and Old World nations.

  C He intends to provoke his listeners by accusing them of immorality and their nation of inhumane crimes.

  D He wishes to reflect on the historical significance of the United States declaring its independence and its principles of equality.

4 Which sentence from the speech best supports the inference that Douglass does not need to argue against slavery because it is clearly immoral?

  A "At a time like this, scorching irony, not convincing argument, is needed."

  B "There is not a man beneath the canopy of heaven who does not know that slavery is wrong for him."

  C "I have better employment for my time and strength than such arguments would imply."

  D "There is not a nation of the earth guilty of practices more shocking and bloody than are the people of these United States at this very hour."

5 Describe how you determined the author's purpose for "The Hypocrisy of American Slavery." Cite at least **two** pieces of textual evidence that led to this inference.

See sample response.

_____

_____

_____

_____

_____

✔ **Self Check**   *Go back and see what you can check off on the Self Check on page 94.*

Integrating Standards

Use these questions and tasks as opportunities to interact with "The Hypocrisy of American Slavery, July 4, 1852."

1 Explain what Douglass means when he says "You have already declared it" in paragraph 1. **(RI.8.4)**

Douglass is referring to "all men are created equal" in the Declaration of Independence.

2 What is the central idea of Douglass's speech and how does he develop it? **(RI.8.2)**

The central idea is that Americans should not celebrate their independence when slaves are not free. Douglass develops the idea by giving examples of the inhumane treatment of slaves and accusing Americans of being hypocrites by celebrating their freedom while slavery exists.

3 Why doesn't Douglass argue against slavery in his speech? Cite evidence from the text. **(RI.8.1)**

Douglass doesn't argue against slavery because he says "To do so would be to make myself ridiculous and to offer an insult to your understanding. There is not a man beneath the canopy of heaven who does not know that slavery is wrong for him."

4 Write a brief summary of the speech. **(W.8.2)**

Students' summaries will vary. Sample response: In a speech on July 4, 1852, Frederick Douglass tries to persuade listeners to see how hypocritical it is to celebrate the nation's independence when people are being treated unjustly as slaves.

5 Discuss in small groups: How does this speech compare with a typical speech you might hear in your community as part of a Fourth of July celebration? **(SL.8.1)**

Discussions will vary. Students might suggest that a contemporary speaker would have a more positive point of view.

Writing Activities

Write a Compare and Contrast Essay (W.8.2, W.8.5)

- Challenge students to compare and contrast "The First Female President" and "White House Deception." How are these editorials alike? How are they different?

- Have students write to compare these two editorials, including which author's point of view they found more persuasive and why. Remind students to provide a concluding statement that supports their reasoning.

- Ask students to share their writing with partners. Then have them revise their writing based on their partner's feedback.

Consult Reference Materials (L.8.4c)

- Direct students to the word *lineage* in paragraph 2 of "American Flag Heroine." Write the word on the board and explain that it means "descendents of a common ancestor."

- Tell students they can use a print or an online dictionary to determine the pronunciation of *lineage*. Have students find the phonetic spelling in a print or online dictionary and an audio pronunciation online. Then have volunteers say the word aloud. Ask students to look up other unfamiliar words from this lesson's passages to determine their meanings and pronunciations.

LISTENING ACTIVITY (SL.8.6)

Listen Closely/Listen to a Dramatic Reading

- Have students read aloud "The Hypocrisy of American Slavery, July 4, 1852," using appropriate rate and expression. Volunteers may wish to take turns each reading a portion of the speech.

- Remind students of Douglass's point of view and encourage them to convey it through their intonation when they read.

- Remind students to listen respectfully and comment constructively on the readings.

DISCUSSION ACTIVITY (SL.8.1, SL.8.2)

Talk in a Group/Discuss Editorials

- Provide recent newspaper editorials.

- Have students form small groups to read and discuss an editorial. Students should determine the point of view expressed in the editorial and identify textual evidence to support it.

- Tell students to discuss whether or not they agree with the author's point of view, and why.

- Allow 10 to 15 minutes for discussion. Then have each group share the results of its discussion with the class.

MEDIA ACTIVITY (RI.8.7)

Be Creative/Watch a Video

- Direct students to videos that contain readings of Frederick Douglass's speech "The Hypocrisy of American Slavery" in its entirety.

- Have students compare the experience of reading a speech with hearing it spoken. How does the expression in the speaker's voice contribute to their understanding? How does it differ from what they "hear" or "see" when they read?

RESEARCH ACTIVITY (W.8.7, W.8.8; SL.8.4)

Research and Present/Give a Presentation

- Have students use "The Hypocrisy of American Slavery, July 4, 1852" as a starting point for an oral presentation on abolitionists.

- Ask students to use print and digital sources for information about Frederick Douglass and other abolitionists, such as Harriet Tubman, William Lloyd Garrison, John Brown, or Sojourner Truth.

- Students should take notes and write a brief report for their oral presentation. Suggest that they include a visual display, such as photographs or handbills.

Analyzing How Authors Respond

LESSON OBJECTIVES

- Identify an author's viewpoint.
- Identify conflicting evidence or viewpoints.
- Analyze how an author addresses conflicting evidence or viewpoints.

THE LEARNING PROGRESSION

- **Grade 7:** CCSS RI.7.6 requires students to analyze how the author distinguishes his or her position from that of others.

- **Grade 8: CCSS RI.8.6 builds on the Grade 6 standard by requiring students to not only consider the author's point of view but also to consider how he or she responds to opposing evidence or viewpoints.**

- **Grade 9:** CCSS RI.9.6 requires students to analyze how the author uses rhetoric to advance a particular point of view or purpose.

PREREQUISITE SKILLS

- Identify an author's purpose, perspective, and point of view.

- Recognize descriptive statements and word choices that make clear the text is expressing the author's point of view.

- Analyze different points of view on the same topic.

- Recognize how one point of view conflicts with another point of view.

TAP STUDENTS' PRIOR KNOWLEDGE

- Tell students that they will be working on a lesson about analyzing how an author responds to opposing points of view. Ask students to explain what *point of view* means. (*"what a person thinks about a topic"*)

- Present students with the following scenario: You and your friend are going to the movies. You want to see different films. How would you try to convince your friend to change his or her mind to want to see your movie instead? What would you say? What techniques would you use to prove your point?

- Have students share their ideas for accomplishing the goal.

- Point out that there are many persuasive techniques used to try to convince people to think or act in a certain way. Sometimes when authors want readers to share their point of view on a topic, they will explain why other points of view are not as sound as theirs. By responding to conflicting points of view, authors can make their argument stronger.

- Explain that analyzing how an author responds to conflicting points of view will help students better understand the author's argument and purpose for writing. It will also help them to gain a more well-rounded understanding of the topic.

Ready *Teacher Toolbox*   *teacher-toolbox.com*

	Prerequisite Skills	RI.8.6
Ready Lessons	✓	✓
Tools for Instruction		
Interactive Tutorials		✓

CCSS Focus

RI.8.6 … analyze how the author acknowledges and responds to conflicting evidence or viewpoints.

ADDITIONAL STANDARDS: *RI.8.2, RI.8.3, RI.8.4, RI.8.5, RI.8.7; L.8.1d, L.8.4, L.8.4a, L.8.4b, L.8.4d; W.8.1, W.8.2, W.8.6; SL.8.1, SL.8.4 (See page A39 for full text.)*

AT A GLANCE

Through analyzing a persuasive paragraph, students learn that some authors include opposing viewpoints in their writing. Students identify the author's point of view in a text and use that information to help them identify conflicting viewpoints. Students analyze how the author responds to these viewpoints.

STEP BY STEP

- Read aloud the first two paragraphs and introduce the idea of conflicting viewpoints. Then have students read the text about solar power. Tell them to underline the sentence with a point of view that conflicts with the author's point of view.

- Explain that the chart shows how the author of the paragraph acknowledges an opposing viewpoint and responds to it. Read the conflicting viewpoint listed in the chart, and have students compare it to the sentence they underlined. Then ask students to consider how the author's response to the conflicting viewpoint strengthens his argument.

- Ask students to share other examples they have encountered that were successful at using conflicting viewpoints to strengthen an original argument. Students might mention debates, political advertisements, and other persuasive formats.

- Remind students that, as persuasive writers themselves, they should not be afraid to include conflicting viewpoints when expressing their own

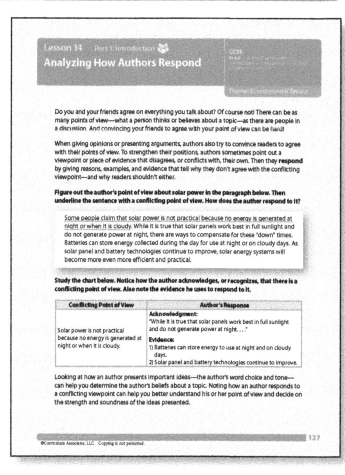

opinions on topics. When carefully presented, conflicting viewpoints can be shown to be invalid or irrelevant, which credibly strengthens the writer's argument.

Genre Focus

Informational Texts: Persuasive Essay

Tell students that in this lesson they will read persuasive essays. A persuasive essay is a text in which an author persuades the reader to agree with his or her opinion. The author states claims and supports them with evidence. Persuasive essays often have the following features:

- express a point of view and support it with evidence, such as facts, examples, statistics, expert opinions, and direct quotations

- rely on logic and reason to accomplish a goal

- include and respond to conflicting viewpoints

Based on these characteristics, ask students to recall persuasive essays that they have read or written themselves. Invite volunteers to share their experiences with the genre.

Explain that "Not Recycling? What's Your Excuse?" in this lesson is a persuasive essay that presents the viewpoint that recycling is important and beneficial.

The editorial "Realistic Environmentalism" is a kind of persuasive essay that is written for inclusion in a newspaper or magazine.

The introduction from the book *Before the Lights Go Out* is also a type of persuasive essay that prefaces a more in-depth analysis of the topic.

AT A GLANCE

Students read a persuasive essay about recycling. They evaluate the author's response to conflicting viewpoints.

STEP BY STEP

- Invite volunteers to tell what they learned on the previous page about how authors acknowledge conflicting points of view and respond to them.

- Tell students that in this lesson they will practice analyzing the author's point of view, a conflicting point of view, and the author's response.

- Read aloud "Not Recycling? What's Your Excuse?"

- Read the questions: "What is the author's point of view about recycling? How does the author respond to a point of view that conflicts with his own?"

- Tell students you will use a Think Aloud to demonstrate a way to answer the questions.

Think Aloud: I will look for details that provide clues about the author's point of view. I see that the word choice in the title provides the first clue. The word *excuse* has a negative connotation, which suggests that the author supports recycling. The second sentence states how the author feels about recycling. I'll use these clues to figure out the author's point of view.

- Direct students to the chart. Review that it helps them identify the conflicting views and the evidence the author uses.

Think Aloud: Now I'll look for a conflicting point of view and see how the author responds. In the second paragraph, this view seems to contradict the author's: "Sending trash to landfills is working fine, so why should I recycle?" In the sentences that follow, I see that the author responds by naming problems that make landfills a less-than-perfect solution. For example, he says not all of the trash in landfills breaks down.

- Point out the conflicting point of view in the first column of the chart.

- Have students record evidence that the author provides in response to the conflicting viewpoint. Invite volunteers to share their responses.

- Finally, have students discuss with partners whether they think the author has presented reasonable and convincing evidence.

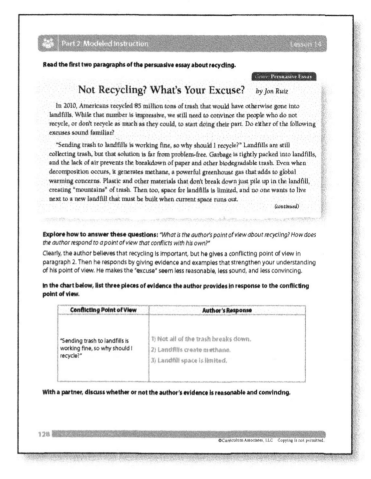

ELL Support: Compound Words

- Explain to students that a compound word is made up of two smaller words. Tell students that to figure out the meaning of a compound word, they can first identify the two smaller words that make up the compound word. Then they can think about the meanings of those words.

- Direct students to the word *landfills* in paragraph 1. Have students identify the two smaller words that make up this compound word. (*land* and *fill*) Discuss how the individual meanings of *land* and *fill* relate to the meaning of *landfill*. (Landfill means "an area of land that is filled with garbage.")

- Have students locate the compound word *breakdown* in paragraph 2. Have students identify its meaning. ("*to break down physically, or decompose*") **(L.8.4)**

AT A GLANCE

Students continue reading the persuasive essay about recycling. They answer a multiple-choice question and identify the evidence that the author of the passage presents to support his response to conflicting views.

STEP BY STEP

- Tell students that they will continue reading the persuasive essay.

- The Close Reading helps students identify the conflicting point of view in the essay as well as the author's response to it. The Hint will help them identify the author's response to the conflicting point of view.

- Have students read the essay, circle the author's acknowledgment of a conflicting viewpoint, and underline text that reveals his response to it, as directed by the Close Reading. Ask volunteers to share the conflicting point of view that they identified as well as the evidence the author uses in response to it.

- Point out that students' answers to the Close Reading will help them answer the Show Your Thinking. Encourage students to consider how the essay would be different if the author did not include conflicting viewpoints.

ANSWER ANALYSIS

Choice A is incorrect. It reflects the conflicting viewpoint, not the author's response or viewpoint.

Choice B is incorrect. The author shares this idea to explain why people might think this way, but it does not reflect the response to the conflicting viewpoint.

Choice C is correct. The author's response to the conflicting viewpoint discusses both the cost- and resource-saving features of recycling.

Choice D is incorrect. This statement is not supported by the text. The essay notes that manufacturers do want to reduce costs, but it does not say they will do this by recycling plastics.

ERROR ALERT: Students who did not choose C may have thought they were looking for the conflicting point of view rather than the author's response to it. Guide students to reread the question and restate it in their own words.

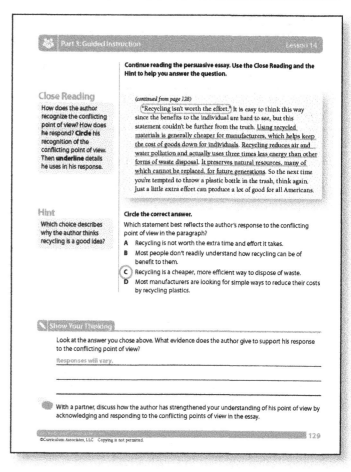

Tier Two Vocabulary: *Resources*

- Point out the word *resources*. Remind students that context clues are often found in the words and sentences nearest to the unfamiliar word. Ask students to identify words and phrases that help them understand the meaning of *resources*. ("*natural*," "*cannot be replaced*") Then have them tell what *resources* means. ("*materials on Earth*") Then have students use a dictionary to verify the meaning. **(RI.8.4; L.8.4a, L.8.4d)**

- Ask students to give examples of natural resources. (*oil, water, land*)

AT A GLANCE

Students read a passage twice about environmentalism. After the first reading, you will ask three questions to check your students' understanding of the passage.

STEP BY STEP

- Have students read the passage silently without referring to the Study Buddy or Close Reading text.

- Ask the following questions to ensure students' comprehension of the passage:

  Why won't a purist definition of *environmentalism* work? (*It is not realistic; humans cannot stop having an effect on the environment because there are so many people on the planet.*)

  If humans cannot stop affecting the environment, how can these issues ever be solved? (*Humans must make changes to how they affect the environment.*)

  How might technology benefit environmentalism? (*If environmentalists stopped seeing technology as an enemy, they might be able to use technological advances to solve environmental problems.*)

- Then ask students to reread the first paragraph and look at the Study Buddy think aloud. What does the Study Buddy help them think about?

Tip: The Study Buddy reminds students the order in which to approach their analysis of the editorial: first identify the topic and the author's point of view. Then look for any conflicting viewpoints and, once they identify them, analyze how the author responds to them. Following this approach will lead students logically through an analysis of persuasive writing.

- Have students read the rest of the passage. Tell them to follow the directions in the Close Reading.

Tip: Remind students that not all authors will directly state their point of view as this author does. Explain that students will need to infer the point of view of some persuasive texts based on what the author is trying to convince them to agree with.

- Finally, have students answer the questions on page 131. Use the Answer Analysis to discuss correct and incorrect responses.

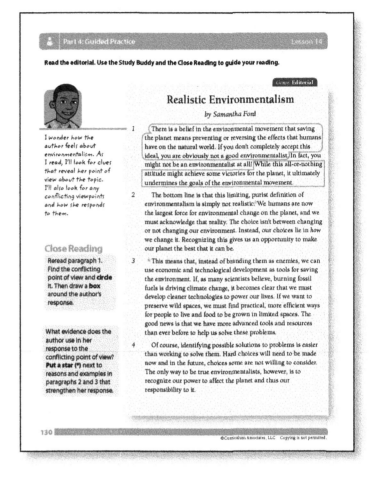

Tier Two Vocabulary: *Purist*

- Direct students to the word *purist* in paragraph 2. Have students look for context clues that help them understand the meaning of this word. Remind them that they can also use word parts to help them figure out the meaning of an unfamiliar word.

- Ask students to identify the base word in *purist*. (*pure*) Tell students that, in this usage, the suffix -*ist* refers to "following a certain idea or principle." Work with students to define a *purist* as "a person who follows a certain idea strictly." **(RI.8.4; L.8.4b)**

STEP BY STEP

- Have students read questions 1–3, using the Hints to help them answer the questions.

Tip: If students have trouble answering question 2, they might be looking for an opposing viewpoint. Discuss the difference between opposite and conflicting ideas. Point out that conflicting ideas do not have to differ from each other in every way.

- Discuss with students the Answer Analysis below.

ANSWER ANALYSIS

1 The correct choice is A. It states the author's point of view. Choice B is incorrect. The author believes in environmentalism, just not a narrow view of it. Choice C contradicts the author's statement about how complicated these environmental problems are. Choice D reflects the conflicting viewpoint.

2 The correct choice is C. The author disagrees with the opinion that humans can reverse the changes. Choice A reflects the author's viewpoint. Choice B states a fact about scientists' beliefs. The author's beliefs coincide with this statement. Choice D presents a belief of the author's.

3 Sample response: The author says that all-or-nothing environmentalism harms the movement. She gives the reasons that humans will change the environment no matter what and that technological advances and newer resources can help solve, not worsen, the environmental problems. She recognizes that hard choices need to be made but claims that since people will be changing the environment, we should plan to do so responsibly.

RETEACHING

Use a chart to answer question 3. Draw the chart below, and work with students to fill in the boxes.

Conflicting Point of View	Author's Response
All-or-nothing environmentalism: humans must prevent or reverse the effects of humans on the environment	• There are too many humans in the environment to leave it unaffected. • Humans must figure out how to better interact with the environment. • Humans can use technology for help.

Part 4: Guided Practice — Lesson 14

Use the Hints on this page to help you answer the questions.

Hints

Review the author's point of view in paragraph 2. What does she think about the purist definition of environmentalism?

1 What is the author's point of view about the topic of environmentalism in this editorial?

(A) It must be realistic to be effective.

B There is no need for environmentalism.

C Environmental problems have simple solutions.

D People who compromise aren't true environmentalists.

Which answer best summarizes the point of view that you circled in from paragraph 1?

2 Which statement best describes the point of view that conflicts with the author's?

A Environmentalists can help us decide on the best ways to change the planet.

B Many scientists believe we need to find cleaner energy sources that will power our lives.

(C) We must reverse the changes that humans have made to the natural world.

D People with advanced tools and resources can help solve environmental problems.

What statement did you draw a box around in your Close Reading? What reasons, evidence, and examples did you star?

3 Explain how the author responds to the conflicting point of view and strengthens her point of view. Use at least two details from the text in your response.

See sample response.

131

©Curriculum Associates, LLC Copying is not permitted.

Integrating Standards

Use these questions to further students' understanding of "Realistic Environmentalism."

1 Write a brief summary of the central ideas in "Realistic Environmentalism." *(RI.8.2)*

Sample response: The author counters the opinions of the environmental purists by saying that humans must be realistic—we will always impact the environment. She suggests that we use our tools and resources to solve our problems and impact the environment in responsible ways.

2 Evaluate the structure of the editorial. How well does the presentation of ideas work? *(RI.8.5)*

Sample response: The author begins the essay by stating the counterpoint first and then explaining why it won't work. I am not sure this was the best presentation of ideas because I was confused at first, thinking that she was stating her beliefs.

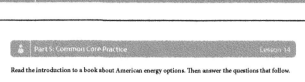

Read the introduction to a book about American energy options. Then answer the questions that follow.

from *Before the Lights Go Out*

by Maggie Koerth-Baker

1   Today, somewhere on the order of 60 percent of us believe that climate change is a serious threat supported by evidence. Yet depending on the poll and the specific questions being asked, between 70 percent and 90 percent of us support increasing funding for alternative energy and mass transit, raising fuel efficiency standards for cars, instituting tougher energy efficiency standards in other areas of our lives, and requiring utility companies to get more of their energy from renewable sources. Even a majority of self-described Republicans support alternative energy and energy-change policies that you might suspect they'd be against. Sometimes, you can even find low belief in climate change and high support for alternative energy *in the exact same poll*. In addition, since the year 2000, large majorities of Americans have made personal choices that reflect energy-conscious values: 90 percent of us have recycled in the last year, 85 percent of us reduced our household energy use in some way, and 81 percent replaced standard lightbulbs with compact fluorescents.

2   When I told my family that I was writing a book about the future of energy in the United States, I got pretty much the same response from everyone, whether liberal or conservative. They were curious. They were excited. They had ideas they wanted to contribute and questions they wanted to ask. The United States has an energy problem. Americans may not agree on the cause or the solutions, but we can all tell that something needs to change.

3   I was born in 1981. In the years I've been alive, the United States has made some big changes to the way we use energy. Specifically, we've become more efficient, able to get more—more work, more conveniences, more money—out of the same amount of energy. Back when I was born, we had to consume more than 12,000 British thermal units (BTUs) of energy to produce $1 of gross domestic product. Today, each dollar costs us only about 7,500 BTUs. Yet at the same time that energy efficiency increased, reliance on fossil fuels has barely budged. In 1980, coal, oil, and gas made up 89 percent of the energy we used. In 2010, those fuels accounted for 83 percent of our energy use. Americans used only a little less energy per person in 2009 than we did in 1981 (and in 2007, we used more). Overall, our total energy use has gone up. Basically, our energy efficiency has made us wealthier, but it hasn't done much to solve our energy problems.

4   Americans may not agree on the reasons for conservation, but most of them support the idea of using less fossil fuel. Actually doing that, though, takes more than just superficial support. We need to break with more than a century of steadily increasing dependence.

5   Today, we use 25 percent more energy in a year than we did when I was a baby. We're currently on a course to use 28 percent more energy a year in 2030 than we do now. If that comes to pass, we'll need more of everything: more coal, more oil, more gas, more wind, more solar, and a whole lot more money to pay for it all. "Staying the course" will not be as simple as it sounds. Meanwhile, making a change—tacking toward a world where we use less energy overall and getting it from different places than we do today—is unlikely to be any easier or cheaper. Nuclear energy is incredibly expensive and unpopular. Clean coal, as we'll see, isn't yet a reality and will cost a lot of money. Wind and solar are "free" but will require huge investments

---

and the creation of new technologies. More oil at ever-higher prices? Some of it from countries that hate us? You already know the problem with that.

6   Where we stand with energy today is a little like finding yourself deep in debt on a low-paying job. At that point, change is inevitable. The future won't be like the present, because the present isn't working. Neither are there any simple, pain-free ways to crawl out of that hole. How do you solve a problem like that? You make hard choices, and you do what you have to do.

7   Today in the United States, our choice isn't between the energy system we have and what somebody, somewhere says we *ought* to be doing. Rather, the choice we are left with is whether or not we want some control over what happens next. That's not happy talk. We probably won't get everything right. We might not love the future we plan. Yet we'll probably like it a lot more than the future that will happen to us if we simply do nothing.

Answer the questions. Mark your answers to questions 1–3 on the Answer Form to the right.

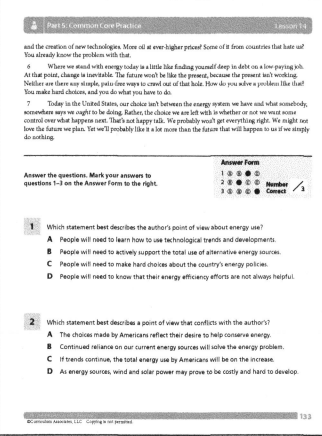

1 Which statement best describes the author's point of view about energy use?

  A People will need to learn how to use technological trends and developments.

  B People will need to actively support the total use of alternative energy sources.

  C People will need to make hard choices about the country's energy policies.

  D People will need to know that their energy efficiency efforts are not always helpful.

2 Which statement best describes a point of view that conflicts with the author's?

  A The choices made by Americans reflect their desire to help conserve energy.

  B Continued reliance on our current energy sources will solve the energy problem.

  C If trends continue, the total energy use by Americans will be on the increase.

  D As energy sources, wind and solar power may prove to be costly and hard to develop.

AT A GLANCE

Students independently read a longer persuasive essay and answer questions in a format that provides test practice.

STEP BY STEP

- Tell students to use what they have learned about reading closely and analyzing how authors respond to read the passage on pages 132 and 133.

- Remind students to underline or circle important word choices.

- Tell students to answer the questions on pages 133 and 134. For questions 1–3, they should fill in the correct circle on the Answer Form.

- When students have finished, use the Answer Analysis to discuss correct responses and the reasons for them. Have students fill in the Number Correct on the Answer Form.

ANSWER ANALYSIS

1 Choice C is correct. The author believes people will need to make hard choices. Choice A might be true, but it does not best reflect the author's point of view. Choice B presents a scenario that the author does not suggest. Choice D includes a detail, but it does not describe the author's point of view. **(DOK 3)**

2 Choice B is correct. The author explains why "staying the course" is not an option. The author would most likely accept the viewpoint in Choice A. Choice C summarizes the main idea of paragraph 5, so it expresses the author's opinion. The author would likely support the opinion expressed in Choice D. **(DOK 3)**

Theme Connection

- How do all of the passages in this lesson relate to the theme of the environment?

- How might one author respond to the conflicting views of another?

ANSWER ANALYSIS

3 Choice D is correct. The author's opinion conflicts with the idea that people need to "stay the course," and she instead explains that people need to make some tough choices and do some hard work. Choice A provides a detail from the text, but it does not reflect the author's response to the conflicting point of view. Choice B is incorrect because it directly conflicts with information provided in paragraphs 3 and 5. Choice C is not supported by the information in the essay. **(DOK 3)**

4 Sample response: The author believes that there is no simple way to solve our energy problems. Total energy use has gone up, and "We're currently on a course to use 28 percent more energy a year in 2030 than we do now." Today this energy comes mostly from fossil fuels, but the author claims that we'll soon need more energy from many sources and more money to pay for it. Using less energy will not be easy, and getting it from alternative sources will not necessarily be cheaper. The author hopes, however, that Americans will be willing to control the choices made about future energy sources. **(DOK 3)**

> **Part 5: Common Core Practice** Lesson 14
>
> **3** Which statement best reflects the author's response to the conflicting point of view about the future of energy use in America?
>
> **A** Different polls show that Americans support alternative energy use and fuel efficiency standards for cars.
>
> **B** Americans have been able to get more work and power more conveniences from the same amount of energy.
>
> **C** Currently, Americans need fewer British thermal units (BTUs) to produce the same amount of gross domestic product.
>
> **D** Americans need to work harder to become less dependent on coal, oil, and gas for our increasing energy needs.
>
> **4** Explain how the author responds to the prevailing point of view about the future of energy. Include at least three pieces of evidence from the text to support your response.
>
> See sample response.
>
> ✓ **Self Check** *Go back and see what you can check off on the Self Check on page 94.*
>
> 134   ©Curriculum Associates, LLC Copying is not permitted.

Integrating Standards

Use these questions and tasks as opportunities to interact with "Before the Lights Go Out."

1 In paragraph 6, the author compares the energy problem to "finding yourself deep in debt on a low-paying job." Explain how this analogy helps you understand her message about our energy policy. **(RI.8.3)**

By continuing in the same job, a person will get deeper and deeper in debt. In the same way, following today's energy policies will produce "deeper" problems that will be even harder to solve.

2 Analyze the author's choices in paragraph 3, such as mentioning her birth and providing statistics. How effective is this approach in expressing the central idea of the paragraph? **(RI.8.5)**

The author refers to the time she was born in order to create a comparison point. She compares energy use at the beginning of her life to energy use today, several decades later. This approach, combined with sharing relevant statistics, is effective in expressing

the key concept of the paragraph, which is how energy use has increased over this time period.

3 Write about what, according to the author, is the one thing Americans agree on, even if we have different views about the environment. Include details that support this opinion. **(W.8.2)**

Sample response: The author says that everyone agrees we have an energy problem, no matter what ideas they have to solve it. To support this idea, the author explains the reactions of her diverse family members to the idea of her writing a book about energy. Everyone had a question, an idea, or something to contribute to the topic.

4 Discuss the following question in small groups: Does the author effectively present her argument? Cite evidence supporting your answer. **(SL.8.1)**

Discussions will vary. Remind students that their evaluations should be supported by details from the text and that they should consider whether the author's evidence is sound and sufficient.

Writing Activities

Write a Persuasive Essay (W.8.1)

- Have students review the viewpoints on environmental issues that are expressed in this lesson's passages.

- Challenge them to write their own persuasive essay to express their opinion about a topic presented in one or more of the passages.

- Tell students to use the information in the lesson essays as the evidence and support for their viewpoint.

- Allow time for students to share their essays in class.

Shift in Verb Tense (L.8.1d)

- Have students read the first sentence of "Before the Lights Go Out" and identify the verb tense. (*present*) Then have them read the first sentence of paragraph 2 and identify the tense in that sentence. (*past*) Discuss the change in verb tense with students. Explain that writers should generally maintain consistency in their verb tenses, although sometimes a change in tense is necessary and effective.

- Have students write a paragraph that includes incorrect shifts in verbs tense. Then have partners correct each other's paragraphs.

LISTENING ACTIVITY (SL.8.1)

Listen Closely/Answer Questions

- After reading "Before the Lights Go Out," have students each write three questions that can be answered using information in the essay.

- Have students work in pairs to ask and answer each other's questions orally.

- Remind students that they must listen closely to their partner's questions before they answer them with information from the essay.

DISCUSSION ACTIVITY (SL.8.1)

Talk in a Group/Compare Points of View

- Have students form small groups to compare the points of view on the environment that are expressed in this lesson's passages.

- Provide the following discussion prompts: Which of the authors was the most effective at presenting his or her opinion? Why? Which author's point of view most closely reflected your own ideas about the environment?

- Allow 10 to 15 minutes for discussion. Appoint one group member to take notes, and have groups share the results of their discussion with the class.

MEDIA ACTIVITY (RI.8.7; SL.8.4)

Be Creative/Evaluate Media

- Have students work in pairs to research and evaluate a piece of persuasive media.

- Invite pairs to use the Internet to find an interview, news clip, commercial, or other piece of persuasive media that includes a conflicting view.

- Have pairs analyze how the conflicting view is presented and whether its use is successful at strengthening the creator's stance.

RESEARCH ACTIVITY (W.8.6; SL.8.4)

Research and Present/Photo Essay

- Ask students to use the information in this lesson's passages to make a photo essay about an environmental topic.

- Have students research photos on the Internet or in old magazines, and collect the ones that they plan to use to reflect their topic.

- Ask students to create a description of each photo. They may research additional information for their descriptions.

- Have students share their photo essays in groups. Encourage others to ask any questions they have.

SCORING GUIDE AND ANSWER ANALYSIS

Informational Passage Answer Analysis

1A Ⓐ Ⓑ Ⓒ ●   3 Ⓐ Ⓑ Ⓒ ●

1B Ⓐ ● Ⓒ Ⓓ   4 ● Ⓑ Ⓒ Ⓓ

2 ● Ⓑ Ⓒ Ⓓ   5 Ⓐ Ⓑ Ⓒ ●

1   **Part A:** Choice D is correct. The author argues that low-fat diets are unhelpful, listing facts to support this claim. Choices A and B are not included in the text. Choice C is incorrect because the benefits are given only passing mention, with the bulk of the text devoted to the drawbacks. *(RI.8.6; DOK 3)*

     Part B: Choice B is correct. The word "fortunately" indicates the author thinks people should not go on a low-fat diet. He clearly sees the results of new studies that cause people to turn away from low-fat diets as a good thing. Choice A is incorrect. It only defines a low-fat diet but does not opine on the worth of such diets. Choices C and D actually mention possible benefits of a low-fat diet; as such, they do not support the statement. *(RI.8.6; DOK 3)*

2   Choice A is correct. It introduces the author's main point that there are not as many benefits to this diet as people may think.

     Choice B is incorrect. The sentence introduces the idea that a low-fat diet may not be as healthy as people thought, but it does not explain why. Choice C is incorrect. It explains that low-fat diets are not always as nutritious as you might think. Choice D is also incorrect. The diet is not shown as difficult or costly, just not completely nutritious. *(RI.8.5; DOK 2)*

3   Choice D is correct. In paragraphs 2–4, the author explains why some fats are good for you and some are bad. In the past, people on low-fat diets tended to cut back on all fats, including the healthy unsaturated fats found in sources such as nuts and avocados.

     Choice A supports the importance of fat in a diet, but it doesn't say why low-fat diets can be unhealthy. Choice B offers a reason to support low-fat diets. Choice C describes an event related to low-fat diets, not a reason for or against following such a diet. *(RI.8.6; DOK 2)*

4   Choice A is correct. *Empty calories* means that a food can be low in fat but not necessarily nutritious.

     Choice B is incorrect. The idea of empty calories has nothing to do with choosing foods that are low in fat. Instead, it means that they are not good for you. Choice C is incorrect. The word *empty* does not mean foods with healthy fats. It means foods with little nutritional value. Choice D is also incorrect. *Empty calories* demonstrates the idea that a food has little value. It doesn't explain which foods are nutritious. *(RI.8.4; DOK 3)*

5   Choice D is correct. The author of "The Skinny on Low-Fat Diets" uses paragraph 5 to show the few health benefits associated with this way of eating. He describes a scientific study that supports his argument that low-fat diets are not necessarily good for you.

     Choice A is incorrect. Although the author does explain earlier in the passage how these diets came to be popular over time, that is not the point of paragraph 5. Choice B is incorrect. Paragraph 5 does talk about women who follow a low-fat way of eating. However, this paragraph is more about the results of the study than about the women themselves. Choice C is also incorrect. Earlier, the author provided information about the dietary restrictions on this way of eating, such as the avoidance of foods like avocados and nuts. However, paragraph 5 is meant to describe the study that shows the few benefits of low-fat eating. *(RI.8.5; DOK 2)*

SAMPLE RESPONSES

Short Response

6 The author's comparison of frustrated dieters to King Arthur and his knights shows the similarity between searching for the perfect weight-loss solution and searching for the Holy Grail. By making this allusion to a famous legend, the author is showing readers that the low-fat diet was considered the diet all dieters were searching for. The author supports this idea by explaining that the diet was considered the perfect balance of foods. Just as the Knights of the Round Table were searching for the Holy Grail and experienced frustration, dieters were frustrated while searching for the best diet. **(RI.8.4; DOK 3)**

7 The author compares superfoods to superheroes so readers will recognize the important role of "fatty" foods such as oil and nuts. Superheroes usually have great powers that let them save citizens from bad situations, so the analogy suggests that superfoods possess similar powers. These substances help the body to deal with bad situations, such as high cholesterol and uncontrolled blood sugar. And because superheroes are considered strong and positive, the analogy suggests that superfoods are strong and positive, too. **(RI.8.4; DOK 3)**

8 The author of "The Skinny on Low-Fat Diets" believes that fats are an important part of a healthy diet. He mentions that fats are one of the substances needed to make the human body work properly. He also mentions that some fats, such as saturated fats, can cause health problems. The author makes the point that people should understand the difference between good fats, such as those found in oils and nuts, and bad fats, such as those found in meats and dairy products. This knowledge will help people understand how to best incorporate fats into their diet and make good choices when considering low-fat foods. **(RI.8.6; DOK 3)**

Performance Task

9 The author of "The Skinny on Low-Fat Diets" includes the information in paragraphs 6 and 7 to show that others have a different point of view from his own. He wants to show that while studies show that low-fat diets do not provide for health benefits such as weight loss and protection from certain cancers, other people disagree. This conflicting viewpoint also supports the author's statement at the beginning of the passage that recommendations about diets can differ greatly and can be confusing to non-experts.

Paragraph 6 mentions an expert, Dr. Dean Ornish, who disagrees with the author's argument and the results of the study. Dr. Ornish questions the study because he feels that it may not have followed "the participants for a long enough period to show how low-fat diets can affect health." He also points out that there is no way of knowing how carefully the study participants complied with the study.

Paragraph 7 builds on this expert questioning by suggesting that people might continue to follow a low-fat diet for other reasons. For example, if they have experienced weight loss or a feeling of health, people might choose to eat that way no matter what the study says.

The author of "The Skinny on Low-Fat Diets" responds to this position by pointing out that it is best for people to be informed and to take a moderate approach to their eating plan. He points out the federal guidelines that suggest that reducing saturated and trans fat is a way in which people can become healthier. He describes specifically which food items might be chosen in order to eat enough good fats. He also says that people should read labels so that they are informed as to the content of the foods they eat. **(RI.8.5, RI.8.6; DOK 3)**

SCORING RUBRICS

Short-Response Rubric

2 points The response is accurate, complete, and fulfills all requirements of the task. Text-based support and examples are included. Any information that goes beyond the text is relevant to the task.

1 point The response is partially accurate and fulfills some requirements of the task. Some information may be inaccurate, too general, or confused. Support and examples may be insufficient or not text-based.

0 points The response is inaccurate, poorly organized, or does not respond to the task.

Performance Task Rubric

4 points The response
- Fulfills all requirements of the task
- Uses varied sentence types and some sophisticated vocabulary
- Includes relevant and accurate details from the texts as well as text-based inferences
- Demonstrates a thorough understanding of the texts
- Maintains a clear focus and organization
- Is fluent and demonstrates a clear voice
- Uses correct spelling, grammar, capitalization, and punctuation

3 points The response
- Fulfills all requirements of the task
- Uses simple sentences and grade-level vocabulary
- Includes relevant and accurate details from the texts
- Demonstrates a mainly literal understanding of the texts
- Maintains a mostly clear focus and organization
- Is fluent and demonstrates some sense of voice
- Uses mostly correct spelling, grammar, capitalization, and punctuation

2 points The response
- Fulfills some requirements of the task
- Uses simple sentences, some fragments, and grade-level vocabulary
- Includes some relevant and accurate details from the texts
- Demonstrates some misunderstandings or gaps in understanding of the texts
- Attempts to maintain a clear focus and organization
- Is difficult to read, includes some inaccuracies, and demonstrates little or no sense of voice
- Contains some inaccurate spelling, grammar, capitalization, and punctuation that may hinder understanding

1 point The response
- Fulfills few requirements of the task
- Uses sentence fragments and below-grade-level vocabulary
- Includes no details or irrelevant details to support the response
- Demonstrates very little understanding of the texts
- Does not establish a clear focus or organization
- Is difficult to read, contains many inaccuracies, and demonstrates no sense of voice
- Uses incorrect spelling, grammar, capitalization, and punctuation to an extent that impedes understanding

0 points The response is irrelevant, poorly organized, or illegible.

Determining Word Meanings

LESSON OBJECTIVES

- Determine the meanings of words and phrases used in a text.

- Analyze the effect of figurative and connotative language on literary texts.

- Identify and analyze different types of figurative language, including similes, metaphors, and personification.

THE LEARNING PROGRESSION

- **Grade 7:** CCSS RL.7.4 requires students to determine the meaning of words and phrases, including figurative and connotative meanings.

- **Grade 8: CCSS RL.8.4 builds on the Grade 7 standards by requiring students to deepen their understanding of specific word choices, including figurative and connotative meaning. This helps students prepare for the analysis required at Grade 9.**

- **Grade 9:** CCSS RL.9.4 requires analyzing the cumulative impact of word choice.

PREREQUISITE SKILLS

- Determine the meaning of words as they are used in fiction and poetry.

- Identify similes, metaphors, and personification in poetry and fiction.

- Analyze the effect of figurative language in stanzas or sections of a story or play.

- Analyze the impact of words with connotative meanings.

TAP STUDENTS' PRIOR KNOWLEDGE

- Tell students they will be working on a lesson about using figurative language, such as personification, simile, and metaphor.

- First, ask students how poets sometimes treat things that are not human as if they were human. (*A poet can personify something, or give it human traits.*) Invite students to give examples of personification. (*The train whistle called to people.*)

- Next, focus on simile and metaphor. Point out that with both elements, poets are comparing two things. A simile uses the words *like* or *as*, while a metaphor often uses a form of the verb *to be*. Ask students for an everyday example of each. (*Simile: He's as skinny as a string bean. Metaphor: The room is a furnace.*)

- Point out that people use figurative language in everyday conversation without realizing it, but poets use it in careful ways to express specific thoughts and feelings. Recognizing the meanings of the figurative language an author uses will help students to better understand and appreciate the literary texts they read.

Ready *Teacher Toolbox*   *teacher-toolbox.com*

	Prerequisite Skills	*RL.8.4*
Ready Lessons	✓	✓
Tools for Instruction	✓ ✓	✓ ✓
Interactive Tutorials	✓	✓

CCSS Focus

RL.8.4 Determine the meaning of words and phrases as they are used in a text, including figurative and connotative meanings ....

ADDITIONAL STANDARDS: **RL.8.1, RL.8.2; L.8.1, L.8.2a, L.8.4a, L.8.5c; W.8.2, W.8.4, W.8.7, W.8.8; SL.8.1, SL.8.4, SL.8.5** (*See page A39 for full text.*)

AT A GLANCE

Through a cartoon that includes lines from a Shakespearean play, students are introduced to the way poets use figurative language. They determine the type of comparison being made to help them recognize figurative language and how poets use it.

STEP BY STEP

- Read aloud the definition of *figurative language*. Then read the second paragraph, which defines types of figurative language.

- Have students study the cartoon, and identify the type of figurative language that is used. (*metaphor*)

- Have students circle the things that are being compared in the lines. Then have them note how the two things are alike.

- Then point to the chart. Read the first column and explain that the comparisons in the cartoon are metaphors.

- Now, read the second column, and ask students to compare what they circled with the words listed

- Finally, read the meaning of the first metaphor, and ask volunteers to share what they wrote for the second metaphor. (*Sample response: In life, people act out their roles.*)

- Discuss the possible effects of these metaphors. Ask students if the metaphors are effective and why or why not. Then discuss whether or not they agree or disagree with the ideas that are being expressed.

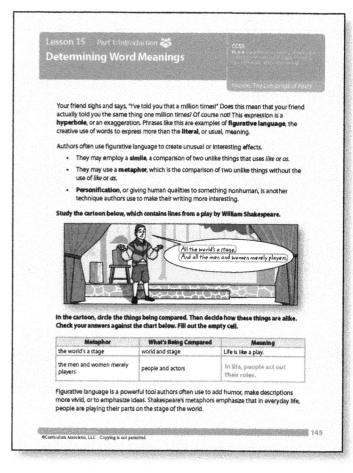

- Challenge students to suggest other metaphors or similes that express a similar idea. (*Life is a game of chess. Regular citizens are merely pawns.*)

Genre Focus

Literary Texts: Sonnet

Tell students that they will read a sonnet by William Shakespeare. Explain that a sonnet is a type of lyric poem. A lyric poem is a poem in which a speaker expresses thoughts or feelings. It often features different types of figurative language.

Explain that a sonnet has 14 lines that are written in iambic pentameter, which is a pattern of units of unstressed and stressed syllables.

Another feature of the sonnet is its rhyme scheme. Remind students that rhyme is the use of repeated sounds at the ends of words. The Shakespearean

sonnet has a specific rhyme scheme. At an appropriate point in the lesson, read the poem aloud several times and ask students to identify the rhyme scheme. (*ABAB, CDCD, EFEF, GG*)

Tell students that another lyric poem in this lesson is "A Winter Twilight" by Angela W. Grimke. This poem has a strong rhythm, or pattern of stressed syllables. It also has a rhyme scheme, but unlike the sonnet by Shakespeare, the rhyme is not always at the end of each line, and it is not regular. For example, in the second stanza, the end of the second and third line rhyme, and the ends of the fourth and sixth lines rhyme.

AT A GLANCE

Students read a Shakespearean sonnet and identify the sonnet's figurative language to determine its meaning.

STEP BY STEP

- Invite volunteers to tell what they learned on the previous page about figurative language.

- Tell students that they will now read a sonnet by Shakespeare.

- Read aloud "Sonnet XVIII."

- Then read the question: "How does the speaker in this poem use figurative language to describe the person he cares about?"

- Tell students you will use a Think Aloud to demonstrate a way to answer the question.

Think Aloud: None of the lines in the poem tell me exactly how the person is like a summer's day. But some phrases or lines are very vivid and descriptive. These phrases help me see how this person could be as lovely and wonderful as a day in summer. I will look for examples of figurative language.

- Direct students to the chart. Point out that it helps them to identify and determine the meaning of figurative language in a text.

Think Aloud: The phrase "the eye of heaven shines" is an example of personification. It gives heaven a shining eye, which I think is the sun. I know the sun is hot and shines. It is also round like an eye. So, this figurative language means that the sun beats down warmly.

- Point out this meaning in the chart.

Think Aloud: In line 9, I read "thy eternal summer shall not fade." I think this is a metaphor. It compares a person's "summer" to never fading eternity. I think the speaker is saying that the person's youthfulness and beauty will last forever.

- Have students write the meaning of this metaphor in the chart.

- Then have students complete the rest of the chart. Once they have determined the type of figurative language and its meaning, ask them to determine what the speaker is comparing.

- When students have completed the chart, have them work with a partner to discuss the author's purpose.

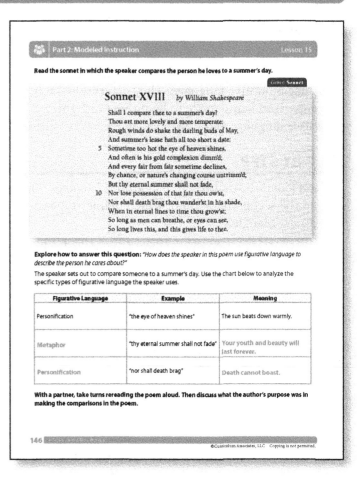

Tier Two Vocabulary: *Temperate*

- Have students reread the first three lines of the poem. Point out the word *temperate*.

- Ask them to use the context to determine what the person's behavior is being compared to. (*weather in May*)

- Have students use the context to determine the meaning of *temperate*. (*mild weather*) **(RL.8.4; L.8.4a)**

- Tell students that this word can also describe a person's behavior. Ask them what they think the word means when it describes a person. (*mild mannered; easy to get along with*)

AT A GLANCE

Students read another poem and use context to determine the connotation of words and phrases.

STEP BY STEP

- Tell students they will read a poem by Muriel Stuart.

- Remind students that good readers pay attention to a poet's word choice to help them understand what the speaker is trying to express. The Close Reading helps students understand that certain words can express certain feelings. The Hint will help them identify a metaphor and describe the feelings expressed in it.

- Have students read the poem and underline words with negative connotations, as directed by the Close Reading. Ask volunteers to share the words they underlined. Then have them explain why they chose those words.

- Have students circle the answer to the question, using the Hint to help. Then have them respond to the questions in Show Your Thinking. Place students in pairs to discuss the final question.

ANSWER ANALYSIS

Choice A is incorrect. The metaphor is positive, not neutral, and the images in the first three lines are negative.

Choice B is correct. Words such as *quiet, faded, crumbled, forlorn, ashes, shriveled, scentless,* and *dry* express negative feelings, which contrasts with meadows and gardens.

Choice C is incorrect. The descriptive words in the first three lines present a negative image, and the metaphor is positive, not frightening.

Choice D is incorrect. The metaphor is positive and contrasts with the negative feelings expressed in the first three lines.

ERROR ALERT: Students who did not choose B may not understand the concept of connotation. List adjectives and ask students if they are positive, negative, or neutral. Then write the metaphor and help students determine its meaning. Finally, compare the words with the meaning of the metaphor to help them understand how they contrast.

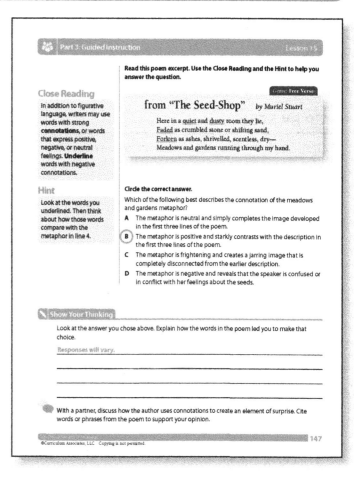

👥 Part 3: Guided Instruction — Lesson 15

Read this poem excerpt. Use the Close Reading and the Hint to help you answer the question.

Close Reading

In addition to figurative language, writers may use words with strong **connotations**, or words that express positive, negative, or neutral feelings. **Underline** words with negative connotations.

Hint

Look at the words you underlined. Then think about how those words compare with the metaphor in line 4.

from "The Seed-Shop"   *by Muriel Stuart*

Genre: Free Verse

Here in a quiet and dusty room they lie,
Faded as crumbled stone or shifting sand,
Forlorn as ashes, shrivelled, scentless, dry—
Meadows and gardens running through my hand.

Circle the correct answer.

Which of the following best describes the connotation of the meadows and gardens metaphor?

A   The metaphor is neutral and simply completes the image developed in the first three lines of the poem.

B   The metaphor is positive and starkly contrasts with the description in the first three lines of the poem.

C   The metaphor is frightening and creates a jarring image that is completely disconnected from the earlier description.

D   The metaphor is negative and reveals that the speaker is confused or in conflict with her feelings about the seeds.

Show Your Thinking

Look at the answer you chose above. Explain how the words in the poem led you to make that choice.

Responses will vary.

With a partner, discuss how the author uses connotations to create an element of surprise. Cite words or phrases from the poem to support your opinion.

©Curriculum Associates, LLC   Copying is not permitted.   147

Tier Two Vocabulary: *Forlorn*

- Direct students to the word *forlorn* in line 3. Point out the word *as*, and explain that this word is used to show comparisons. Ask students what words come after *as*. (*ashes, shriveled, scentless, dry*) Ask them what these words mean and their connotations, or how they make the reader feel. (*These words all have a sad connotation.*) **(L.8.5c)**

- Have students use the context to determine the meaning of *forlorn* and to decide what other words would make sense in its place. (*sad, hopeless*) **(RL.8.4; L.8.4a)**

AT A GLANCE

Students read a poem twice. After the first reading, you will ask three questions to check your students' understanding of the poem.

STEP BY STEP

- Have students read the poem silently without referring to the Study Buddy or the Close Reading text.

- Ask the following questions to ensure students' comprehension of the poem:

  In the first line, what does the speaker compare silence to? *(death)*

  How does the speaker describe the sky? What does this description make you visualize? What is she describing? *(green-gold; It makes me visualize light shining behind green trees. She is describing a sunset.)*

  How does the speaker end the poem? Why do you think she ends it this way? *(She ends it by describing the fields as brown. This shows that the sun has finally set and it is night in the field.)*

- Then ask students to reread the first stanza and look at the Study Buddy think aloud. What does the Study Buddy help them think about?

Tip: The Study Buddy tells students to underline two things the poet is comparing in the first stanza. Identifying what the poet is comparing will help them recognize and analyze figurative language.

- Have students read the rest of the poem. Tell them to follow the directions in the Close Reading.

Tip: The Close Reading guides students to identify words with negative and positive connotations. Learning to recognize words with certain connotations will help them understand the ideas and feelings the speaker is trying to express. Encourage students to use this strategy when they read poetry.

- Finally, have students answer the questions on page 149. Use the Answer Analysis to discuss correct and incorrect responses.

ELL Support: Contractions

- Explain to students that a contraction is a word or words that have been shortened from their original form. The apostrophe shows where letters are missing.

- Explain that most contractions join two words, such as *don't* instead of *do not*.

- Point out the word *'gainst* in line 5. Explain that this is a contraction for *against*. The apostrophe shows the missing letter *a*. Removing the *a* makes this word one syllable.

- Write *cannot, he is, I will, they have,* and *you had* on the board. Help students join these words to form contractions. *(can't, he's, I'll, they've, you'd)* **(L.8.1)**

STEP BY STEP

• Have students read questions 1–3, using the Hints to help them answer the questions.

Tip: The Study Buddy has students identify types of figurative language and then look for context clues that might help them understand it.

• Discuss with students the Answer Analysis below.

ANSWER ANALYSIS

1   The correct choice is D. The words "inking their cress" describes the way the "lean, naked, and cold" trees form a silhouette of treetops against the setting sun. Choices A and C are not described by the phrase in question: while the poem does mention the appearance of the twilight sky and sounds of the air moving. Choice B somewhat fits the image of black images of trees, but shadows are not what the phrase describes.

2   The correct choice is B. The image of a group of trees "lean, naked, and cold" tells the reader the trees are bare, conveying that the words describe the bare black branches of the trees—their crests, or "cress"—against the fading light of evening. Choices A, C, and D are incorrect. Choice A suggests the sounds of a light wind. Choice C describes an "unyielding" fir tree. Choice D describes the brown fields of winter.

3   Sample response: The speaker personifies the star by saying that it is "softly leaning down" over the lonely fir tree. This creates an image of a parent leaning over a child in a gentle, loving way, which gives a peaceful tone to the poem.

RETEACHING

Use a graphic organizer to verify the correct answer to question 3. Draw the graphic organizer below, leaving the boxes blank. Work with students to fill in the boxes. Sample responses are provided.

Personification	What's Being Compared	Meaning
over it softly leaning down/ One star	a star to a person	The star leans over the tree like a parent gently leans over a child.

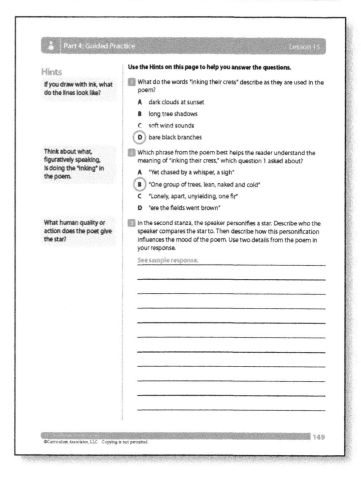

Integrating Standards

Use these questions to further students' understanding of "A Winter Twilight."

1   What can you infer about the speaker's feelings about twilight in winter? Cite evidence from the poem to support your inference. *(RL.8.1)*

The speaker seems to be focusing on a specific moment that is sad and lonely, because the trees are "naked and cold" and the firs are "lonely, apart, and unyielding." It is also beautiful with the trees against the "green-gold" sky and nature whispering and breathing.

2   What do you think is the theme of this poem? *(RL.8.2)*

I think the theme is that nature is powerful and beautiful, but it can also be sad and lonely.

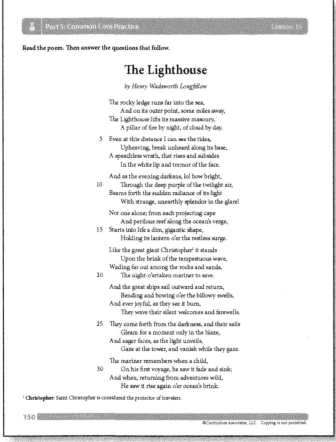

Read the poem. Then answer the questions that follow.

The Lighthouse

by Henry Wadsworth Longfellow

The rocky ledge runs far into the sea,
    And on its outer point, some miles away,
The Lighthouse lifts its massive masonry,
    A pillar of fire by night, of cloud by day.

5 Even at this distance I can see the tides,
    Upheaving, break unheard along its base,
A speechless wrath, that rises and subsides
    In the white lip and tremor of the face.

And as the evening darkens, lo! how bright,
10   Through the deep purple of the twilight air,
Beams forth the sudden radiance of its light
    With strange, unearthly splendor in the glare!

Not one alone; from each projecting cape
    And perilous reef along the ocean's verge,
15 Starts into life a dim, gigantic shape,
    Holding its lantern o'er the restless surge.

Like the great giant Christopher¹ it stands
    Upon the brink of the tempestuous wave,
Wading far out among the rocks and sands,
20   The night-o'ertaken mariner to save.

And the great ships sail outward and return,
    Bending and bowing o'er the billowy swells,
And ever joyful, as they see it burn,
    They wave their silent welcomes and farewells.

25 They come forth from the darkness, and their sails
    Gleam for a moment only in the blaze,
And eager faces, as the light unveils,
    Gaze at the tower, and vanish while they gaze.

The mariner remembers when a child,
30   On his first voyage, he saw it fade and sink;
And when, returning from adventures wild,
    He saw it rise again o'er ocean's brink.

¹ **Christopher:** Saint Christopher is considered the protector of travelers.

150

©Curriculum Associates, LLC   Copying is not permitted.

Steadfast, serene, immovable, the same
    Year after year, through all the silent night
35 Burns on forevermore that quenchless flame,
    Shines on that inextinguishable light!

It sees the ocean to its bosom clasp
    The rocks and sea-sand with the kiss of peace;
It sees the wild winds lift it in their grasp,
40   And hold it up, and shake it like a fleece.

The startled waves leap over it; the storm
    Smites it with all the scourges of the rain,
And steadily against its solid form
    Press the great shoulders of the hurricane.

45 The sea-bird wheeling round it, with the din
    Of wings and winds and solitary cries,
Blinded and maddened by the light within,
    Dashes himself against the glare, and dies.

A new Prometheus,² chained upon the rock,
50   Still grasping in his hand the fire of Jove,
It does not hear the cry, nor heed the shock,
    But hails the mariner with words of love.

"Sail on!" it says, "sail on, ye stately ships!
    And with your floating bridge the ocean span;
55 Be mine to guard this light from all eclipse,
    Be yours to bring man nearer unto man!"

² **Prometheus:** In Greek mythology, Prometheus was chained to rocks and attacked by birds as a punishment for stealing fire.

1 Which of the phrases from the poem best helps the reader to understand the meaning of the phrase "restless surge" in line 16?

  A "A pillar of fire by night"

  B "that rises and subsides"

  C "from each projecting cape"

  D "a dim, gigantic shape"

©Curriculum Associates, LLC   Copying is not permitted.

151

AT A GLANCE

Students independently read a longer poem and answer questions in a format that provides test practice.

STEP BY STEP

- Tell students to use what they have learned about reading closely and thinking about figurative language and connotations to read the poem on pages 150 and 151.

- Remind students to underline or circle important word choices.

- Tell students to answer the questions on pages 151 and 152. For questions 1–4, they should fill in the correct circle on the Answer Form.

- When students have finished, use the Answer Analysis to discuss correct responses and the reasons for them. Have students fill in the Number Correct on the Answer Form.

ANSWER ANALYSIS

1 Choice B is correct. When the poet writes of the "restless surge," he is referring to the constant motion of the ocean's waves, a "speechless wrath" that "rises and subsides." Choices A and D are incorrect. Both describe the lighthouse. Choice C is also incorrect. It describes the common location for lighthouses, a "projecting cape" of rock out into the ocean. **(DOK 3)**

Theme Connection

- How do all the poems in this lesson use figurative and connotative language to express emotions and ideas?

- What example of figurative or connotative language in these poems did you find most descriptive or expressive? Why?

©Curriculum Associates, LLC   Copying is not permitted.

ANSWER ANALYSIS

2 The correct choice is C. The word *like* shows that the lines contain a simile, comparing the lighthouse with a giant that protects sailors against unseen dangers. Choices A and B are incorrect because metaphors and personification do not contain the word *like*. Choice D is incorrect because the word *like* indicates a comparison in the form of a simile. **(DOK 3)**

3 Choice B is correct. The words *steadfast*, *serene*, and *immovable* have positive connotations that express the feelings of admiration and reliability, which gives the sailors comfort in the dangerous oceans. Choices A, C, and D are incorrect because the words the speaker uses to describe the lighthouse have positive, not negative, connotations. **(DOK 3)**

4 Choice C is correct. The word "inextinguishable" refers to the fact that the lighthouse cannot be put out by the wind and rain, but "burns on" through the night in all circumstances, a "quenchless flame." Choices A, B, and D are incorrect. Choice A refers to the "gleam" from the lighthouse shining "for a moment only" on the sails of passing ships. Choice C contributes to the image of the always reliable lighthouse, but not to the meaning of the word in question. Choice D refers to the ocean's waves passing over the rocks and sands of the shore. **(DOK 2)**

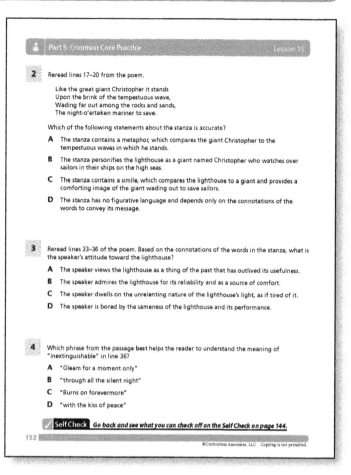

Integrating Standards

Use these questions and tasks as opportunities to interact with "The Lighthouse."

1 What is the central theme of the poem? Use examples from the poem to support your response. **(RL.8.2)**

The theme is man versus nature. Nature is stronger than man, but man has found ways to survive, such as building a lighthouse. The lighthouse is an extension of man, which is shown through personification.

2 What inferences can you draw about the speaker's feelings about the lighthouse? Use examples to support your analysis. **(RL.8.1)**

The speaker sees the lighthouse as the sailors' welcome home and their farewell. It is always there to guide them and protect them. In the last two stanzas, the poet uses personification to show how the lighthouse is the protector.

3 Write a brief summary of the first three stanzas of this poem. **(RL.8.2; W.8.4)**

After a long ocean journey, the speaker is nearing the shore and sees the welcoming light from the lighthouse. He can see the wind and waves beat against it, but it holds steady and gives the sailors light and guidance.

4 Discuss in small groups: How did the figurative language make descriptions more vivid and emphasize ideas in this poem? Give specific examples and explain why you found them to be most vivid. **(SL.8.1)**

Discussions will vary. Encourage students to find examples of the types of figurative language and to think about which examples they found most descriptive and vivid. Remind students that something that is vivid is something they can easily picture in their mind.

©Curriculum Associates, LLC   Copying is not permitted.

Writing Activities

Write an Informative Essay (W.8.2)

- Have students think about what they have learned about how authors use words with connotative meaning to convey a feeling, tone, theme, or message.

- Then have students write a brief informative essay that explains what word connotations are and how poets use them. Also ask students to provide specific examples of different types. Encourage students to write to a clear audience, such as a group of younger students who have not yet learned about connotative meaning.

- Have students exchange essays with a partner and then revise them based on their partner's comments.

Quotation Marks (L.8.2a)

- Have students reread the last stanza of "The Lighthouse." Explain that this sentence includes quotation marks to indicate dialogue, or someone's exact words.

- Explain that when writing dialogue, periods and commas go inside closing quotation marks. If the statement is an exclamation, as they are here, the exclamation mark also goes inside the quotation mark.

- Have students write a line of dialogue. Be sure they punctuate the dialogue correctly.

LISTENING ACTIVITY (SL.8.1)

Listen Closely/Listen to a Recording

- Play a recording several times of one of the poems from the lesson or another short poem.

- Ask students to listen carefully and then discuss how hearing the poem is different from reading it. Students should recognize that hearing the rhythm and inflection can make the poem more powerful and easier to relate to or understand.

DISCUSSION ACTIVITY (SL.8.1)

Talk in a Group/Talk about Language

- Have students choose their favorite poem from this lesson or another poem they have read. Ask them to think about how the figurative language and word connotations helped them understand that poem.

- Have students form small groups. Have each person discuss the poem they chose as their favorite and give reasons to support their choice.

- Appoint one member of each group to take notes. Allow 10 to 15 minutes for discussion. Then have each group share their ideas with the class.

MEDIA ACTIVITY (RL.8.4)

Be Creative/Illustrate a Poem

- Have students choose examples of figurative language from a poem in this lesson. Then have them find digital images or draw pictures that visually represent the description or idea expressed in the figurative language.

- Then ask students to use their images to create an illustrated version of the poem. Allow students to share their illustrated poems.

RESEARCH ACTIVITY (W.8.7, W.8.8; SL.8.4, SL.8.5)

Research and Present/Research a Poet

- Have students choose one of the featured poets they would like to learn more about. Then have them ask themselves questions about the poet's life and work. Have have them use multiple digital and print sources to find the answers.

- Have students use their research to create and give a short presentation on their poet. Encourage them to include visuals, such as a time line, and audio clips of poems.

Analyzing Analogies and Allusions

LESSON OBJECTIVES

- Analyze the impact of specific word choice on meaning and tone, including analogies or allusions to other texts.

THE LEARNING PROGRESSION

- **Grade 7:** CCSS RL.7.4 requires students to analyze the effect figurative language, rhymes, and repetition has on poetry, stories, and drama.

- **Grade 8: CCSS RL.8.4 builds on the Grade 7 standard and prepares students for Grade 9 by requiring students to analyze how the author's use of analogies, allusions, and other figurative language impacts the meaning and tone of a text.**

- **Grade 9:** CCSS RL.9.4 requires students to consider the cumulative impact of word choices on meaning and tone.

PREREQUISITE SKILLS

- Identify figurative language and determine the author's intended meaning.

- Identify and understand analogies.

- Connect allusions to other texts and explain their use.

- Analyze how word connotations affect the tone of a text.

- Determine an author's point of view.

TAP STUDENTS' PRIOR KNOWLEDGE

- Tell students they will be working on a lesson about analyzing analogies and allusions. They will analyze how allusions and analogies affect meaning and tone in a text.

- Ask students how they can determine people's attitudes when talking to them. (*by how they say things; the words they choose; their facial and vocal expressions*) Point out that a person's attitude on a subject is often reflected in the tone of his or her voice, which may reveal inner feelings.

- Next, remind students that authors' attitudes are reflected in the tone of their writing. They choose specific words and phrases to help the reader understand how they feel about the topic. One way authors do this is through the use of analogies and allusions.

- Review the definitions of analogies and allusions. Give an analogy (*a topic as broad and deep as an ocean*), and discuss ways the two can be considered alike. Repeat with an allusion (*Achilles' heel*).

- Explain that analogies and allusions are tools a writer can use to express his or her feelings or to help readers visualize a scene.

Ready Teacher Toolbox		teacher-toolbox.com
	Prerequisite Skills	*RL.8.4*
Ready Lessons	✓	✓
Tools for Instruction	✓ ✓	✓
Interactive Tutorials		✓

CCSS Focus

RL.8.4 ...analyze the impact of specific word choices on meaning and tone, including analogies and allusions to other texts.

ADDITIONAL STANDARDS: **RL.8.1, RL.8.2, RL.8.3; L.8.2a, L.8.4, L.8.4a, L.8.4b, L.8.4d; W.8.3, W.8.7, W.8.8; SL.8.1, SL.8.4, SL.8.5**
(*See page A39 for full text.*)

AT A GLANCE

Through a cartoon, students are introduced to the idea of how allusions affect tone and meaning. Students will learn that analyzing analogies and allusions are strategies they can use when reading to determine the author's attitude and intended meaning.

STEP BY STEP

- Read the first paragraph that includes the definition of *tone*.

- Then have students read the excerpt. Explain that the author's word choice helps the reader visualize the act of sculpting. Ask students to point out the descriptive words or phrases the author uses. (*like a tiny dancer, dancer stretches; slender column; delicate fingers; widens gracefully; elegant ballet*)

- Ask what tone the description expresses. (*The author is full of admiration for the potter's abilities.*)

- Read the paragraph below the excerpt and discuss the definition of *analogy* and *allusions*.

- Next, direct students to the cartoon, and have them study the image and words. Have them identify the allusions and think about how they affect the cartoon's tone and meaning.

- Finally, review the chart. Explain that it lists the allusions the cartoonist makes and their impact on meaning. Tell students that using a chart will help them consider the impact of allusions and analogies.

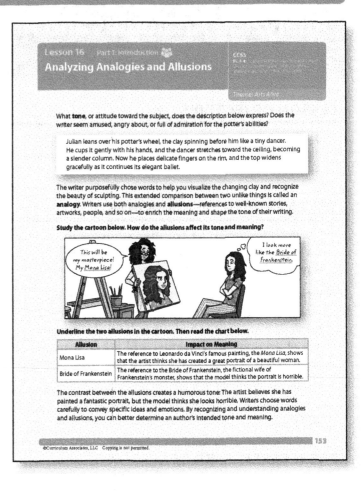

Genre Focus

Literary Texts: Realistic Fiction

Tell students that realistic fiction is a fiction story with characters who take part in activities that could really happen. In realistic fiction, the characters, setting, and situations are believable, but the story is made up. The story may be based on real events, or it may be set in a real place.

Explain that in some realistic fiction pieces, certain characters are actual people. While their actions and words may be based on fact, the author has invented much of what they are thinking, doing, and saying in the story.

Based on these characteristics, ask students to name realistic fiction books they have read that were about

real people. Who were the stories about? What did they like about these stories?

Tell students that "A Trip over the Rainbow" is a realistic fiction story about students who meet the famous painter Jackson Pollock. In the story, the author accurately describes how Pollock painted and where he lived, as well as how he felt about painting. The author researched Pollock and found these details in biographies, articles, and other accounts of his work.

Explain that "An Artist at Work" is also a piece of realistic fiction about a true-life painter. In "Any fool can get into an ocean ..." the poet describes a realistic setting in a unique and imaginative way.

AT A GLANCE

Students identify and analyze how analogies and allusion impact a story's meaning and tone.

STEP BY STEP

- Invite volunteers to tell what they learned on the previous page about analogies and allusions.

- Explain that in this lesson, they will learn how to identify allusions and analogies in a passage and then analyze them.

- Read aloud the passage "An Artist at Work."

- Then read the question: "How does the use of analogy and allusion impact the meaning and tone of the story?"

- Tell students you will use a Think Aloud to demonstrate a way to answer the question.

Think Aloud: I'll look for descriptive words and phrases to see if I can determine the analogy and allusions the author includes. In the first paragraph, the author describes how the paintbrush "swoops like a swallow," flits, and glides. Based on these descriptions, the author is comparing the paintbrush and the artist's painting style to a bird flying. The comparison helps me visualize how the artist paints and suggests that the author admires the artist and his style.

- Direct students to the chart and ask where they've seen a similar chart before. Remind them it will help them record their ideas about the impact of analogies and allusions on meaning and tone.

Think Aloud: In the second paragraph, the visitors compare the artist's painting style to Pablo Picasso and Jackson Pollock. I know that both of these men were very famous and respected painters—Picasso in the early 20th century, and Pollock in the mid-20th century. This reference must be important.

- Ask students why comparing Kang's work to that of two famous artists helps them understand more about Kang's art. How does this comparison help them understand the author's meaning and tone, or how he feels about Kang?

- Finally, have students complete the chart and discuss the question at the bottom of the page with a partner. Invite students to share their thoughts with the class.

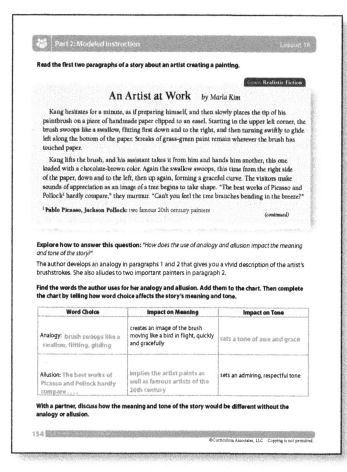

ELL Support: Suffixes

- Explain that a suffix is a word part added to the end of a word. It often changes the word's part of speech. For example, the suffix *-ly* changes a base word to an adverb.

- Remind students that an adverb modifies a verb or an adjective. It tells how, when, or to what extent.

- Point out the word *slowly*. Explain that *slow* is the base word of *slowly*. Ask students what *slow* means. Then ask them how adding *-ly* changes this meaning.

- Have them use their knowledge of the word *slow* and the suffix *-ly* to explain how *slowly* modifies the word *places*. Repeat with the word *swiftly*. **(RL.8.4; L.8.4b)**

AT A GLANCE

Students continue reading about Kang's artistic style. They answer a multiple-choice question and analyze the analogies that helped them select the correct answer.

STEP BY STEP

- Tell students they will continue reading about the artist Kang.

- The Close Reading helps students identify the new analogy in the first paragraph. The Hint will help them pay attention to details in order to select the best answer.

- Have students read the passage and underline the two places where the author uses a new analogy, as directed by the Close Reading.

- Ask volunteers to share the phrases they underlined that show the analogy. Discuss how this comparison is different from the analogy on the previous page and what it helps them understand. If necessary, ask, "What impact on the meaning does this analogy have? How does it affect the tone?"

- Have students circle the answer to the question, using the Hint to help. Then have them respond to the questions in Show Your Thinking.

ANSWER ANALYSIS

Choice A is incorrect. The author mentions the colors Kang is using but does not describe blending colors.

Choice B is incorrect. The author is not comparing the artist's perspective to a tiger's behavior.

Choice C is incorrect. Words such as *fiercely* and *quick* do not indicate the use of more delicate brushstrokes.

Choice D is correct. On this page, the author compares the brushstrokes to a powerful tiger, rather than the graceful swallow. The comparison shows that Kang is now using a stronger style.

> **ERROR ALERT:** Students who did not choose D may not have understood the author's new analogy. Guide these students to complete a chart in which they analyze the analogy and the impact that it has on the meaning of the text.

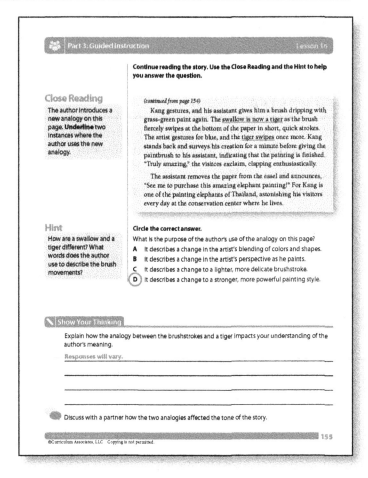

Tier Two Vocabulary: *Surveys*

- Direct students to the word *surveys* in the first paragraph. Have students identify context clues that help them figure out the meaning of the word (*stands back; for a minute*). Based on these context clues, have students tell what Kang is doing. (*looking carefully and thoroughly at the painting*)

- Ask students to describe other instances when they might *survey* a place or thing. Then have students compare this use of the word to the process of *surveying* people or groups by gathering information and opinions. **(RL.8.4; L.8.4a, L.8.4d)**

AT A GLANCE

Students read a poem twice about reading poetry. After the first reading, you will ask three questions to check your students' understanding of the poem.

STEP BY STEP

- Have students read the poem silently without referring to the Study Buddy or Close Reading text.

- Ask the following questions to ensure students' comprehension of the poem:

  What does the speaker compare the ocean to in lines 4 and 5? (*poems and labyrinths*)

  What does the speaker compare swimming in the ocean to? (*reading or writing poetry and understanding or creating metaphors*)

  What does the speaker compare labyrinths to in the last two lines of the poem? How are they alike? (*love and memory; responses will vary.*)

- Then ask students to reread the poem and look at the Study Buddy think aloud. What does the Study Buddy help them think about?

Tip: The Study Buddy suggests that students reread the poem several times to be sure they understand what the speaker is saying. Remind students that rereading is an important strategy to use to help them comprehend any genre of text.

- Tell students to follow the directions in the Close Reading.

Tip: The Close Reading guides students to identify the allusions in the poem. Encourage students to use the footnotes on this page to help them understand the allusions. Also remind them to use a dictionary to look up any unfamiliar words.

- Finally, have students answer the questions on page 157. Use the Answer Analysis to discuss correct and incorrect responses.

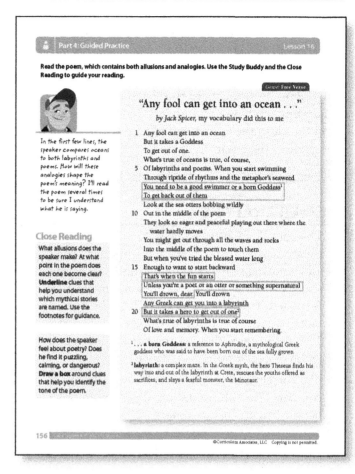

Read the poem, which contains both allusions and analogies. Use the Study Buddy and the Close Reading to guide your reading.

Genre: Free Verse

"Any fool can get into an ocean . . ."
by Jack Spicer, my vocabulary did this to me

1   Any fool can get into an ocean
     But it takes a Goddess
     To get out of one.
     What's true of oceans is true, of course,
5   Of labyrinths and poems. When you start swimming
     Through riptide of rhythms and the metaphor's seaweed
     You need to be a good swimmer or a born Goddess[1]
     To get back out of them
     Look at the sea otters bobbing wildly
10   Out in the middle of the poem
     They look so eager and peaceful playing out there where the
       water hardly moves
     You might get out through all the waves and rocks
     Into the middle of the poem to touch them
     But when you've tried the blessed water long
15   Enough to want to start backward
     That's when the fun starts
     Unless you're a poet or an otter or something supernatural
     You'll drown, dear. You'll drown
     Any Greek can get you into a labyrinth
20   But it takes a hero to get out of one[2]
     What's true of labyrinths is true of course
     Of love and memory. When you start remembering.

[1] . . . a born Goddess: a reference to Aphrodite, a mythological Greek goddess who was said to have been born out of the sea fully grown

[2] labyrinth: a complex maze. In the Greek myth, the hero Theseus finds his way into and out of the labyrinth at Crete, rescues the youths offered as sacrifices, and slays a fearful monster, the Minotaur.

In the first few lines, the speaker compares oceans to both labyrinths and poems. How will these analogies shape the poem's meaning? I'll read the poem several times to be sure I understand what he is saying.

Close Reading

What allusions does the speaker make? At what point in the poem does each one become clear? **Underline** clues that help you understand which mythical stories are named. Use the footnotes for guidance.

How does the speaker feel about poetry? Does he find it puzzling, calming, or dangerous? **Draw a box** around clues that help you identify the tone of the poem.

156

Tier Two Vocabulary: *Supernatural*

- Direct students attention to the word *supernatural* in line 17. Write the word on the board and explain that it is made up of the prefix *super-*, meaning "above" or "beyond," and the base word *natural*. Have students describe how the prefix affects the meaning of *natural* ("*beyond natural*").

- Explain that the dictionary definition for *supernatural* is "beyond scientific explanation or understanding." Have students interpret its use in the poem.

- Then ask students to identify synonyms that make sense in this line (*mystical, magical, otherworldly*). (**RL.8.4; L.8.4a**)

STEP BY STEP

- Have students read questions 1–3, using the Hints to help them answer the questions.

> **Tip:** Remind students to think about the clues they underlined to help them understand the analogy and the clues they identified to help them determine the tone of the poem.

- Discuss with students the Answer Analysis below.

ANSWER ANALYSIS

1 The correct answer choice is A. The first eight lines illustrate this idea. Choice B is incorrect. The ocean and a poem are described as dangerous, captivating, and playful, but not all at the same time. Choice C is incorrect. The poem doesn't describe fighting monsters to gain freedom. Choice D is incorrect. The poem states that getting *into* an ocean or a poem does not pose a challenge.

2 The correct answer choice is D. The allusion compares the interpretation of a poem to the way people can get lost in a maze. Choice A is incorrect. The poem does not compare the abilities of a goddess and a hero. Choice B is incorrect. A poem often has layers of meaning, but the speaker is not trapped, just confused by the language used. The meaning is unclear, so Choice C is incorrect.

3 Sample response: The speaker uses a cautionary tone to tell readers to beware of the dangers that come with reading—or perhaps writing— poetry. The analogy drawn between a poem and an ocean, with its hidden hazards such as riptides and seaweed, suggest a sense of danger, but the reference to sea otters strikes a playful note. The allusion to the mythical labyrinth also contributes to the tone by creating a sense of danger, but it suggests mystery and excitement as well.

RETEACHING

Use a chart to verify the correct answer to question 2. Draw the chart below, and work with students to fill in the boxes. Sample answers are provided.

Allusion	Impact on Meaning
Labyrinth	The readers can get lost and confused in a maze or in the meaning of a poem.

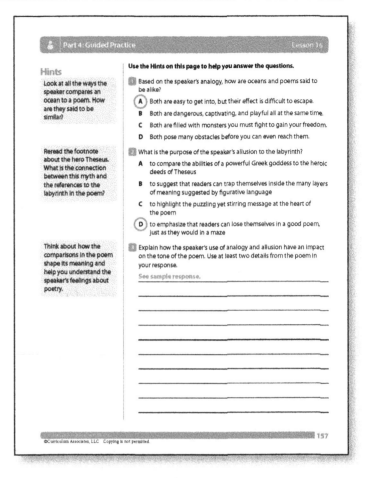

Integrating Standards

Use these questions to further students' understanding of "Any fool can get into an ocean..."

1 Based on the allusions, what inference can you draw about the speaker's knowledge of the world? **(RL.8.1)**

The speaker is very educated and understands or appreciates Greek mythology.

2 What is the theme of the poem? What details helped you determine this theme? **(RL.8.2)**

The theme is that poetry is beautiful, complex, mysterious, and powerful, just like nature or folklore. Readers must respect poets and poetry if they want to understand them. Lines 17 through 20 help readers understand the power of art and nature by describing how the reader will "drown" in a poem.

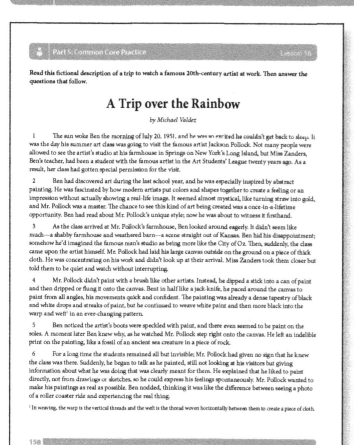

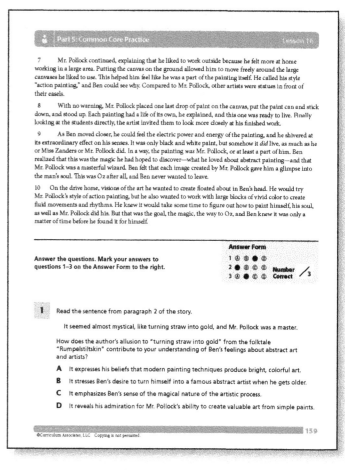

AT A GLANCE

Students independently read a longer realistic fiction story and answer questions in a format that provides test practice.

STEP BY STEP

- Tell students to use what they have learned about reading closely and analyzing analogies and allusions to read the story on pages 158 and 159.

- Remind students to underline or circle important word choices or language.

- Tell students to answer the questions on pages 159 and 160. For questions 1–3, they should fill in the correct circle on the Answer Form.

- When students have finished, use the Answer Analysis to discuss correct responses and the reasons for them. Have students fill in the Number Correct on the Answer Form.

ANSWER ANALYSIS

1   The correct choice is C. It alludes to the tale in which a princess is locked in a tower and magically spins straw into gold. This allusion helps readers understand how modern, abstract art seems magical for Ben. Choice A mentions modern painting, but for Ben, it is the process and impact, not the colors, that make the art magical. Choice B mentions Ben's desire to become an artist, but the analogy does not compare his desire with a magical process. Choice D talks about the artist's ability to paint something of value, which is of no interest to Ben. Instead, he admires the creative process and the feelings an artist can express in a painting. **(DOK 3)**

Theme Connection

- How do the stories and poems in this lesson relate to the theme of the power of art?

- What is one idea you learned about art or artists from each passage in this lesson?

©Curriculum Associates, LLC   Copying is not permitted.

ANSWER ANALYSIS

2 The correct choice is A. A tapestry is a wall hanging in which thread is woven to create a pattern. This helps readers visualize Pollock's painting. Choice B is incorrect. Pollock's shoe makes a fossil-like pattern. Choice C is incorrect. Pollock doesn't sketch. Choice D is incorrect. The analogy doesn't reveal that the pattern grew as he paced. (**DOK 3**)

3 The correct choice is B. These words create a sense of excitement. Choice A is incorrect. Ben respects Pollock, but the phrase *electric power and energy* doesn't suggest a solemn tone. Choice C is incorrect. Ben has been interested throughout the story. Choice D is incorrect. The words do not create mystery, and Ben shows no interest in Pollock's personal life. (**DOK 3**)

4 Sample response: References to Kansas represent an ordinary place, like Dorothy's farm in the book. In contrast, references to Oz and the wizard reflect the magic and power that abstract art holds for Ben. Referring to a magical place emphasizes what art means to him and adds to the author's tone of excitement, respect, and awe. (**DOK 3**)

---

2 Read this line from paragraph 4 of the story.

> The painting was already a dense tapestry of black and white drops and streaks of paint. . . .

What does the analogy of the tapestry reveal about the painting?

A The many lines and layers of paint created an abstract pattern on the canvas.

B The thick canvas and thread-like paint streaks made fossil-like prints and patterns.

C The artist used a sketch he had made to reproduce a tapestry in black and white.

D The black and white pattern grew as the artist paced around the canvas.

3 What is the purpose of the author's use of phrases such as "electric power and energy" and "shivered at its extraordinary effect" in paragraph 9?

A They create a solemn, respectful tone about the painter's unusual style.

B They reflect a tone of excitement and intensity about the painting.

C They signal a change from a tone of indifference to one of interest in the artist's explanation.

D They build a sense of suspense and mystery about the life of the artist.

4 Explain how the allusions to *The Wonderful Wizard of Oz* contribute to the meaning and tone of the story. Use at least **two** details from the text in your response.

See sample response.

_____

_____

_____

_____

_____

_____

✓ **Self Check** *Go back and see what you can check off on the Self Check on page 144.*

160

©Curriculum Associates, LLC   Copying is not permitted.

Integrating Standards

Use these questions and tasks as opportunities to interact with "A Trip Over the Rainbow."

1 How do Ben's feelings about Pollock's studio and farmhouse change over the course of the story? Why do they change? Cite evidence from the text to support your answer. (**RL.8.1**)

At first, Ben is disappointed that the farmhouse and studio are "shabby" and nothing special, like an ordinary farm in Kansas. After watching Pollock paint, however, Ben realizes that the place is "Oz after all," as the painting comes to life, like magic.

2 What is the theme or central idea of the story? How does it develop over the course of the story? (**RL.8.2**)

The theme is that modern art can be powerful and expressive. At the beginning of the story, Ben is interested in modern, abstract art. When he watches Pollock paint, he realizes that the art provides a powerful message. This inspires Ben to work hard and search for an expressive artistic style of his own.

3 What does the phrase "other artists were statues in front of their easels" reveal about how Ben feels about other artists compared to Pollock? (**RL.8.3**)

This comparison shows that Ben pictures other artists as standing completely still as they work. He realizes why Pollock's abstract paintings seem so alive and expressive—because the painter was active and moving about as he painted, not sitting motionless behind an easel and creating dull, static pictures.

4 Discuss in small groups: Which descriptive words or phrases helped you visualize Pollock's style and paintings and understand Ben's reactions to them? (**SL.8.1**)

Discussions will vary. Encourage students to quote evidence from the text that helped them visualize the work and Ben's response. Remind students to follow rules for discussions.

Writing Activities

Another Point of View (W.8.3)

- Challenge students to think about how Jackson Pollock would feel about an art class visiting his studio. How would he feel about students watching him work? How would he explain his process? How would the theme change? Briefly discuss student ideas.

- Have students write a narrative from Pollock's point of view. Encourage them to use details from "A Trip over the Rainbow" to inform their stories. Allow time for students to share their stories.

Dashes (L.8.2a)

- Have students reread the third sentence in paragraph 9 of "A Trip over the Rainbow." Explain that dashes are used to show a break in thought or to emphasize an idea. Ask students to identify the phrase set off with dashes (*"what he loved about abstract painting"*). Discuss how the use of dashes affects the sentence and how it would be read aloud.

- Ask students to write a short paragraph describing an art form, hobby, or sport they enjoy and how it makes them feel. Have them include at least one sentence that uses dashes to emphasize an important idea.

LISTENING ACTIVITY (SL.8.1)

Listen Closely/Summarize

- Have students work in small groups and take turns reading "An Artist at Work." Have the students pass along the story and read one paragraph. The listeners will summarize the paragraph that was read.

- When they've finished, have students discuss how listening to the story was different from reading it.

DISCUSSION ACTIVITY (SL.8.1)

Talk in a Group/Talk about Art and Artists

- Ask students to think about the art forms and artists they read about in this lesson's passages. Have them discuss the characteristics of an artist and the creation of art.

- Have students form small groups to discuss other artists that they admire, including musicians, actors, or authors. Group members should list the common characteristics that make these people great artists.

- Allow 10 to 15 minutes for discussion. Then have groups share their lists to come up with a class description of an artist's characteristics.

MEDIA ACTIVITY (RL.8.4)

Be Creative/Create a Cartoon

- Have students review the cartoon on page 153 that used allusions to create meaning and tone.

- Challenge students to create a cartoon of their own that includes allusions or analogies.

- Then ask students to exchange cartoons and discuss how the allusions or analogies affected the tone or meaning of each cartoon.

RESEARCH ACTIVITY (W.8.7; SL.8.4)

Research and Present/Give a Presentation

- Ask students to use the information in "A Trip over the Rainbow" to plan an oral presentation on Pollock and abstract art. Students should explain more about the artist's style and how it conveys meaning, as well as his influence on modern art.

- Have students use the Internet to search for information about Pollock's works and to find images of his art to include in their presentations.

- Encourage students to refer to the images while they give their presentations. Then allow time for students to answer questions from their peers about their presentations.

Comparing and Contrasting Structure

LESSON OBJECTIVES

- Identify key features of particular text structures in two or more literary texts, including poetry.

- Compare and contrast the effects of different kinds of structures in literary texts.

- Analyze how the differing structure of each text contributes to its meaning and style.

THE LEARNING PROGRESSION

- **Grade 7:** CCSS RL.7.5 emphasizes that students need to understand how form and structure help an author develop meaning.

- **Grade 8: CCSS RL.8.5 builds on the grade 7 standard by having students compare texts and consider how form contributes to the meaning and style of each.**

- **Grade 9:** CCSS RL.9.5 asks students to analyze how an author's choices concerning how to structure a text create such effects as mystery, tension, or surprise.

PREREQUISITE SKILLS

- Recognize and identify forms and structures in literary texts, including poetry.

- Identify main ideas and themes in literary texts, including poetry.

- Recognize and analyze the connection between form/structure and meaning and style.

- Recognize rhyme, repetition, and rhythm in poetry.

TAP STUDENTS' PRIOR KNOWLEDGE

- Tell students that in this lesson they will learn about text structure and how it impacts the meaning of a text. Ask students to review what text structure is. (*how the text is organized*)

- Retell a familiar story such as "Stone Soup" or "Jack and the Beanstalk." Explain that the story is told in narrative form.

- Then ask students to retell the story using a different text structure, such as in the form of a poem. Students may choose to write a rhyming verse, a free verse, a sonnet, a haiku, or another structure of their choosing.

- Have volunteers share their creative rewrites. Discuss how the new versions are alike and different from the original text structure. Talk about how the different structure contributes to the meaning and style of the story.

- Point out that looking at the form an author chooses will help them better understand the way that form and structure contribute to a text's overall meaning and style.

Ready *Teacher Toolbox*		teacher-toolbox.com
	Prerequisite Skills	**RL.8.5**
Ready Lessons	✓ ✓	✓
Tools for Instruction	✓	
Interactive Tutorials		✓

CCSS Focus

RL.8.5 Compare and contrast the structure of two or more texts and analyze how the differing structure of each text contributes to its meaning and style.
ADDITIONAL STANDARDS: **RL.8.1, RL.8.2, RL.8.4; L.8.4, L.8.4c, L.8.5a; W.8.4, W.8.7; SL.8.1, SL.8.4, SL.8.6** (*See page A39 for full text.*)

AT A GLANCE

Students will read a poem and analyze how its structure contributes to the tone and meaning.

STEP BY STEP

- Read aloud the introductory paragraph and discuss the example about the different types of building structures. Ask students what different purposes such buildings might serve, and what structures architects might devise to ensure those buildings meet those purposes.

- Now discuss the definitions of *structure, stanzas*, and *rhythm*.

- Read aloud the poem, emphasizing the rhythm and rhyme scheme. Then have students read aloud the poem, lightly tapping their desks to mirror the rhythm.

- After students read the poem, have them read it again. This time, guide students in marking the rhyme scheme of the poem. Then have students underline repeated words.

- Read aloud the text below the poem. Discuss the tone and meaning that this poem imparts. Ask students what parts of the poem help contribute to the poem's style. Talk about how the meaning of the poem would be different if it had been written in narrative form. How would it be different if it had been written as a letter?

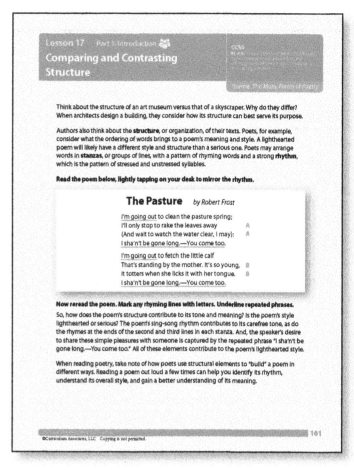

- Reinforce the idea that authors choose specific text structures to deliver the meaning they wish to impart. Understanding a text's structure will help students better understand a text's meaning.

Genre Focus

Literary Texts: Elegy

Tell students that in this lesson they will read different types of poems. Review that a poem is a piece of writing that uses language in an unusual way to express emotions, ideas, or experiences. Poems often use language that is descriptive and speaks to the senses. One type of poem is an elegy, which is a poem that mourns the loss of someone or something. Elegies often share the following characteristics:

- couplets, or sets of two lines, that form a unit, contain one complete idea, and often rhyme

- each couplet has a strong rhythm, which is repeated throughout the poem

- may use repetition of words and phrases

- express strong feelings of love and sorrow

Have students discuss why authors might choose to write an elegy such as "Annabel Lee." How might writing an elegy help an author express feelings about the loss of someone or something close to him or her? Discuss how the structure and meaning of an elegy might be different from another type of poem, such as free verse, which has no rhyme scheme or rhythm.

Tell students that they will study the text structure of an elegy and other types of poems, such as lyric poems and a sonnet, in this lesson. They will analyze how the structures affect the poems' meanings and styles.

AT A GLANCE

Students read a lyric poem. They then describe the poem's text structure and its impact on the poem's meaning and style.

STEP BY STEP

- Invite volunteers to tell what they learned on the previous page about analyzing poetic structure.

- Explain that in this lesson they will read a poem by Emily Dickinson and evaluate the poem's text structure and its impact on meaning and style.

- Read the poem aloud. Then read aloud the prompt: "Describe the poem's structure. Use details from the poem to develop your description of the structure."

- Tell students you will use a Think Aloud to demonstrate a way to answer the question.

Think Aloud: I know that structure is how a text is organized. This poem is written with three uniform stanzas of four lines each. Each stanza has its own rhyme scheme, with a sing-song rhythm pattern that gives a light, whimsical tone. I will record this information in the box labeled "Structure."

- Direct students to the chart on the next page. Point out that it helps them compare and contrast the structures and meanings of two different texts.

- Have students write about the structure of "Hope is the thing with feathers" in the appropriate box.

Think Aloud: Now I will think about the poem's meaning. I think the author delivers a positive message about hope and how hope can overcome challenges. The author compares hope to a bird, and how this bird can survive even the harshest storms.

- Have students complete the Meaning box for this poem in the chart.

- Next, have students use the information they recorded to describe how the structural elements impact the meaning and style of the poem. (*Sample response: By organizing the poem into three stanzas, the poet builds on the definition of hope. The poet uses a metaphor to compare hope to a singing bird in stanza 1, and in stanza 2 describes hope [the bird] surviving in difficult times [a storm]. The poet continues the metaphor in stanza 3.*)

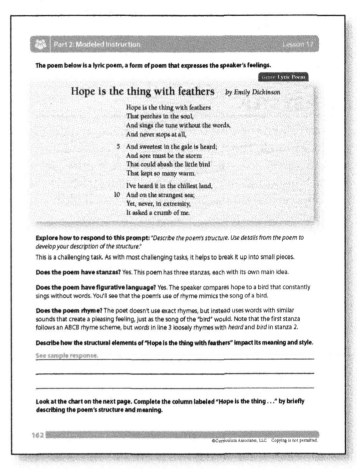

ELL Support: Superlatives

- Explain to students that superlatives are words that compare three or more things. Place three different-sized books on the desk. Write the word *biggest* on the board. Have a volunteer point to the biggest book. Then write the word *smallest* on the board and ask a volunteer to point to the smallest book. Circle the letters -est in each word and explain that superlatives use the letters -est to compare three or more objects or attributes.

- Point out the word *sweetest* in stanza 2. Ask students what is being compared. (*all songs*) Then point out the words *chillest* and *strangest* in stanza 3. Pair students and ask partners to determine what is being compared by each superlative. Have volunteers share their responses.

AT A GLANCE

Students read another lyric poem and compare the text structure and meaning of this poem with those of the poem on the previous page.

STEP BY STEP

- Tell students they will read another lyric poem and analyze its text structure. Then they will compare this poem to the poem from the previous page.

- The Close Reading helps students analyze how the stanzas are arranged in this poem and compare this structure to the previous poem. The Hint will help students compare the rhythm and rhyme patterns of each poem.

- Have students read "Dream Deferred."

- Then direct students to the chart and remind them that it helps to compare and contrast the structure and meaning of these two poems. Have students use the Close Reading and the Hint to complete the rest of the chart on this page.

- Next, have students respond to the Show Your Thinking. Place students into pairs to discuss the final question. Guide students to think about how the poets' chosen text structures impacts the meaning and style of the poems.

ANSWER ANALYSIS

Sample response: In "Hope is a thing with feathers," the poet organizes the poem into three stanzas of equal length. In "Dream Deferred," the poet organizes the text into different sized stanzas with the first and last stanzas only made up of one line. "Hope is a thing with feathers" has a more positive message about hope while "Dream Deferred" focuses more on the loss of hopes and dreams.

> **ERROR ALERT:** Students who could not correctly identify the structure of "Dream Deferred" may have had difficulty with the irregular and unpredictable stanza and line length pattern in the poem. Review the poem with these students to point out the one-line stanzas at the beginning and end of the poem.

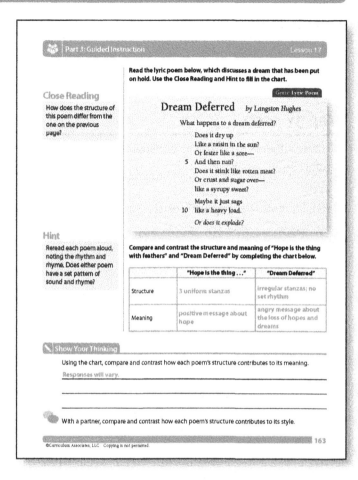

Tier Two Vocabulary: *Deferred*

- Point out the word *deferred* in the title and line 1 of the poem. Tell students that they may need to use word parts or dictionaries to understand the meaning of an unfamiliar word in a poem because poems do not always provide many context clues to suggest the word's meaning.

- Have students use a print or online dictionary to look up the meaning of *deferred* ("to put off or delay"). Then have them use this meaning to tell what the subject of the poem is. (*a dream that is put off until later*) **(RL.8.4; L.8.4c)**

AT A GLANCE

Students read a poem twice. After the first reading, you will ask three questions to check your students' understanding of the poem.

STEP BY STEP

- Have students read the poem silently without referring to the Study Buddy or the Close Reading text.

- Ask the following questions to ensure students' comprehension of the poem:

  Who is Annabel Lee? (*Annabel Lee is a maiden whom the speaker loved.*)

  What happens to Annabel Lee? (*She dies from an illness caused by a chill.*)

  How does the speaker remember his young love? (*He remembers her when the moon shines and when the stars sparkle.*)

- Then ask students to reread the poem and look at the Study Buddy think aloud. What does the Study Buddy help them think about?

Tip: The Study Buddy informs students that this poem is an elegy. Discuss with students that an elegy is a poem that mourns the loss of something or someone. Point out that knowing that this poem is an elegy will help them to identify the theme.

- Tell students to follow the directions in the Close Reading.

Tip: The Close Reading helps students identify the phrases in the poem that help create a fairy-tale feel. Discuss with students what a fairy-tale feel is and have them look for examples of creatures or other elements that are commonly found in fairy tales.

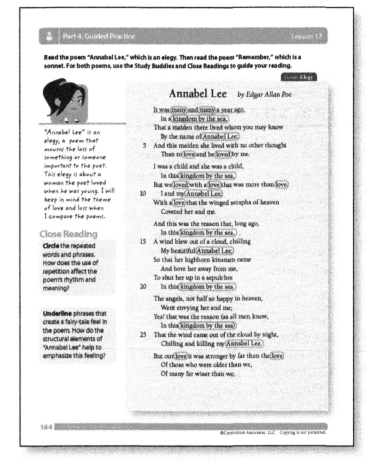

ELL Support: Compound Words

- Explain to students that a compound word is made up of two smaller words. Tell students that they can look at the two smaller words to figure out the meaning of the compound word.

- Point out the compound words *highborn* and *kinsmen* in line 17 of "Annabel Lee." Have partners work together to define the two compound words using the meanings of the smaller words. Have volunteers share their definitions with the class (highborn: *"born in a high rank,"* kinsmen: *"people of the same family"*). **(RL.8.4; L.8.4)**

AT A GLANCE

Students read another poem twice. After the first reading, you will ask three questions to check your students' understanding of the poem.

STEP BY STEP

- Have students read the poem silently without referring to the Study Buddy or the Close Reading text.

- Ask the following questions to ensure students' comprehension of the poem:

  Who is the speaker of the poem and who is the speaker addressing? (*The speaker is someone who is living, addressing someone who knows the speaker.*)

  What is the speaker asking the listener to do? (*The speaker wants the listener to remember her when she's gone and be happy in the memories.*)

  Why is "Remember" a suitable title? (*The poem is about remembering someone when he or she is gone.*)

- Then ask students to reread the poem and look at the Study Buddy think aloud. What does the Study Buddy help them think about?

Tip: The Study Buddy points out that "Remember" is a sonnet with 14 lines and encourages students to think about how the different forms of the two poems contribute to their styles. Point out that "Remember" expresses complex feelings in a compact form. Have students consider how the two poems might be different if their structures were reversed. How might "Remember" change if it were an elegy? How might "Annabel Lee" change if it were a sonnet?

- Tell students to follow the directions in the Close Reading.

Tip: The Close Reading guides students to mark the rhyme scheme and underline repeated words and phrases. Point out that by repeating these words and phrases, the poet is reinforcing the poem's theme that she wants her reader to remember her after she is gone. Point out that the rhyme scheme gives the poem a lyrical tone that imparts a sense of comfort, adding to the poem's theme of remembering.

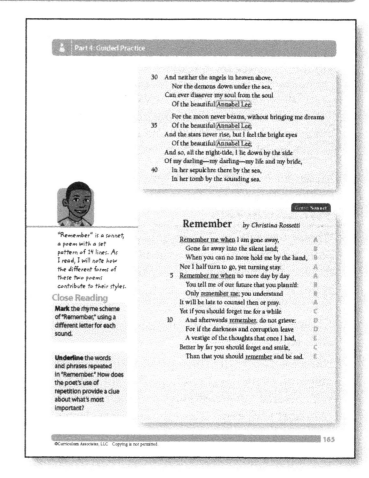

- Finally, have students answer the questions on page 166. Use the Answer Analysis to discuss correct and incorrect responses.

Tier Two Vocabulary: *Vestige*

- Point out the word *vestige* in line 12 of "Remember." Review with students that they may need to use reference books to determine the meanings of unfamiliar words in poetry that they read. Have partners use a dictionary to look up the word *vestige* ("*a trace or remnant*").

- Then have students use this definition to rewrite lines 11 and 12, using a synonym for the word *vestige*. Have volunteers share their new versions of lines 11 and 12. **(RL.8.4; L.8.4c)**

STEP BY STEP

- Have students read questions 1–3, using the Hints to help them answer the questions.

Tip: If students have trouble answering question 3, encourage them to read each poem aloud to help them get a feel for the rhythm and rhyme scheme that each poem has.

- Discuss with students the Answer Analysis below.

ANSWER ANALYSIS

1 Choice B is correct. The rhythm and the rhyme pattern lend themselves to the fairy-tale feeling. Choice A is incorrect. The speaker's love of the sea is not reflective of the theme. Choice C is incorrect because the poem does have rhyme and rhythm. Choice D is incorrect because the tone is longing and sadness, not anger.

2 Choice C is correct. The repetition in "Remember" emphasizes the speaker's hope that she will be remembered after she's gone, and the repetition in "Annabel Lee" emphasizes the speaker's deep sense of loss. Choice A is incorrect because the speaker in "Remember" is not mourning the loss of a loved one. Choices B and D are inaccurate representations of the poems' meanings.

3 Sample response: In "Annabel Lee," the speaker mourns his lost love by repeating her name. Even thought the poem's overall meaning is about death, the poet uses a sing-song rhythm to convey a fairy tale feel. In "Remember," the poet repeats the words *remember* and *remember me* to show that the speaker wants people to remember her after she's gone. The first two stanzas have the same rhyme scheme, but the third stanza has a different pattern, indicating a change in the speaker's thoughts.

RETEACHING

Use a chart to answer question 3. Draw the chart below, and work with students to fill in the boxes. Sample responses are provided.

	"Annabel Lee"	"Remember"
Structure	14-line sonnet, repetition, rhyme	6 stanzas, repetition, rhyme
Meaning	mourns lost love	wants to be remembered

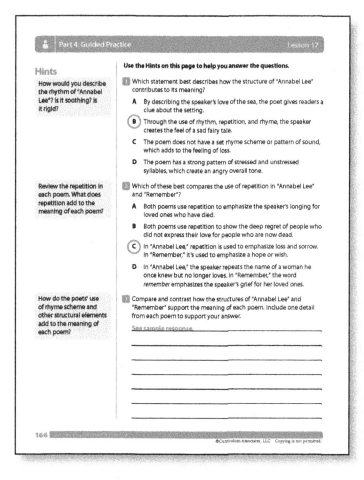

Integrating Standards

Use these questions and tasks as opportunities to interact with "Annabel Lee" and "Remember."

1 Summarize "Annabel Lee" and "Remember." **(RL.8.2)**

Summaries will vary. Students should mention the theme of mourning a lost love in "Annabel Lee" and hoping to be remembered by loved ones in "Remember," using details to support the main ideas.

2 What does the speaker in "Remember" mean when she says: "Better by far that you should forget and smile, / Than that you should remember and be sad"? **(RL.8.4)**

The speaker means that even if her loved ones forget her briefly, she wants them to remember her fondly rather than with sadness.

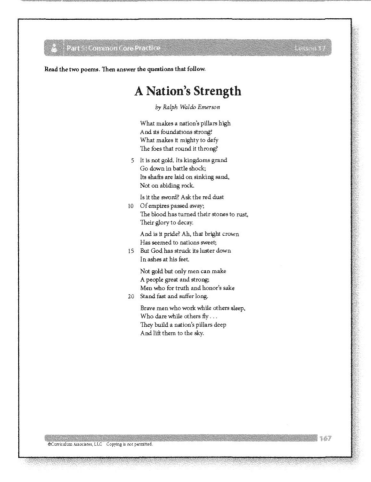

AT A GLANCE

Students independently read two poems and answer questions in a format that provides test practice.

STEP BY STEP

- Tell students to use what they have learned about reading closely and comparing text structure to read the poems on pages 167 and 168.

- Remind students to underline or circle repeated words or phrases or words that evoke meaning. Tell students to pay attention to whether each poem has a regular rhythm and rhyme pattern.

- Tell students to answer the questions on pages 168–170. For questions 1–4, they should fill in the correct circle on the Answer Form.

- When students have finished, use the Answer Analysis to discuss correct responses and the reasons for them. Have students fill in the Number Correct on the Answer Form.

ANSWER ANALYSIS

1 Choice A is correct. This response accurately defines the structure of the two poems. Choice B is incorrect because Whitman's poem is not a sonnet. Choice C is incorrect because Emerson's poem does have a set rhyme scheme. Choice D is incorrect because Emerson's poem does have a repeated rhythm pattern. **(DOK 3)**

Theme Connection

- How do all the poems in this lesson relate to the theme of the many forms of poetry?

- What is one fact or idea that you learned about poem forms and structures from each poem in this lesson?

©Curriculum Associates, LLC   Copying is not permitted.

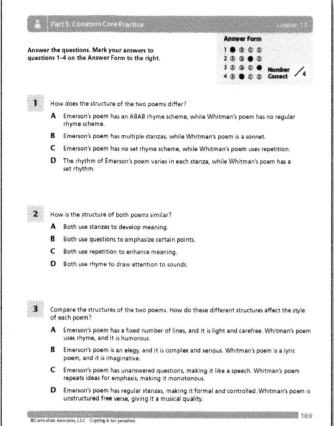

ANSWER ANALYSIS

2 Choice C is correct. Both poems use repetition. Choices A, B, and D are incorrect because "I Hear America Singing" does not use stanzas, questions to emphasize certain points, or rhyme. **(DOK 3)**

3 Choice D is correct; it correctly describes the structure of both poems. Choice A is incorrect; Whitman's poem is unstructured free verse, not rhyming or humorous. Choice B is incorrect; Emerson's poem is not an elegy. Choice C is incorrect; Emerson's poem poses questions, then answers the questions throughout the stanzas. **(DOK 3)**

4 Choice B is correct. It's common for poets using a set rhyme scheme, such as Emerson's ABAB pattern, to use stanza breaks to emphasize both their rhymes and their ideas. Whitman, on the other hand, wouldn't have wanted a reader to pause within the flow of language, so he chose a single stanza. Choice A is incorrect because no evidence supports the idea that either poet wanted to mask his content by the "at-a-glance" look of his poem.

Choice C is incorrect because both poems use varied language and repetitions but different structures. Choice D is incorrect. While both poems use rhythms (a very formal one in Emerson's case), neither does so to imitate specific sounds. **(DOK 3)**

5 Sample response: Emerson and Whitman both structure their poems in stanzas that each explore a single idea related to a main topic. Emerson uses six stanzas in his poem. The first stanza presents the main topic of the poem, which is to answer the question: What makes a nation strong? The following stanzas each explore an idea related to the topic. For example, his second stanza talks about gold, his third about military strength, and his fourth about pride. Whitman's poem, on the other hand, presents a single idea. He writes about all the different kinds of people in our country doing different kinds of work. He imagines each of them happy at their work and "singing." In conclusion, both poets use stanzas to organize ideas in their poems. **(DOK 4)**

Integrating Standards

Use these questions and tasks as opportunities to interact with "I Hear America Singing" and "A Nation's Strength."

1 What is the central theme of "I Hear America Singing"? Use examples from the poem to support your response. **(RL.8.2)**

Whitman's poem celebrates the strengths of America's working population. He describes the many different types of workers in our country. By describing the workers in song, Whitman demonstrates the strength and joy of America's varied workers.

2 What does the speaker in "A Nation's Strength" believe makes a nation strong? **(RL.8.1)**

The speaker believes that the true strength of a nation is in its people. He says that brave and honorable citizens are what make a nation strong.

3 In "A Nation's Strength," what is the speaker describing in stanza 3 when he asks "Is it the sword?" Write your answer. **(RL.8.4; W.8.4)**

The speaker is asking if a nation's strength in battle is what makes it strong, and the answer is no. The speaker goes on to explain that nations who conquered others in bloody wars do not win everlasting strength. Their battle victories are won at the cost of the lost lives of others, and this glory is fleeting.

4 Discuss in small groups: How are the central themes of "I Hear America Singing" and "A Nation's Strength" alike? Use examples from both poems to support your answer. **(SL.8.1)**

Discussions will vary. Students should point out that both poems address the theme that nations are built on the strength of its people. In Whitman's poem, he celebrates the strong and varied American workers, and in Emerson's poem, he describes a nation's strength as being built by the strength and honor of its people.

Writing Activities

More to the Story (W.8.4)

- Have students reread the poem "The Pasture." Explain that the speaker is going into the pasture to do chores. Have students imagine what other kinds of things the speaker might encounter as he goes into the pasture, or when he returns to the farmhouse.

- Point out the rhythm and rhyme scheme of the poem and discuss how these structures contribute to the poem's carefree, cheerful tone. Then challenge students to write two new stanzas for the poem, using the same rhythm and rhyme pattern.

Metaphors (L.8.5a)

- Explain that a metaphor is an implied comparison of two seemingly unrelated things, such as *Life is a journey*. Point out that a metaphor makes a comparison without using the words *like* or *as*.

- Reread "Hope is the thing with feathers." Explain that Dickinson uses a metaphor to compare the emotion of *hope* to a bird. Have students name other emotions, such as *joy, fear, sorrow, love, hate*, and *curiosity*. Have students write a poem of at least two stanzas about one of these emotions, using a metaphor as the first line of the poem. Give an example such as *Love is a roller coaster*.

LISTENING ACTIVITY (SL.8.1, SL.8.6)

Listen Closely/Add to the Rhyme

- Have students practice rhyme and rhythm patterns by having them change a familiar nursery rhyme. For example, you could say: "Humpty Dumpty sat in a tree" then have a student add the next line with a rhyming word for "tree."

- Have each student repeat the previous rhyme before adding a new rhyme, ensuring that each student listens closely.

MEDIA ACTIVITY (RL.8.2, RL.8.4)

Be Creative/Illustrate a Poem

- Have students choose one of the poems from this lesson and create an illustration to represent the poem's central theme or message. Encourage students to use a variety of media in their illustrations.

- Invite students to share their illustrations with the class and explain how their picture represents the poem's message.

DISCUSSION ACTIVITY (SL.8.1)

Talk in a Group/Talk about Dreams

- Have students reread the poem "Dream Deferred." Have them discuss how the speaker feels about not being able to achieve a dream.

- Then place students in small groups. Have them discuss a dream they might have for your school and a dream they might have for your city or town. Have each group make a list of at least one dream for your school and one dream for your city, and talk about ways to achieve these dreams.

- Invite groups to share their dreams with the class.

RESEARCH ACTIVITY (W.8.7; SL.8.4)

Research and Present/Poetry Movement

- Have students use this lesson's poems as a starting point for a research report on a poetry movement. For example, Langston Hughes is a poet from the Harlem Renaissance and Ralph Waldo Emerson was part of the Transcendentalism movement.

- Have students find multiple sources to research their chosen poetry movement. Encourage students to include at least one additional poem from their chosen movement in their report.

- Have students share their reports with the class. Encourage listeners to pose questions.

Analyzing Point of View

LESSON OBJECTIVES

- Analyze the techniques the author uses to shape the audience's or reader's point of view.

- Analyze the ways in which the differing points of view of the characters, narrator, and audience or reader create suspense, humor, or dramatic irony.

THE LEARNING PROGRESSION

- **Grade 7:** CCSS RL.7.6 asks students to analyze the different points of view of various characters and narrators in a text.

- **Grade 8: CCSS RL.8.6 broadens the context by asking students to consider the audience's or reader's point of view, as well as to determine how the author uses differing points of view to create the mood and tone of a text.**

- **Grade 9** CCSS RL.9.6 requires students to analyze a particular point of view or culture reflected in a work of literature from outside the United States.

PREREQUISITE SKILLS

- Identify the narrator's and characters' points of view in a text.

- Recognize the differences between what the narrator knows and what the other characters know.

- Determine the techniques authors use to shape the points of view of their readers.

TAP STUDENTS' PRIOR KNOWLEDGE

- Tell students they will be working on a lesson about analyzing point of view. Review that a character's point of view is revealed through how he or she thinks, believes, or feels about other story characters or events. Note that different characters have different points of view, as does the reader or the audience.

- Using a current movie as an example, discuss how the makers of suspense movies use differing points of view to shape the viewers' experiences. They allow viewers to see and know more information than the characters see and know. This difference in perspective is what builds excitement and suspense.

- Go on to explain how, in some movies, the moviemakers add sudden plot twists that produce unexpected events. This is meant to entertain by adding surprise or humor. Have students describe examples of scenes from this type of movie.

- Point out that authors use similar techniques to shape their readers' points of view. Note that, as readers, students need to be aware of their own points of view as well as those of the characters. This will help students to better understand the author's intentions and sustain interest in what they are reading.

Ready *Teacher Toolbox*		*teacher-toolbox.com*
	Prerequisite Skills	*RL.8.6*
Ready Lessons	✓	✓
Tools for Instruction		✓
Interactive Tutorials		

CCSS Focus

RL.8.6 Analyze how differences in the points of view of the characters and the audience or reader (e.g., created through the use of dramatic irony) creates such effects as suspense or humor.

ADDITIONAL STANDARDS: **RL.8.1, RL.8.2, RL.8.3, RL.8.4, RL.8.7; L.8.2a, L.8.4a, L.8.4d, L.8.5a, L.8.5c; W.8.2, W.8.4, W.8.7; SL.8.1, SL.8.4** (*See page A39 for full text.*)

AT A GLANCE

By studying a cartoon, students learn to recognize points of view. They learn to analyze how the irony in situations can create humor or suspense.

STEP BY STEP

- Read the first two paragraphs that include the definitions of *point of view* and *dramatic irony*. Point out that suspense movies often use the technique of dramatic irony to create excitement.

- Have students study the cartoon. Tell them to look for evidence that helps them understand what is going on and how the viewers' knowledge contrasts with the girl's point of view. (*Viewers see a spider climbing up her leg, but the girl is unaware of it.*)

- Explain that the chart shows how to contrast the points of view of the girl and the audience. Ask students to compare evidence in the second column of the chart with details in the scene.

- Review the third column, and contrast the girl's point of view with the audience's point of view. Ask: How is your point of view shaped by details you know that the girl has yet to realize?

- Emphasize that the way authors shape their readers' point of view can create humor or suspense or both. Share an example of a book that you couldn't put down. Explain how suspense, surprises, and plot twists kept you reading on.

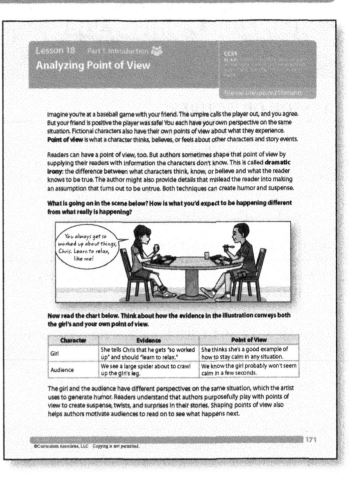

Genre Focus

Literary Texts: Novel

Tell students that in this lesson they will read an excerpt from a novel. Explain that a novel is a longer work of fiction that tells a story about invented characters, settings, and events. Discuss the following characteristics of a novel with students:

- includes a complex plot, setting(s), and theme

- often provides the feelings and perspectives of major characters as well as their words and actions

- involves a problem that one or more characters are trying to solve

- is usually divided into scenes, chapters, or sections

Based on these characteristics, have students name some examples of novels they have read. Discuss the similarities and differences between short fiction stories and novels.

Explain that students will read an excerpt from *Esperanza Rising*, a novel about a young Mexican girl whose change in circumstances force her family to move to the United States. "Homecoming" is a realistic fiction story about a family's trip to the airport for a special surprise. The realistic fiction story "Tutor in Shining Armor" tells about a boy's embarrassing misunderstanding over a situation he overhears in the school cafeteria.

AT A GLANCE

Students read a realistic fiction story. They contrast the reader's point of view with the characters' point of view and analyze how the author achieved this contrast.

STEP BY STEP

- Invite volunteers to tell what they learned on the previous page about point of view and dramatic irony. Tell them that now they will analyze the effects an author achieves by presenting differing points of view.

- Read "Homecoming." Then read the questions: "How does the reader's point of view toward story events differ from that of the characters? How does the author produce this difference in points of view?"

- Now tell students you will use a Think Aloud to demonstrate a way of answering the questions.

Think Aloud: From story details, I learn the characters' differing points of view. Liz and Oscar seem to be planning something that Kate knows nothing about, but it won't make her angry. I also learn their suitcases are empty, so that must be part of their plan.

- Direct students to the chart, and explain that it shows a way of comparing different points of view. Read and discuss Liz and Oscar's points of view, which can be inferred from the evidence.

Think Aloud: Now I'll look for evidence telling how Kate feels about what's happening. The text says she "had her heart set" on going to the concert and is "desperately" hoping to make it there. She seems upset.

- Have students add evidence from the story and Kate's point of view to the chart.

Think Aloud: As the reader, I've learned that Kate's point of view is very different from the cousins'. The author must be giving me, the reader, extra information to create suspense. I'm wondering what exactly is the cousins' plan and how Kate will react to it. The author must want me to read on to find out more.

- Have students add the story evidence and the reader's point of view to the chart. Then have partners respond to the last question. (*Sample response: Kate thinks Liz and Oscar are taking a trip somewhere and need her to drive them to the airport. The reader knows that the cousins are planning some kind of surprise.*)

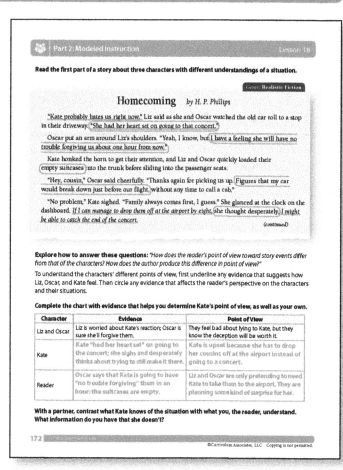

ELL Support: Idioms

- Explain that idioms are phrases with meanings that are different from the meanings of the individual words.

- Point out the idiom *she had her heart set on* in sentence 2. Ask students how they know that Kate wants to go to the concert. (*Liz thinks Kate will be upset that she is not going; Kate's thoughts at the end of paragraph 5.*) Now ask students what they think *she had her heart set on* means. (*She wants it very much; she has a strong desire to go the concert.*)

- Have students find the idiom *picking us up* in paragraph 4. Have partners work together to illustrate the literal meaning of the words and the meaning of the idiom. (**RL.8.4; L.8.5a**)

AT A GLANCE

Students continue reading about the trip to the airport. They complete a chart and analyze the effect achieved by knowing the characters' differing points of view.

STEP BY STEP

- Tell students they will continue reading about Liz, Oscar, and Kate's trip to the airport.

- The Close Reading helps students identify clues that something special is about to happen at the airport. The Hint will help them analyze the characters' and reader's feelings about story events.

- Have students read the passage and underline clues that helped them recognize that something was about to happen, as directed by the Close Reading.

- Ask volunteers to share the text they underlined. Have them explain how each clue helped them know that something special was about to happen.

- Have students complete the activities on the page. Then discuss their responses. (*Sample response to Show Your Thinking: The author provides details about the cousins' plan that Kate doesn't know but holds back on the surprise itself until the end. This creates suspense for the reader. At the end, even though the reader knows more than Kate, the mother's appearance is an unexpected twist.*)

ANSWER ANALYSIS

Sample response for Evidence—*Liz and Oscar:* Oscar jumps out of car, comes out grinning. *Kate:* asks why they are going to Arrivals, questions suitcase weight; cries tears of joy. *Reader:* knows characters' differing viewpoints, woman in army garb hurries out, woman is Kate's mom, "the best lie they ever told"

Sample response for Point of View—*Liz and Oscar:* eager for their plan to succeed. *Kate:* confused, then grateful for the surprise. *Reader:* aware of the cousins' deception as events unfold, Kate appreciates her cousins' surprise and her mom's visit.

ERROR ALERT: Students who have difficulty identifying Kate's point of view about the ending may not have understood that a character's point of view can change. Have them reread the story conclusion, focusing on what Kate says and does.

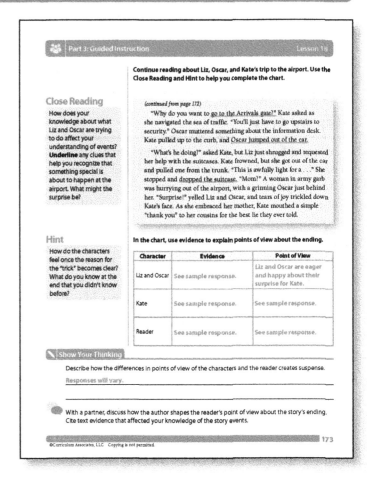

Tier Two Vocabulary: *Trickled*

- Direct students to the word *trickled* in paragraph 2. Have students use context clues to figure out what *trickled* means. (*"dripped slowly"*) Ask students to name the clues in the sentence that helped them determine the meaning of the word. (*"tears;" "down Kate's face"*) (**RL.8.4; L.8.4a**)

- Have students rewrite the sentence using a synonym for *trickled*, such as *dripped*, *leaked*, or *streamed*.

AT A GLANCE

Students read a story about a misunderstanding. After the first reading, you will ask three questions to check your students' comprehension of the story.

STEP BY STEP

• Have students read the story silently without referring to the Close Reading. Then ask questions to ensure students' comprehension of the text:

What are Chloe and Ava practicing? (*They are doing an acting exercise.*)

Why does James offer to help Ava with Algebra? (*He has a crush on Ava, and he overhears her say that she is failing Algebra.*)

Does Ava really need tutoring? How do you know? (*No; she is just acting. Paragraph 1 tells she is doing an acting exercise with Chloe. The text also says she is a straight-A student.*)

• Ask students to reread paragraph 1 and look at the Study Buddy think aloud. What does the Study Buddy help them think about?

Tip: The Study Buddy guides students to think about each character's point of view. Review that the author may give readers information that only one character knows or that none know. Recognizing these differences will help students understand what the author is trying to achieve by using this technique. Ask students to think about why the author chose to reveal this information to readers and how it impacts their point of view of story events.

• Have students read the rest of the story. Tell them to follow the directions in the Close Reading.

Tip: Point out that authors don't always state the reasons for a character's actions. Readers have to make inferences. Ask students how they think James feels about Ava and why these feelings might prompt him to offer to tutor her.

• Finally, have students answer the questions on page 175. Use the Answer Analysis to discuss correct and incorrect responses.

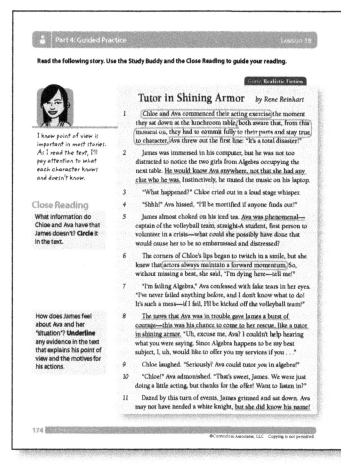

Tier Two Vocabulary: *Immersed*

• Point out the word *immersed* in paragraph 2. Explain that the word can mean "dip into or cover with liquid" or "deeply involved in." Have students use context clues to figure out its meaning here. (*"deeply involved in"*) Encourage students to use a dictionary or a thesaurus to verify this meaning. (**RL.8.4; L.8.4a, L.8.4d**)

• Have students suggest synonyms for *immersed* that would make sense in the sentence context. (*absorbed, engrossed, involved*)

STEP BY STEP

- Have students read questions 1–3, using the Hints to help them answer those questions.

> **Tip:** Students who have trouble answering question 1 may not have understood that James doesn't know what the reader knows. Point out that the girls began acting as soon as they sat down, so James doesn't know what they are really doing.

- Discuss with students the Answer Analysis below.

ANSWER ANALYSIS

1   The correct choice is D. James overhears the girls talking about Ava failing Algebra. Choice A is incorrect. Ava says she might get kicked off the team for failing Algebra. Choice B is incorrect. James doesn't know the girls are acting. Choice C is incorrect. It doesn't describe James's point of view.

2   The correct choice is A. The reader knows Ava is pretending, so it is humorous when James rushes in to help. Choice B is incorrect. Readers don't know whether or not Ava is a tutor. Choice C is incorrect. Ava is acting, not trying to play a joke. Choice D is incorrect. Ava is only pretending to be failing.

3   Sample response: James doesn't know that the girls are only doing acting exercises, while Chloe and Ava don't know that James is listening in and believes that Ava is really failing her Algebra class. The reader, however, knows everything, including that James has a crush on Ava. The author supplies the differing points of view in order to set up a humorous situation.

RETEACHING

Use a chart to answer question 3. Draw the chart below, and work with students to fill in the boxes. Sample responses are provided.

Character	Evidence	Point of View
Chloe and Ava	commenced acting exercise	find James's offer humorous
James	would know Ava anywhere	concerned, embarrassed, happy
Reader	The girls are acting but James doesn't know; James is listening in.	knows that the situation is humorous

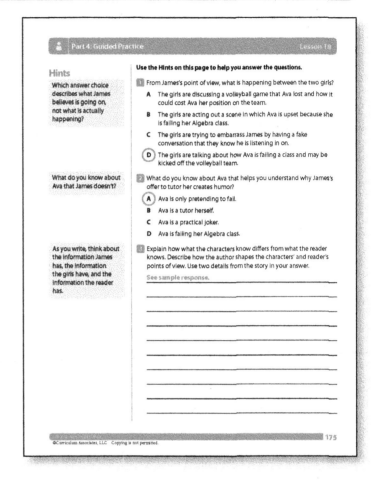

Integrating Standards

Use these questions to further students' understanding of "A Tutor in Shining Armor."

1   Ava says, "That's sweet, James. We were just doing a little acting, but thanks for the offer. Want to listen in?" What does this dialogue tell you about her character? **(RL.8.3)**

This dialogue shows that Ava is polite and sensitive to the feelings of others. She makes James feel better about misunderstanding the situation.

2   James tries to come to Ava's rescue, like a "tutor in shining armor." What does this phrase allude to? What does it tell you about James? **(RL.8.4; L.8.5a)**

This phrase is an allusion to being a white knight in shining armor, or a hero who rides in to save the helpless heroine. It shows that James wants to be a hero and help Ava.

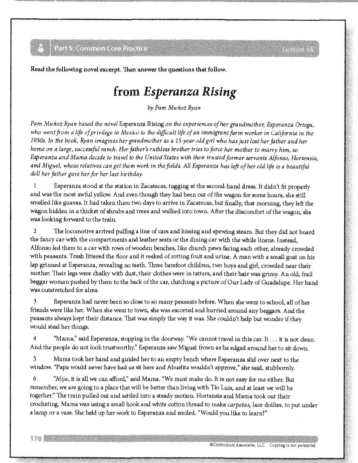

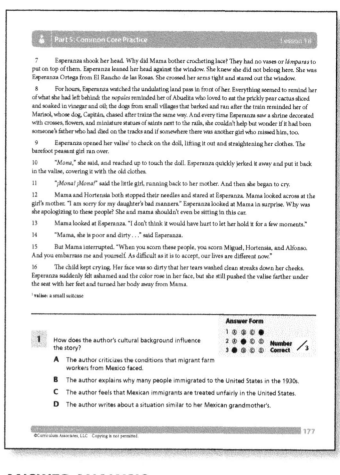

AT A GLANCE

Students independently read an excerpt from a novel and answer questions in a format that provides test practice.

STEP BY STEP

- Tell students to use what they have learned about reading closely and analyzing different points of view to read the novel excerpt on pages 176 and 177.

- Tell students to underline or circle important details about the characters' points of view.

- Tell students to answer the questions on pages 177 and 178. For questions 1–3, they should fill in the correct circle on the Answer Form.

- When students have finished, use the Answer Analysis to discuss correct responses and the reasons for them. Have students fill in the Number Correct on the Answer Form.

ANSWER ANALYSIS

1 Choice D is correct. The author tells a story based on a situation similar to her grandmother's life. Choices A and C are incorrect. The author does not express an opinion about the conditions of migrant farm workers or the treatment of Mexican immigrants. Choice B is incorrect. The author explains why one family immigrates to the U.S. **(DOK 3)**

2 Choice B is correct. Esperanza's actions show she is unhappy and does not want to change. This creates suspense. Choice A is incorrect. Esperanza's behavior does not add humor. Choice C is incorrect. Esperanza's actions don't show she agrees with her mother. Choice D is incorrect. The reader knows only what the characters know. **(DOK 2)**

Theme Connection

- How do all the texts in this lesson relate to the theme of unexpected moments?

- Compare two of the unexpected moments.

3 Choice A is correct. Mama tells Esperanza that she should have let the girl hold her doll and should not scorn people. Choice B is incorrect. Mama says that their lives are different, but she does not agree with Esperanza's treatment of people. Choice C is incorrect. Mama does not show regret that they have to work. She says their lives will be better than if they had stayed with Tío Luis. Choice D is incorrect. Mama thinks Esperanza should share her doll, not protect it. **(DOK 2)**

4 Sample response: Pam Muñoz Ryan based the novel on her grandmother's experiences as a Mexican migrant farm worker, and Ryan expresses her sympathy toward peasants in Mama's character. Mama shows her compassion for the peasant girl by disapproving of Esperanza's behavior with the doll. Mama tells Esperanza, "'When you scorn these people, you scorn Miguel, Hortensia, and Alfonso. And you embarrass me and yourself.'" Mama is willing to see everyone as equal and expresses kindness toward people who are less fortunate, much like Ryan must have understood that her grandmother deserved respect in spite of the difficult life she led. **(DOK 3)**

---

2 Reread this sentence from paragraph 16:

   Esperanza suddenly felt ashamed and the color rose in her face, but she still pushed the valise farther under the seat with her feet and turned her body away from Mama.

What effect does Esperanza's point of view have on the story?

A It creates humor by emphasizing Esperanza's silly and selfish behavior.

B It creates suspense by raising doubt that Esperanza will ever adjust to her new life.

C It creates surprise by revealing how Mama and Esperanza really agree with each other.

D It creates dramatic irony by introducing information that the characters don't have.

3 Which statement best describes Mama's point of view in the story?

A Mama thinks all people, even the poor and dirty, deserve respect and compassion.

B Mama secretly agrees with Esperanza but has to act as if she likes the peasants.

C Mama regrets that she and Esperanza have to work because they are poor now.

D Mama thinks Esperanza should protect the doll because it was her father's last gift.

4 Explain how the author's cultural background is reflected in Mama's point of view about peasants in the story. Cite at least two details from the text to support your answer.

   See sample response.

   _____

   _____

   _____

   _____

   _____

   _____

   ☑ **Self Check**   *Go back and see what you can check off on the Self Check on page 144.*

170   ©Curriculum Associates, LLC Copying is not permitted.

Integrating Standards

Use these questions and tasks as opportunities to interact with "Esperanza Rising."

1 Why do you think Esperanza is struggling with the idea of riding the train with peasants? Support your answer with details from the text. **(RL.8.1)**

Esperanza is probably struggling because she is nervous and afraid. The text says that she used to be "escorted and hurried around any beggars." When she was rich, she never associated with peasants because they "always kept their distance."

2 How does Esperanza's refusal to share her doll propel the story's action? **(RL.8.3)**

After Esperanza refuses to share her doll, Mama lectures her, saying that she must accept her new life. Esperanza's actions indicate she is not ready to do so.

3 In paragraph 10, what does *jerked* mean? What connotation does this word have that helps you understand Esperanza's actions? **(RL.8.4; L.8.5c)**

Jerked means "pulled away quickly." It has a negative connotation, showing that Esperanza yanked the doll away quickly with a negative attitude toward the girl.

4 Summarize: Write a summary of this story. **(RL.8.2; W.8.4)**

Esperanza and Mama are moving to California with their servants to avoid having to live with Tío Luis. It is difficult for both of them, but Mama is determined to make the best of the situation. Esperanza, however, is disgusted by the people and conditions and refuses to accept that this situation is her new life.

5 Discuss in small groups: What is the theme, or life lesson, that the author conveys in this story? What details help you understand this theme? **(RL.8.2; SL.8.1)**

Discussions will vary. Encourage students to think about what the characters learn from the events and how their perspectives change as the story develops.

Writing Activities

Compare Works from Diverse World Cultures (W.8.2)

- Challenge students to compare the excerpt from *Esperanza Rising* by Pam Muñoz Ryan with a novel by an author from another world culture, such as *The Year of Impossible Goodbyes* by Sook Nyul Choi or *The Not-So-Star-Spangled Life of Sunita Sen* by Mitali Perkins.

- Begin by discussing how the characters of Esperanza and her mother reflected the experiences of the author's Mexican grandmother. Ask students to cite text details that reveal something about Mexican culture.

- Have students write an essay to compare and contrast the two novels. They should describe how the culture of each author is revealed and how the author has drawn on his or her background to create the story. Allow time for students to share their essays. Then discuss the cultural perspectives communicated in each work.

Punctuation: Dashes (L.8.2a)

- Have a few students read aloud the last sentence in paragraph 6 of "Tutor in Shining Armor." Explain that the dash is used to indicate a pause or break in the sentence. Point out that when they read the text aloud, they paused at the dash before reading the second part. Also discuss the dash in the last sentence in paragraph 7.

- Have students write lines of dialogue between two friends, using two or more dashes to indicate pauses.

LISTENING ACTIVITY (SL.8.4)

Listen Closely/Cumulative Retell

- Divide students into small groups to retell events from "A Tutor in Shining Armor," one event at a time in sequence.

- Each student must repeat the event named by the previous student before saying the next one, making each student have to listen closely.

DISCUSSION ACTIVITY (SL.8.1)

Talk in a Group/Talk About Respect for Others

- Ask students to recall that in "Tutor in Shining Armor," Chloe makes fun of James when he offers to tutor Ava. In contrast, Ava makes James feel important and invites him to join them. Point out that treating others with respect, as Ava does, helps make school a better place to learn.

- Have students form small groups to discuss ways to treat their fellow students with respect. Have them make a list of "Dos" and "Don'ts" for treating others.

- Allow 10 to 15 minutes for discussion. Then have each group share its results with the class.

MEDIA ACTIVITY (RI.8.7)

Evaluate Mediums/Surprise Party Invitation

- Remind students that when they plan a surprise party, they have information that the guest of honor doesn't, which results in a surprise.

- Tell students to work in groups to plan a surprise party and create a print or e-invite. The invitation should include important party details and how the element of surprise will be incorporated.

- Have students discuss the advantages and disadvantages of print or electronic invitations.

RESEARCH ACTIVITY (W.8.7; SL.8.4)

Research and Present/Give a Presentation

- Tell students that conditions were difficult for migrant workers in the first half of the 1900s. Cesar Chavez and Dolores Huerta were two leaders who worked for change.

- Ask students to choose one of these leaders to research. Have them prepare an oral presentation on the life and work of the leader they chose. Tell them to include visuals such as time lines and audio clips of the leader speaking.

- Have students present their reports to the class.

SCORING GUIDE AND ANSWER ANALYSIS

Literary Passage Answer Analysis

1 Ⓐ Ⓑ Ⓒ ●   4 ● Ⓑ Ⓒ Ⓓ

2 Ⓐ Ⓑ Ⓒ ●   5 Ⓐ ● Ⓒ Ⓓ

3A ● Ⓑ Ⓒ Ⓓ   7 Ⓐ ● Ⓒ Ⓓ

3B ● Ⓑ Ⓒ Ⓓ

1   Choice D is correct. Katie is acting in a serious manner. She leads the hike and takes charge.

Choice A is incorrect. Although Katie is serious about the hike, nothing in the text suggests she's not enjoying it. Choice B is incorrect. There is no evidence that Katie spends all of her time working hard. She just knows a lot about nature. Choice C is also incorrect. Katie and Jim are on a hike together. It's not her job to lead her older cousin. It has just turned out that way. *(RL.8.4; DOK 2)*

2   Choice D is correct. Jim's allusion to Alice's adventure with the mushroom in Wonderland suggests that at this point, he is unconvinced of his cousin's superior knowledge of the outdoors. He is joking about her warning not to eat the plants.

Choice A is incorrect. Jim follows Katie's instructions and avoids touching or eating the pokeberries. His allusion to a fantasy story shows that he is not convinced of Katie's superior knowledge. Choice B is incorrect. Jim does not seem to believe that the woods are a magical place. Choice C is also incorrect. Jim does not seem too worried about the hidden dangers of the woods. He makes the allusion to make fun of Katie's knowledge of the woods. *(RL.8.4; DOK 3)*

3   **Part A:** Choice A is correct. Botanists study plants, enabling them to recommend which fruits are safe to eat. The other choices describe people who may know about edible berries, but with less authority than botanists. *(RL.8.4; DOK 2)*

Part B: Choice A is correct. This word indicates that pokeberry is part of a plant, which plant scientists know the most about. Choices B and D are incorrect because the words do not give information about what a pokeberry or botanists are. Choice C is incorrect because it is not a common word, so it's not helpful in identifying another unknown word. *(RL.8.4; DOK 2)*

4   Choice A is correct. The dramatic irony in the story is created when Jim assumes he knows more than his younger cousin. The reader can see that Katie knows more than he does.

Choice B is incorrect. Katie is younger than Jim but she doesn't act older. She just has more information about the plants and birds in the woods. This is not dramatic irony. Choice C is incorrect. Jim's question about animals eating plants that may be poisonous does hint that he knows less than he had thought. However, the irony is that the reader can tell that he doesn't know more than Katie. Choice D is also incorrect. Jim's belief that he knows more than Katie about the outdoors is obviously incorrect and he does start to realize that. But this is not an example of dramatic irony or humor. *(RL.8.6; DOK 3)*

5   Choice B is correct. The word "debatable" indicates that scientists disagree on the danger of the pokeberry plant.

Choice A is incorrect. Scientists are not baffled by the pokeberry. They know that it is not always clear at what point the plant is toxic for people. Choice C is incorrect. There is no evidence in the story that berry-bearing plants are often dangerous. Choice D is also incorrect. The word "debatable" does not indicate that botanists are quarrelsome. They just don't agree on how dangerous the plant may be. *(RL.8.4; DOK 2)*

7   Choice B is correct. The word *learn'd* suggests that the astronomer has book knowledge but lacks imagination and an appreciation of nature.

Choice A is incorrect. Although the astronomer is a great scholar, the word *learn'd* makes fun of the astronomer. He understands facts, but he has no imagination. Choice C is incorrect. The speaker is not impressed by the astronomer or by his lecture. The speaker feels that the lecturer focuses only on facts and data, and not the beauty and wonder of nature. Choice D is also incorrect. There is no evidence in the poem that the lecturer is humble. The word *learn'd* shows that the scientist understands facts but has no appreciation for nature. *(RL.8.4; DOK 3)*

SAMPLE RESPONSES

Short Response

6 Jim starts out feeling very confident about his knowledge of the woods. He also uses the fact that he is older than Katie to suggest that he knows more than she does. The reader sees through this immediately because Katie corrects everything Jim says. Jim's information is wrong or confused. Katie's information about the birds and the plants is correct. It shows that Jim does not know as much as she does. The reader is not fooled by Jim's opinion of himself. It's clear that Katie is more knowledgeable. *(RL.8.6; DOK 3)*

8 The narrator of the poem is very happy at the end of the poem to be standing outside staring up at actual stars in "perfect silence." This is a very positive moment for him, and it contrasts with his negative feelings earlier on. In the first part of the poem, he expresses how "tired and sick" he felt after listening to the astronomer. The narrator obviously did not enjoy the astronomer's lecture, with all of its proofs, figures, charts, and diagrams. All the talk about stars meant little to him compared with looking at the stars themselves. *(RL.8.4; DOK 3)*

9 In the poem, the speaker wants the reader to side with him in his negative view of the astronomer and his lecture. He mentions the charts and diagrams and all the math that went with them so that the reader understands precisely what he found dull. Listening to the astronomer and then hearing "much applause" from others for his lecture makes the narrator feel "tired and sick." He does not share the audience's enthusiasm for the lecture. His strong point of view attempts to draw the reader into sharing his opinion of the event. *(RL.8.6; DOK 3)*

Performance Task

10 The poem "When I Heard the Learn'd Astronomer" and the story "The Expert" have different structures. The poem is structured like a monologue that expresses only the speaker's thoughts and feelings. The short story expresses ideas through a setting, characters, and plot. Both the poem and the story are narratives but they have different structures and tell their stories in different ways.

In the poem, the speaker shows us how he feels about the lecture. He leaves because he doesn't agree with the astronomer's lecture. There is no dialogue or other point of view in the poem. We know that the speaker is reacting to "the proofs, the figures...the charts and the diagrams." The speaker goes outside to look up and enjoy the night sky "in perfect silence." He does not want to learn facts about nature. We never see what the audience at the lecture thinks. We only know what the speaker thinks.

In the story, we see things mainly from Jim's point of view. We also learn how Katie views things by reading the dialogue. Jim sees only beauty, but Katie sees both beauty and danger in the woods. In the first part of the story, Jim thinks he must know more than Katie because he is older than her. By the end of the story, he respects her knowledge. Jim changes what he thinks in response to Katie. The structure allows the reader to see that Jim's opinion of himself is not correct and that Katie knows what she is talking about.

The poem shows only what the speaker thinks, and he never changes. The plot of the story shows us what each character thinks, how they react to each other, and how Jim changes. In each case, the author uses the structure to help develop the meaning of the text. *(RL.8.5; DOK 4)*

SCORING RUBRICS

Short-Response Rubric

2 points   The response is accurate, complete, and fulfills all requirements of the task. Text-based support and examples are included. Any information that goes beyond the text is relevant to the task.

1 point   The response is partially accurate and fulfills some requirements of the task. Some information may be inaccurate, too general, or confused. Support and examples may be insufficient or not text-based.

0 points   The response is inaccurate, poorly organized, or does not respond to the task.

Performance Task Rubric

4 points   The response
- Fulfills all requirements of the task
- Uses varied sentence types and some sophisticated vocabulary
- Includes relevant and accurate details from the texts as well as text-based inferences
- Demonstrates a thorough understanding of the texts
- Maintains a clear focus and organization
- Is fluent and demonstrates a clear voice
- Uses correct spelling, grammar, capitalization, and punctuation

3 points   The response
- Fulfills all requirements of the task
- Uses simple sentences and grade-level vocabulary
- Includes relevant and accurate details from the texts
- Demonstrates a mainly literal understanding of the texts
- Maintains a mostly clear focus and organization
- Is fluent and demonstrates some sense of voice
- Uses mostly correct spelling, grammar, capitalization, and punctuation

2 points   The response
- Fulfills some requirements of the task
- Uses simple sentences, some fragments, and grade-level vocabulary
- Includes some relevant and accurate details from the texts
- Demonstrates some misunderstandings or gaps in understanding of the texts
- Attempts to maintain a clear focus and organization
- Is difficult to read, includes some inaccuracies, and demonstrates little or no sense of voice
- Contains some inaccurate spelling, grammar, capitalization, and punctuation that may hinder understanding

1 point   The response
- Fulfills few requirements of the task
- Uses sentence fragments and below-grade-level vocabulary
- Includes no details or irrelevant details to support the response
- Demonstrates very little understanding of the texts
- Does not establish a clear focus or organization
- Is difficult to read, contains many inaccuracies, and demonstrates no sense of voice
- Uses incorrect spelling, grammar, capitalization, and punctuation to an extent that impedes understanding

0 points   The response is irrelevant, poorly organized, or illegible.

Evaluating an Argument

LESSON OBJECTIVES

- Identify the main argument made in a text.
- Identify claims made to develop the main argument.
- Identify and evaluate reasons and evidence given to support the claims.
- Identify evidence that isn't related to the claim.

THE LEARNING PROGRESSION

- **Grade 7:** CCSS RI.7.8 requires students to trace and evaluate the argument and specific claims in a text, assessing whether the reasoning is sound and the evidence is relevant and sufficient to support the claims.

- **Grade 8: CCSS RI.8.8 builds on the Grade 7 standard by requiring students to evaluate an author's effectiveness in supporting claims with relevant and sufficient evidence and to recognize irrelevant evidence within a text.**

- **Grade 9:** CCSS RI.9.8 requires students to evaluate an argument's overall effectiveness by assessing the soundness of the claims and evidence provided and by identifying false statements and fallacious reasoning.

PREREQUISITE SKILLS

- Identify an author's argument.
- Trace an author's argument by recognizing how specific claims contribute to the whole.
- Evaluate an argument by assessing whether claims exhibit sound reasoning and are supported by relevant and sufficient evidence.

TAP STUDENTS' PRIOR KNOWLEDGE

- Tell students they will be working on a lesson about evaluating an author's argument and the reasons and evidence he or she uses to support the argument.

- Provide an example of a claim with a reason and evidence. Say: Tom wants to convince his mom that he should get a raise in his allowance. He gives the following reason: *I am doing more chores around the house.* His evidence is:

  1) *I am mowing the lawn.*

  2) *I am brushing the dog daily.*

  3) *My friend got a raise in his allowance.*

- Ask students what Tom's claim is. (*He should get a raise in his allowance.*) Ask what his reason is. (*He has been doing more chores around the house.*)

- Then have them evaluate the evidence Tom supplies to support his claim. Which evidence is relevant to his argument? (*1 and 2*) Which evidence is irrelevant? (*3*)

- Explain that good readers evaluate an author's evidence to make sure it supports a claim and look for evidence that is not relevant.

Ready *Teacher Toolbox*   *teacher-toolbox.com*

	Prerequisite Skills	RI.8.8
Ready Lessons	✓	✓
Tools for Instruction	✓	✓
Interactive Tutorials	✓	✓

CCSS Focus

RI.8.8 Delineate and evaluate the argument and specific claims in a text, assessing whether the reasoning is sound and the evidence is relevant and sufficient; recognize when irrelevant evidence is introduced.

ADDITIONAL STANDARDS: **RI.8.1, RI.8.2, RI.8.3, RI.8.4, RI.8.5, RI.8.6, RI.8.7; L.8.4a, L.8.4b, L.8.4d; W.8.1, W.8.4, W.8.7; SL.8.1, SL.8.3, SL.8.4** (*See page A39 for full text.*)

AT A GLANCE

Students evaluate the claims, reasoning, and evidence offered by two opposing points of view in a cartoon.

STEP BY STEP

- Read aloud the first paragraph and the definitions of *argument, claim, evidence, relevant,* and *sufficient.* Then have students study the cartoon about funding the U.S. space program. Tell students to look for the evidence that each speaker gives to support his or her claim.

- Explain that the chart identifies each speaker's claim, reasoning, and the evidence to support the claim. Discuss the first row of the chart that describes the woman's claim, reasoning and evidence. Explain that some of the evidence is irrelevant because it does not support the claim.

- Read and discuss the man's claim, reasoning, and relevant evidence in the second row of the chart. Then have students complete the chart by identifying evidence that does not support the claim "We should not fund the space program."

- Remind students to watch for irrelevant or insufficient evidence when they evaluate an author's claims.

- Reinforce the skill by giving an example of a claim, such as "Schools should offer computer classes in kindergarten." Then work with students to develop reasons and evidence to support this claim.

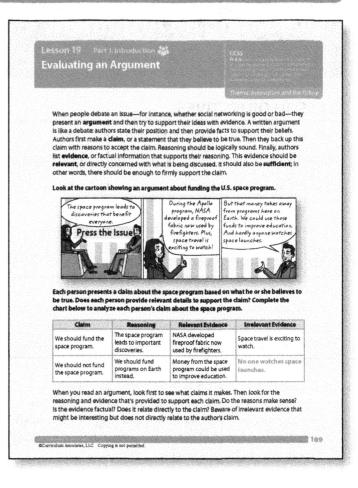

Genre Focus

Informational Texts: Editorial

Tell students that one type of informational text is an editorial. Explain that the purpose of an editorial is to persuade readers to agree with a certain opinion about a topic. An editorial writer might try to persuade readers to vote a certain way on an issue or to take action on a specific concern. Editorials usually contain the following:

- a statement of the author's position

- claims, or statements the author believes to be true that support the position

- evidence to support the claims

Ask students to name publications where they might find editorials. (*newspapers, magazines, online news sources*)

Explain that in this lesson, students will read two editorials about the U.S. space program and evaluate them based on the authors' claims and evidence. They will also read two passages that offer arguments. One passage, "Print Is Dead," provides evidence to support the claim that print is declining. The other passage, "Get on the Anti-Cancer Diet," offers evidence to support the argument that a certain diet can improve one's health. Explain to students that they will have the opportunity to evaluate the claims and evidence in each of these articles.

AT A GLANCE

Students read an editorial and evaluate the claims and evidence the author provides to support his argument.

STEP BY STEP

- Invite volunteers to tell what they learned on the previous page about evaluating arguments. Tell students that in this lesson they will evaluate the reasoning and evidence that authors provide to support claims.

- Read "Our Space Program Inspires All."

- Then read the question: "What claim does the author make in this editorial?"

- Tell students you will use a Think Aloud to demonstrate a way of answering the question.

Think Aloud: When I read an editorial, I first look for the author's position on the space program. Often authors will state their position at the beginning of the editorial. In this editorial, the author states his position in the first sentence. I will circle this sentence because this is his primary claim, or what he believes to be true.

- Direct students to the chart and ask where they've seen a similar chart before. Review that it helps them to evaluate an author's claim.

- Point out the claim listed in the chart.

Think Aloud: After I identify the author's claim, I will look for reasons the author gives to support it. The first reason the author provides is that people have an insatiable curiosity about space. The author also states that the space program provides vital advancements in science and technology.

- Point out this reasoning in the chart.

Think Aloud: Next, I will look for evidence the author uses to support his reasoning. He gives the example that curiosity inspired Galileo's work. This shows how curious people are about space. The author goes on to say that Europe's navigation satellite system is named after Galileo. This does not relate to his reasoning about people's curiosity about space, so it is irrelevant.

- Have students complete the chart. Discuss responses.

- Finally, have partners discuss whether the reasoning in each paragraph is sound, or is based on logic. Invite volunteers to share their opinions with the class.

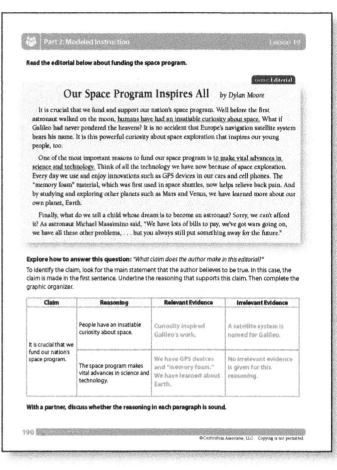

Tier Two Vocabulary: *Insatiable*

- Point out the word *insatiable* in sentence 2. Explain that the base word is *satiate*, which is derived from the Latin word *satis*, meaning "enough or sufficient." Based on the definition, guide students to understand that *satiate* means "to have enough; to be satisfied."

- Then explain that the prefix *in-* means "not." Based on this prefix meaning, plus what they know about the meaning of *satiate*, have students explain what *insatiable* means. If necessary, provide the definition: "not able to be satisfied." **(RI.8.4; L.8.4b)**

AT A GLANCE

Students read another editorial about funding the space program. They answer a multiple-choice question and explain how evidence supports the author's reasoning.

STEP BY STEP

- Tell students they will read another editorial about funding the space program.

- The Close Reading helps students identify the author's reasoning and relevant and irrelevant evidence. The Hint will help students evaluate the answer choices by identifying irrelevant responses.

- Have students read the article. Ask them to underline the author's reasoning, circle key evidence, and mark an "X" next to any irrelevant evidence, as directed by the Close Reading.

- Discuss what students underlined, circled, and marked with "Xs." If necessary, ask: "How is reasoning different from evidence?"

- Have students answer the multiple-choice question, using the Hint to help. Then have them respond to Show Your Thinking and the writing prompt at the bottom of the page.

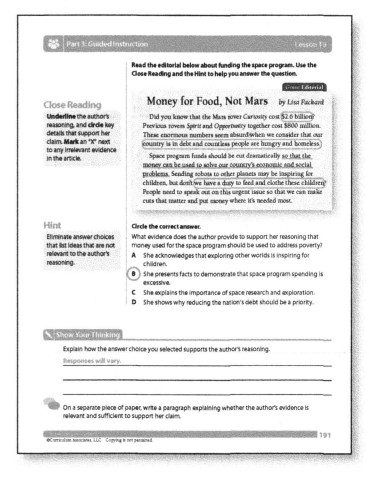

ANSWER ANALYSIS

Choice A is incorrect. It is evidence that goes against the author's reasoning.

Choice B is correct. The author provides specific costs of the space program to support the reasoning that the money should be used to address poverty.

Choice C is incorrect. It describes reasoning that is opposite from the author's reasoning.

Choice D is incorrect. The author does not claim that reducing the nation's debt should be a priority.

ERROR ALERT: Students who did not choose B may have had difficulty determining which evidence supports this reasoning. Encourage students to look back at the sentence they underlined. Then have students reread each choice to see if the evidence is relevant to the author's reasoning.

ELL Support: Multiple-Meaning Words

- Explain that words with more than one meaning are multiple-meaning words. Tell students that they can use other words in a text to help them know which meaning of a multiple-meaning word is being used.

- Direct students to the words *cut* and *cuts* in the first and last sentences of paragraph 2. Help students come up with different meanings for the word. (*"to divide into pieces;" "a long, narrow opening," "a reduction in amount or size"*)

- Work with students to figure out which meaning is used in this context. (*"a reduction in amount"*) Have students share which context clues they used to determine the correct meaning of the word. (*"funds," "put money where it's needed"*) **(RI.8.4; L.8.4a)**

AT A GLANCE

Students read an excerpt twice from a book about the state of printed books in the digital age. After the first reading, you will ask three questions to check students' comprehension of the passage.

STEP BY STEP

- Have students read the passage silently without referring to the Study Buddy or the Close Reading text.

- Ask the following questions to ensure students' comprehension of the text:

  What does the author mean by "print"? (*The author is referring to printed products such as books, magazines, and newspapers.*)

  Where does the author often see the use of print products? (*in airports, on public transportation*)

  Why does the author think that people are moving away from print products? (*He feels digital resources are increasingly taking the place of print products.*)

- Then ask students to reread the title and look at the Study Buddy think aloud. What does the Study Buddy help them think about?

Tip: Point out that authors do not always state their claims at the beginning of a text. Encourage students to read the entire article first, then look at the question posed at the end of paragraph 3. This question indicates that the author doesn't believe that "print can't be dead." The author's main claim is that print truly is declining.

- Have students read the article. Tell them to follow the directions in the Close Reading.

Tip: The Close Reading helps students identify the author's claim, which is the first sentence in paragraph 4, as well as the author's relevant evidence to support the claim. Learning to identify and analyze text evidence will help students evaluate an author's argument in any text they read.

- Finally, have students answer the questions on page 193. When students have finished, use the Answer Analysis to discuss correct and incorrect responses.

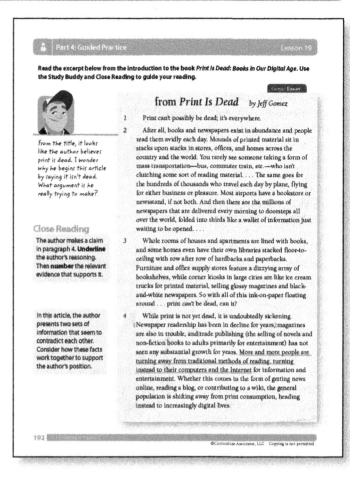

Tier Two Vocabulary: *Array*

- Direct students to the word *array* in paragraph 3. Ask them to list the context clues they use to determine the meaning of the word. (*"dizzying," "bookshelves"*) Guide them to define *array* as "an impressive display or group."

- Ask them to name other words that could be used in place of *array* in the sentence. (*variety, assortment, collection, display*)

- Then have students look up the word *array* in the dictionary to check this meaning and find other meanings. Ask students to use the word in sentences to demonstrate other meanings. (**RI.8.4; L.8.4a, L.8.4d**)

STEP BY STEP

- Have students read questions 1–3, using the Hints to help them answer those questions.

Tip: To help students answer question 3, ask them to consider how the article would be different if the author only presented the facts in paragraph 4. Point out that the comparison of print products to digital products strengthens the author's argument.

ANSWER ANALYSIS

1 Choice C is correct. This response restates the author's claim, which is presented in the first sentence in paragraph 4. Choice A is incorrect. Even though the title is *Print Is Dead,* the author does not claim it is dead. Choice B is incorrect. It does not state a claim. Choice D is incorrect. The article states newspaper and book sales are declining.

2 Choice B is correct. This statement indicates that newspapers, a traditional form of print, are becoming less popular. Choices A, C, and D are incorrect because these responses support the idea that print continues to be popular, which contradicts the reasoning in the question.

3 Sample response: In the author's first claim, he states that print products are everywhere. He backs up his claim by giving examples of the abundance of print products in our lives. He later states that while print is alive, it is "sickening." This claim is supported with evidence that includes a noted decline in newspaper and magazine sales. Then he claims that this decline is due to a shift in people's reading habits from print to "increasingly digital lives." Yet, the author provides no facts to back up this claim.

RETEACHING

Use a chart to answer question 3. Work with students to fill in the boxes. Sample responses are provided.

Claim	Reasoning
Print is still alive.	print products are abundant; bookstores and newsstands are everywhere; commuters read print products
Print is declining.	newspaper and magazine sales are decreasing; trade publishing has flat growth

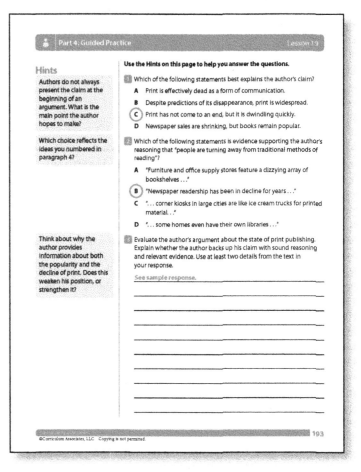

Hints

Authors do not always present the claim at the beginning of an argument. What is the main point the author hopes to make?

Which choice reflects the ideas you numbered in paragraph 4?

Think about why the author provides information about both the popularity and the decline of print. Does this weaken his position, or strengthen it?

Use the Hints on this page to help you answer the questions.

1 Which of the following statements best explains the author's claim?

A   Print is effectively dead as a form of communication.

B   Despite predictions of its disappearance, print is widespread.

C   Print has not come to an end, but it is dwindling quickly.

D   Newspaper sales are shrinking, but books remain popular.

2 Which of the following statements is evidence supporting the author's reasoning that "people are turning away from traditional methods of reading"?

A   "Furniture and office supply stores feature a dizzying array of bookshelves..."

B   "Newspaper readership has been in decline for years..."

C   "... corner kiosks in large cities are like ice cream trucks for printed material..."

D   "... some homes even have their own libraries..."

3 Evaluate the author's argument about the state of print publishing. Explain whether the author backs up his claim with sound reasoning and relevant evidence. Use at least two details from the text in your response.

See sample response.

_____

Integrating Standards

Use these questions to further students' understanding of *Print Is Dead.*

1 According to the author, what is one reason print is declining? **(RI.8.3)**

Consumers are becoming more interested in using digital resources instead of print products for their news and entertainment.

2 What is the author's purpose in *Print Is Dead*? **(RI.8.6)**

His purpose is to convince the reader that print products, while still popular, are slowly being replaced by an increasing popularity of digital media.

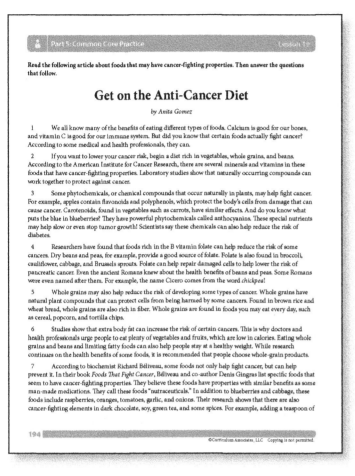

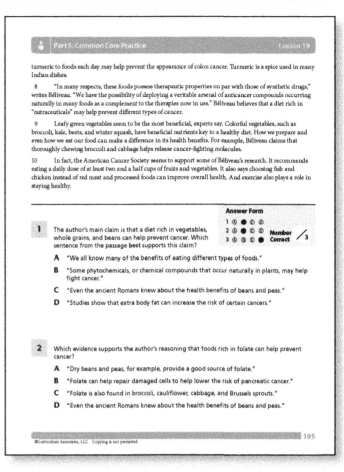

AT A GLANCE

Students independently read a longer article and answer questions in a format that provides test practice.

STEP BY STEP

- Tell students to use what they have learned about reading closely and evaluating arguments to read the article on pages 194 and 195.

- Remind students to underline or circle important claims, reasoning, and evidence in the text.

- Tell students to answer the questions on pages 195 and 196. For questions 1–3, they should fill in the correct circle on the Answer Form.

- When students have finished, use the Answer Analysis to discuss correct responses and the reasons for them. Have students fill in the Number Correct on the Answer Form.

ANSWER ANALYSIS

1 Choice B is correct. All of the foods mentioned in the author's main claim come from plants. The phytochemicals found in plants contribute to certain foods' cancer-prevention properties. Choice A is incorrect because it just makes a broad generalization about food benefits. Choice C is incorrect because it does not directly connect the health benefits of beans and peas with cancer prevention. Choice D is incorrect. While a diet of vegetables, whole grains, and beans may help a person maintain a healthy weight and reduce cancer risks, those connections are not evident in the sentence. **(DOK 2)**

Theme Connection

- How do all the passages in this lesson relate to the theme of innovation and the future?

- Describe how one of the innovative ideas from the lesson texts might impact your future.

2 Choice B is correct. It explains how folate-rich foods can help prevent pancreatic cancer. Choices A and C are incorrect because they list foods that contain folate but don't explain why it helps prevent cancer. Choice D is a fact irrelevant to the claim. **(DOK 3)**

3 Choice D is correct. It addresses the benefits of phytochemicals toward diabetes, not cancer. Choices A, B and C are incorrect because they describes the cancer-fighting benefits of these chemicals, which is relevant evidence. **(DOK 3)**

4 **Part A:** Students select the second claim. The evidence is strongest for this claim because the article cites studies and laboratory research. The first claim has some truth to it, but outside of paragraph 6 there is not much in the article to support it. The passage also supports the third claim to some degree, but nothing backs up the notion that "nutraceuticals" will soon be "more important" than synthetic drugs.

Part B: Sample response: The article offers many examples of studies supporting the claim that plant-based foods can help prevent cancer. For example, paragraph 2 notes that the American Institute for Cancer Research has confirmed "cancer-fighting properties" in vegetables, whole grains, and beans. Paragraph 4 reports researcher findings that folate in beans and vegetables "can help reduce the risk of some cancers." Paragraph 7 reports on the research of

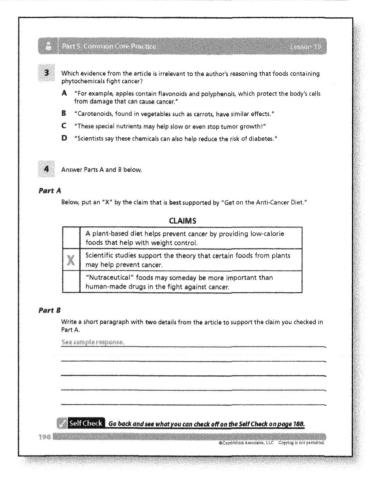

biochemist Richard Béliveau, which has shown many plant foods to have cancer-fighting elements. **(DOK 3)**

Integrating Standards

Use these questions and tasks as opportunities to interact with "Get on the Anti-Cancer Diet."

1 How does paragraph 1 of "Get on the Anti-Cancer Diet" contribute to the author's message? **(RI.8.5)**

This paragraph introduces the author's primary claim—that certain foods fight cancer. The following paragraphs provide evidence to support this claim.

2 What examples of whole grain foods does the author include? **(RI.8.1)**

The author names brown rice, wheat bread, cereal, popcorn, and tortilla chips as rich in whole grains.

3 What is the author's point of view about a healthy diet? Give reasons for your response. **(RI.8.6)**

The author believes that it is important to eat a healthy diet, including cancer-fighting foods, to promote good health and fight possible disease. The

author cites many examples of foods that can promote health, and the tone of her article indicates that she is encouraging her readers to eat these foods.

4 Write a summary of the article, including details that support the central idea. **(RI.8.2; W.8.4)**

The author claims that a diet rich in certain foods can reduce a person's risk of getting cancer. She uses research to show the effectiveness of eating each type of food in preventing cancer.

5 Discuss in small groups: How does the author's word choices help make her claim convincing and her reasoning sound? Cite examples. **(SL.8.1)**

Discussions will vary. Encourage students to consider how the author's use of technical language helps convince readers that she is knowledgeable about the topic. Remind students to follow discussion rules.

Writing Activities

Advocate Persuasively and Address Issues Creatively (W.8.1)

- Have students review one of the editorials they read. Discuss what it means to advocate for a cause. Explain that an advocate is someone who passionately and publicly supports a cause.

- Have students think about the texts they read in this lesson, and how these topics might translate to action, such as choosing to buy or not to buy printed materials or eating a diet that will help prevent cancer. Have students choose one of these ideas, or another idea of their choosing that is related to innovation. Challenge them to write their own persuasive editorial in which they advocate for their opinion about the topic.

- Remind students to state their claim and then support it with sound reasoning and relevant evidence. How will they address the issue in a creative way that will effectively persuade their audience to agree with their point of view or take action?

- Ask students to trade editorials with a partner. Have partners circle the claim in the editorial, underline the reasoning and supporting evidence, and mark an "X" next to any irrelevant evidence.

- After peer review, have students revise their editorials to strengthen their writing. Invite volunteers to share their editorials with the class.

LISTENING ACTIVITY (SL.8.3)

Listen Closely/Listen for Details

- Have student pairs take turns reading aloud paragraphs from "Get on the Anti-Cancer Diet."

- After each paragraph is read, the listener should identify two or more details that he or she heard and classify them as a claim, reasoning, relevant evidence, or irrelevant evidence.

DISCUSSION ACTIVITY (SL.8.1)

Advocate For or Against the Space Program

- Have students reread the two editorials about funding the U.S. space program. Then have students form two groups—one in support of continued funding of the space program, and one in support of reduced funding for the space program.

- Give each group time to formulate their argument in support of their position. Remind students to list evidence to support their claim. Have each group include one detail that provides irrelevant evidence that does not support their claim.

- Have each group present their argument to the class. Have the listening group identify the irrelevant evidence from the group's presentation.

MEDIA ACTIVITY (RI.8.7)

Design an Ad for Healthful Food Choices

- Reread "Get on the Anti-Cancer Diet." Then tell students they have been hired by the American Cancer Society to design an ad to encourage young children to eat healthful, cancer-fighting foods.

- Have students decide what media they will use for their ad. They may choose to write a script for a radio ad, design a print ad for children's magazines, or create a poster to distribute to elementary campuses. Have students create their ads and share them with the class.

RESEARCH ACTIVITY (W.8.7; SL.8.4)

Research and Present/Give a Presentation

- Have students use the information in this lesson about funding the space program to give a presentation about the various claims people make about this topic.

- Students should research other people's arguments surrounding this issue, which may be found in sources such as speeches and news interviews.

- Have students present the different claims they found related to this topic and explain which claim has the most sound reasoning.

Analyzing Conflicting Information

LESSON OBJECTIVES

- Compare and contrast two informational texts on the same topic that have conflicting information.
- Analyze the ways in which different authors present information on the same topic, identifying where the texts disagree on matters of fact and interpretation.

THE LEARNING PROGRESSION

- **Grade 7:** CCSS RI.7.9 requires students to analyze how two or more authors writing about the same topic shape their presentations of key information by emphasizing different evidence or advancing different interpretations of facts.

- **Grade 8: CCSS RI.8.9 focuses on comparing and contrasting conflicting information about matters of fact and interpretation.**

- **Grade 9:** CCSS RI.9.9 requires students to analyze seminal U.S. documents of historical and literary importance, focusing on how they address related themes and concepts.

PREREQUISITE SKILLS

- Recognize how authors use evidence to support claims and information about a topic.
- Understand that different authors interpret and present facts differently.
- Compare and contrast two texts on the same topic.

TAP STUDENTS' PRIOR KNOWLEDGE

- Tell students they will be working on a lesson about analyzing conflicting information in different texts that are about the same topic. Review that facts are statements that can be proven true. Ask students what an opinion is. (*what someone thinks, feels, or believes*) Remind students that authors often use facts and other information to support their opinion.

- Ask students to think about reading reviews of a movie they want to see. Have them suppose that one reviewer gives the movie a high rating. She explains that the film is action-packed and keeps viewers on the edge of their seats. Another reviewer gives the movie a moderate score, citing that the film is full of action but lacks realistic dialogue and events.

- Have students discuss how the two opinions about the same topic differ based on the reviewer's personal preferences. Point out that by reading both reviews, they are more informed about what to expect from the movie.

- Point out to students that reading conflicting information will help them to better understand a topic.

📦 Ready *Teacher Toolbox*   *teacher-toolbox.com*

	Prerequisite Skills	RI.8.9
Ready Lessons	✓	✓
Tools for Instruction	✓	
Interactive Tutorials		✓

CCSS Focus

RI.8.9 Analyze a case in which two or more texts provide conflicting information on the same topic and identify where the texts disagree on matters of fact or interpretation.

ADDITIONAL STANDARDS: **RI.8.1, RI.8.2, RI.8.4, RI.8.6, RI.8.7; L.8.1c, L.8.2b, L.8.4a, L.8.4b, L.8.4c, L.8.5a; W.8.1, W.8.8; SL.8.1, SL.8.4** (*See page A39 for full text.*)

AT A GLANCE

Students read and compare two short product reviews and then determine how the authors give conflicting information about the same product.

STEP BY STEP

- Read aloud the first paragraph and explain the definitions of *conflicting* and *interpretations*.

- Ask students to study the product reviews and circle details that show that the reviews are about the same topic. Have them underline details that show conflicting information.

- Explain that the chart shows how the reviews are alike and different. Read the information in each column, and have students compare it to the details they noticed.

- Discuss how both reviews talk about the same product, but they have very different interpretations of its features and value.

- Ask students to share advertisements they have seen or read. Have students discuss points made by the advertiser. Then ask students to offer a different interpretation of the features of the product based on their experience with it.

- Read the final paragraph on the page and reinforce the idea that articles that present conflicting information are valuable because they allow readers to get a broader understanding of a topic.

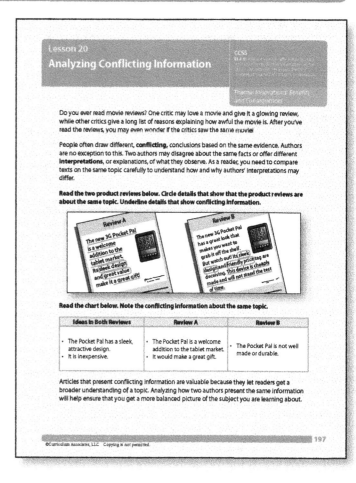

Genre Focus

Informational Texts: Scientific Account

Tell students that in this lesson they will read scientific accounts. Explain that a scientific account is a piece of writing that provides information about a scientific topic. Its purpose is to explain or inform. Scientific accounts often share the following characteristics:

- The opening usually engages the reader's attention, and the body of the article gives facts, examples, reasons, descriptions, and so on.

- It often answers *who*, *what*, *when*, *where*, *why*, and *how* questions and has an objective tone.

- It may include the author's interpretation of facts.

- The ending sums up the author's message.

Ask students to tell about scientific accounts they have read. What was the topic and purpose of each? Did the author successfully answer the questions *who*, *what*, *when*, *where*, *why*, and *how* about the topic? Did the author offer his or her opinion or interpretation of the facts?

Two of the scientific accounts in this lesson are "Are You Eating GM Food?," which is about genetically modified (GM) foods and their potential dangers, and "GM Crops are Superfoods," which gives a positive interpretation of facts about GM foods.

AT A GLANCE

Students read a scientific account about genetically modified foods and determine how the author interprets facts about the topic.

STEP BY STEP

- Invite volunteers to tell what they learned on the previous page about analyzing conflicting accounts of the same topic.

- Tell students that in this lesson they will read two scientific accounts about genetically modified foods and compare them.

- Read "Are You Eating GM Food?"

- Then read the question: "How does the author interpret facts about genetically modified foods?"

- Tell students you will use a Think Aloud to demonstrate a way of answering the question.

Think Aloud: In the first paragraph, I see that the author explains what genetically modified (GM) foods are and lists some possible benefits. I see that the second paragraph describes possible dangers of GM foods, such as unknown side effects. I will put these ideas together to figure out how the author interprets facts about GM foods.

- Direct students to the chart and ask where they've seen a similar chart before. Explain that they can use it to compare and then analyze the conflicting information.

- Have students fill in a point of interpretation from the second paragraph of this article.

Think Aloud: In the third paragraph, I see that the author points out that GM foods do not have warning labels on their products about the unknown and potential dangers. I think the author believes this information should be made known to consumers.

- Have students complete the second column of the chart with another point of interpretation from this article about GM foods.

- Then tell students that they will read another article about this topic and complete the chart on this page.

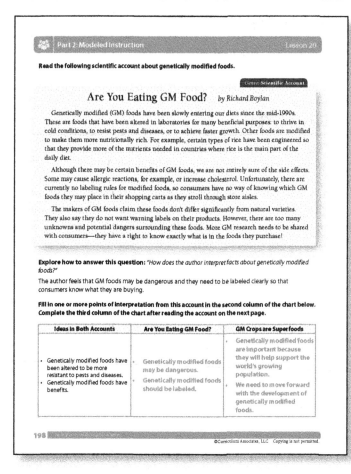

Read the following scientific account about genetically modified foods.

Genre: Scientific Account

Are You Eating GM Food?   *by Richard Boylan*

Genetically modified (GM) foods have been slowly entering our diets since the mid-1990s. These are foods that have been altered in laboratories for many beneficial purposes: to thrive in cold conditions, to resist pests and diseases, or to achieve faster growth. Other foods are modified to make them more nutritionally rich. For example, certain types of rice have been engineered so that they provide more of the nutrients needed in countries where rice is the main part of the daily diet.

Although there may be certain benefits of GM foods, we are not entirely sure of the side effects. Some may cause allergic reactions, for example, or increase cholesterol. Unfortunately, there are currently no labeling rules for modified foods, so consumers have no way of knowing which GM foods they may place in their shopping carts as they stroll through store aisles.

The makers of GM foods claim these foods don't differ significantly from natural varieties. They also say they do not want warning labels on their products. However, there are too many unknowns and potential dangers surrounding these foods. More GM research needs to be shared with consumers—they have a right to know exactly what is in the foods they purchase!

Explore how to answer this question: *"How does the author interpret facts about genetically modified foods?"*

The author feels that GM foods may be dangerous and they need to be labeled clearly so that consumers know what they are buying.

Fill in one or more points of interpretation from this account in the second column of the chart below. Complete the third column of the chart after reading the account on the next page.

Ideas in Both Accounts	Are You Eating GM Food?	GM Crops are Superfoods
• Genetically modified foods have been altered to be more resistant to pests and diseases. • Genetically modified foods have benefits.	• Genetically modified foods may be dangerous. • Genetically modified foods should be labeled.	• Genetically modified foods are important because they will help support the world's growing population. • We need to move forward with the development of genetically modified foods.

198

©Curriculum Associates, LLC   Copying is not permitted.

Tier Two Vocabulary: *Engineered*

- Direct students to the word *engineered* in paragraph 1. Remind them that context clues can be synonyms of the word. Have students identify the context clues that help them to understand the meaning of this word. (*"modified"*) Then ask them to define *engineered*. (*"changed or designed in a particular way"*)

- Then ask students to use a dictionary to verify this definition and identify slight differences in meaning this word can have depending on the context in which it is used. **(RI.8.4; L.8.4a, L.8.4c)**

AT A GLANCE

Students read another scientific account about GM foods. They answer a multiple-choice question and analyze the conflicting information in the articles.

STEP BY STEP

- Tell students they will read another scientific account about genetically modified foods, or GMs.

- The Close Reading helps students compare and contrast details in this article to those in "Are You Eating GM Food?" The Hint will help students consider each author's interpretation of the topic.

- Ask volunteers to share the details they marked in the two articles. Discuss how the two accounts are alike and different.

- Have students read the first column of the chart on page 198 and complete the third column with points of interpretation from "GM Crops Are Superfoods."

- Then have students complete the bottom of the page. (*Sample response for Show Your Thinking: In "Are You Eating GM Food?," Boylan suggests that GM foods may be dangerous and should be labeled. In "GM Crops Are Superfoods," Silva puts forth the conflicting idea that people should move ahead with the development of GMs because they will help support the world's growing population.*)

ANSWER ANALYSIS

Choice A is correct. It tells the conflicting interpretations the two authors, Boylan and Silva, offer about GMs.

Choice B is incorrect. Boylan also includes the positive arguments for GMs in his article.

Choice C is incorrect. Silva thinks that the benefits of GMs are very significant.

Choice D is incorrect. The opposite is true. Boylan thinks the unknown dangers of GMs are a concern while Silva feels that GMs are safe.

ERROR ALERT: Students who did not choose A may not have understood how the two authors disagree. Have students read each choice and eliminate those choices that tell how the two authors agree and have them use their charts to select the correct answer.

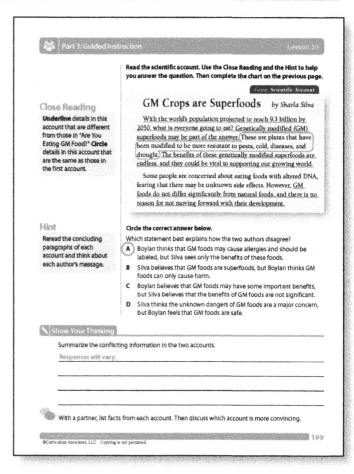

ELL Support: *Prefixes*

- Explain to students that many English words have prefixes. A prefix is a group of letters added to the beginning of a word to change its meaning. Work with students to show how the meaning of a word changes with a prefix. Point out the word *superfoods* in the title and paragraph 1. Explain to students that *super-* is a prefix that means "above, over, or beyond." Have students use this meaning to explain what *superfoods* are. (*foods that are beyond regular foods*) Then have students list and discuss the meanings of other words with the prefix *super-*. (*supermarket, superabundant, superhero*)

- Point out the word *unknown* in paragraph 2. Have students identify the prefix (*un-*) and base word (*known*). Then have them explain how the prefix changes the meaning of *known*. (*It changes known to mean "not known."*) **(RI.8.4; L.8.4b)**

AT A GLANCE

Students read a scientific account about the mystery of King Tut twice. After the first reading, you will ask three questions to check your students' understanding of the article.

STEP BY STEP

- Have students read the article silently without referring to the Study Buddy or Close Reading text.

- Ask the following questions to ensure students' comprehension of the text:

  What does the author propose in the first paragraph when he uses the phrase *foul play*? (*He proposes that King Tut's death might have been murder. Foul play is an unfair or underhanded action, including murder.*)

  What evidence is offered to support the idea of murder? (*An X-ray in 1968 showed a piece of bone floating inside Tut's skull.*)

  What other details does the author offer to support his proposition? (*He offers the opinions of experts and the use of forensic science.*)

- Then ask students to reread paragraph 1 and look at the Study Buddy think aloud. What does the Study Buddy help them think about?

Tip: The Study Buddy points out to students that the title indicates the author is going to present a "case" and encourages them to look for details and facts that support this case. Being able to recognize an author's argument will help students prepare for comparing this text to another text that presents conflicting information on the same topic.

- Have students read the rest of the article. Tell them to follow the directions in the Close Reading.

Tip: Point out to students that the information they are identifying using the Close Reading are the author's central claim and the evidence he offers to support it. Help students analyze the evidence to distinguish between the facts themselves and the author's interpretation of what they signify.

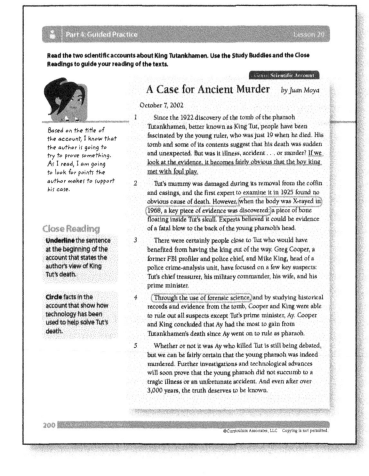

Read the two scientific accounts about King Tutankhamen. Use the Study Buddies and the Close Readings to guide your reading of the texts.

Genre: Scientific Account

A Case for Ancient Murder   by Juan Moya

October 7, 2002

Based on the title of the account, I know that the author is going to try to prove something. As I read, I am going to look for points the author makes to support his case.

1   Since the 1922 discovery of the tomb of the pharaoh Tutankhamen, better known as King Tut, people have been fascinated by the young ruler, who was just 19 when he died. His tomb and some of its contents suggest that his death was sudden and unexpected. But was it illness, accident . . . or murder? If we look at the evidence, it becomes fairly obvious that the boy king met with foul play.

2   Tut's mummy was damaged during its removal from the coffin and casings, and the first expert to examine it in 1925 found no obvious cause of death. However, when the body was X-rayed in 1968, a key piece of evidence was discovered: a piece of bone floating inside Tut's skull. Experts believed it could be evidence of a fatal blow to the back of the young pharaoh's head.

3   There were certainly people close to Tut who would have benefited from having the king out of the way. Greg Cooper, a former FBI profiler and police chief, and Mike King, head of a police crime-analysis unit, have focused on a few key suspects: Tut's chief treasurer, his military commander, his wife, and his prime minister.

4   Through the use of forensic science, and by studying historical records and evidence from the tomb, Cooper and King were able to rule out all suspects except Tut's prime minister, Ay. Cooper and King concluded that Ay had the most to gain from Tutankhamen's death since Ay went on to rule as pharaoh.

5   Whether or not it was Ay who killed Tut is still being debated, but we can be fairly certain that the young pharaoh was indeed murdered. Further investigations and technological advances will soon prove that the young pharaoh did not succumb to a tragic illness or an unfortunate accident. And even after over 3,000 years, the truth deserves to be known.

Close Reading

Underline the sentence at the beginning of the account that states the author's view of King Tut's death.

Circle facts in the account that show how technology has been used to help solve Tut's death.

200

Tier Two Vocabulary: *Succumb*

- Point out the word *succumb* in paragraph 5. Encourage students to determine the meaning of this word based on the context. (*"give in to"*)

- Remind them that they can use reference materials, such as print or online dictionaries, to help them determine the meaning of an unfamiliar word. Ask students to look up the meaning of *succumb* and any other unfamiliar words in this passage that they have difficulty understanding in the given context. **(RI.8.4; L.8.4d)**

AT A GLANCE

Students read another scientific account about the mystery of King Tut twice. After the first reading, you will ask three questions to check your students' understanding of the article.

STEP BY STEP

- Have students read the article silently without referring to the Study Buddy or Close Reading text.

- Ask the following questions to ensure students' comprehension of the text:

  What does the author propose caused King Tut's death? *(malaria and a leg fracture)*

  Why did the researchers test King Tut's DNA? *(to learn more about possible genetic disorders and diseases he might have had)*

  Why was Tut buried with about 100 canes in his tomb? *(He likely had disorders that caused him to need a cane to be able to walk.)*

- Then ask students to reread paragraph 1 and look at the Study Buddy think aloud. What does the Study Buddy help them think about?

Tip: The Study Buddy guides students to look for clues to this author's ideas about King Tut's death. Have students first identify the author's main claim. Then have them identify the reasoning and evidence the author provides to convince readers of her claim.

- Have students read the rest of the article. Tell them to follow the directions in the Close Reading.

Tip: Close Reading suggests that students return to the previous scientific account and reread the sentence they underlined. Then they think about how the facts in these two articles differ. This information will help students evaluate the conflicting interpretations of the facts.

- Finally, have students answer the questions on page 202. Use the Answer Analysis to discuss correct and incorrect responses.

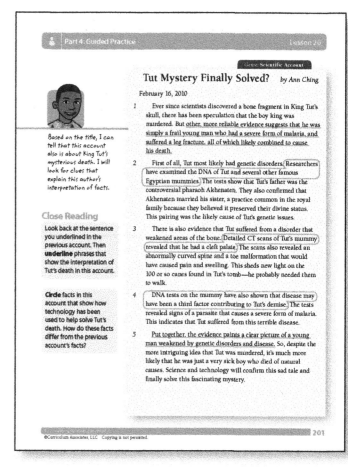

ELL Support: Regular Plural Nouns

- Explain to students that nouns name people, places, or things. Students can look at the endings of nouns to know *how many*.

- Work with students to identify the plural forms of regular nouns in this article. Point out the word *scientists* and *issues* and have students tell how this plural was formed. *(add -s)*

- Direct students to the word *status* in paragraph 2 and ask how they would form the plural of this singular noun. *(add -es, statuses)*

- Finally, explain to students that some nouns, called noncount nouns, have the same spelling when used in the singular and the plural, such as the word *evidence* in this article. **(L.8.1, L.8.2b)**

STEP BY STEP

- Have students read questions 1–3, using the Hints to help them answer the questions.

> **Tip:** If students have trouble answering question 2, remind them to review their marked text. Have them look back at the sentences they underlined in each article to help them determine the best answer to this question.

- Discuss with students the Answer Analysis below.

ANSWER ANALYSIS

1   The correct choice is C. Both accounts mention the damage to the back of King Tut's skull. Choice A is incorrect. Only the second account mentions the broken leg. Choices B and D are incorrect. Tut's age and when the tomb was found are mentioned only in the first account.

2   The correct choice is D. The authors do not agree on what caused Tut to die. Choice A is incorrect. Ching does not discuss who might have gained from Tut's death. Choice B is incorrect. The authors agree on the basic time of death. Choice C is incorrect. Both turn to experts to support their interpretations.

3   Sample response: Moya's article explains how technology revealed a possible cause of King Tut's death. Moya emphasizes the importance of X-rays and forensic science in the search for evidence of foul play. Ching's article examines the evidence provided by CT scans and DNA tests. Ching uses these results to build a case that confirms Tut's poor health. Both authors use evidence from technological advances to support their conclusions about Tut's death.

RETEACHING

Use a chart to answer question 3. Draw the chart below, and work with students to fill in the boxes. Sample responses are provided.

Ideas in Both Articles	"A Case for Ancient Murder"	"Tut Mystery Finally Solved?"
Technology is used to study King Tut's mummy.	relies on X-rays and forensic science	examines evidence of poor health from scans and tests

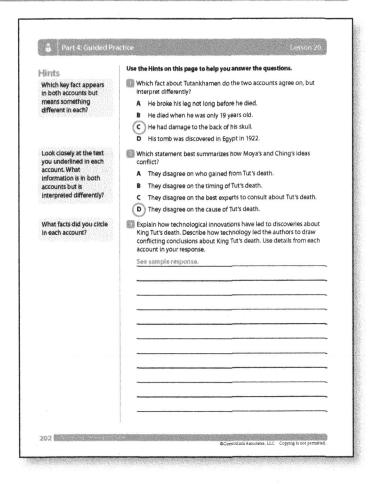

Hints

Which key fact appears in both accounts but means something different in each?

Look closely at the text you underlined in each account. What information is in both accounts but is interpreted differently?

What facts did you circle in each account?

Use the Hints on this page to help you answer the questions.

1   Which fact about Tutankhamen do the two accounts agree on, but interpret differently?

   A   He broke his leg not long before he died.
   B   He died when he was only 19 years old.
   (C)   He had damage to the back of his skull.
   D   His tomb was discovered in Egypt in 1922.

2   Which statement best summarizes how Moya's and Ching's ideas conflict?

   A   They disagree on who gained from Tut's death.
   B   They disagree on the timing of Tut's death.
   C   They disagree on the best experts to consult about Tut's death.
   (D)   They disagree on the cause of Tut's death.

3   Explain how technological innovations have led to discoveries about King Tut's death. Describe how technology led the authors to draw conflicting conclusions about King Tut's death. Use details from each account in your response.

See sample response.

202   ©Curriculum Associates, LLC   Copying is not permitted.

Integrating Standards

Use these questions to further students' understanding of "A Case for Ancient Murder" and "Tut Mystery Finally Solved?"

1   What can you infer about which argument may be more accurate, based on the dates at the beginning of each article? **(RI.8.1)**

The dates show the first article was written in 2002 while the second was written in 2010. The author of the second article may have worked with more recent technological evidence than the first author. This suggests the second article may be more accurately based on the latest technology.

2   Give an example of how the author of "Tut Mystery Finally Solved?" acknowledges and responds to a conflicting view. **(RI.8.6)**

In paragraph 5, the author mentions the conflicting view that Tut was murdered. She responds to it by saying that it is unlikely, even though it may be "the more intriguing idea."

Read these passages about technology and the human brain. Then answer the questions.

Your Brain on Technology

by Annabelle Jordan

December 3, 2010

1　How many things do you do at once when you are in front of a computer? Do you think of yourself as a multitasker? As computer and Internet use grows, allowing us access anywhere to multiple sources of information and entertainment, so too do concerns about its impact on our lives. Technology isn't just changing the way we do things; studies show that it's changing our brains. But for better or for worse?

2　There is no doubt that Internet-connected devices give us access to more information than ever before. If you want to know the news of the day, check what your friends are doing, watch a music video or a movie, or look for a great deal on a product, it's all instantly available. While the Internet is a powerful tool, allowing us to quickly access all sorts of useful facts, keeping up with all of the available information can also be distracting and overwhelming. Academic and professional achievement still requires the ability to focus for extended periods on complex tasks. However, some research shows that the distractions of the modern world are impairing this ability.

3　Have you ever been working on something and thought, "I'll just quickly check if I have any messages"? How long did it take you to get back to your original task? People who multitask, or do more than one thing at a time, often feel they are more productive by doing so, but studies show that is not the case. Researchers have found that heavy multitaskers actually take longer to switch between tasks, are not as good as non-multitaskers at ignoring distracting information, and actually feel more stress. Despite this, people are multitasking more. Studies indicate that computer users at work change windows or switch to other programs such as email almost 37 times every hour. That's more than once every two minutes.

4　All this multitasking seems to be actually changing our brains. When users juggle information, it provides stimulation that triggers the release of dopamine, a chemical that activates the pleasure centers in the brain. In other words, their brains reward them for switching between activities. Evidence shows that doing this on a regular basis retrains the brain to prefer switching activities. This can cause problems in situations in which people need to focus on one thing for more than a few minutes, such as working on longer tasks or in social situations. Heavy technology users report getting distracted even when they don't want to be, such as when spending time with their families. Without the constant release of dopamine, they feel bored.

5　Dopamine is also the brain chemical associated with addiction, leading to the worry that excessive technology use may cause dysfunctional behavior similar to other addictions. And given the effects on adult brains, experts worry that this will be even more pronounced in the still-developing brains of children and teenagers. The lives of countless young people are intertwined with technology; many youths send hundreds of text messages a day, not to mention the time spent on social networking, video games, or browsing the Internet. Students admit that their use of technology takes time away and distracts them from schoolwork. How can you not check your phone if a text comes in while you're doing homework? And then you have to reply, right?

6　The loss of focus during a task isn't the only way technology impairs learning. One study tracked how well 12- to 14-year-old boys remembered vocabulary words after two different activities. They either watched TV or played video games for two hours between studying the words and going to sleep. The results showed that playing video games both reduced the quality of sleep and significantly reduced their ability to remember the vocabulary words the next day. Researchers believe the intense stimulation of a video game after learning may have kept the brain from remembering the words. Evidence indicates that the brain needs a time of lower activity to process information. If we are always online, our brains are not getting that downtime.

7　Technology isn't all bad, of course. Research also shows that the brains of people who use the Internet find information more efficiently, and video games can improve the brain's ability to process images. Technology is here to stay, so it's not a question of should we use it, but of how we manage it. We can only do that effectively if we understand how it affects us, especially our brains. As with many things, finding a balance may be the key to maximizing the potential of our brains on technology.

from "The New Literacy"

by Clive Thompson, Wired Magazine

August 24, 2009

1　As the school year begins, be ready to hear pundits fretting once again about how kids today can't write—and technology is to blame. An age of illiteracy is at hand, right?

2　Andrea Lunsford isn't so sure. Lunsford is a professor of writing and rhetoric at Stanford University, where she has organized a mammoth project called the Stanford Study of Writing to scrutinize college students' prose. From 2001 to 2006, she collected 14,672 student writing samples—everything from in-class assignments, formal essays, and journal entries to emails, blog posts, and chat sessions. Her conclusions are stirring.

3　"I think we're in the midst of a literacy revolution the likes of which we haven't seen since Greek civilization," she says. For Lunsford, technology isn't killing our ability to write. It's reviving it—and pushing our literacy in bold new directions.

4　The first thing she found is that young people today write far more than any generation before them. That's because so much socializing takes place online, and it almost always involves text. Of all the writing that the Stanford students did, a stunning 38 percent of it took place out of the classroom—life writing, as Lunsford calls it. Those [online] updates and lists of 25 things about yourself add up.

5　It's almost hard to remember how big a paradigm[1] shift this is. Before the Internet came along, most Americans never wrote anything, ever, that wasn't a school assignment. Unless they got a job that required producing text (like in law, advertising, or media), they'd leave school and virtually never construct a paragraph again.

[1] **paradigm:** an example or framework

AT A GLANCE

Students independently read two longer articles and answer questions in a format that provides test practice.

STEP BY STEP

- Tell students to use what they have learned about analyzing conflicting information on the same topic to read the articles on pages 203–205.

- Remind students to pay attention to clues and important details that reveal the authors' interpretations of the facts.

- Tell students to answer the questions on pages 205 and 206. For questions 1–3, they should fill in the correct circle on the Answer Form.

- When students have finished, use the Answer Analysis to discuss correct responses and the reasons for them. Have students fill in the Number Correct on the Answer Form.

ANSWER ANALYSIS

1　Choice B is correct. Jordan's article focuses on how multitasking affects the brain and a person's ability to focus. But Jordan suggests managing rather than abandoning technology. Choice A is incorrect because it is a detail of the article, not the main interpretation Jordan puts forward. Choice C is incorrect since Jordan suggests managing rather than stopping the use of technology. Choice D is incorrect since Jordan is suggesting a moderate approach to using technology. Jordan does not mention that technology is damaging our brains; she says it is changing brain activity. ***(DOK 2)***

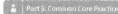

Theme Connection

- How do the articles in this lesson relate to the benefits and consequences of innovations?

- What is one fact or idea you learned about innovations from each article?

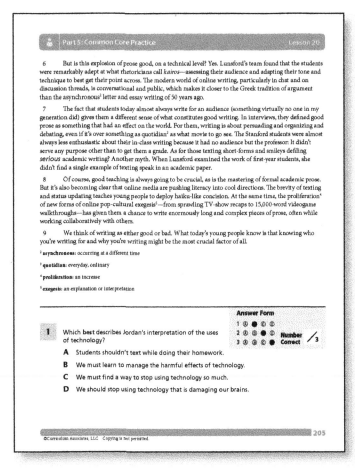

6   But is this explosion of prose good, on a technical level? Yes. Lunsford's team found that the students were remarkably adept at what rhetoricians call *kairos*—assessing their audience and adapting their tone and technique to best get their point across. The modern world of online writing, particularly in chat and on discussion threads, is conversational and public, which makes it closer to the Greek tradition of argument than the asynchronous[2] letter and essay writing of 50 years ago.

7   The fact that students today almost always write for an audience (something virtually no one in my generation did) gives them a different sense of what constitutes good writing. In interviews, they defined good prose as something that had an effect on the world. For them, writing is about persuading and organizing and debating, even if it's over something as quotidian[3] as what movie to go see. The Stanford students were almost always less enthusiastic about their in-class writing because it had no audience but the professor: It didn't serve any purpose other than to get them a grade. As for those texting short-forms and smileys defiling *serious* academic writing? Another myth. When Lunsford examined the work of first-year students, she didn't find a single example of texting speak in an academic paper.

8   Of course, good teaching is always going to be crucial, as is the mastering of formal academic prose. But it's also becoming clear that online media are pushing literacy into cool directions. The brevity of texting and status updating teaches young people to deploy haiku-like concision. At the same time, the proliferation[4] of new forms of online pop-cultural exegesis[5]—from sprawling TV-show recaps to 15,000-word videogame walkthroughs—has given them a chance to write enormously long and complex pieces of prose, often while working collaboratively with others.

9   We think of writing as either good or bad. What today's young people know is that knowing who you're writing for and why you're writing might be the most crucial factor of all.

[2] **asynchronous:** occurring at a different time

[3] **quotidian:** everyday, ordinary

[4] **proliferation:** an increase

[5] **exegesis:** an explanation or interpretation

1 Which best describes Jordan's interpretation of the uses of technology?

   A Students shouldn't text while doing their homework.

   B We must learn to manage the harmful effects of technology.

   C We must find a way to stop using technology so much.

   D We should stop using technology that is damaging our brains.

©Curriculum Associates, LLC   Copying is not permitted.   205

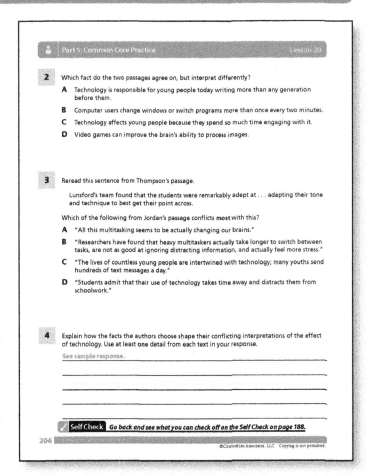

2 Which fact do the two passages agree on, but interpret differently?

   A Technology is responsible for young people today writing more than any generation before them.

   B Computer users change windows or switch programs more than once every two minutes.

   C Technology affects young people because they spend so much time engaging with it.

   D Video games can improve the brain's ability to process images.

3 Reread this sentence from Thompson's passage.

   Lunsford's team found that the students were remarkably adept at . . . adapting their tone and technique to best get their point across.

   Which of the following from Jordan's passage conflicts **most** with this?

   A "All this multitasking seems to be actually changing our brains."

   B "Researchers have found that heavy multitaskers actually take longer to switch between tasks, are not as good at ignoring distracting information, and actually feel more stress."

   C "The lives of countless young people are intertwined with technology; many youths send hundreds of text messages a day."

   D "Students admit that their use of technology takes time away and distracts them from schoolwork."

4 Explain how the facts the authors choose shape their conflicting interpretations of the effect of technology. Use at least one detail from each text in your response.

   See sample response.

   _____

   _____

   _____

   _____

   _____

   ✓ **Self Check** *Go back and see what you can check off on the Self Check on page 188.*

206   ©Curriculum Associates, LLC   Copying is not permitted.

ANSWER ANALYSIS

2 Choice C is correct. Both authors cite the amount of time that young people spend using technology. Choice A is incorrect. Only Thompson discusses this information. Choice B is incorrect because only Jordan mentions how often computer users switch between programs or windows. Choice D is incorrect since only Jordan mentions the brain's improved ability to process images. **(DOK 3)**

3 Choice D is correct. Lunsford's study stresses how technology has helped students improve their writing skills, while Jordan points out the distractions technology often presents students. Choice A is incorrect because it has no bearing on the question. Choice B is incorrect because it has more to do with switching tasks rather than remaining focused on writing and schoolwork. Choice C is incorrect because it is in agreement with the interpretation of the second author. **(DOK 3)**

4 Sample response: The authors choose different facts about the effects of technology on people's lives. Jordan focuses mostly on the damaging effects of technology on the brain. Thompson focuses on the positive effects of technology on students' writing skills. As a result, Jordan interprets the effects as mainly negative, while Thompson sees the effects as being positive. **(DOK 4)**

Integrating Standards

Use these questions to further students' understanding of both articles, "Your Brain on Technology" and "The New Literacy."

1 In the first article, what can you infer about the vocabulary retention of the boys who watched TV? **(RI.8.1)**

I can infer that boys who watched TV retained vocabulary better than the boys who played video games. The study compares the two groups and concludes that "the intense stimulation of a video game after learning may have kept the brain from remembering the words." It does not draw the same conclusion about boys who watched TV.

2 What is the central idea of each article? How are they different from each other? **(RI.8.2)**

The central idea of the first article is that technological multitasking is bad for people's focus. The central idea of the second article is that the increase in student writing through the use of technology has been beneficial to students' writing and their ability to fine-tune their writing to different audiences.

3 What does the phrase "get their point across" mean in paragraph 6 of "The New Literacy"? **(RI.8.4; L.8.5a)**

It means that someone is able to communicate his or her idea successfully.

4 Discuss in small groups: What is each author's point of view? How does each author develop his or her claims and support them with evidence? Which article do you find most convincing? **(SL.8.1)**

Discussions will vary. Guide students to outline the claims, reasoning, and evidence each author presents and then discuss which they find to be more convincing and why. Remind them to take one another's opinions into account.

Writing Activities

Write a Scientific Argument (W.8.1)

- Have students think about how an author might use scientific facts to craft an argument. Do authors have a responsibility to curb their bias and stick to the facts? How might an author's interpretation influence the facts and details he or she chooses to include?

- Ask students to write an argument about a subject related to innovation that interests them. Students can take either side of the issue, but they should support their claims with clear reasoning and relevant evidence.

Imperative Mood (L.8.1c)

- Explain to students that the imperative mood is used to convey a command or direction. Point out that sentences using the imperative mood often end with an exclamation point, which adds emphasis to the command or direction.

- Point out the last sentence of "Are You Eating GM Food?" and discuss with students the imperative mood the author expresses. (*Consumers have a right to know what is in the food they purchase.*)

- Have students revise the essays they wrote to include at least one imperative statement.

LISTENING ACTIVITY (SL.8.4)

Listen Closely/Present Claims and Findings

- Have small groups of students reread the articles about innovations. Then have them orally present the claims from each text. Have them use relevant facts and details to support each author's interpretations of the facts.

- Students must listen closely to the oral arguments. They should be able to summarize what they hear and explain how these claims are a result of the authors' viewpoint and their purpose for writing.

DISCUSSION ACTIVITY (SL.8.1)

Talk in a Group/Evaluate Arguments

- Ask students to compare and contrast the information presented in the two articles about genetically modified foods.

- Have students evaluate the claims made in each. Which are based in fact? Are any based in personal experience? Which are based on newly uncovered facts? Students should be able to identify claims that are supported by evidence.

- Appoint one member of each group to take notes. Allow 10 to 15 minutes for discussion, and then have each group share its results with the class.

MEDIA ACTIVITY (RI.8.7)

Be Creative/Select a Media Format

- Have students consider the mystery surrounding King Tut's death. How would they best portray to others the information they have learned? What type of media would be most effective and why? Have students consider printed and digital text, video, and other forms of multimedia.

- Have students outline how they would use their chosen media format to inform others about King Tut and then write a paragraph to explain why it is the best format to use.

RESEARCH ACTIVITY (W.8.8; SL.8.4)

Research and Present/Give a Presentation

- Ask students to research more about the life of King Tut. What important events in his life were not mentioned in either of this lesson's articles about him?

- Remind students to assess the credibility of each source they choose and quote or paraphrase their conclusions.

- Students should present their findings orally to the class. Have them create a time line and a bibliography.

SCORING GUIDE AND ANSWER ANALYSIS

Informational Passage Answer Analysis

1 ● Ⓑ Ⓒ Ⓓ   4 Ⓐ Ⓑ ● Ⓓ

2 ● Ⓑ Ⓒ Ⓓ   5 Ⓐ Ⓑ Ⓒ ●

3 Ⓐ Ⓑ Ⓒ ●

1 Choice A is correct. This sentence clearly states the author's strong opinions about limiting human interaction with Antarctica.

Choices B, C, and D are incorrect. Choice B describes an opinion—that Antarctica could be a useful place for many human activities—that is opposite to the author's. Choice C supports the author's views about protecting Antarctica, but elsewhere the author expresses skepticism about whether the treaty will hold if valuable resources are discovered. Choice D is a circumstance the author approves of, but it doesn't support the statement in question. **(RI.8.8; DOK 2)**

2 Choice A is correct. In the last paragraph of "A New Land of Opportunity," the author states that "in recent years tens of thousands of tourists" have visited Antarctica. He then uses this idea to lead into a claim that people love the continent's adventure and beauty.

Choice B is incorrect. The author does estimate that relatively few people are residents of Antarctica. However, this information would seem contrary to the idea that people love Antarctica. Choice C is incorrect. The author explains the work international scientists are doing in Antarctica. However, he addresses science separately from "adventure and beauty." Choice D is also incorrect. The author talks about possible technological advances that will allow colonization, but he presents this idea after talking about how people love the adventure and beauty of Antarctica, not as an introduction. **(RI.8.8; DOK 2)**

3 Choice D is correct. While the nations of the world have so far honored agreements about mining and drilling in Antarctica, the author makes it clear she believes that this is because no large deposits have been discovered. If they are, she claims, nations will be quick to fight over them. Choices A, B, and C are incorrect. Each choice describes the current situation with regard to mineral and oil deposits in Antarctica and does not suggest what might happen in different circumstances. **(RI.8.8; DOK 2)**

4 Choice C is correct. In "A New Land of Opportunity," the author writes that there are large amounts of important minerals such as coal, iron, and gold. However, the author of "The Last Wilderness Preserve" writes that not many large mineral deposits have been found in Antarctica and those which do exist are protected by regulations.

Choice A is incorrect. Both authors note that few people live on Antarctica on a regular basis. Choice B is incorrect. The passages both note the wild nature of Antarctica as well as its icy cold climate. Choice D is also incorrect. Both passages mention the Antarctic Treaty, the agreement that protects Antarctica in various ways. The authors mention different aspects of the treaty but they both acknowledge its existence and purpose. **(RI.8.9; DOK 3)**

5 Choice D is correct. The author of "A New Land of Opportunity" praises the scientific research (such as archaeology and astronomy) in Antarctica as fascinating and beneficial. The author of "The Last Wilderness Preserve," however, writes that it would be better to conduct this sort of research on other continents instead.

Choice A is incorrect. Both of the authors address the effects of climate change and agree that global warming may be causing large amounts of Antarctica's ice to melt. Choice B is incorrect. The authors focus on different aspects of the treaty, but they do not have clearly differing interpretations of its details. Choice C is also incorrect. The authors of both passages write about the difficult living conditions in Antarctica. **(RI.8.9; DOK 3)**

SAMPLE RESPONSES

Short Response

6 **Part A:** Students select the third claim. Most of the article revolves around the author's main claim that Antarctica possesses resources and features potentially of great benefit to humankind. He endorses taking advantage of these benefits before the continent's ice melts any more. The first claim is suggested by the author, but there is little to support it beyond some generalizations in paragraph 2. The second claim is also made by the author, but most of what he offers to support it is briefly stated in paragraph 6. *(RI.8.8; DOK 3)*

Part B: Sample response: In the first paragraph, the author says that people should "take the opportunity" to explore Antarctica while it "exists in its present state." Much of what he describes in the rest of the article goes beyond exploring and has to do with making use of various features of the continent. For example, the author discusses Antarctica's wealth of natural resources, including minerals, oil, and fish, and he supports the idea that people should "take advantage" of these resources. He later supports the idea that scientists and tourists should make more use of and enjoy the "unique qualities" of Antarctica while they still exist." *(RI.8.8; DOK 3)*

7 The author of "The Last Wilderness Preserve" believes that people are not supposed to visit Antarctica. She describes the harsh conditions on the continent—such as the cold, wind, and lack of water and plants—and its isolated location. I think this evidence shows that it would be hard to reach and live in Antarctica, but it does not prove that people should never go there. *(RI.8.8; DOK 3)*

8 The authors of "The Last Wilderness Preserve" and "A New Land of Opportunity" agree that climate change is melting much of Antarctica's ice. This climate change is likely caused by global warming brought on by human pollution. The authors disagree, however, on what should be done about it. The author of "The Last Wilderness Preserve" writes that people should stay away from Antarctica and let the land heal. The author of "A New Land of Opportunity" encourages more people to visit and find remedies for the problem. *(RI.8.9; DOK 4)*

Performance Task

9 There is no correct answer. Students can choose either passage as having the stronger argument.

The authors of "The Last Wilderness Preserve" and "A New Land of Opportunity" offer many ideas about the way human actions are impacting Antarctica. In "The Last Wilderness Preserve," the author takes an unfavorable view of it. She explains that people can be greedy and destructive, and believes that people should not explore Antarctica because that might bring damage to the continent. The author presents evidence that Antarctica is not a feasible place to live and people have few, if any, good reasons to go there.

Meanwhile, the author of "A New Land of Opportunity" takes the opposite view. He believes that Antarctica has much to offer. He writes that people should visit Antarctica to learn about it and its offerings. The author describes some scientific work that takes place on the continent as well as its animals and minerals. "A New Land of Opportunity" closes with the idea that in the future, technology may provide ways for people to live and work in Antarctica without causing damage.

I think both of the authors made strong arguments. However, the author of "The Last Wilderness Preserve" used some especially convincing facts and examples. She described the difficulty of living in Antarctica as well as the damage people have done to many regions of the world. She also uses factual information from the Antarctic Treaty to show weaknesses in the other author's claims. *(RI.8.8, RI.8.9; DOK 4)*

SCORING RUBRICS

Short-Response Rubric

2 points   The response is accurate, complete, and fulfills all requirements of the task. Text-based support and examples are included. Any information that goes beyond the text is relevant to the task.

1 point   The response is partially accurate and fulfills some requirements of the task. Some information may be inaccurate, too general, or confused. Support and examples may be insufficient or not text-based.

0 points   The response is inaccurate, poorly organized, or does not respond to the task.

Performance Task Rubric

4 points   The response
- Fulfills all requirements of the task
- Uses varied sentence types and some sophisticated vocabulary
- Includes relevant and accurate details from the texts as well as text-based inferences
- Demonstrates a thorough understanding of the texts
- Maintains a clear focus and organization
- Is fluent and demonstrates a clear voice
- Uses correct spelling, grammar, capitalization, and punctuation

3 points   The response
- Fulfills all requirements of the task
- Uses simple sentences and grade-level vocabulary
- Includes relevant and accurate details from the texts
- Demonstrates a mainly literal understanding of the texts
- Maintains a mostly clear focus and organization
- Is fluent and demonstrates some sense of voice
- Uses mostly correct spelling, grammar, capitalization, and punctuation

2 points   The response
- Fulfills some requirements of the task
- Uses simple sentences, some fragments, and grade-level vocabulary
- Includes some relevant and accurate details from the texts
- Demonstrates some misunderstandings or gaps in understanding of the texts
- Attempts to maintain a clear focus and organization
- Is difficult to read, includes some inaccuracies, and demonstrates little or no sense of voice
- Contains some inaccurate spelling, grammar, capitalization, and punctuation that may hinder understanding

1 point   The response
- Fulfills few requirements of the task
- Uses sentence fragments and below-grade-level vocabulary
- Includes no details or irrelevant details to support the response
- Demonstrates very little understanding of the texts
- Does not establish a clear focus or organization
- Is difficult to read, contains many inaccuracies, and demonstrates no sense of voice
- Uses incorrect spelling, grammar, capitalization, and punctuation to an extent that impedes understanding

0 points   The response is irrelevant, poorly organized, or illegible.

Evaluating Presentation Mediums

LESSON OBJECTIVE

• Evaluate the advantages and disadvantages of using different mediums such as print, video, and multimedia to present a topic or idea.

THE LEARNING PROGRESSION

Grade 7: CCSS RI.7.7 required students to compare and contrast a text to an audio, video, or multimedia version of the text, "analyzing each medium's portrayal of the subject."

Grade 8: CCSS RI.8.7 builds on the Grade 7 standard by requiring students to "evaluate the advantages and disadvantages of using different mediums" to present a topic or idea.

Grade 9: CCSS RI.9–10.7 requires students to analyze various accounts of a subject presented in different mediums and determine "which details are emphasized in each account."

TAP STUDENTS' PRIOR KNOWLEDGE

• Ask students to recall a memorable event in American history that they've read about in school or on their own. What details do they remember?

• Now ask the class for examples of recent news events they saw on TV or watched video of online. What do they remember most about the event?

• Explain that the way we learn about events affects how we understand the information being conveyed. The various mediums we rely on for information have unique characteristics, and each has distinct advantages and disadvantages.

• For example, if you learn about a tornado from a newscast, the image of a man crying as he looks at his destroyed house may affect you greatly—but what has the image told you of the breadth and scope of the tornado's devastation? If you read an article online about the tornado and its effects, a quote from the tearful man will be only one quote among other information about the tornado.

• Tell students they will look at the benefits and drawbacks of three popular mediums: print, the Internet, and multimedia. They will use this information to evaluate which medium is best suited to present a particular topic or idea.

Ready *Teacher Toolbox*   *teacher-toolbox.com*

	Prerequisite Skills	*RI.8.7*
Ready Lessons	✓	✓
Tools for Instruction		
Interactive Tutorials		✓

CCSS Focus

RI.8.7 Evaluate the advantages and disadvantages of using different mediums (e.g., print or digital text, video, multimedia) to present a particular topic or idea.

ADDITIONAL STANDARDS: **W.8.3, W.8.7; SL.8.2, SL.8.5**

AT A GLANCE

By evaluating the advantages and disadvantages of using different mediums to present an idea or topic, students will make decisions about which medium best suits a topic they want to explore.

STEP BY STEP: PAGE 215

- Before students look at page 215, ask them where they go to get information on something that interests them. (*The Internet* will likely be the overwhelming answer.) Do they watch video presentations? Do they read articles? Survey the class to see how many students *watch* sources to get information and how many *read* sources for information. Remind students that often when they watch a video about something that interests them, they get less information than when they read an article (online or in print) about something.

- Have a volunteer read the introduction on page 215. Define a tribute (something that is done to show respect or appreciation) and point out that creating a tribute to a band or artist can be done in many ways. Provide some examples, such as a television show or a CD of artists covering the band's songs.

- Read the lines above the chart on page 215. Be sure students understand the format of the chart. Explain that each column presents the major pros and cons of each medium.

- Remind students to think about how each medium may or may not work to create their tribute.

- **Print:** Review the bullet points in each row. Point out that print sources, like magazine articles, are often more in-depth, easier to follow, and allow for greater analysis of a subject than other sources. Writers can include information from other sources, such as interviews, to create a detailed understanding of the subject. Once published, articles are difficult to update with new information.

- **Internet:** Review the bullet points in each row. Point out that Web sites have the great advantage of being able to be updated regularly. They can also bring together various forms of media: print articles, video, and audio. Web sites allow readers to interact with the site, often from anywhere in the world. Tell students it's hard to tell a story on a Web site (other

than in print articles housed on the site), and creating a Web site requires some technical ability.

- **Multimedia:** Review the bullet points in each row. The personal nature of a multimedia presentation allows the creator to express him or herself creatively. The creator can incorporate a variety of mediums to tell a story. Technological concerns can be a drawback to these presentations.

- After reviewing the chart, have small groups of students discuss the pros and cons of each medium and determine which would be best suited for a tribute to a band or artist.

STEP BY STEP: PAGE 216

- Divide students into small groups (you may wish to keep the discussion groups from Part 1 in place). Tell students that they are going to plan their tribute as a group and determine which medium will work best for their purpose and audience.

- Read aloud the directions on page 216. Tell students to make notes in the chart about their responses to each step. They will use these responses to choose a medium.

- **Step 1:** Students can stick with the band tribute idea or choose a different subject for a tribute, such as a local hero or favorite author, that they all agree on.

- **Step 2:** Have students set a clear purpose for their tribute: to inform, entertain, persuade, or share information. Ask them to imagine a specific type of person who would be interested in their tribute.

- **Step 3:** Urge students to brainstorm here. Have them make detailed notes on all the possible content they might want to include in their tribute. This will help them to determine which medium can best handle what they want to do.

- **Step 4:** Have students review the chart on page 215 and add to their notes. Remind them that considering the benefits or drawbacks of a medium will help them decide which one to use for their tribute.

- When the groups have completed the first three steps in the planner, they should decide which medium they will use for their tribute. Have each group explain why they chose the medium and provide specific details.

CREATE MULTIMEDIA *(SL.8.5)*

- Have small groups of students create a multimedia piece incorporating four different mediums. Tell students to brainstorm an idea about one of the following topics: a famous protest or revolution; an important invention; a U.S. president; a favorite film or TV show.

- Tell students to use the copymaster on page 203 to make notes on the various mediums they will incorporate into their multimedia piece. Have them use at least four of the following mediums: video, music or audio, print, photographs or visual art, animation, and performance.

- Each group will decide their topic and make notes about which mediums they should use to best present their subject matter. Remind students to set a clear purpose for the multimedia piece, use the mediums to clarify information and add interest, and consider their audience. Once the pieces are completed, have each group present their work to the class.

WRITE A NEWS STORY *(W.8.3)*

- Have students find a photo online, in a magazine, or at home to use as inspiration to write a news story. Tell them to look for a photo that suggests a story. It can be of an individual, a group, or of a place—the important thing is that when the student looks at it he or she can begin to conjure a story from the image.

- Students will use the photo as the basis for a news story that they will make up. Have them pretend that they are reporters filing their stories based on the image. Remind them to include lots of details and quotes (which they will make up). When they are finished, other students should be able to read the article and look at the photo and learn a complete story.

MAKE IT VISUAL *(SL.8.5)*

- Have student pairs find a news story online or in a newspaper or magazine that deals with a local, national, or international story. Tell students they will adapt the print story to a one-minute broadcast story.

- Students will need to describe the visuals, voice over, and text that will be used in their adaptation. Remind them that a broadcast story relies on visuals to show the viewer what the news story uses words to describe.

- Have students use a simple format such as this:

VISUAL: Hurricane winds blowing through trees.

VOICEOVER: Hurricane Edna is making her presence know all across the Gulf Coast tonight. Just ask weatherman Bob Aggers of New Orleans.

INTERVIEW: This doesn't feel so bad right now, but just wait a couple of hours—Edna's going to be a tough one.

- Ask volunteers to read or perform their broadcasts for the class.

ANALYZE A WEBSITE HOMEPAGE *(SL.8.2)*

- Have students visit an entertainment, news, or political Web site (it must be appropriate for class) and analyze the media elements used on the homepage. Is there video? How is the homepage organized? Is it easy for a first time visitor to figure out where and how to find information on the site?

- Tell students to make notes as they examine the homepage to identify the media elements employed. Then have them write a two-paragraph analysis of the homepage where paragraph one describes the media elements used and paragraph two evaluates the reasons or motives for using those elements.

RESEARCH IN A HURRY *(W.8.7)*

- Give each student a topic to research overnight. Topics should be straightforward, such as what causes dog allergies, when babies start laughing, who is the fastest person on the planet, etc.

- Tell students they need to return to school the next day with a one- or two-paragraph answer to their topic. Encourage them to use at least two media sources to find the answer, and have them list the media sources they used. Discuss with the class how they found the answers and which medium provided the best answers.

Name_____ Date_____

DIRECTIONS: Use this chart to brainstorm and organize your ideas about sources for the different possible mediums you can use in your presentation. Try to give some thought to each of the six mediums as your group discusses how to create your multimedia piece.

Topic: _____
_____

AVAILABLE MEDIA		
VIDEO	**MUSIC/AUDIO**	**PRINT**
PHOTOS/VISUAL ART	**ANIMATION**	**PERFORMANCE**

Which mediums did you decide were most effective for the piece you want to present? Explain your rationale for each of the four mediums you decided to use.

Cut along the dotted line.

Analyzing Elements of Modern Fiction

Theme: *From Myth to Modern Fiction*

LESSON OBJECTIVES

- Compare and contrast modern pieces of fiction with myths and traditional tales.

- Analyze how authors of modern fiction incorporate elements from myths and traditional tales, such as themes, events, or character types.

- Explain the ways in which material from myths and traditional tales is reinterpreted or rendered new in modern fiction.

THE LEARNING PROGRESSION

- **Grade 7:** Grade 7: CCSS RL.7.9 requires students to compare fictional portrayals of historical events as a means to understand how fiction authors use or alter history.

- **Grade 8: CCSS RL.8.9 builds on the Grade 7 standard by having students analyze how modern fiction draws on traditional stories and myths, including how the material is rendered new.**

- **Grade 9:** CCSS RL.9.9 requires students to analyze how authors draw on and transform older works.

PREREQUISITE SKILLS

- Identify and analyze plot, setting, and character types.

- Understand that many themes are timeless and appear across centuries.

- Compare and contrast two works of fiction.

- Understand the elements of myths, legends, and traditional tales.

TAP STUDENTS' PRIOR KNOWLEDGE

- Tell students that in this lesson they will analyze the elements of modern fiction and how modern stories often draw on past works, such as myths and traditional stories.

- Remind students that the theme of a story is the central message about life or human nature that the author wants to share with the reader.

- Ask students if they have seen movies or read books that have similar themes, such as good conquers evil. Discuss the movies or books and how they conveyed the theme.

- Next, ask students if they have seen movies or read books that have similar plots and characters. Choose two stories and draw plot diagrams on the board to compare the plots.

- Point out that many character types and themes are universal, or found in literature throughout all time periods. It is important to recognize how authors have drawn on past works for inspiration. This will help students better appreciate the stories they read.

Ready *Teacher Toolbox*   *teacher-toolbox.com*

	Prerequisite Skills	RL.8.9
Ready Lessons	✓	✓
Tools for Instruction		
Interactive Tutorials	✓	✓

CCSS Focus

RL.8.9 Analyze how a modern work of fiction draws on themes, patterns of events, or character types from myths, traditional stories, or religious works, such as the Bible, including describing how the material is rendered new.

ADDITIONAL STANDARDS: **RL.8.1, RL.8.2, RL.8.3, RL.8.4, RL.8.5, RL.8.7; L.8.1, L.8.2a, L.8.4a, L.8.5b, L.8.5c; W.8.3, W.8.4, W.8.7; SL.8.1, SL.8.4, SL.8.5** (*See page A39 for full text.*)

AT A GLANCE

By studying a cartoon, students are introduced to the idea that myths and legends are often retold by modern writers. They compare the theme, pattern of events, and character types in both versions.

STEP BY STEP

- Read the first paragraph, which includes the definitions of *pattern of events, character types,* and *theme.* Point out that the cartoon shows two stories. The first panel illustrates a Greek myth about King Midas. The second panel illustrates a retelling of the story. Then encourage students to read the cartoon and look for clues in the pictures and words that help them note what is similar in both panels.

- Explain that the chart compares the theme, pattern of events, and character types in both versions. Review each column.

- Ask students to share the notes they made and discuss how they compare with the notes in the chart.

- Reinforce the idea that comparing a modern story to a traditional version helps readers recognize how certain themes, character types, and events have withstood the test of time. Analyzing the comparisons will help students better understand the meaning and appreciate the modern version.

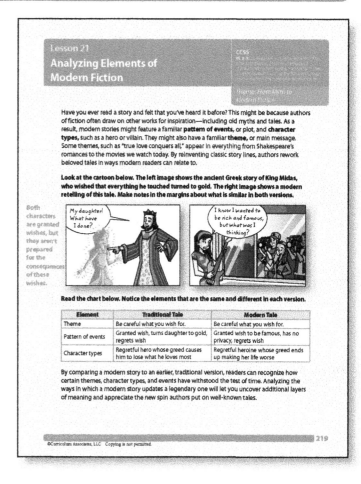

Genre Focus

Literary Texts: Legend and Myth

Explain that legends are stories that get passed down from generation to generation. They are often told as if they were true stories. Explain that legends usually have the following characteristics:

- A focus on the deeds and acts of humans rather than gods or goddesses.

- A main character who is highly ethical and moral.

- Events that demonstrate the character's traits, such as bravery and honesty.

A myth is a fiction story that often explains something about human behavior or the natural world. Myths are closely tied to the beliefs and ideals of a particular culture. The characters are often gods, goddesses, or godlike beings with extraordinary powers. The heroes possess traits valued by the culture.

Ask students what legends and myths they are familiar with. Who are the main characters? What are the plot events? What is the theme? Students may be familiar with the legend of King Arthur and Greek or Roman myths.

Explain that "Mulan's Ballad" is a legend about Hua Mulan, a Chinese emperor's daughter who becomes a great warrior. Tell students they will read myths about a labyrinth and about the Sphinx. They will also read a modern version of each text.

AT A GLANCE

Students read a traditional legend and identify the themes, pattern of events, and character types. This will help them compare this traditional legend with the modern retelling they will read next.

STEP BY STEP

- Invite volunteers to tell what they learned on the previous page about how modern stories often draw on elements of traditional tales.

- Tell students that in this lesson they will compare a legend with a story set in modern times.

- Read "Mulan's Ballad." Then read the questions: "Based on text evidence, what kind of character is Mulan? What theme is suggested by her actions?"

- Tell students you will use a Think Aloud to demonstrate a way to answer the questions.

Think Aloud: The author uses Mulan's words and actions to describe her. I'll look for clues that tell me what kind of person Mulan is. First, she challenges the emperor to a duel, which shows she is strong and brave. That she disguised herself as a man shows that she is smart and bold.

- Have students underline details in the text pertaining to the theme, patterns of events, and character types.

- Direct students to the chart, and review how it helps them compare and contrast the aspects of two versions of a story.

- Have students record in the chart details about the type of character Mulan is.

Think Aloud: The theme is also not directly stated, so I need to think about what message Mulan's character traits and the pattern of events reveal. The first event is her challenge of the emperor. The next events are Mulan's rise to the rank of general and then her revelation that she is the emperor's daughter.

- Have students think about these events and Mulan's character traits, and then discuss possible themes with a partner, as prompted at the bottom of the page. *(Sample response: One possible theme is women can do anything men can do. Women are not allowed in the army, but Mulan ends up becoming a general and one of the greatest warriors in China.)*

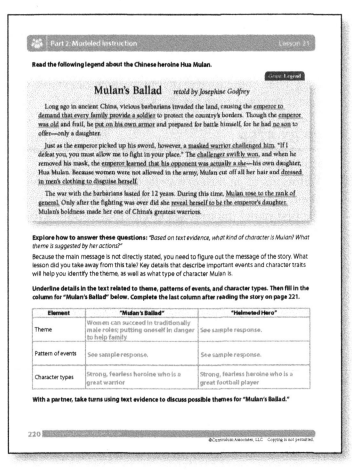

ELL Support: Possessives

- Point out the possessive nouns *country's* and *men's*. Explain that possessive nouns show ownership or relationship. Tell students that most possessive nouns are formed by adding an apostrophe and -s to the end of singular nouns and an apostrophe to the end of plural nouns that end with s.

- Point out the phrase *country's borders*. Have students identify the meaning of this phrase. *("borders of the country")*

- Then point out the possessive pronouns *his* and *her*. Explain that these are the possessive forms of the pronouns *he* and *she*. **(L.8.1)**

AT A GLANCE

Students read a story set in modern times that draws on the legend of Mulan. They answer a multiple-choice question and analyze how the modern version conveys the same theme as the legend.

STEP BY STEP

- Tell students they will read a story that is set in modern times.

- The Close Reading helps students identify aspects of the Mulan tale that the author has drawn upon. The Hint will help them think about the characters and the events in order to understand the theme.

- Have students read the story and underline details about the theme, events, and character types, as directed by the Close Reading. After students finish, have them complete the chart on page 220.

- *(Sample responses: Theme: Women can succeed in traditionally male roles. Pattern of Events: Eric's team is down a player, an unfamiliar figure helps win the game, the player is a girl.)*

- Then have students respond to Show Your Thinking.

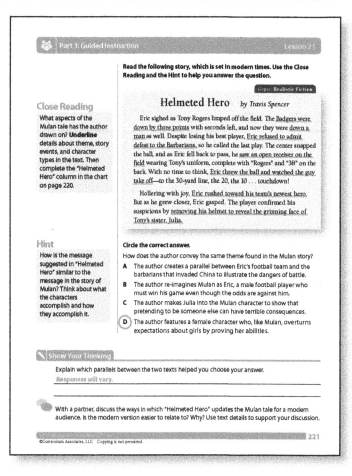

ANSWER ANALYSIS

Choice A is incorrect. The parallel the author creates is between Julia and Mulan, not between the football team and the barbarians.

Choice B is incorrect. The author re-imagines Mulan as Julia, not as Eric.

Choice C is incorrect. The author does make Julia into the Mulan character, but the theme is not that pretending to be someone else can have terrible consequences.

Choice D is correct. Like Mulan, Julia dresses as a boy and then proves that she has as much strength and talent to be a football player.

ERROR ALERT: Students who did not choose D might not have recognized the similarities between Julia and Mulan and how they reveal the theme. Point out details that show similarities between the two characters. Note only D conveys these details.

ELL Support: Irregular Past Tense

- Explain to students that verbs are action words. The past tense of a verb tells that the action has already happened. The past tense of a regular verb ends in *-ed*. The past tense of an irregular verb does not end in *-ed*. Irregular verbs have special forms in the past tense.

- Read the second sentence. Point out the verb *were*. Tell students that this is the past tense of the verb *be*. Explain that the past tense of *be* does not follow a pattern. Then point out the verbs *saw, fell, threw,* and *grew*. Explain that these are also irregular past tense verbs. Have students name the present tense of each verb. (*see, fall, throw, grow*) **(L.8.1)**

AT A GLANCE

Students read a myth about Theseus twice. After the first reading, you will ask three questions to check your students' understanding of the passage.

STEP BY STEP

- Have students read the passage silently without referring to the Study Buddy or Close Reading text.

- Ask the following questions to ensure students' comprehension of the text:

  What does King Minos do each year? Why does he do it? (*He makes the king of Athens choose 14 Athenian men and women to enter the maze to be sacrificed to the Minotaur. He does this as revenge for his son's death in Athens.*)

  Why does Theseus volunteer to enter the labyrinth? (*He wants to defeat the Minotaur and end his kingdom's sacrifices.*)

  How does Theseus survive the labyrinth? (*Ariadne gives him a ball of string. He leaves a trail of string behind him so he can find the Minotaur and then find his way out of the maze.*)

- Then ask students to reread paragraph 1 and look at the Study Buddy think aloud. What does the Study Buddy help them think about?

Tip: The Study Buddy has students underline details about the main characters. Underlining details will help students understand what the characters are like and what their motives are. These details will also help them determine the theme.

- Have students read the rest of the passage. Tell them to follow the directions in the Close Reading.

Tip: The Close Reading guides students to mark main plot points and story details. Recognizing details and understanding the plot points will help students determine the theme. It will also prepare them for comparing the legend with a modern day story.

Tier Two Vocabulary: *Steeled*

- Direct students to the word *steeled* in paragraph 4. Have students use the context of the sentence and the paragraph to determine the meaning of the word. ("*strengthened*")

- Have students identify the context clues they used to help them determine the meaning of the word. They should recognize that the word *but* signals that the sentence contains an antonym or opposite feeling of *frightened*.

- Ask students to come up with two synonyms for the word and then consider why the author chose to use the word *steeled* instead of the other words. **(RL.8.4; L.8.4a, L.8.5b)**

AT A GLANCE

Students read a modern version of the Theseus myth twice. After the first reading, you will ask three questions to check your students' understanding of the passage.

STEP BY STEP

- Have students read the passage silently without referring to the Study Buddy or Close Reading text.

- Ask the following questions to ensure students' comprehension of the text:

  Why is Thea in a new school? How does she feel about being there? (*Her father got a new job. She feels that she sacrificed her friends and everything she loved for the good of her family.*)

  What did Aaron send Thea? Why did he send it? (*He sent her a map of the new school. He hoped it would help keep her from getting lost in the school's maze of hallways.*)

  What "battle" did Thea win? (*She used the map to conquer her fear of getting lost in her new school and faced her Biology teacher even though she was afraid of getting in trouble for being late.*)

- Then ask students to reread paragraph 1 and look at the Study Buddy think aloud. What does the Study Buddy help them think about?

Tip: The Study Buddy tells students to pay attention to characters that are similar to those in the myth. Recognizing the similarities between characters will help them understand how the author drew on the myth to create the modern version of the story.

- Have students read the rest of the passage. Tell them to follow the directions in the Close Reading.

Tip: The Close Reading guides students to think about how details suggest a theme that is similar to the myth. It also tells them to identify familiar events. Identifying the similarities will help them recognize how the author drew inspiration from the myth.

- Finally, have students answer the questions on page 224. Use the Answer Analysis to discuss correct and incorrect responses.

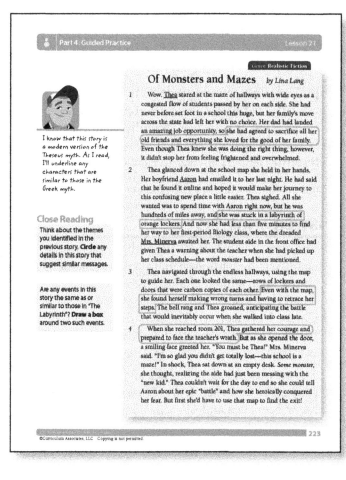

Tier Two Vocabulary: *Congested*

- Point out the word *congested* in paragraph 1. Have students use context clues to determine its meaning. (*"crowded"*)

- Have students list synonyms. Then remind them that synonyms do not have the exact same meanings and often have different connotations, or feelings attached to them. Ask students if the word *congested* has a negative, positive, or neutral connotation. (*negative*)

- Ask students why they think the author chose *congested* instead of a word such as *crowded*. (*Congested makes the reader think of being sick and unable to breathe. It helps the reader understand how Thea feels.*) **(RL.8.4; L.8.4a, L.8.5c)**

STEP BY STEP

- Have students read questions 1–3, using the Hints to help them answer the questions.

Tip: The Hints remind students to think about the similarities between the stories. Tell students to read each question and answer carefully. Remind them they can reread parts of the story to help them determine the best answer to each question.

- Discuss with students the Answer Analysis below.

ANSWER ANALYSIS

1 The correct choice is C. The author updates the characters by putting them in similar situations and giving them similar characteristics. Choice A incorrectly states that Thea must use a ball of string. Choice B is incorrect. The story doesn't highlight a parallel between the father and the king. Choice D incorrectly states that Aaron defies his father.

2 The correct choice is B. Thea and Theseus find the courage to face their fears. Choices A and C are incorrect. Thea and Theseus do not ask for help and do not disobey their parents. Choice D is incorrect. Only the modern version suggests this theme.

3 Sample response: Both stories' plots are similar. The heroes (Theseus and Thea) have to make their way through a maze to find a "monster" (the Minotaur and Mrs. Minerva). They are given a tool by someone they care about to help keep them from getting lost—Ariadne gives Theseus a ball of string, and Aaron gives Thea a map. "Of Monsters and Mazes" is made new in that the monster turns out not to be a monster after all.

RETEACHING

Use a chart to verify the correct answer to question 2. Draw the chart below, and work with students to fill in the boxes. Sample responses are provided.

Element	"The Labyrinth"	"Of Monsters and Mazes"
Pattern of Events	enters labyrinth to end sacrifices, uses string, faces fears	sacrifices friends to move, uses map, faces fears
Character Types	Theseus: brave, honorable Ariadne: helpful	Thea: brave, loyal Aaron: helpful

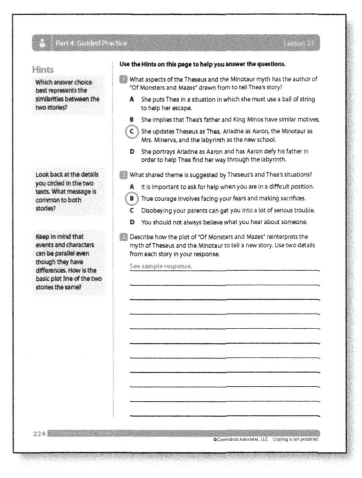

Integrating Standards

Use these questions to further students' understanding of "The Labyrinth" and "Of Monsters and Mazes."

1 In "The Labyrinth," Theseus volunteers to face the Minotaur. How does this decision propel the action, and what does it reveal about Theseus? **(RL.8.3)**

His decision shows that he is willing to sacrifice himself to save others. His decision moves the plot forward and introduces the conflict.

2 In "Of Mazes and Monsters," what can you infer about Aaron based on his actions? How do his actions affect the plot? **(RL.8.1, RL.8.3)**

It shows that he cares about Thea, and even though he is not with her, he wants to help her succeed. Without Aaron's map, Thea might not have had the courage or ability to face her fears.

Part 5: Common Core Practice · Lesson 21

Read the two stories. Then answer the questions that follow.

Oedipus and the Sphinx

adapted by Alice Denbrough

1 In the tales of ancient gods and goddesses, heroes and monsters, there was a wandering traveler by the name of Oedipus who journeyed aimlessly through the countryside in the hope of eluding his destiny. After a number of years traveling, he one day arrived at the exalted city of Thebes, whose gates were barred to prevent anyone from entering or leaving.

2 A horrific creature called the Sphinx guarded these gates. She had the body of a lion, wings of an eagle, and the head of a human woman. The Sphinx allowed no one passage through the gates . . . not without first answering a riddle. If the person could not give the correct answer, the Sphinx would devour him. For many years, the brave and the foolish stood before the Sphinx and demanded she pose her riddle. None had given the correct answer, and therefore none had survived the challenge. The city of Thebes continued to be isolated from the rest of the world.

3 Then came the day Oedipus stood before the Sphinx. "I request admittance into the city," he said.

4 "No one may enter Thebes," the Sphinx replied, "without first answering my riddle."

5 Oedipus was a well-traveled man who had seen a great many things in his days. He felt confident he could answer the Sphinx's riddle—and if not, he kept his hand resting on the hilt of his sword.

6 "Then ask," he said, "for I do not fear any test you might put before me."

7 The Sphinx had not eaten in many weeks, and so she rose to her full, fearsome height, eager to have her next meal. "What walks on four legs in the morning, two legs at noon, and three legs in the evening?"

8 This gave Oedipus pause, since he'd seen all manner of beasts, from the winged to the finned to the hoofed, but never had he seen a creature such as this. The Sphinx read the hesitation in the man's face and knew she had bested another.

9 But then, a thought came to Oedipus. "It is man. Man crawls on all fours as a baby (in the morning), walks on two legs during adulthood (at noon), and leans on a cane in his old age (in the evening)."

10 He had done it. He'd answered correctly, and the Sphinx was so enraged that someone had finally answered her riddle that she flung herself off the city walls and down into the sea, where she was never seen or heard from again.

11 The city gates of Thebes were opened once again, and the city's inhabitants hailed Oedipus as a hero for ridding them of the terrible monster that had kept them prisoners for so long.

225

Part 5: Common Core Practice · Lesson 21

from *The Grey King*

by Susan Cooper

The Grey King is part of Susan Cooper's The Dark Is Rising sequence of popular fantasy novels that are steeped in classic Welsh and Celtic mythology. This volume of the series tells the story of 12-year-old Will Stanton, who is sent to a farm in Wales to recuperate from a terrible illness but soon discovers that he is really an "Old One" of legend doing battle against modern-day dark forces.

In the following scene, Will and his new friend Bran have begun a quest to find a Golden Harp, whose music will help them defeat "The Dark." They find themselves in a dimly-lit chamber where three hooded figures pose riddles the boys must answer in order to prove themselves worthy of the harp.

1 The soft-voiced lord in the lightest robe, who had spoken first, swiftly stood. His cloak swirled round him like a blue mist; bright eyes glinted from the thin pale face glimmering in the hood.

2 "Answer the three riddles as the law demands, Old One, you and the White Crow your helper there, and the harp shall be yours. But if you answer wrong, the doors of rock shall close, and you be left [defenseless] on the cold mountain, and the harp shall be lost to the Light forever."

3 "We shall answer," Will said. . . .

4 The hall seemed darker, filled with dancing shadows from the flickering light of the fire. A sudden flash and crackle came from behind the boys, as a log fell and the flames leapt up; instinctively Will glanced back. When he turned forward again, the third figure, who had not spoken or moved until now, was standing tall and silent before his throne. His robe was a deep, deep blue, darkest of the three, and his hood was pulled so far forward that there was no hint of his face visible, but only shadow.

5 His voice was deep and resonant, like the voice of a cello, and it brought music into the hall.

6 "Will Stanton," it said, "what is the shore that fears the sea?"

7 Will started impulsively forward, his hands clenching into fists, for this voice caught into the deepest part of him. Surely, surely . . . but the face in the hood was hidden, and he was denied all ways of recognition. Any part of his senses that tried to reach out to the great thrones met a blank wall of refusal from the High Magic. Once more Will gave up, and put his mind to the riddle.

8 He said slowly, "The shore that fears the sea . . ."

9 Images wavered in and out of his mind: great crashing waves against a rocky coast . . . the green light in the ocean, the realm of Tethys, where strange creatures may live . . . a gentler sea then, washing in long slow waves an endless golden beach. The shore . . . the beach . . . the beach . . .

10 The image wavered and changed. It dissolved into a green dappled forest of gnarled ancient trees, their broad trunks smooth with a curious light grey bark. Their leaves danced above, new, soft bright with a delicate green that had in it all of springtime. The beginnings of triumph whispered in Will's mind.

226

AT A GLANCE

Students independently read a longer myth and modern story and answer questions in a format that provides test practice.

STEP BY STEP

- Tell students to use what they have learned about reading closely and analyzing elements of modern fiction to read the passages on pages 225–227.

- Remind students to underline or circle important details about theme, patterns of events, and character types.

- Tell students to answer the questions on pages 227 and 228. For questions 1–3, they should fill in the correct circle on the Answer Form.

- When students have finished, use the Answer Analysis to discuss correct responses and the reasons for them. Have students fill in the Number Correct on the Answer Form.

ANSWER ANALYSIS

1 The correct choice is D. Oedipus and Will must both answer riddles. Choice A is incorrect. The Sphinx is not a character in *The Grey King*. Choice B is incorrect. Neither Oedipus nor Will use their swords to fight those who ask the riddles. Choice C is incorrect. The hooded figures who guard the Golden Harp do not resemble the people of Thebes. They mirror the Sphinx, who guards the entrance to Thebes. **(DOK 3)**

Theme Connection

- Which of the modern stories in this lesson do you think was the best example of an author drawing on a myth or legend? Why?

- What is one thing you learned by comparing traditional stories to modern fiction?

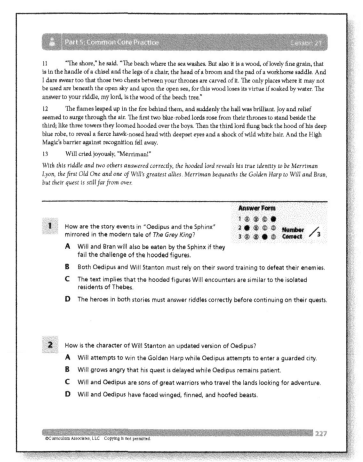

ANSWER ANALYSIS

2 The correct choice is A. In order to get the Golden Harp, Will must answer the riddles of the hooded men who guard the harp. This is similar to Oedipus, who must answer the Sphinx's riddle to enter Thebes. Choice B is incorrect. Will remains calm while he solves the riddle. Choice C is incorrect. The texts do not describe Will or Oedipus as sons of great warriors who travel for adventure. Choice D is incorrect. Will does not have to face a beast, and the Sphinx isn't finned— she is part lion, part eagle, and part human. **(DOK 3)**

3 The correct choice is C. Will and Oedipus are posed with difficult riddles. They must think carefully and creatively to defeat the guardians and achieve their goals. Choice A is incorrect. Oedipus does not have an ally that helps him defeat the Sphinx. Choice B is incorrect. Neither Will nor Oedipus cheat in order to be victorious. Choice D is

incorrect. True heroes do not face adversity just to be famous. Will and Oedipus faced challenges to help or protect others. **(DOK 3)**

4 Sample response: *The Grey King* is set in modern times, but many of the events in the excerpt are similar to those in "Oedipus and the Sphinx." Both Will Stanton and Oedipus are on journeys and have riddles they must answer. Rather than using force to get what they want, both heroes stay calm and use their heads to solve the riddles. **(DOK 4)**

Integrating Standards

Use these questions and tasks as opportunities to interact with "Oedipus and the Sphinx" and *The Grey King*.

1 In "Oedipus and the Sphinx," what causes the city of Thebes to be isolated from the world? *(RL.8.1)*

No one had answered the Sphinx's riddle correctly, so no one was able to pass through the gates into Thebes.

2 In "Oedipus and the Sphinx," what does the author mean by "This gave Oedipus pause" in paragraph 8? What mood does it create? *(RL.8.5)*

The phrase means that Oedipus was confused by the Sphinx's riddle and was concerned he could not answer it. This creates a feeling of suspense.

3 Write a brief summary of the excerpt from *The Grey King*, including key details. *(RL.8.2; W.8.4)*

Sample response: Will is told he must answer three riddles in order to receive the harp. If the answers are wrong, he will be trapped alone on a mountain. Will

thinks he knows one of the hooded men who asks a question. Will answers it correctly. The hooded man reveals himself as Will's ally.

4 What lines or descriptions reveal aspects of Will's and Oedipus's character? *(RL.8.3)*

The lines "[Oedipus] felt confident he could answer the Sphinx" and "'I do not fear any test'" show Oedipus is confident and brave. The description of how Will thinks out the answer shows he is creative, smart, and determined.

5 Discuss in small groups: What are some possible themes of each story? Which themes do the stories share and which are unique? Cite evidence to support each theme. *(SL.8.1)*

Discussions will vary. Students should discuss what the author wants readers to learn. In both stories, thinking creatively can have great rewards.

Writing Activities

Write a Modern Version (RL.8.9; W.8.3)

- Have students choose one of the myths or legends in this lesson that they enjoyed reading. Then have them reread the tale and review the character types, pattern of events, and theme.

- Challenge students to retell the tale and set it in modern times. Remind students to base the events, characters, and themes on the original story. Encourage students to use dialogue and vivid details.

- Invite volunteers to read their stories to the class. Have the class determine which myths or legends volunteers are retelling and discuss how they drew on the original stories.

Punctuation with Phrases and Clauses (L.8.2a)

- Explain that commas and dashes are often used to separate phrases and clauses from the rest of the sentence. Read sentence 2 in paragraph 1 of "The Labyrinth." Point out the appositive phrase and explain that an appositive phrase identifies or renames a preceding noun. Nonessential appositives are often set off with commas but can also follow dashes. Then point out the introductory phrase. Explain that these are also separated by commas.

- Have students write a paragraph that contains phrases or clauses set off by commas or dashes.

LISTENING ACTIVITY (SL.8.1)

Listen Closely/Retell a Tale

- Have students form small groups. Provide them with a short myth or legend, or assign one from the lesson.

- Have students take turns reading the story aloud. After each paragraph, have the listeners summarize the paragraph. After the entire story has been read, have students determine the theme.

DISCUSSION ACTIVITY (SL.8.1)

Talk in a Group/Discuss Personal Connections

- Ask students to review each of this lesson's paired stories and the themes they portray.

- Have students form small groups to discuss their personal connections or experiences related to each of the stories' themes. How does the theme of this story relate to their own experiences or the experiences of people they know?

- Encourage students to evaluate the stories and determine which theme is most relevant to their lives. Which pair of stories did they connect with most? Why?

- Have each group share its results with the class.

MEDIA ACTIVITY (RL.8.7)

Be Creative/Watch a Film or Production

- Have students watch a film or recorded production based on one of the myths or legends in this lesson. They may watch a clip related to the excerpt of the story that they read. For example, students may watch an animated version of *Mulan*.

- Have students evaluate the choices that the director or actors made in producing the film or production version. Ask them to compare this version to the text they read. How are the stories similar? In what ways does the film depart from the written work?

RESEARCH ACTIVITY (W.8.7; SL.8.4, SL.8.5)

Research and Present/Give a Presentation

- Have students choose one hero or monster from the myths they read. Have them research that character to learn about his or her characteristics and roles in myths or modern stories.

- Have students use their research to plan a presentation. Students should produce a visual display to show ways the character is depicted in different versions of the story.

- Have students present their information.

SCORING GUIDE AND ANSWER ANALYSIS

Literary Passage Answer Analysis

1 ● ⓑ ⓒ ⓓ   4 ⓐ ⓑ ● ⓓ

2 ⓐ ● ⓒ ⓓ   5A ● ⓑ ⓒ ⓓ

3 ⓐ ● ⓒ ⓓ

1   Choice A is correct. Madison's nickname "The Songbird" most likely refers to the idea that both she and the Rainbow Crow have admirable abilities. In this case, they are both great singers.

Choice B is incorrect. Rainbow Crow volunteered to go on a difficult journey, but this does not relate to Madison's nickname. Choice C is incorrect. The Great Sky Spirit recognizes the sacrifices made by Rainbow Crow, but this idea is not directly related to Madison's nickname. Choice D is incorrect. The Great Sky Spirit was impressed by Rainbow Crow, but this does not help to explain Madison's actions or her nickname "The Songbird." **(RL.8.9; DOK 3)**

2   Choice B is correct. In both "The Rainbow Crow" and "The Silent Songbird," the main characters show the virtuous behaviors of caring and giving. The Rainbow Crow sacrifices his beauty and talent to save his friends from the cold, while Madison gives up the leading role in the play so that the production is able to happen.

Choice A is incorrect. Only "The Rainbow Crow" takes place in a natural outdoor setting. "The Silent Songbird" takes place at a theater. Choice C is incorrect. Only in "The Rainbow Crow" does a character go on a dangerous quest. Choice D is also incorrect. Only "The Rainbow Crow" deals with the symbolism of cold and warmth. The author of "The Silent Songbird" does not draw on this element. **(RL.8.9; DOK 3)**

3   Choice B is correct. In "The Rainbow Crow," the author refers to Rattlesnake as "mean" and "selfish." The reference to rattlesnakes in "The Silent Songbird" most likely connects Abigail with the selfishness of Rattlesnake.

Choice A is incorrect. In "The Rainbow Crow," the rattlesnake is described as "mean" and "selfish," not boastful. Choice C is incorrect. None of the characters in "The Rainbow Crow" are portrayed as sneaky. Choice D is also incorrect. In "The

Rainbow Crow," the other animals doubt the Crow's abilities. The Rattlesnake, however, is known to be mean, which is similar to how Abigail is described. **(RL.8.9; DOK 3)**

4   Choice C is correct. The characters in "The Silent Songbird" are young people who are putting on a theatrical production. These characters are realistic since they are acting in ways real people act. The characters in "The Rainbow Crow" are not realistic because they are animals that talk.

Choice A is incorrect. The characters in both stories need help. The characters in "The Rainbow Crow" need help because they do not want to be cold during the winter. The characters in "The Silent Songbird" also need help because they cannot have a play without a theater assistant. Choice B is incorrect. Both Rattlesnake in "The Rainbow Crow" and Abigail in "The Silent Songbird" are selfish. This is not a way in which the characters differ. Choice D is incorrect. In "The Silent Songbird," the characters face the problem of having to cancel the play if they don't find a theater assistant. The animals in "The Rainbow Crow" also face problems, such as the dangers of the coming winter. **(RL.8.9; DOK 3)**

5   **Part A:** Choice A is correct. Rainbow Crow gives up his feathers but brings much-needed fire to his friends, and Madison gives up a stage role in order to keep the play from being canceled. Choices B and C are not shown in either story. Choice D is a theme of "The Rainbow Crow" but not "The Silent Songbird." **(RL.8.9; DOK 3)**

Part B: Students' choice of sentences will vary. Possible sentence: "Losing his beauty did not seem like such a sacrifice when he saw the animals gathering around a warm fire to await the cold weather." **(RL.8.9; DOK 3)**

Part C: Students' choice of sentences will vary. Possible sentence: "She knew she might not be gaining the most praise and attention, but she felt proud that she'd done so much to make the production a success." **(RL.8.9; DOK 3)**

SAMPLE RESPONSES

Short Response

6 The character of Madison in "The Silent Songbird" seems to be drawn from the character of Rainbow Crow. Madison is a caring person willing to make important sacrifices, such as giving up the lead role in the play, to help others. Rainbow Crow does the same thing when he gives up his colorful feathers and singing voice to bring fire to the animals. Madison also has great talent for singing, just like Rainbow Crow. In addition, the character of Abigail in "The Silent Songbird" acts meanly and selfishly, like the Rattlesnake in "The Rainbow Crow." *(RL.8.9; DOK 4)*

7 "The Rainbow Crow" tells a powerful story with important lessons about how people should act toward one another. The author of "The Silent Songbird" drew on these elements but wrote them into a new story in a modern setting. Instead of using talking animals in a dangerous situation, the author uses realistic young people in a school play. "The Silent Songbird" may be easier for modern readers to relate to, since it is more realistic and contains more familiar ideas and situations. *(RL.8.9; DOK 4)*

8 Both "The Silent Songbird" and "The Rainbow Crow" follow a similar pattern of events. The stories begin with an introduction of the main characters, the talented Rainbow Crow and Madison. Then, the characters discover a problem: the cold of winter in "The Rainbow Crow" and the lack of a theater assistant in "The Silent Songbird." The main characters then volunteer to make sacrifices to help others and work hard to bring positive changes. In the end, both characters are proud of the contributions they made. *(RL.8.9; DOK 4)*

Performance Task

9 The stories "The Rainbow Crow" and "The Silent Songbird" are about important sacrifices made by characters to help others. The Rainbow Crow gave up his beautiful colored feathers and wonderful singing voice to carry the torch of fire to the other animals. Madison gave up her leading role in the play to become the theater assistant, a position that was necessary for the production. Both characters were brave and caring, and they gave up what was important to themselves to help others.

Their sacrifices were different in some ways, though. The Rainbow Crow risked his life and was forever changed by his sacrifice. He knew that he was going to help his friends survive the winter, so it was a very serious matter. Madison did a great thing, too, but she did not take nearly as much risk. She gave up a role in a play, which was important to her but not necessary for her life. Her sacrifice was not as serious or life-changing as Rainbow Crow's.

I think both sacrifices were important in their own ways, but overall Rainbow Crow's had to be more important. Rainbow Crow took an almost impossible journey, met the Great Sky Spirit, and carried a flaming torch in his beak. He showed great bravery and was willing to endure pain and permanently lose some of his good qualities. It was worth it in the end, however, because he saved his friends from terrible suffering in the cold winter. *(RL.8.9; DOK 4)*

SCORING RUBRICS

Short-Response Rubric

2 points   The response is accurate, complete, and fulfills all requirements of the task. Text-based support and examples are included. Any information that goes beyond the text is relevant to the task.

1 point   The response is partially accurate and fulfills some requirements of the task. Some information may be inaccurate, too general, or confused. Support and examples may be insufficient or not text-based.

0 points   The response is inaccurate, poorly organized, or does not respond to the task.

Performance Task Rubric

4 points   The response
- Fulfills all requirements of the task
- Uses varied sentence types and some sophisticated vocabulary
- Includes relevant and accurate details from the texts as well as text-based inferences
- Demonstrates a thorough understanding of the texts
- Maintains a clear focus and organization
- Is fluent and demonstrates a clear voice
- Uses correct spelling, grammar, capitalization, and punctuation

3 points   The response
- Fulfills all requirements of the task
- Uses simple sentences and grade-level vocabulary
- Includes relevant and accurate details from the texts
- Demonstrates a mainly literal understanding of the texts
- Maintains a mostly clear focus and organization
- Is fluent and demonstrates some sense of voice
- Uses mostly correct spelling, grammar, capitalization, and punctuation

2 points   The response
- Fulfills some requirements of the task
- Uses simple sentences, some fragments, and grade-level vocabulary
- Includes some relevant and accurate details from the texts
- Demonstrates some misunderstandings or gaps in understanding of the texts
- Attempts to maintain a clear focus and organization
- Is difficult to read, includes some inaccuracies, and demonstrates little or no sense of voice
- Contains some inaccurate spelling, grammar, capitalization, and punctuation that may hinder understanding

1 point   The response
- Fulfills few requirements of the task
- Uses sentence fragments and below-grade-level vocabulary
- Includes no details or irrelevant details to support the response
- Demonstrates very little understanding of the texts
- Does not establish a clear focus or organization
- Is difficult to read, contains many inaccuracies, and demonstrates no sense of voice
- Uses incorrect spelling, grammar, capitalization, and punctuation to an extent that impedes understanding

0 points   The response is irrelevant, poorly organized, or illegible.

Comparing Media: Evaluating Artistic Choices

LESSON OBJECTIVES

- Analyze the extent to which a filmed version of a print story stays faithful to the original text.

- Evaluate the artistic choices made by the director, actors, and screenwriter.

THE LEARNING PROGRESSION

Grade 7: CCSS RL.7.7 requires students to compare and contrast written and filmed versions of texts by "analyzing the effects of techniques unique to each medium."

Grade 8: CCSS RL.8.7 builds on the Grade 7 standard by requiring students to analyze how faithful a filmed or stage version of a story is to the original text, "evaluating the choices made by the director or actors."

Grade 9: CCSS RL.9-10.7 requires students to analyze a subject or key scene in two different artistic mediums, including what is "emphasized or absent in each treatment."

TAP STUDENTS' PRIOR KNOWLEDGE

- Ask the class for examples of movies they've seen that were based on a book they've read. (*Holes, The Outsiders, The Hunger Games, etc.*) When they were watching the movie, were they comparing it to the book? Or were they just swept up in the story?

- Discuss how it can be difficult not to compare the movie version to the original. As we read a book, we picture characters and actions in our mind, based on the descriptions the writer provides. But what happens when we see the movie? We get someone else's images and ideas about the characters and plot—which can sometimes conflict with our own mind's eye version.

- Explain that when adapting a book to the big screen, the director, actors, and screenwriter need to make countless artistic choices about how to best represent the original written text. They know they are working with material that already has an established audience with specific ideas about the characters and plot. The filmmakers' challenge is to find a way to capture the spirit of the original book and translate it onto a big screen without alienating viewers already familiar with the work.

- Tell students they will look at the roles of the decision-makers in adapting a book or story to the stage or screen. They will also consider the artistic choices and questions that inform an adaptation.

Ready *Teacher Toolbox*   teacher-toolbox.com

	Prerequisite Skills	RL.8.7
Ready Lessons	✓	✓
Tools for Instruction		
Interactive Tutorials		✓

CCSS Focus

RL.8.7 Analyze the extent to which a filmed or live production of a story or drama stays faithful to or departs from the text or script, evaluating the choices made by the director or actors.

ADDITIONAL STANDARDS: **W.8.1, W.8.3, W.8.7**

AT A GLANCE

By evaluating the choices made by film directors in adapting a story to the screen, students will be able to assess how faithful an adaptation is to the original material.

STEP BY STEP: PAGE 237

- Have a volunteer read the introduction on page 237 aloud to the class. Ask students what they know about how movies are made. Have them consider all the various elements that go into a production—script writing, lighting, costuming, makeup, rehearsals, sound effects, camera angles, editing, etc.

- Read through the Key Decision-Makers section on page 237.

   Screenwriter/Playwright: Explain that in addition to writing a script, the screenwriter also provides detailed information on the setting of a scene, the camera angles and shots, and the lighting and sound.

- **Director:** The director is like an orchestra conductor, bringing all the parts of the filmmaking process—acting, filming, editing—together.

   Actor: An actor's appearance, movements, and speech are usually carefully planned by the performer and the director, even when they seem spontaneous.

- Before students look at the Questions for Adaptation section, ask them what they think would be the most challenging part of adapting a novel or story for the stage or screen. Ask them to explain their choice.

- Read the introduction to the Questions for Adaptation. As you go through each section of the chart, you might want to apply the questions to a book or novel your students have recently read. For each section, ask students which of the key decision-makers most likely has the most influence in determining the answers.

- **Character:** The screenwriter uses information from the book to suggest the look and actions of the characters and to create the dialogue. Casting, makeup, and costumes are suggested by other members of the team. An actor would be concerned not only with how the character looks, but also with how the character speaks, moves, and interacts with other characters. Ultimately, though, most final decisions are made by the director.

- **Plot:** The screenwriter has the greatest impact on the plot of a story adaptation. He or she will reduce the original story to a logical plot progression for a viewer. Screenwriters frequently delete entire scenes and chapters to fit a novel into a movie's time frame. The director will later work with the screenwriter to make changes to the original script.

- **Setting:** Explain that, once again, the director has the most say in determining how the settings will appear onscreen. However, directors need the expertise of set designers, prop masters, and the cinematographer—the person in charge of the camera and lighting crews—to achieve their vision.

- As an alternative to the discussion activity, you may wish to choose a story the students have read for class and discuss ideas for adapting it for the stage or screen.

STEP BY STEP: PAGE 238

- Tell students that when they analyze the written and filmed versions of a story, it helps to evaluate the specific artistic choices the filmmakers made. Even though a film can be different from the original book, the artistic choices that were made often result in an equally good, and sometimes improved, version of the original.

- Draw students' attention to the chart on page 238, and explain that they will have the opportunity to do a similar comparison later on. Read the labels down the left side, and then the questions across the top. Explain that this chart provides a good model for evaluating a movie adaptation, and that they might even want to add additional categories to evaluate.

- Provide a brief summary of *Holes*: it is a novel about a boy named Stanley who is sent to a detention camp where boys are disciplined by being forced to dig and refill large holes every day. Eventually, Stanley realized that the warden is actually having them dig the holes because she is searching for something.

- Have students read the student's evaluations, pointing out the specific details that were used. Then have them mark up the text before completing the discussion activity that follows the chart. Students' text markings should identify critical language such as "good choice," "it bothered me," "very creative," "what's important," "made me enjoy it even more."

BE A SCREENWRITER *(W.8.3)*

- Have students assume the role of screenwriter to adapt a short scene from a story or novel they have read as a script. They will choose the scene and write descriptive copy detailing how the scene will be filmed and where the scene will be set. They will also adapt or create dialogue from the original source. For example:

EXTERIOR. Blustery winter night. Snow is falling. A streetlight illuminates the road. A man in shorts and a t-shirt [BILL] is talking to a man bundled up in winter clothes [MAX].

BILL

You're sure it's only 10 degrees?

MAX

That's what they said on the news.

BILL

Doesn't seem that cold.

MAX

You're not from these parts, are you?

Have students present their screenplay adaptation to the class and explain some of the artistic choices they had to make in writing it.

CHARACTER STUDY *(RL.8.7)*

- Have students choose a story they've read that was made into a movie. Ask them to choose one character and compare how that character was presented in the two versions.

- Suggest they begin by taking notes on how the character in the book looks, what she wears, how she talks, and any other important information the author provides. Then have them do the same for the movie version.

- After they've made their notes, have students compare the results. What changes were made in the film version? Which version of the character did the student connect with more closely?

ACTOR'S NOTEBOOK *(W.8.7)*

- Explain that actors cast in a historical drama often do copious research on the era. Then tell students that they have been cast as a merchant in a historical drama adaptation of a book series.

- In small groups, have students do the research an actor would conduct to prepare for a role in such a movie. Suggest the group choose from one of the following historical eras: the Civil War, Ancient Greece, Medieval England, or World War II.

- Direct each group to write a one paragraph profile of the merchant they will be playing based on their research Have them include details about what they would wear, where they would do business, what they would sell, who their customers would be, and how they would sell their goods.

FILM CRITIC *(W.8.1)*

- Have students write a movie review of an adapted book or story. Refer students to page 238 of the lesson in the student edition for ideas about how to analyze the artistic choices that were made in translating the book or story into a movie version.

- Hand out the copymaster from page 221 of this Teacher Guide and tell students to use it to record their ideas. Encourage them to create other categories as well, and to provide as much detail as possible.

If students are having trouble thinking of a book and movie to compare, suggest these titles, many of which they may have read when they were younger, and all of which have been made into movies:

Charlotte's Web
Charlie and the Chocolate Factory
Harry Potter
The Chronicles of Narnia
Dr. Dolittle
Diary of a Wimpy Kid
The Bridge to Terebithia
Freak the Mighty
James and the Giant Peach
The Secret Garden

- Tell students the primary focus of their review should be assessing whether or not the film version was faithful to the original book or story, and how successful any changes were. Remind students that the more specific they make the details they cite from the film, the more effective their analysis will be.

- Ask students to share their reviews in small groups.

Name_____ Date_____

DIRECTIONS: Use this chart to compare a book or story to the movie version. Consider the artistic choices the screenwriter, actors, and ultimately the director made. Then determine if the production remained faithful to the original story, and if any changes that were made were successful.

Book/Film Title: _____

Element	What were the differences between the two versions?	How successful were the changes?	How did the changes affect your enjoyment of the movie?
Character			
Plot			
Setting			

How faithful was the adaptation to the original book or story?

Ready® *Common Core* Language Handbook

The **Ready Common Core** Language Handbook was created to help students develop proficiency with the Common Core State Standards for Language. Each lesson uses scaffolded instruction, beginning with an introduction and guided practice and then moving students into fully independent practice of the skills and strategies behind the Common Core.

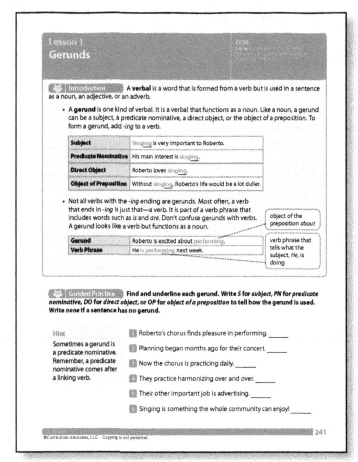

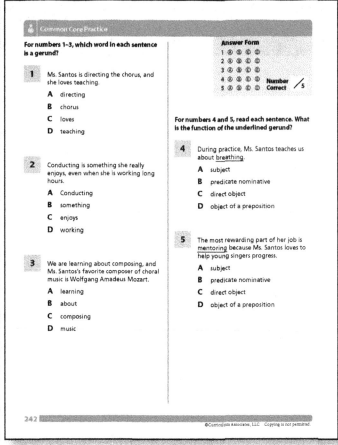

Lesson 1: Gerunds

Guided Practice, page 241

1 <u>performing</u>: *OP*

2 <u>Planning</u>: *S*

3 <u>none</u>

4 <u>harmonizing</u>: *DO*

5 <u>advertising</u>: *PN*

6 <u>Singing</u>: *S*

Common Core Practice, page 242

1   D

2   A

3   C

4   D

5   B

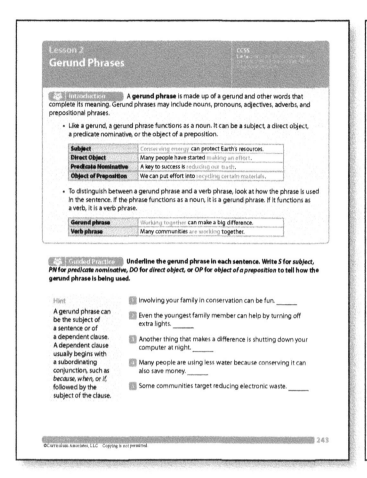

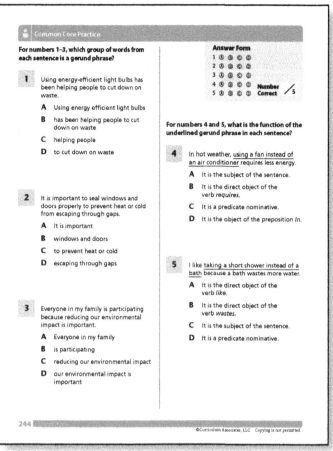

Lesson 2: Gerund Phrases

Guided Practice, page 243

1 <u>Involving your family in conservation</u>: *S*

2 <u>turning off extra lights</u>: *OP*

3 <u>shutting down your computer at night</u>: *PN*

4 <u>conserving it</u>: *S*

5 <u>reducing electronic waste</u>: *DO*

Common Core Practice, page 244

1 A

2 D

3 C

4 A

5 A

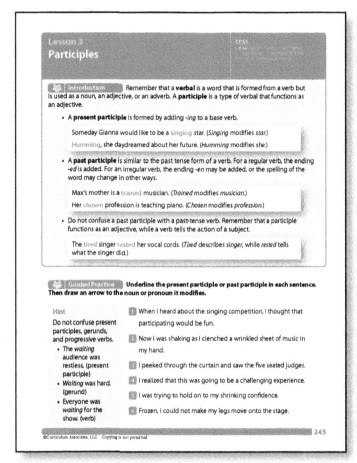

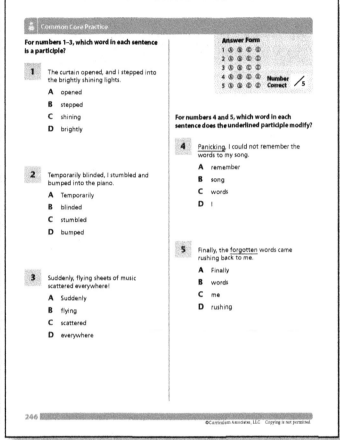

Lesson 3: Participles

Guided Practice, page 245

1 <u>singing</u>, arrow to *competition*

2 <u>wrinkled</u>, arrow to *sheet*

3 <u>seated</u>, arrow to *judges*

4 <u>challenging</u>, arrow to *experience*

5 <u>shrinking</u>, arrow to *confidence*

6 <u>Frozen</u>, arrow to *I*

Common Core Practice, page 246

1 C

2 B

3 B

4 D

5 B

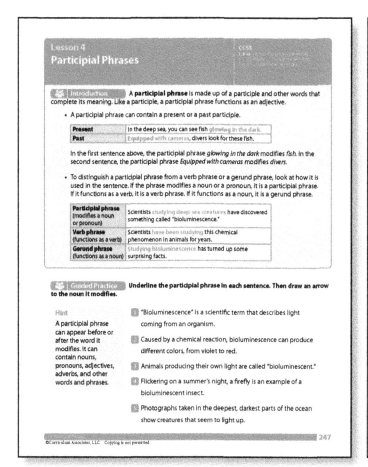

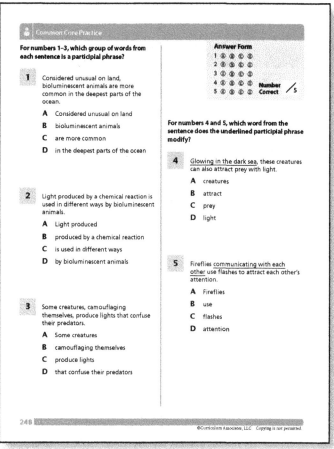

Lesson 4: Participial Phrases

Guided Practice, page 247

1 <u>coming from an organism</u>: light

2 <u>caused by a chemical reaction</u>: bioluminescence

3 <u>producing their own light</u>: Animals

4 <u>flickering on a summer's night</u>: firefly

5 <u>taken in the deepest, darkest parts of the ocean</u>: Photographs

Common Core Practice, page 248

1 A

2 B

3 B

4 A

5 A

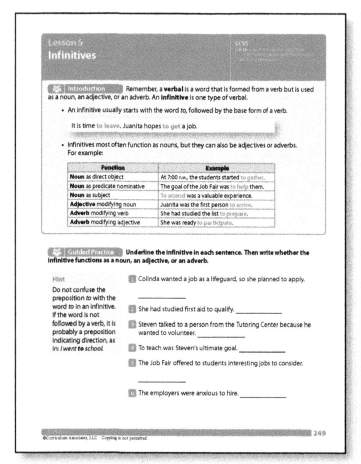

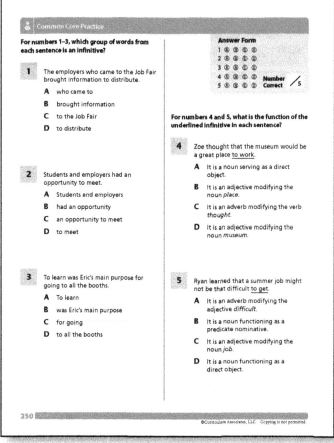

Lesson 5: Infinitives

Guided Practice, page 249

1 <u>to apply</u>: noun

2 <u>to qualify</u>: adverb

3 <u>to volunteer</u>: noun

4 <u>To teach</u>: noun

5 <u>to consider</u>: adjective

6 <u>to hire</u>: adverb

Common Core Practice, page 250

1 D

2 D

3 A

4 B

5 A

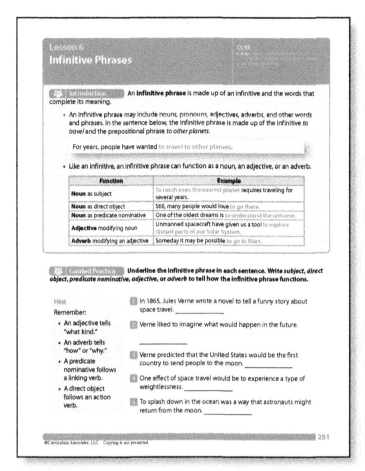

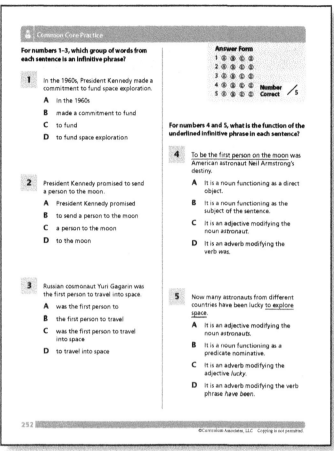

Lesson 6: Infinitive Phrases

Guided Practice, page 251

1 <u>to tell a funny story about space travel</u>: adverb

2 <u>to imagine what would happen in the future</u>: direct object

3 <u>to send people to the moon</u>: adjective

4 <u>to experience a type of weightlessness</u>: predicate nominative

5 <u>To splash down in the ocean</u>: subject

Common Core Practice, page 252

1 D

2 B

3 D

4 B

5 C

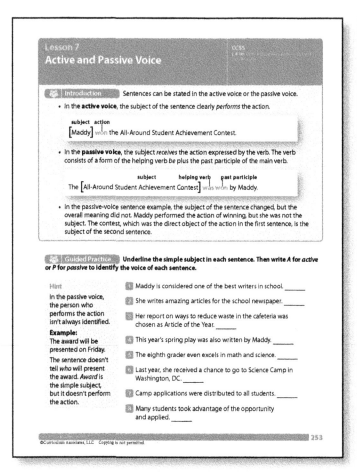

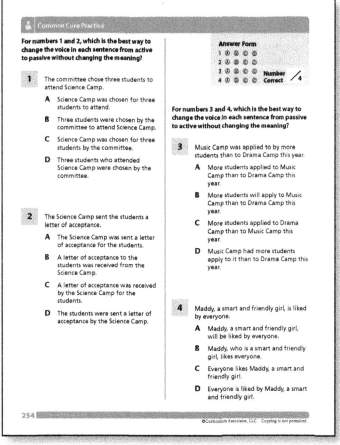

Lesson 7: Active and Passive Voice

Guided Practice, page 253

1 <u>Maddy</u>: P

2 <u>She</u>: A

3 <u>report</u>: P

4 <u>play</u>: P

5 <u>eighth grader</u>: A

6 <u>she</u>: A

7 <u>applications</u>: P

8 <u>students</u>: A

Common Core Practice, page 254

1 B

2 D

3 A

4 C

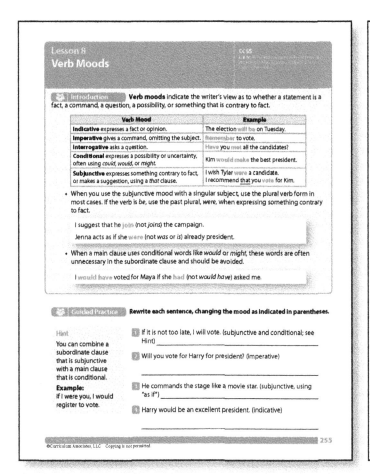

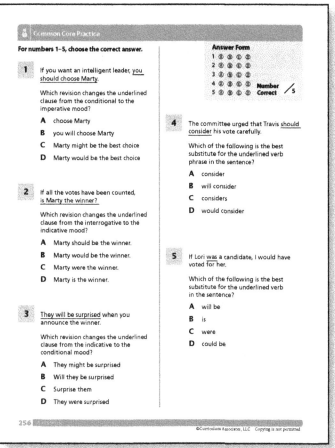

Lesson 8: Verb Moods

Guided Practice, page 255

Responses will vary. Sample answers:

1 If it were not too late, I would vote.

2 Vote for Harry for president.

3 He commands the stage as if he were a movie star.

4 Harry will be an excellent president.

Common Core Practice, page 256

1 A

2 D

3 A

4 A

5 C

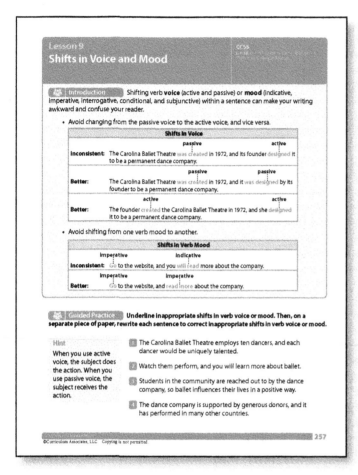

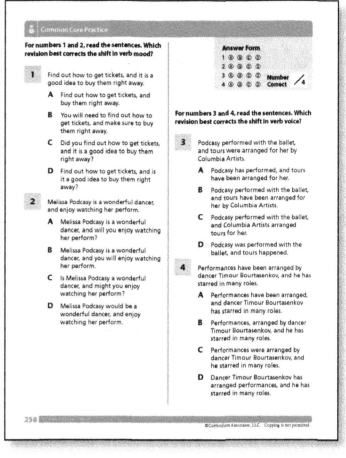

Lesson 9: Shifts in Voice and Mood

Guided Practice, page 257

Answers will vary. Sample answers given.

1 go; The Carolina Ballet Theatre employs ten dancers, and each dancer is uniquely talented.

2 will learn; Watch them perform, and learn more about ballet.

3 are reached; The dance company reaches out to students in the community, so ballet influences their lives in a positive way.

4 is supported; Generous donors support the ballet company, and it has performed in many other countries.

Common Core Practice, page 258

1 A

2 B

3 C

4 D

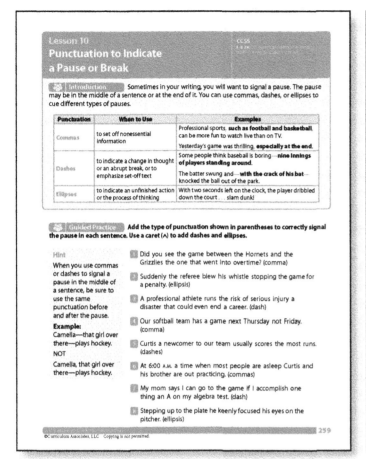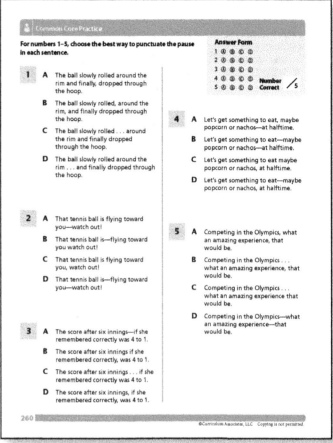

Lesson 10: Punctuation to Indicate a Pause or Break

Guided Practice, page 259

1 Did you see the game between the Hornets and the Grizzlies, the one that went into overtime?

2 Suddenly the referee blew his whistle . . . stopping the game for a penalty.

3 A professional athlete runs the risk of a serious injury—a disaster that could even end a career.

4 Our softball team has a game next Thursday, not Friday.

5 Curtis—a newcomer to our team—usually scores the most runs.

6 At 6:00 A.M., a time when most people are asleep, Curtis and his brother are out practicing.

7 My mom says I can go to the game if I accomplish one thing—an A on my algebra test.

8 Stepping up to the plate . . . he keenly focused his eyes on the pitcher.

Common Core Practice, page 260

1 D
2 A
3 D
4 B
5 C

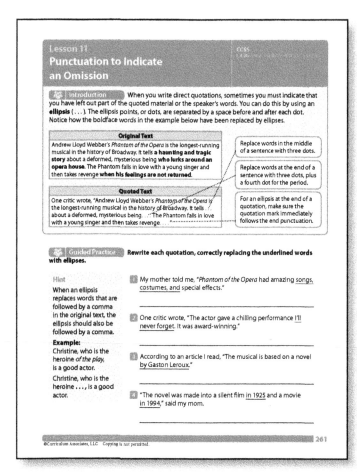

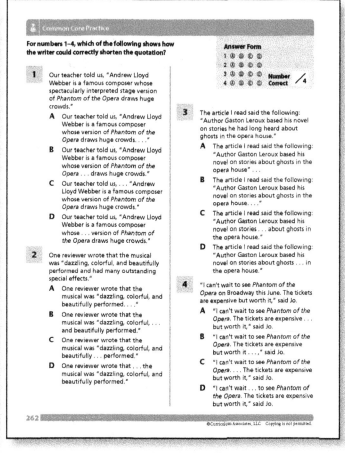

Lesson 11: Punctuation to Indicate an Omission

Guided Practice, page 261

1 My mother told me, "*Phantom of the Opera* had amazing . . . special effects."

2 One critic wrote, "The actor gave a chilling performance. . . . It was award-winning."

3 According to an article I read, "The musical is based on a novel. . . ."

4 "The novel was made into a silent film . . . and a movie . . . ," said my mom.

Common Core Practice, page 262

1 D

2 A

3 C

4 C

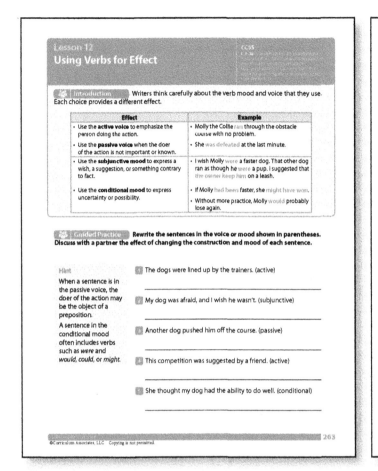

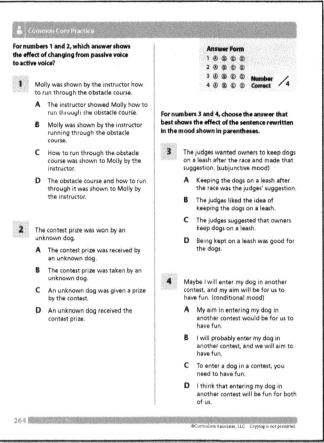

Lesson 12: Using Verbs for Effect

Guided Practice, page 263

Responses will vary. Sample answers:

1. The trainers lined up the dogs.

2. I wish that my dog were not afraid.

3. My dog was pushed off the course by another dog.

4. A friend suggested this competition.

5. She thought my dog would have done well.

Common Core Practice, page 264

1. A

2. D

3. C

4. A

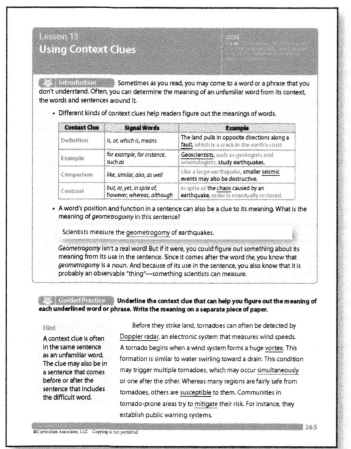

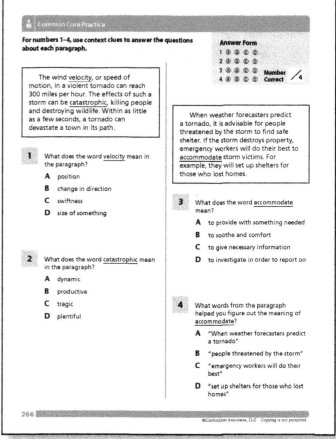

Lesson 13: Using Context Clues

Guided Practice, page 265

Responses will vary. Sample answers:

1 Doppler radar: <u>an electronic system that measures wind speeds</u>; definition same as clue

2 vortex: <u>formation is similar to water swirling toward a drain</u>; a swirling formation

3 simultaneously: <u>or one after the other</u>; at the same time—*not* one after the other

4 susceptible: <u>Whereas…fairly safe from tornadoes</u>; vulnerable to—*not* safe from

5 mitigate: <u>For instance, they establish public warning systems</u>; lessen

Common Core Practice, page 266

1 C

2 C

3 A

4 D

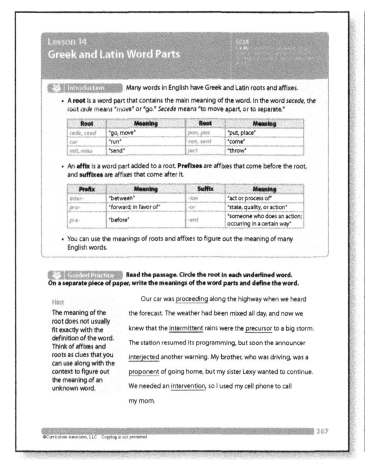

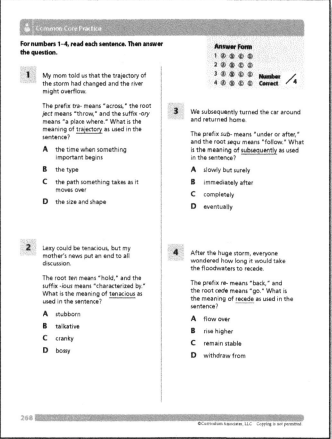

Lesson 14: Greek and Latin Word Parts

Guided Practice, page 267

Responses will vary. Sample answers:

1 proceeding: *ceed* means "move or go"; *pro-* means "forward"; *proceeding* means "moving or going forward."

2 intermittent: *inter-* means "between"; *mit* means "send;" *-ent* means "occurring in a certain way"; *intermittent* means "sent between other things" or "not continuous."

3 precursor: *pre-* means "before"; *cur* means "run"; *-or* means "state, quality, or action"; *precursor* means "something that comes before something else."

4 interjected: *inter-* means "between"; *ject* means "throw"; *-ed* indicates past tense; *interjected* means "inserted between other elements, or interrupted something that is going on."

5 proponent: *pro-* means "forward"; *pon* means "put or place"; *-ent* means "someone who"; *proponent* means "someone who is in favor of a position, or one side of an issue."

6 intervention: *inter-* means "between"; *vent* means "come"; *-ion* means "act or process of"; *intervention* means "an action that comes between two sides of a conflict to help resolve it."

Common Core Practice, page 268

1 C

2 A

3 B

4 D

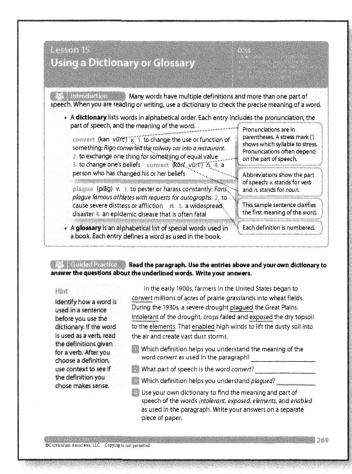

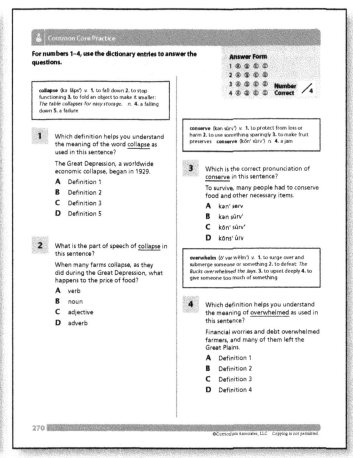

Lesson 15: Using a Dictionary or Glossary

Guided Practice, page 269

1 definition 1

2 verb

3 definition 2

4 intolerant: *adjective* unable to survive under
    certain conditions

   exposed: *verb* lay it open to something harmful

   elements: *noun* the forces of weather

   enabled: *verb* made possible or allowed

Common Core Practice, page 270

1 D

2 A

3 B

4 C

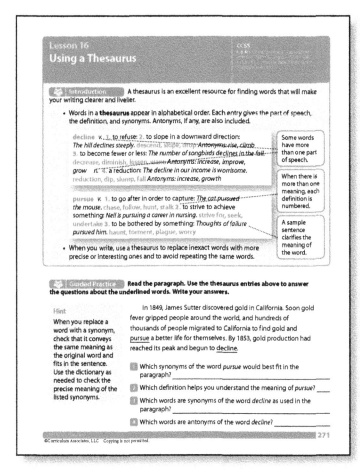

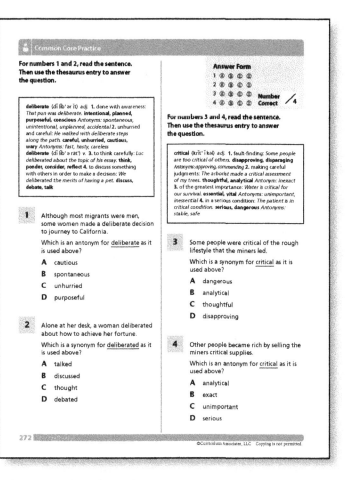

Lesson 16: Using a Thesaurus

Guided Practice, page 271

1 strive for, seek

2 definition 2

3 decrease, diminish, lessen, wane

4 increase, improve, grow

Common Core Practice, page 272

1 B

2 C

3 D

4 C

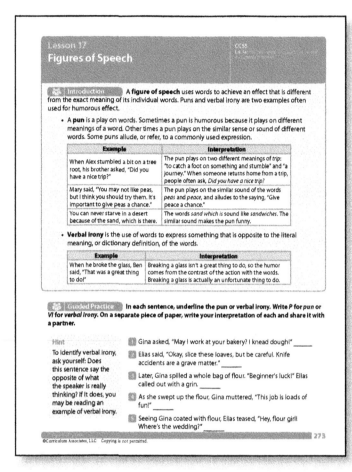

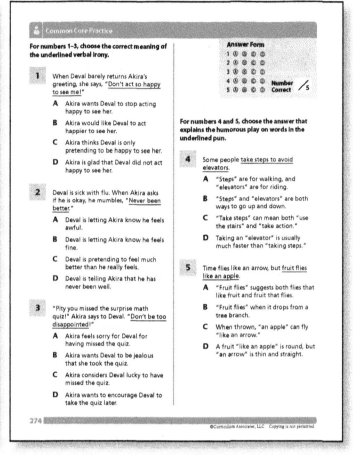

Lesson 17: Figures of Speech

Guided Practice, page 273

1   I knead dough: *P*; The words *knead dough* sound like *need dough*, which means "need money." Both meanings are true: Gina can knead dough and she needs money.

2   grave matter; *P*; The words *grave matter* mean both "a very serious matter" and "a matter related to graves," because a knife accident could be fatal.

3   Beginner's luck! *VI*; Spilling a bag of flour is an *un*lucky thing to have done.

4   This job is loads of fun: *VI*; Sweeping up a mess you made would be unpleasant, not fun.

5   flour girl: *P*; The phrase *flour girl* refers to her being covered in flour and also sounds like *flower girl*, a girl who carries flowers at a wedding.

Common Core Practice, page 274

1   B

2   A

3   C

4   C

5   A

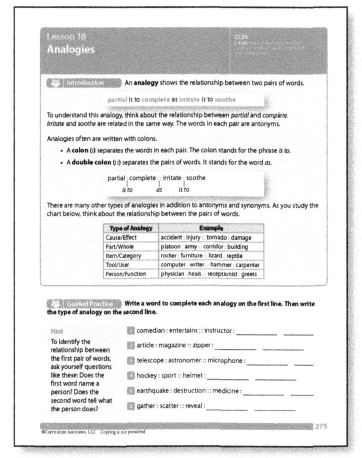

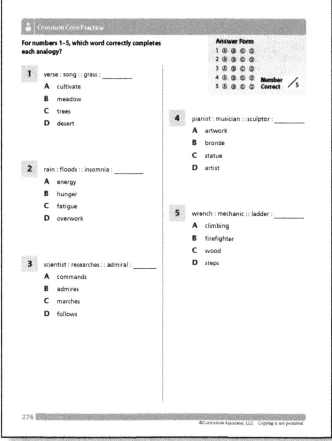

Lesson 18: Analogies

Guided Practice, page 275

Responses will vary. Sample answers:

1   teaches; person/function

2   jacket; part/whole

3   announcer; tool/user

4   equipment; item/category

5   healing; cause/effect

6   conceal or hide; antonym

Common Core Practice, page 276

1   B

2   C

3   A

4   D

5   B

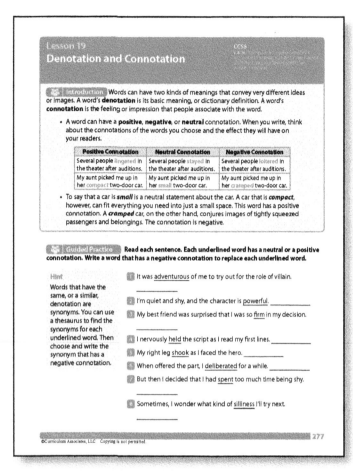

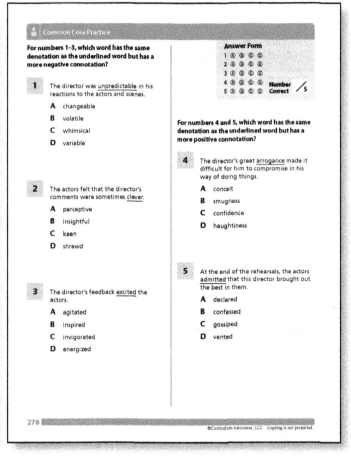

Lesson 19: Denotation and Connotation

Guided Practice, page 277

Responses will vary. Sample answers:

1 reckless
2 pushy, dominating
3 stubborn, obstinate
4 clutched
5 wobbled, trembled
6 agonized, worried
7 wasted, squandered
8 antics, escapades

Common Core Practice, page 278

1 B
2 D
3 A
4 C
5 A